STRE[ET]
East Sussex

published in 1994 by

's, a division of
us Publishing Group Ltd
Heron Quays, London E14 4JP

nd colour edition 2001
nd impression 2002

0-540-07972-3

ilip's 2001

Ordnance
Survey®

product includes mapping data licensed
Ordnance Survey® with the permission
e Controller of Her Majesty's Stationery
e. © Crown copyright 2001. All rights
ved. Licence number 100011710

ance Survey and the OS Symbol are
tered trademarks of Ordnance Survey,
ational mapping agency of Great Britain

ed and bound in Spain
ayfosa-Quebecor

Contents

III **Key to map symbols**

IV **Key to map pages**

VI **Route planning**

VIII **Administrative and Postcode boundaries**

1 **Street maps** at 2½ inches to 1 mile

189 **Street map of Brighton city centre** at 5 inches to 1 mile

190 **Town maps** of Chichester and Crawley

191 **Town maps** of Horsham and Worthing

192 **Index** of towns and villages

193 **Index** of streets, hospitals, industrial estates, railway stations, schools, shopping centres and universities

Digital Data

The exceptionally high-quality mapping found in this book is available as digital data in TIFF format, which is easily convertible to other bit-mapped (raster) image formats.

The index is also available in digital form as a standard database table. It contains all the details found in the printed index together with the National Grid reference for the map square in which each entry is named.

For further information and to discuss your requirements, please contact Philip's on 020 7531 8439 or ruth.king@philips-maps.co.uk

Symbol	Description
	Motorway with junction number
	Primary route – dual/single carriageway
	A road – dual/single carriageway
	B road – dual/single carriageway
	Minor road – dual/single carriageway
	Other minor road – dual/single carriageway
	Road under construction
	Pedestrianised area
	Postcode boundaries
	County and unitary authority boundaries
	Railway
	Tramway, miniature railway
	Rural track, private road or narrow road in urban area
	Gate or obstruction to traffic (restrictions may not apply at all times or to all vehicles)
	Path, bridleway, byway open to all traffic, road used as a public path
	The representation in this atlas of a road, track or path is no evidence of the existence of a right of way
	Adjoining page indicators
	The map area within the pink band is shown at a larger scale on the page indicated by the red block and arrow

Symbol	Description
Walsall	Railway station
	Private railway station
	Bus, coach station
	Ambulance station
	Coastguard station
	Fire station
	Police station
	Accident and Emergency entrance to hospital
H	Hospital
+	Place of worship
i	Information Centre (open all year)
P	Parking
P&R	Park and Ride
PO	Post Office
X	Camping site
	Caravan site
	Golf course
	Picnic site
Prim Sch	Important buildings, schools, colleges, universities and hospitals
River Medway	Water name
	Stream
	River or canal – minor and major
	Water
	Tidal water
	Woods
	Houses
House	Non-Roman antiquity
VILLA	Roman antiquity

Abbr	Full	Abbr	Full
Allot Gdns	Allotments	Meml	Memorial
Acad	Academy	Mon	Monument
Cemy	Cemetery	Mus	Museum
C Ctr	Civic Centre	Obsy	Observatory
CH	Club House	Pal	Royal Palace
Coll	College	PH	Public House
Crem	Crematorium	Recn Gd	Recreation Ground
Ent	Enterprise	Resr	Reservoir
Ex H	Exhibition Hall	Ret Pk	Retail Park
Ind Est	Industrial Estate	Sch	School
Inst	Institute	Sh Ctr	Shopping Centre
Ct	Law Court	TH	Town Hall/House
L Ctr	Leisure Centre	Trad Est	Trading Estate
LC	Level Crossing	Univ	University
Liby	Library	Wks	Works
Mkt	Market	YH	Youth Hostel

The dark grey border on the inside edge of some pages indicates that the mapping does not continue onto the adjacent page

■ The small numbers around the edges of the maps identify the 1 kilometre National Grid lines

The scale of the maps is 3.92 cm to 1 km
2 inches to 1 mile 1: 25344

0	¼	½	¾	1 mile
0	250 m	500 m	750 m	1 kilometre

The scale of the maps on pages numbered in red
7.84 cm to 1 km 5 inches to 1 mile 1: 12672

0	220 yards	440 yards	660 yards	½ mile
0	125 m	250 m	375 m	½ kilometre

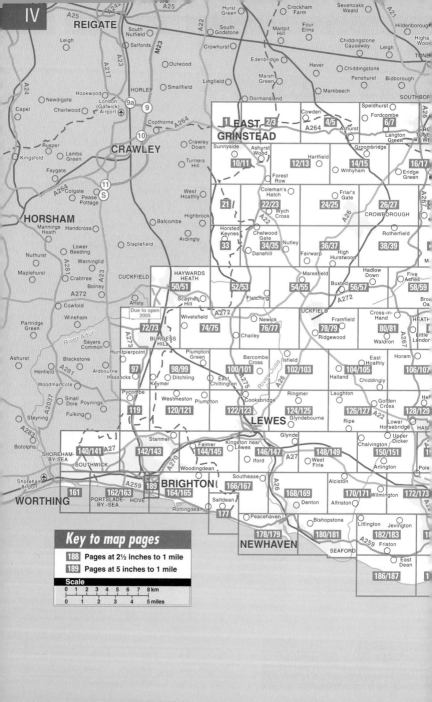

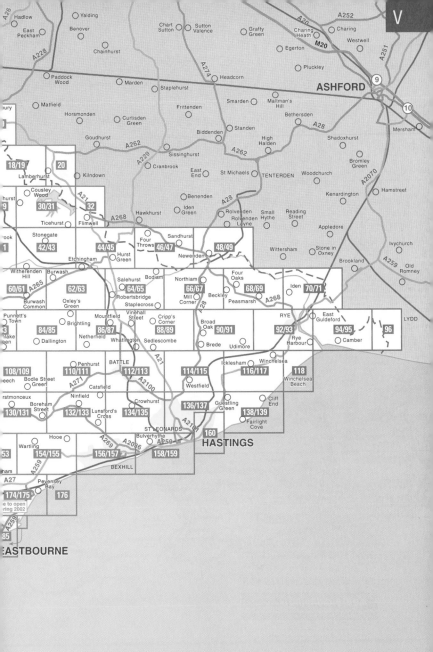

VI

Route planning

Scale

| 0 | 1 | 2 | 3 | 4 | 5 | 6 | 7 | 8 km |

| 0 | 1 | 2 | 3 | 4 | 5 miles |

Major administrative and Postcode boundaries

County and unitary authority boundaries
District boundaries
Postcode boundaries
Area covered by this atlas

Scale

0 ___ 5 ___ 10 ___ 15 km
0 ___ 5 ___ 10 miles

Surrey

West Sussex

Kent

East Sussex

Wealden

Rother

Lewes

Eastbourne

Hastings

City of Brighton & Hove

TN29
TN29
Camber
Winchelsea
Rye
TN31
TN36
TN30
Pett
TN35
Broad Oak
Northiam
TN17
Baldslow
Hastings
St Leonards
Newenden
Sandhurst
TN18
TN38
TN37
Salehurst
TN32
Battle
TN33
Pebsham
TN39
TN40
Bexhill
Lamberhurst
TN12
TN17
Wadhurst
TN5
Burwash
TN19
Rushlake
Green
TN21
Pevensey
Bay
TN1
TN2
TN11
Royal
Tunbridge Wells
TN4
TN3
Mayfield
TN20
Heathfield
Hailsham
BN27
BN24
Langney
BN22
BN23
Groombridge
Crowborough
TN6
East
Heathly
Lower
Willingdon
BN26
Alfriston
Eastbourne
BN21
BN20
Cowden
TN8
Hartfield
TN7
Nutley
TN22
Uckfield
Ringmer
BN8
East
Dean
BN25
Seaford
RH7
East
Grinstead
RH19
Forest Row
RH18
Horsted
Keynes
RH17
Newick
Lewes
BN7
Newhaven
BN9
BN10
Peacehaven
Hayward's
Heath
RH16
Keymer
BN6
RH15
Burgess Hill
RH17
Pycombe
BN45
Woodingdean
Patcham
BN1
Brighton
BN2
Hove
BN3
Portslade-
by-Sea
BN41
Southwick
Shoreham-
by-Sea
BN43
BN42

TQ TR
TV

TQ
TV

C1
1 THE BROWNINGS
2 BYRON GR
3 CHAUCER AVE
4 TENNYSON RISE
5 THE SAYERS
6 WORDSWORTH RISE

D2
1 YEW CT
2 BIRCH HO
3 BEECH CL
4 ELM CT
5 FERNSIDE
6 SOUTHWICK HO

E1
1 GLENSIDE
2 GREGORY CT
3 WHITEHALL PAR
4 CANTELUPE MEWS

3

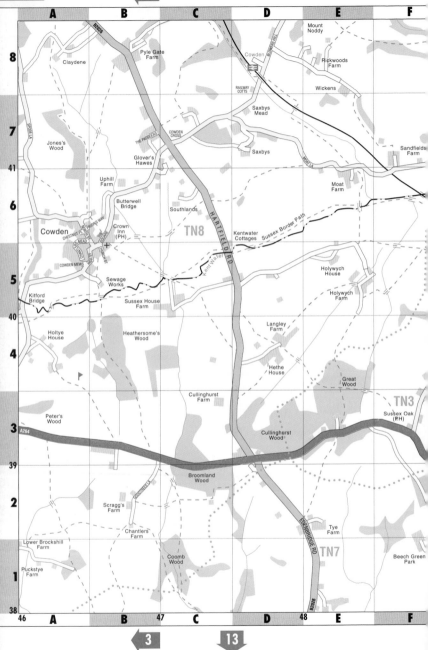

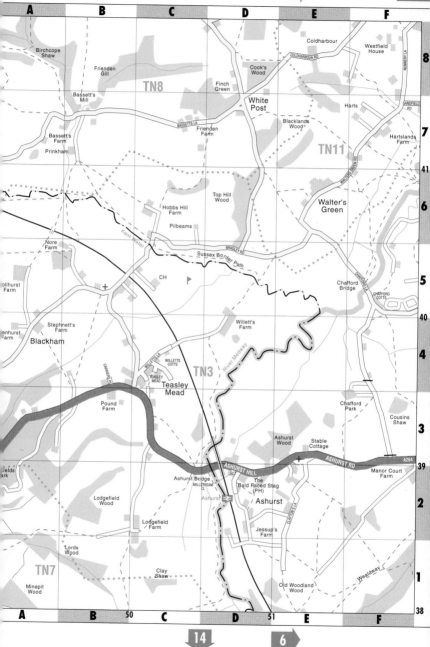

A B C D E F

8

Smart's
Hill

PH

B2188 NEW RD

SAINTS HILL

Poundsbridge

Stone
Wood

FURZ

Hallborough

TN11

Saint's
Hill

River Medway

7

41

Colliersland
Bridge

SPRING HILL

SANDFIELD RD

Hamsell
Farm

COOPERS LA

POUNDSBRIDGE HILL

ASHOURST RD

BULLINGSTONE
COTTS

Cock Pit
Wood

Bullingstone

BULLINGSTONE LA

6

Springhill
Farm

CROCKS LANE PARK CL

Palmers
Farm

Little
Hickman's

Hickman's
Farm

Avery's
Wood

Danemore
Park

FRENCHAM LA

Chafford
Farm

Danemore
Farm

5

CHAFFORD LA

PH

Sch

STONE
ROW

REEVES
CT

PADDOCK

THE LANE

Fordcombe

Silcocks
Farm

LEGGS LA

OLD HOLES LA

WATERFFL
COTTS

STUDOOD LA

40

Fitchetts
Farm

Westaway

Mitre Farm

Shirley
Hall

High Weald Wlk

BIRCHDEN RD

4

Black Lion
House

Stubbs
Wood

FORDCOMBE RD

TN3

Priest Wood

Ashurst
Place

WINSTONE SCOTT WAY

COURTENWELL

THE GREEN

WIDBURY

GREE

PO

HAZEL

3

H
The Tunbridge
Wells Ind

SHERWOOD

Langton Green
Cty Prim
Sch

Langton Green

LITTLE MALLET

KNOWLE

STONEWALL

B2110

Park
Farm

LANGTON RD

HOLMEWOOD RIDGE

39

A264

Stone Cross
Farm

Queens
Spinney

ASHURST RD

BROOM PK

Broomlands

Stone
Cross

GROOMBRIDGE RD

CROCKERS HATCH
CNR

Broom
Farm

BROOM LA

2

Stone Cross
Wood

B2110

The
Hollonds

Burrs
Wood

Newpark
Wood

The
Moltens

Hollonds
Wood

1

Top Hill
Farm

GROOMBRIDGE HILL

STONE ROW
COTTS

High Weald
Wlk

38

Harness Well
Wood

B2110

Sewage Works

F8
1 MIDDLE ROW
2 FOREST LODGE
3 SACKVILLE CT
4 GREAT HOUSE CT
5 PORTLAND HO
6 CORNWALL GDNS
7 NORMANDY CL
8 WILLOW MEAD
9 KINGS COPSE
10 REGAL DR
11 BECKETT WAY

EAST GRINSTEAD

Sunnyside

RH19

Great Wood
Coles Wood
Hill Place Farm
Brook Manor
Brook House Farm
High Grove
Crockshed Wood
HAZELDEN CROSS
Coombe Hall Sch
Bulrushes Farm
The Meads Cty Primry Sch
MILL COTTS
Dunnings Mill L Complex
Hazleden Farm
Coombe Hall Farm
Tobias Sch of Art
The Plantation
Imberley
Dunning's Wood
Eurythmy Sch
Boyles Farm
Playing Field
Rockwood Park
The Beechcroft Towse
Rushett's Shaw
High Wood
Playing Field
Rockingshill Wood
The Rough
Saint Hill Green
Saint Hill Manor
Jenkin's Wood
Ridge Hill Manor
Hen Robin Wood
Saint Hill Farm
Standen Farm
Busses Farm
Cock Robin Wood
Cycle Trial
Standen (National Trust)
Jenhurst Wood
Mary Wood
Busses Wood
River Medway
Stone Hill House
Sussex Border Path
Mill Place Farm
Weir Wood Resr
Bluebell Rly
Pit Shaw
Willet's Bridge
Admiral's Bridge Wood
Birch Farm Nursery
Weir Wood Resr (Nature Reserve)
Charlwood Farm
Alder Moors
Neylands Farm
LEIGHSEATH LA

TURNER'S HILL RD
SAINT HILL RD
WEST HOATHLY RD
COOMBE HILL RD
ADMIRAL'S BRIDGE LA
B2110

8 7 37 6 5 36 4 3 35 2 1 34

37 A B 38 C D 39 E F

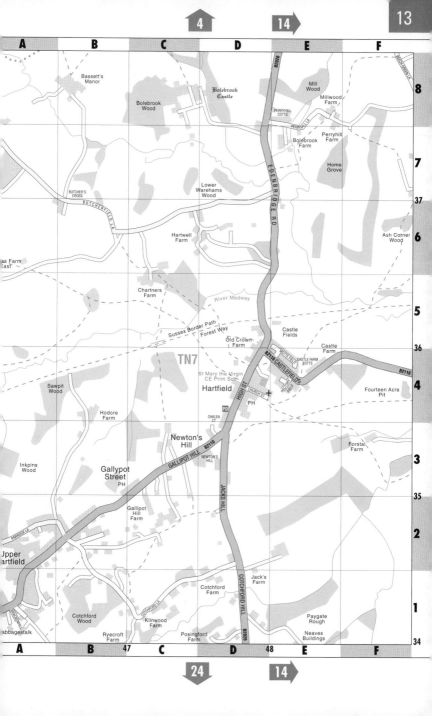

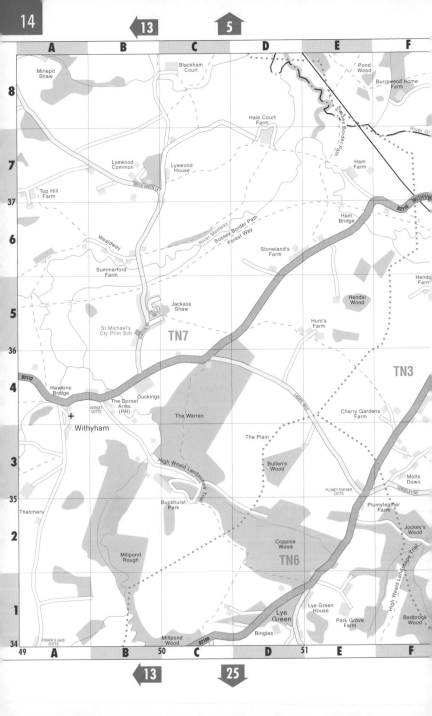

Spa Valley Rly

Ramslye
Wood

TN4

Ramslye
Farm

EASTLANDS CL.

EBRIDGE RD

Sch

RAMSLYE RD

STUART CT.

WATTS

SCHOOL CL.

CHANDOS DR.

FUNHOL

EMERALD DR.

RAMSLYE
COTTS

Strawberry
Hill

BROADWATER
CT.

KENTISH GDNS

BROADWATER DOWN

ST ANDREWS

ST ANDREW'S CL.

Ruffet
Wood

The Firs

STRAWBERRY CL.

HARGATE CL.

1 LEICES
2 DEVONS
3 BROAD

BANG

ST MARY'S RI.

Broadwater
Down

TN2

8

Broadwater
Forest

Spratsbrook
Farm

Strawberry Hill
Farm

7

37

Broadwater
Lodge

Sprat's Brook

Firtree
Plantation

Hargate
Forest

6

The Warren

The
Roundabouts

BUNNY LA.

Bohemia

5

White
Wood

Eridge
Rocks

TN3

36

Warren
Farm

The Nevill
Crest & Gun
(PH)

Eridge
Park

Eridge
Park

4

WARREN FARM LA.

Eridge
Green

Crown
House

Mill
Wood

3

A26

35

Steel
Bridge

High Weald Landscape Trail

Keepers
Cottages

2

Steel Bridge
Farm

Forge
Wood

Eridge
Old Park

Bushy
Wood

Great Robbins
Shaw

Bushy
Shaw

1

34

55   A   B   56   C   D   57   E   F

RH19

8

Kidbrooke
Wood

Tompset's
Bank

BALFOUR GDNS

TOMPSET'S BANK

Greenhall
Cottage

LEWES RD
A22

Fernhill

Wych
Warren

7

Lavender
Platt

PRIORY RD

Old Cherry
Orchard

33

Broadstone Warren
Scout Camp

Broadstc
Warre

6

RH19

Hindleap
Warren

RH18

PRIESTLEY LA

PLAW HATCH
LA

Hindleap Farm

Hindleap Warren
Activity Ctr

COLEMANS HATCH RD

5

Pillow
Mounds

Eighteen Acre
Wood

32

Smockfarthing

Wych
Cross

Roebuck
Hotel

Half M
Cop

4

Wych Cross
Place

Wych Cross
Fruit Farm

A275

Ashdown
Llama Farm

Garde

3

Suttons Farm

Hillsdown
Farm

Press Ridge
Warren

31

P

RH17

2

BROADHILL LA

Stumblewood
Common

Mill Brook

Isle of Thorns
(Univ of Sussex)

TN2

Birch Grove
House

Dane hill Brook

1

Gosses
Farm

LEWES RD
A275

BIRCHGROVE RD

Red Lion
(PH)

LUXFORD LA

The White
House

PO

30

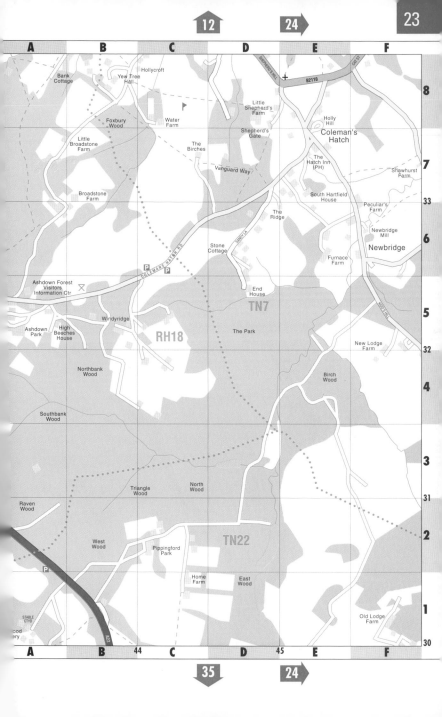

	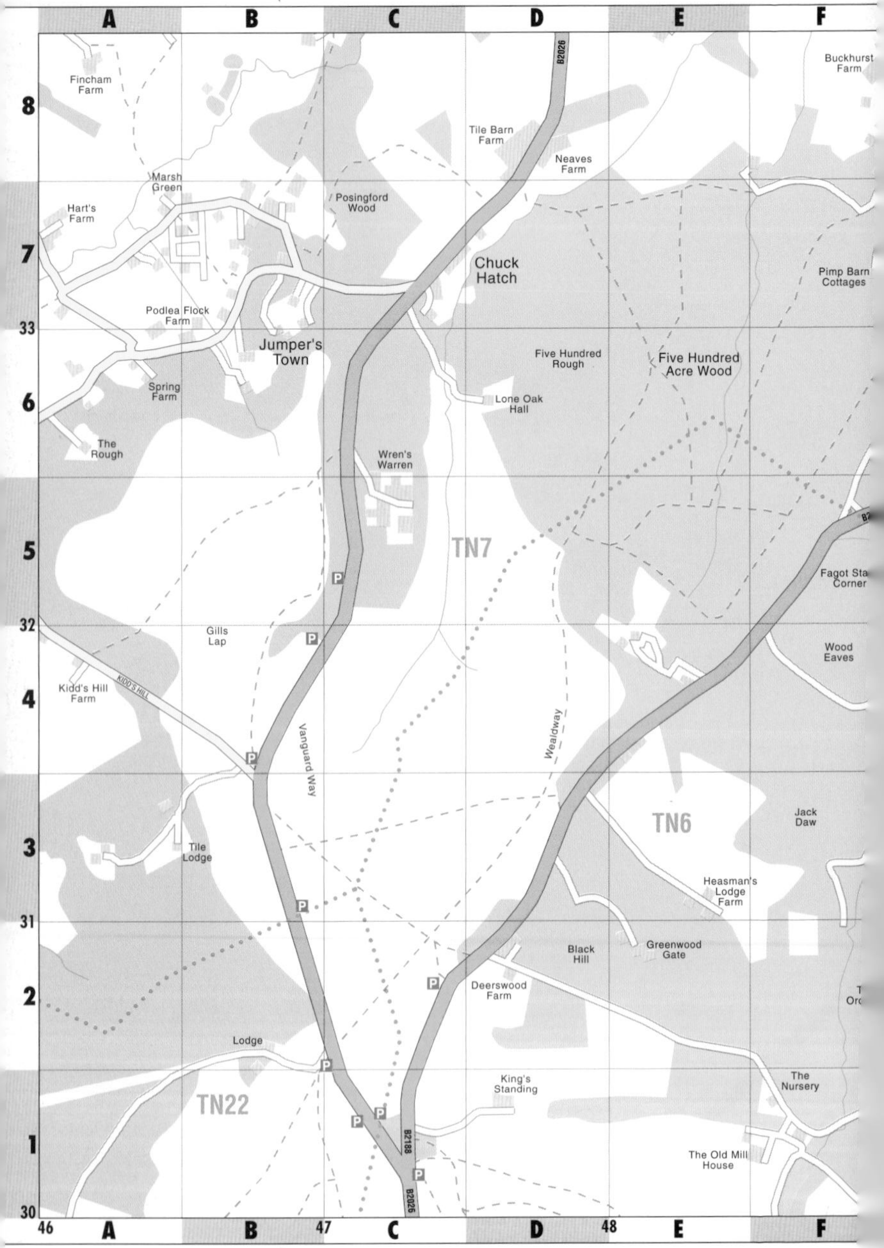 A	B	C	D	E	F

8
Fincham Farm
Buckhurst Farm
Tile Barn Farm
Neaves Farm
B2026

Marsh Green
/ Posingford Wood

7
Hart's Farm
Chuck Hatch
Pimp Barn Cottages

33
Podlea Flock Farm
Jumper's Town
Five Hundred Rough
Five Hundred Acre Wood

6
Spring Farm
Lone Oak Hall

The Rough
Wren's Warren

5
TN7
Fagot Sta Corner

32
Gills Lap
Wood Eaves

4
Kidd's Hill Farm
KIDD'S HILL
Vanguard Way
Wealdway

3
Tile Lodge
TN6
Jack Daw
Heasman's Lodge Farm

31
Black Hill
Greenwood Gate

2
Deerswood Farm
T Or

Lodge
The Nursery

1
TN22
King's Standing
B2188

B2026
The Old Mill House

30

| 46 | A | B | 47 | C | D | 48 | E | F |

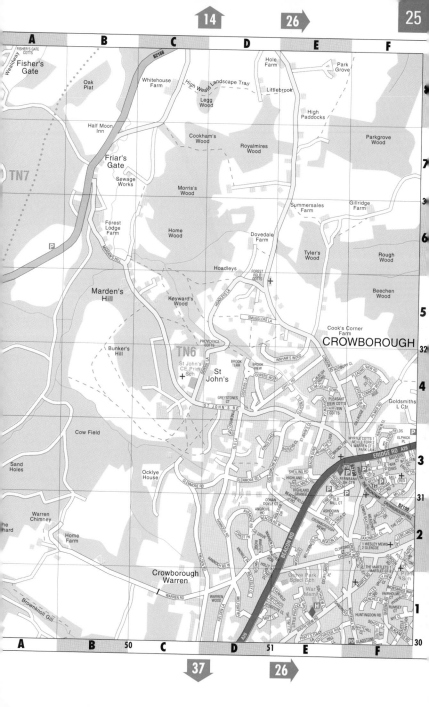

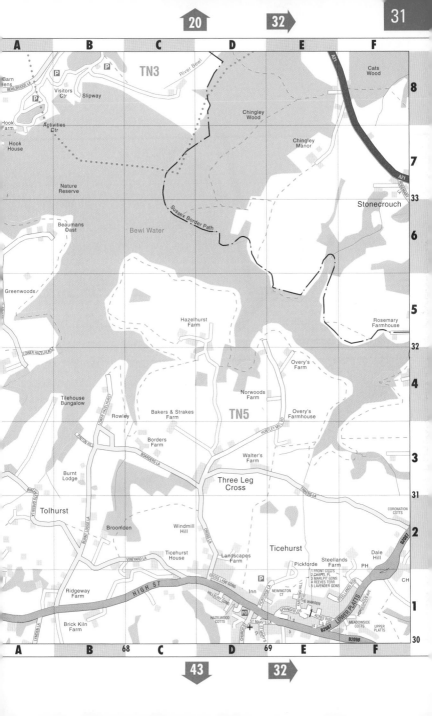

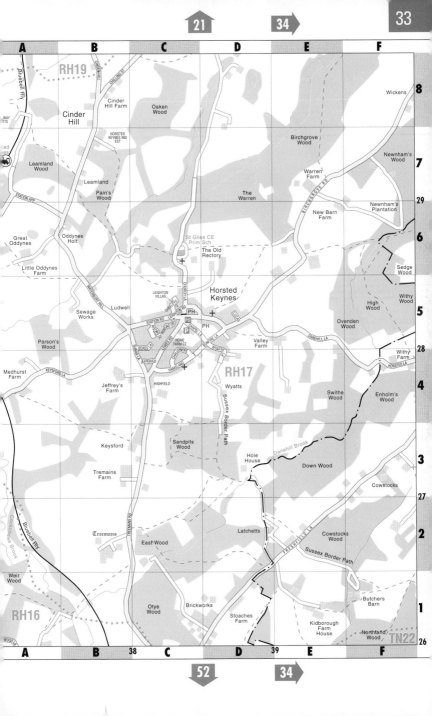

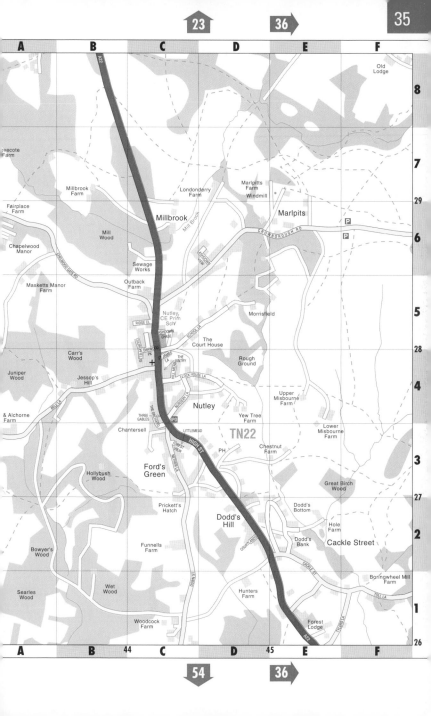

A B C D E F

8

Old
Lodge

7

29

Dovecote
Farm

Millbrook
Farm

Londonderry
Farm

Marlpitts
Farm
Windmill

Marlpits

Fairplace
Farm

Millbrook

Mill Brook

P

P

6

Chapelwood
Manor

Mill
Wood

CROWBOROUGH RD

Masketts Manor
Farm

Sewage
Works

Morrisfield

5

Outback
Farm

Nutley
CE Prim
Sch

CHELWOOD GATE RD

RIDGE CL

SCHOOL LA

28

Carr's
Wood

The
Court House

Rough
Ground

ASHDOWN

Juniper
Wood

CHURCH CL

ASHDOWN
CHASE

OAKWOOD
PK

Jessop's
Hill

ST JAMES
LA

THE
VINTRY

CLOCK HOUSE LA

4

BELL LA

& Alchorne
Farm

Upper
Misbourne
Farm

NURSERY LA

Nutley

Yew Tree
Farm

Lower
Misbourne
Farm

Chantersell

THREE
GABLES

THE PRECINCTS

P

LITTLEMEAD

TN22

27

Hollybush
Wood

Ford's
Green

FOREST
VIEW

HIGH ST

NETHERFIELD

PH

Chestnut
Farm

Great Birch
Wood

3

Prickett's
Hatch

Dodd's
Bottom

Hole
Farm

Bowyer's
Wood

Funnells
Farm

DOWN ST

Dodd's
Hill

COURT LODGE

Dodd's
Bank

CACKLE ST

Cackle Street

2

Boringwheel Mill
Farm

Searles
Wood

Wet
Wood

Hunters
Farm

TOLL LA

26

Woodcock
Farm

A22

Forest
Lodge

TYEHURST LA

A22

A B C D E F

44 45

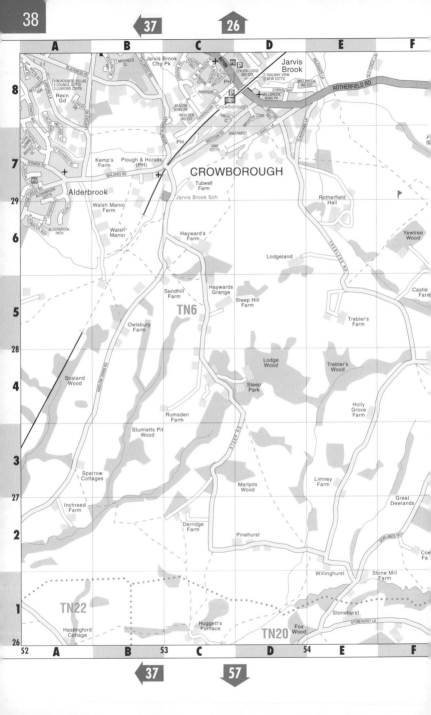

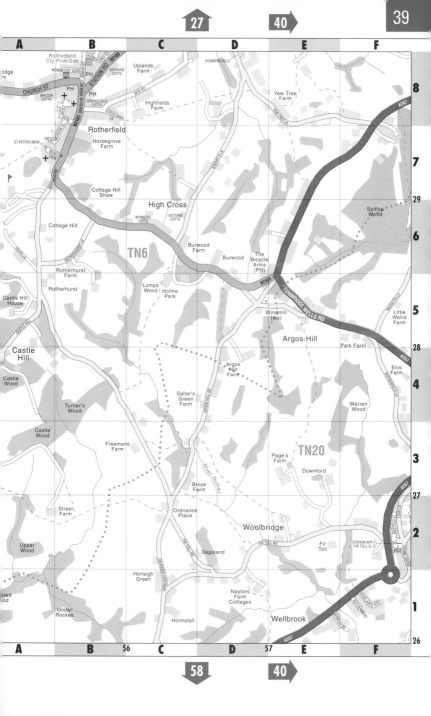

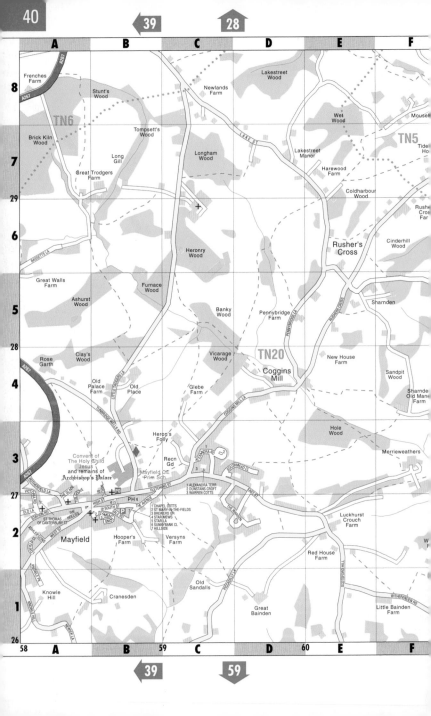

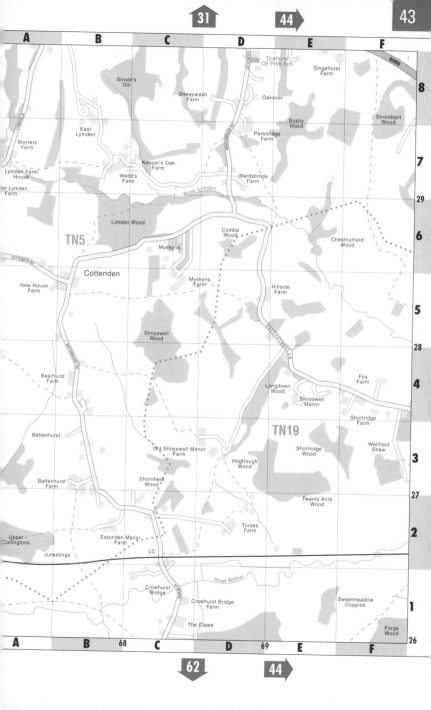

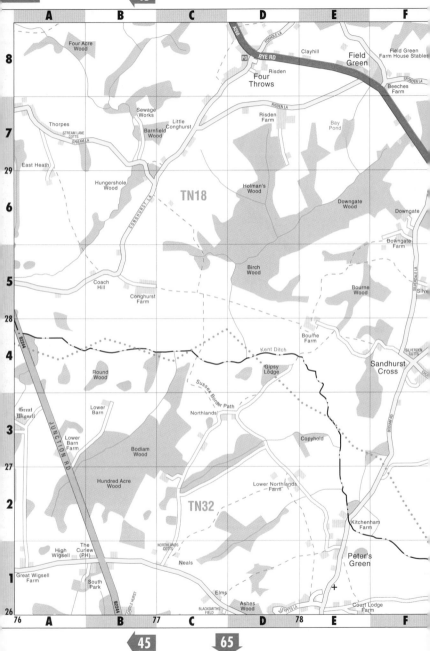

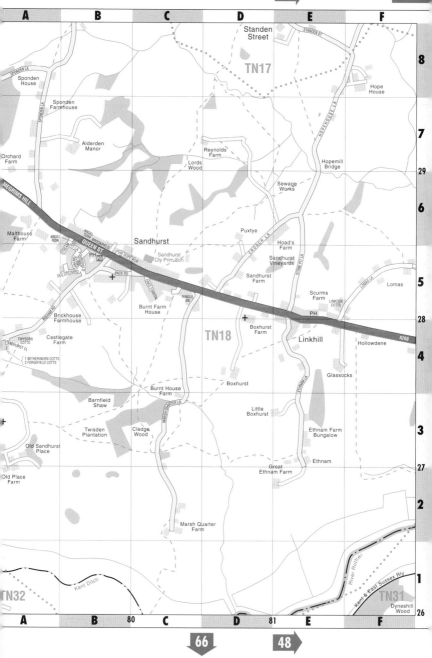

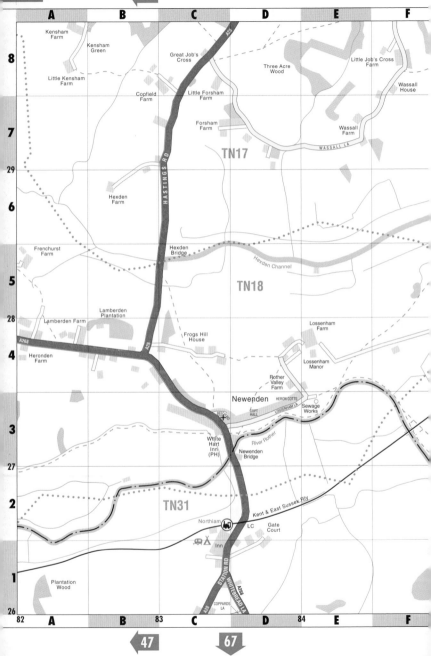

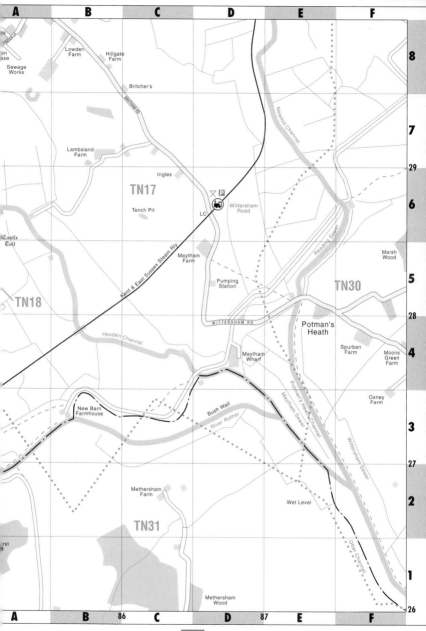

A   **B**   **C**   **D**   **E**   **F**

Sleeches

Buxted Wood

Parkhurst

The Maypole Inn (PH)

CHALLEY LA

RAYNARDS LA

ROYAL OAK LA

CHERRY GDNS

MAYPOLE LA

Holders Farm

Nordens Green

Coxbrook

Tudor Rocks

ROCKS LA

The Hermitage

FOWLER LA

Greenhurst

Grove Wood

Howbourne Farm

Huggett's Farm

Foxhole Farm

HOWBOURNE LA

Coes Rough

Stones Rough

Rosemount

Vanguard Way

CHURCHGATE

BUXTED WOOD LA

New House Farm

River Uck

Dolloways Bank House

TN22

Saxon Court

PEMBROKE LA

SPOTTED COW LA

Parsonage Wood

Sewage Works

Buxted

NURSERY FIELD

PARK VIEW

SPICE GARTH

CHURCH RD

LEWIS CL

HIGH BELTS

Toll Farm

Lowe Wood

Pound Green

Stone's Wood

White Hart (PH)

A272

Buxted

HIGH ST

POST OFFICE

BRITTS ORCH

LIME LA

Popeswood Farm

Lower Totease Farm

FRANKLIN RD

HUGH TRACK

COOMBE LA

G.S.

BUXTED CT

TRIM RD

Potter's Green

Abbotswood House

Bish Wood

Culver Wood

Mascalls Farm

NAN TUCKS LA

TANYARD COTTS

Tanyard Farm

Lower Lowlands Farm

Shepherd's Hill

POUND LA

Etchingwood

STONELEE LA

24

23

22

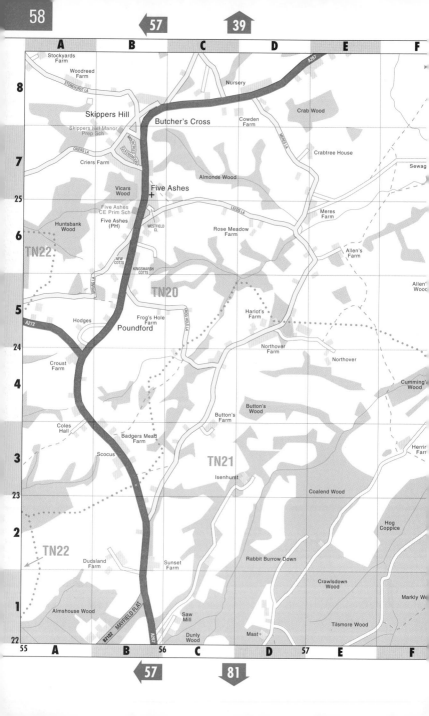

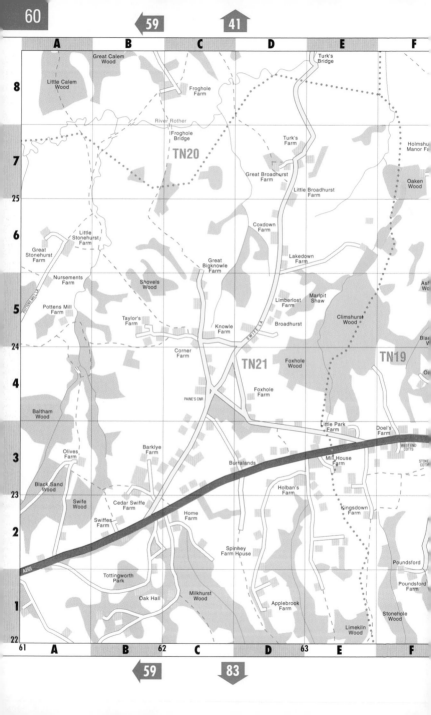

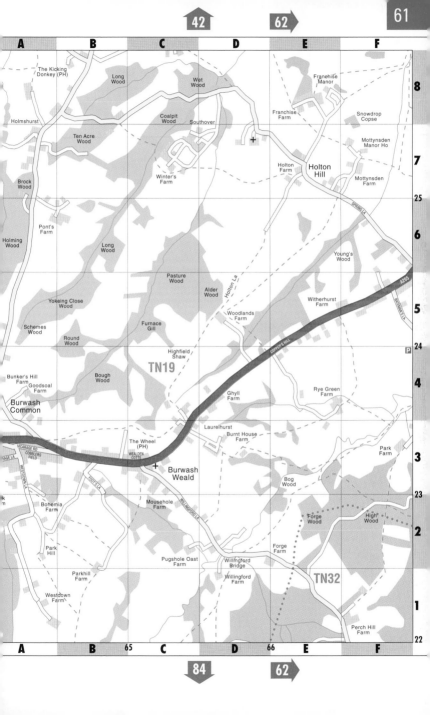

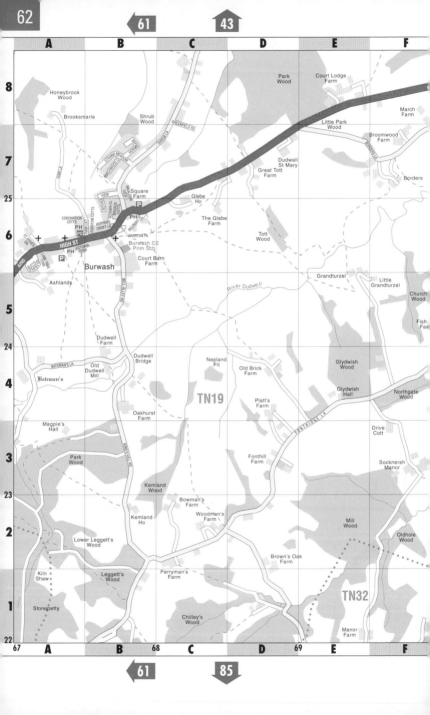

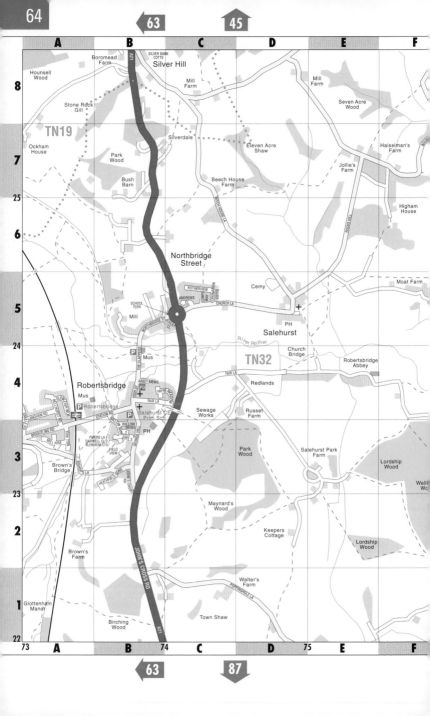

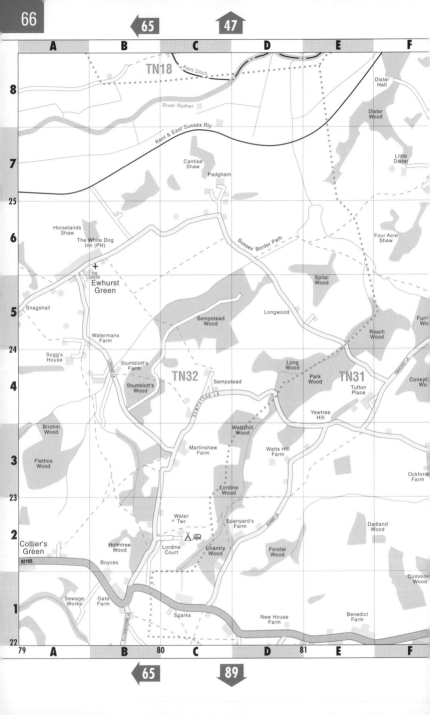

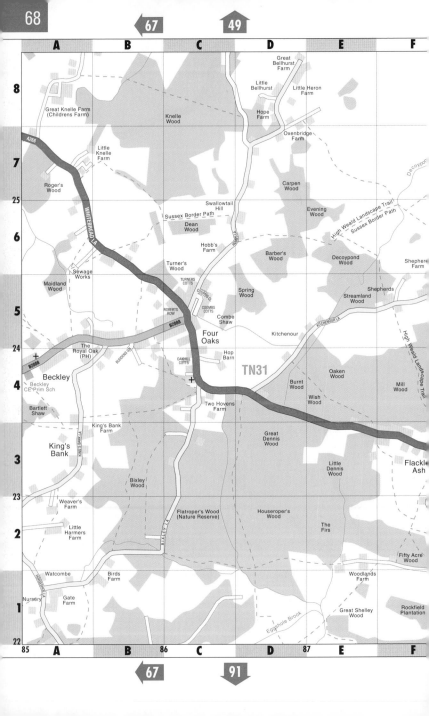

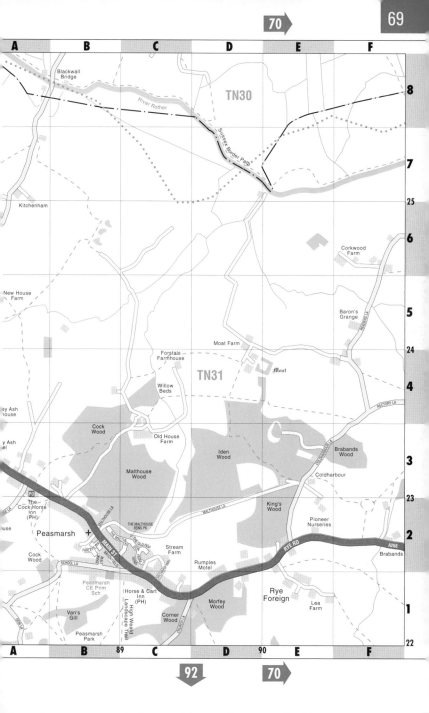

69

A **B** **C** **D** **E** **F**

TN30

Newbridge Farm

RYE RD B2082

Rother Levels

TN30

8

WITTERSHAM RD

New Bridge

7

Sussex Border Path

Thornsdale Farm

25

Sewage Works

GARDNER'S HILL

Varriers Wood

Nirvana

Saxon Shore Way

6

SHETH LA

Oxenbridge Farm

Royal Military Canal

Readers Farm

River Rother

Idenfield Farm

Bosney Farm

5

WITTERSHAM LA

Orchards Farm

24

The Elms

The Bell Inn (PH)

Park Farm

DRIVE LA

TN31

Sunningdale House

Spring Farm

MILITARY RD

RECTORY LA

+

Iden

Cliff Farm

Boonshill Bridge

4

EL MOSREACH

MAIN ST

Saxon Shore Way

Boonsfield Farm

Iden Park

Old Turk

PLAYDEN LA

RANDOLPH LA

HOUGHTON LA

3

IDEN RD

Houghton Wood

Tighe's Wood

23

Mockbeggar

Houghton Green

Scots Float

2

A268

BOWLERS TOWN

Hotel

St Michaels Prim Sch

HOUGHTON GREEN LA

Brook's Bridge

RYE RD

B2082

Union Channel

FOLKESTONE

1

A259

Peace & Plenty (PH)

POPPWIELD

Saltbarn Farm

22

91 **A** **B** **92** **C** **D** **93** **E** **F**

A268

69   93

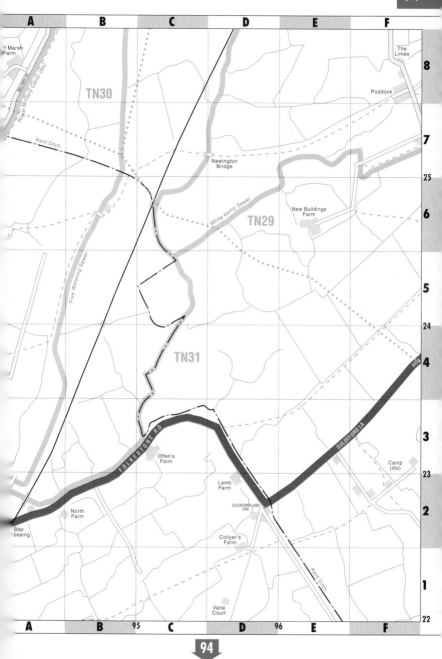

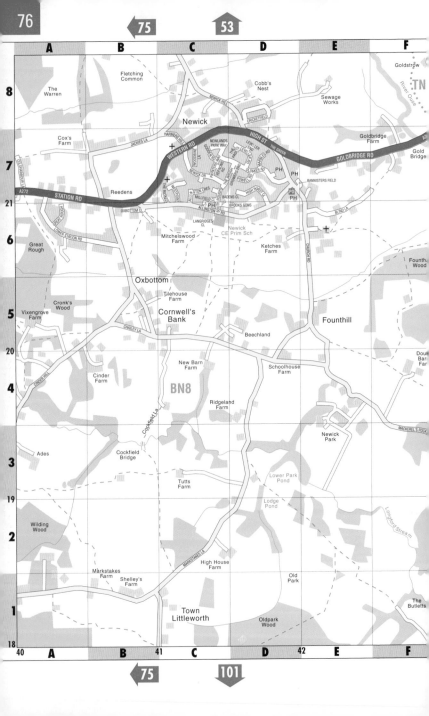

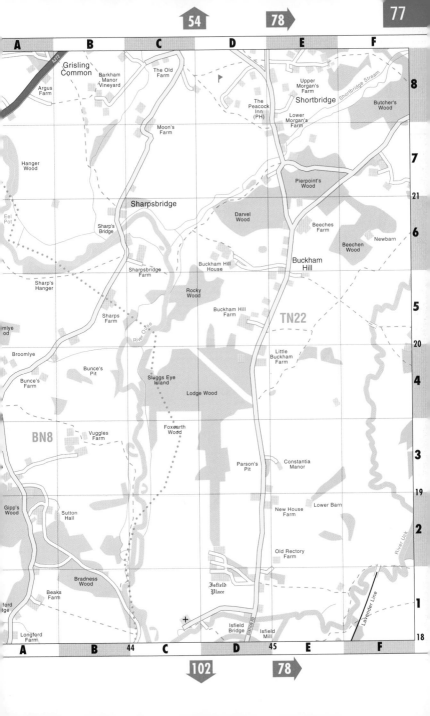

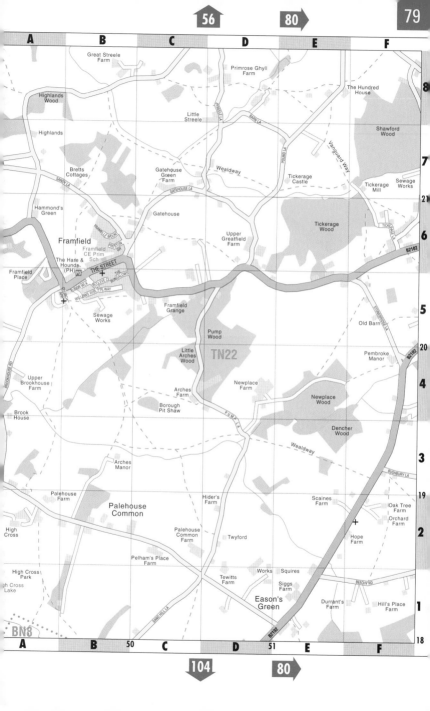

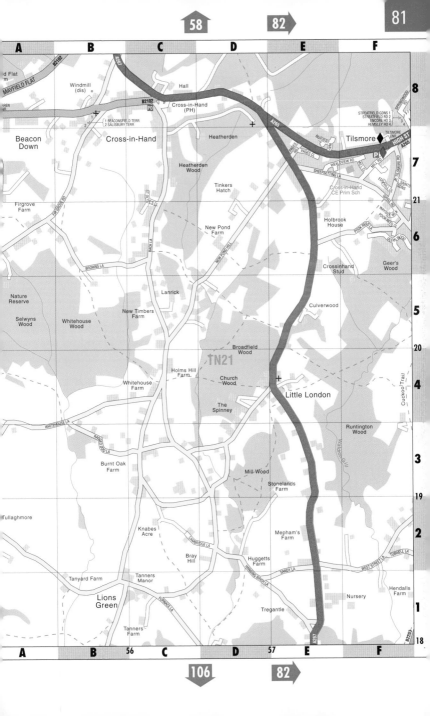

81

59

Map labels:

CHERWELL CT 1
SHEDDEN CT 2
MILL RISE 33

Mutton Hall

The Crown (PH)

BURWASH RD

A265

Little Tottingworth Farm

Ph

MUTTON HALL LA

MUTTON HALL HILL

SPRING PARK

WALDRON

Satinstown Farm

Stores Wood

River Dudwell

Gamelan Wood

A265 HIGH ST

1 LENNOX CT
2 HIGH VIEW
3 STONEGATE WAY
4 MILESTONES
5 PAGE'S COTTS

ROUNDHOUSE COTTS

Heathfield Sch & Com Coll

Streetfield Farm

Ind Est

PROSPECT TERR

Recn Gd

Heathfield L Ctr

7

21

UPPER STATION RD

Tower

HEATHFIELD

Heathfield Park

PORTLAND SQ

Mon

1 CHESTNUT COTTS
2 BROWNING RD
3 MARY BURFIELD CT
4 SHELLEY PK

HAILSHAM RD

1 LANSDOWN TERR
2 PARK VILLAS
3 EAST VIEW
4 OAKLEIGH DR

Heathfield Park

Recn Gd

PH

Cade Street

6

Waldron Gill

Cuckoo Trail

THE AVENUE

THE SPINNEY

GREEN LA

Heathfield CE Prim Sch

Manor Farm

Ind Est

THEOBALDS GN

SANDY CROSS COTTS

BAY TREE

MAGNES

BEECHWOOD LA

ASPEN WLK

Old Heathfield

The Star Inn (PH)

Highlands Farm

St Dunstan's Wood

5

20

ROWAN CL

Sandy Cross

Theobald's Green Farm

Parkside Cty Prim Sch

WEAVERS ROCK LA

Heathfield House

St Dun Far

Barretts Park Farm

TN21

4

The Runt-in-Tun (PH)

White Chimney's Farm

Walnuts Farm

Fountain Wood

St Dun Far

FAIRY WLK

Runtington Manor Farm

Nevilles Farm

New Sapperton Farm

Furnace Wood

Wet Wood

Beck We

3

19

WEST STREET LA

Sapperton Wood

Sapperton Manor Farm

West Street Farm

Nettlesworth Farm

Nettlesworth Place

Pond Farm

Beckington Bridge

Braysland Farm

Cuckoo Trail

2

Maynard's Green Cty Prim Sch

TURNPIKE LA

SICKLEHATCH LA

Springdale Farm

Grantleys Farm

Nettlesworth Wood

FURNACE LA

Maynard's Green

1

18

Stillyans Farm

St Mary's Sch

Hale Hill Farm

Court Lodge Farm

58   A   59   B   C   59   D   60   E   F

81

107

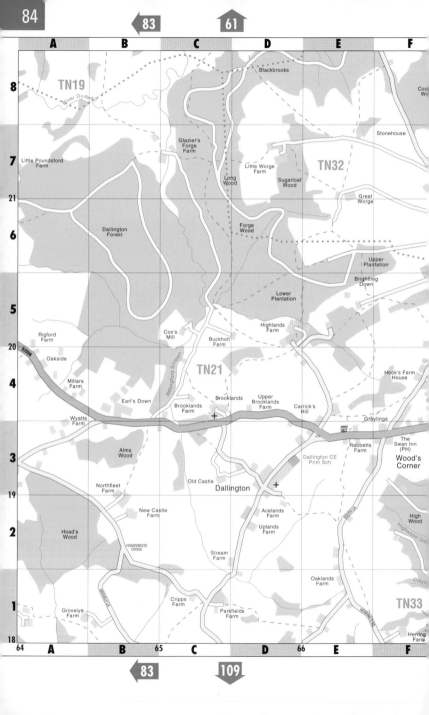

A   B   C   D   E   F

8

TN19

River Dudwell

Blackbrooks

Cool
We

Little Poundsford
Farm

Glazier's
Forge
Farm

7

Stonehouse

Little Worge
Farm

TN32

Long
Wood

Sugarloaf
Wood

21

Great
Worge

6

Dallington
Forest

Forge
Wood

Upper
Plantation

Brightling
Down

5

Lower
Plantation

Highlands
Farm

Upper
Plantation

Rigford
Farm

Cox's
Mill

Buckholt
Farm

20

Oakside

B2096

Hook's Farm
House

Millars
Farm

TN21

4

Earl's Down

Brooklands

Upper
Brooklands
Farm

Carrick's
Hill

Graylings

Brooklands
Farm

Wyatts
Farm

PO

The
Swan Inn
(PH)

Wilmingford Stream

Rabbetts
Farm

Wood's
Corner

3

Alms
Wood

Dallington CE
Prim Sch

Old Castle

Northfleet
Farm

19

Dallington

Acelands
Farm

High
Wood

New Castle
Farm

2

Uplands
Farm

Highwood Gill

Hoad's
Wood

HOADSWOOD
CROSS

Stream
Farm

A2100

SOUTH LA

Oaklands
Farm

Clayto

1

Grovelye
Farm

Cripps
Farm

Parkfields
Farm

TN33

HERRING RD

Herring
Farm

18

64   A   B   65   C   D   66   E   F

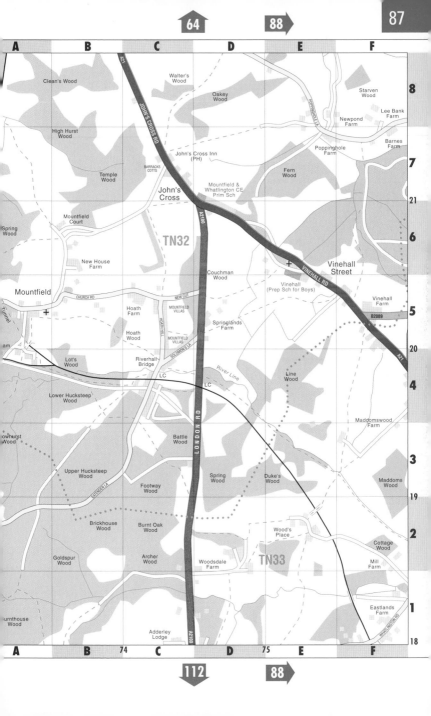

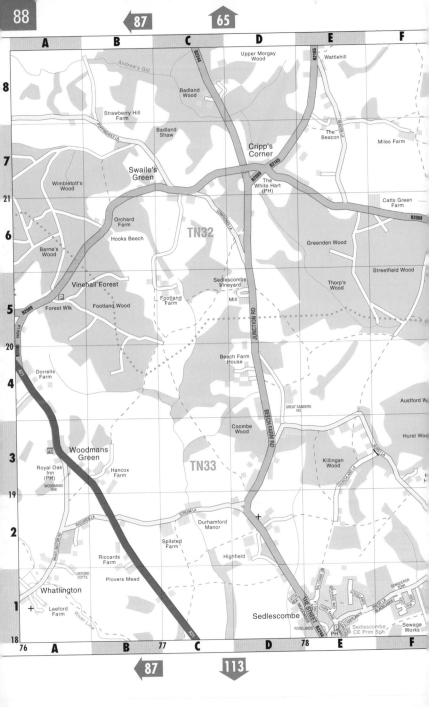

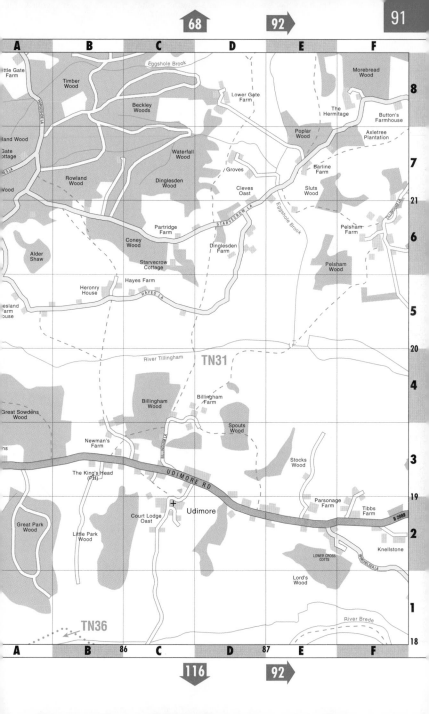

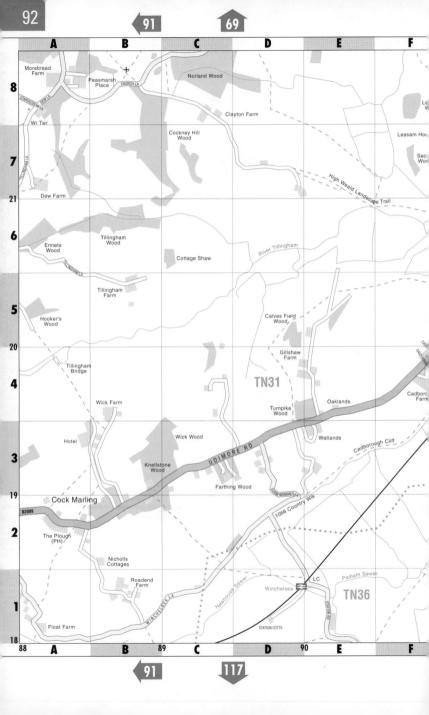

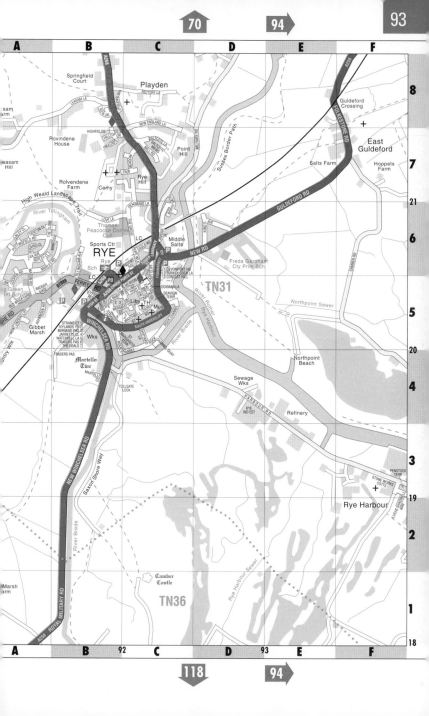

A B C D E F

8

Kent Ditch

Barn Farm

Tressland

7

East Guldeford Level

Moneypenny

21

Guldeford Sewer

Black House Farm

6

Wainway Wall

5

20

Guldeford Sewer

4

Northpoint Beach

CAMBER RD

Point Farm

Pound Field Farm

FARM LA

DRAY'S LA

Holiday Centre

3

1 INKERMAN TERR
2 PAINES COTTS
3 MARY STAMFORD GN

CH

1 COACHHOUSE CI
2 FLEETWAY CI

PH

TRB Sta

COASTGUARD COTTS

OLD WORLD COTTS

P

NEW LYDD RD

Camb

19

OYSTER CREEK

HARBOUR RD

P

JAM WAY

OLD LYDD RD

SECOND AVE

Martello Tier

2

Lime Kiln Cottage

River Rother

Dunes

PETER JAMES CL

MARINE COTTS

P

Dunes

Rye Bay

1

Rye Harbour Nature Reserve

East Pier

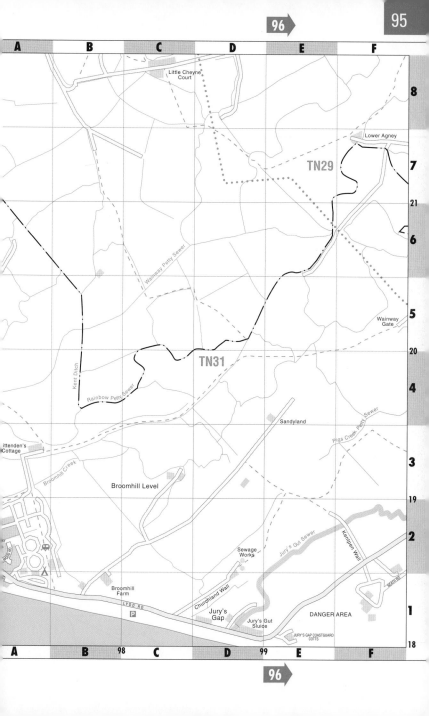

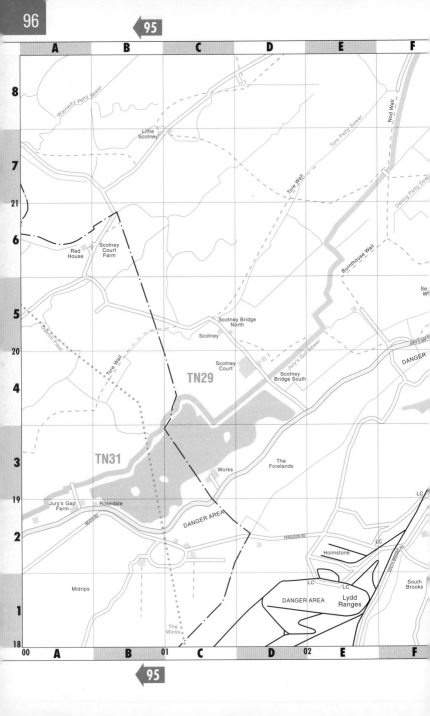

95

8

7

21

6

A B C D E F

Wainway Petty Sewer

Little Scotney

Tore Wall

Tore Petty Sewer

Nod Wall

Dering Petty Sewer

Red House

Scotney Court Farm

Burnthouse Wall

Se W

5

20

4

Scotney Bridge North

Scotney

Scotney Court

Scotney Bridge South

Jury's Gut Sewer

AIRY'S GAP

DANGER

TN29

Tore Wall

TN31

3

19

The Forelands

Works

Jury's Gap Farm

Rosedale

DANGER AREA

FERGUSON RD

LC

2

Midrips

Holmstone

LC

LC

LC

LC

South Brooks

SOUTH BROOK'S RD

1

DANGER AREA

Lydd Ranges

The Wicks

18

00 A B 01 C D 02 E F

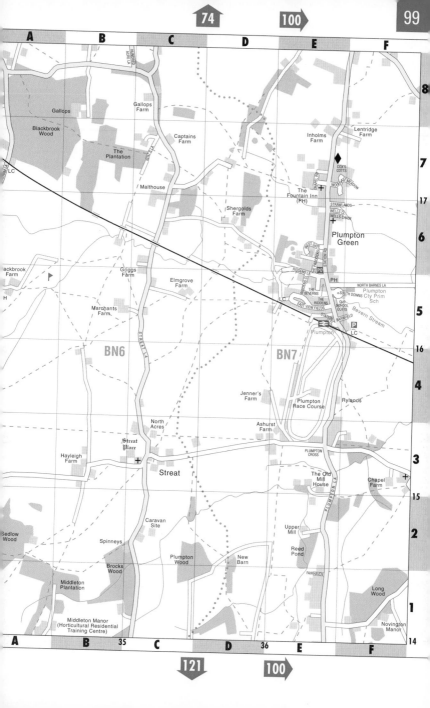

A   B   C   D   E   F

Markstake
Common

Southam
Wood

South
Common

CAVERIDGE LA

Starvecrow
Wood

Works

A275

ST JOHN'S CL 1
OLD FOORD GL 2
ST JOHN BANK

BROCKHOUSE LA

GREEN LA

Kiln
Wood

Balneath
Manor

1 NYM CL
2 MEADOW HO
3 FOLLETT HOLT HO
4 REED HO
5 PALMER HO

Middle Home
Wood

HONEYPOT LA

Chailey Cty
Sec Sch

South
Chailey

SHEPHERD'S LA

MILL LA

MILL
CL

ELLEY CL

BROOKLAND LA

HORNEY CL

SWAN CL

OAKLANDS 1
MAYTREE COTTS 2

Homewoodgate
Farm

Yokehurst

Oldbarns
Farm

The Swan
Inn (PH)

ANDROS
CL

Swan
Wood

BN8

North Barnes
Farm

North
Hall

NORTH BARNES LA

Woodbrooks
Farm

Bevern Bridge
Farm

Hovel
Wood

Hurst
Barns

Works

BEVERN BRIDGE COTTS 1
BEVERN BRIDGE 2

Mount
Pleasant
Cottage

Bevern Stream

HORSHOE LA

Hewenstree
Farm

Brookhouse

BN7

Lower
Burrells

ST PETERS LA

Foll
Woo

RESTING OAK HILL

HOLLYCROFT

SCHOOL
COTTS

LC

Chiltington

Upper
Burrells

Wickham
Barn

WICKHAM LA

CHAPEL LA

NOVINGTON LA

The Jolly
Sportsman
(PH)

East
Chiltington

Wootton
Farm

Whitehouse
Farm

Winterlands
Farm

Stantons
Farm

Spooner's
Farm

Chapel
Farm

Nurs

Novington
Oak

BEECHWOOD LA

Wootton
Shaw

Beechwood
House

ALLINGTON LA

Warningore
Wood

37   A   B   38   C   D   39   E   F

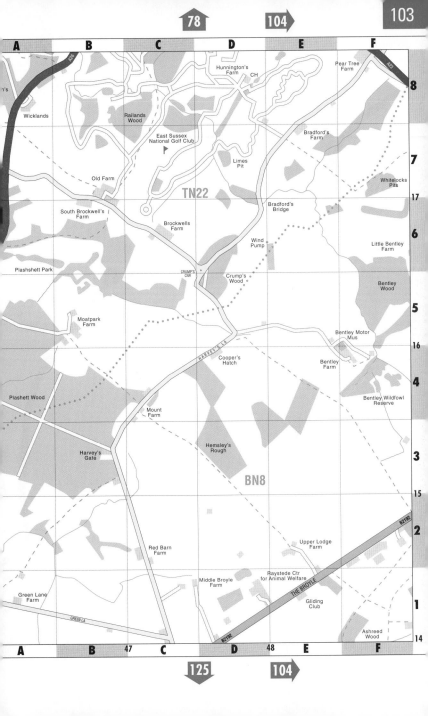

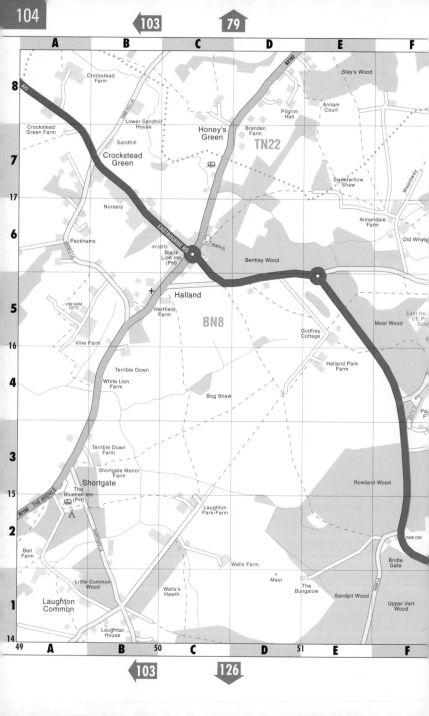

A   B   C   D   E   F

8

A22

Crockstead
Farm

Slay's Wood

Lower Sandhill
House

SAND HILL LA

Crockstead
Green Farm

Annam
Court

Pilgrim
Hall

Honey's
Green

Branden
Farm

B2192

Sandhill

7

Crockstead
Green

TN22

Sweetwillow
Shaw

17

Wealdway

Nursery

Peckhams

KNOWLE LA

EASTBOURNE RD

6

Annandale
Farm

Old Whyly

IVY COTTS

Black
Lion Inn
(PH)

OLD HEATH CL

Bentley Wood

Halland

5

Vine Farm
Cotts

Hartfield
Farm

BN8

Godfrey
Cottage

Moat Wood

East Ho
CE Pr
Sch

16

Vine Farm

Terrible Down

Halland Park
Farm

4

White Lion
Farm

Bog Shaw

Terrible Down
Farm

3

Shortgate Manor
Farm

Rowland Wood

Shortgate

Pa
F

SOUTH ST

15

THE BROYLE

B2192

The
Bluebell Inn
(PH)

SOUTH LA

Laughton
Park-Farm

2

Bell
Farm

PARK CNR

Walls Farm

PARK LA

Bridle
Gate

1

Laughton
Common

Little Common
Wood

Walls's
Hawth

Mast

The
Bungalow

Sandpit Wood

Upper Vert
Wood

14

Laughton
House

A B C D E F

8

Kirby Farm

Crouch's Farm

Piper's Farm

Hope Farm

Scallow Bridge

Longreach Shaw

Convent

Great Wood

Davis's Town

Cinder Wood

Ralph Wood

7

TN21

Firgrove

Barham Farm

Barham House

Graywood Farm

17

Jackmans Farm

llers Wood

Minepit Wood

6

Belmont Farm

Etchingley Wood

Hesmonds Farm

Belmont

THE QUADRANGLE

Scotland Farm

Broomfield Wood

Broomfield Farm

COMAS TURNER DR
CARPENTERS CROFT
LONDON RD
MILL LA
SOUTH ST
STREAM
CLUMP CROFT
BUTTSFIELD LA
CIDER HOUSE WLK
PH

East Hoathly

Gray Wood

HALLAND RD

5

16

Tourle's Farm

Great Ailies Farm

BN8

Clarklye Farm

Vanguard Way

Chiswell's Farm

4

France Wood

Starve Wood

Holdens Farm

ewage Wks

Decoypond Wood

Wealdway

Hilder's Court

3

Martinland Wood

Eggs Wood

15

Coldharbour Farm

Highlands Farm

Frith's Farm

2

Old Land Wood

rice's arm

Parsonage Farm

Chiddingly Place

Chiddingly

A22

Narvic Mink Farm

Whitesmith Farm

The Six Bells (PH)

Little Park Farm

1

14

A B 53 C D 54 E F

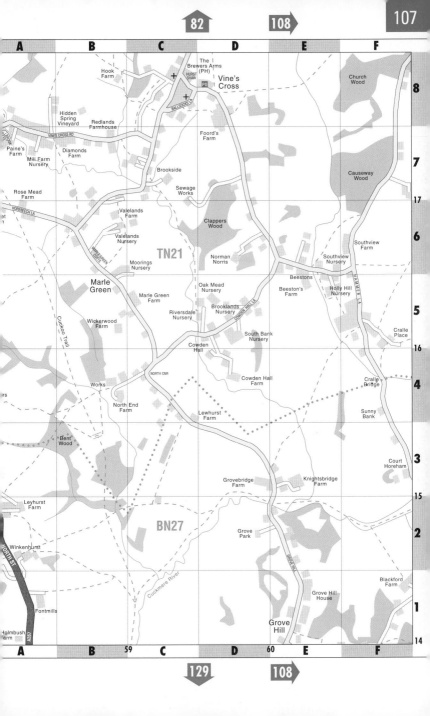

A   B   C   D   E   F

8

The
Brewers
Arms
(PH)
Vine's
Cross
Hook
Farm
HURST SHAW
Church
Wood

BALLSDOCK LA

Hidden
Spring
Vineyard
Redlands
Farmhouse
Foord's
Farm
VINES CROSS RD

7

Paine's
Farm
Mill Farm
Nursery
Diamonds
Farm
Brookside
Causeway
Wood

Rose Mead
Farm
Sewage
Works

17

HOREBEECH LA
Valelands
Farm
Clappers
Wood

6

Valelands
Nursery
MARLE GREEN COTS
TN21
Moorings
Nursery
Norman
Norris
Southview
Farm
Southview
Nursery

Marle
Green
Marle Green
Farm
Oak Mead
Nursery
Beestons
Southview
Nursery

5

Wickerwood
Farm
Riversdale
Nursery
Brooklands
Nursery
Beeston's
Farm
Holly Hill
Nursery
COWDEN HALL LA
HAMMER LA

Cuckoo Trail
South Bank
Nursery
Cralle
Place

16

Cowden
Hall

4

Works
NORTH CNR
Cowden Hall
Farm
Cralle
Bridge

North End
Farm
Lewhurst
Farm
Sunny
Bank

3

Bent
Wood
Court
Horeham

Leyhurst
Farm
Grovebridge
Farm
Knightsbridge
Farm

15

BN27
Grove
Park

2

Winkenhurst
NORTH ST
Blackford
Farm

GROVE HILL

Fontmills
Grove Hill
House

1

Holmbush
arm
A267
Grove
Hill

14

A   B   59   C   60   D   E   F

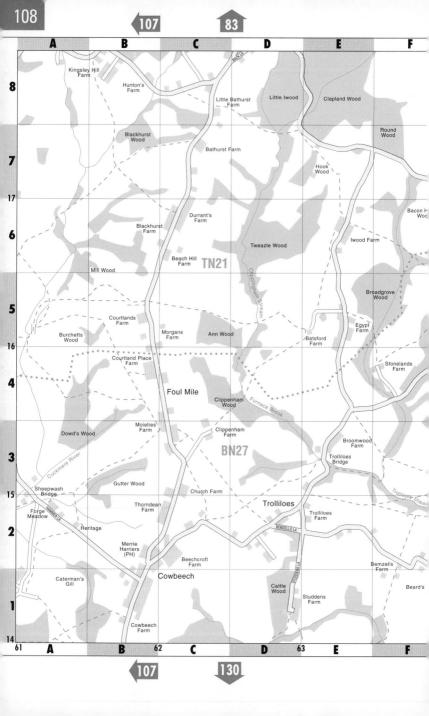

107
83

Kingsley Hill Farm

Hunton's Farm

Little Bathurst Farm

Little Iwood

Clapland Wood

Blackhurst Wood

Bathurst Farm

Round Wood

Hook Wood

Durrant's Farm

Blackhurst Farm

Tweazle Wood

Bacon Woo

Beach Hill Farm

TN21

Iwood Farm

Mill Wood

Clippenham Stream

Broadgrove Wood

Courtlands Farm

Morgans Farm

Ann Wood

Egypt Farm

Burchetts Wood

Batsford Farm

Stonelands Farm

Courtland Place Farm

Foul Mile

Clippenham Wood

Furnace Brook

Dowd's Wood

Moieties Farm

Clippenham Wood

Broomwood Farm

BN27

Trolliloes Bridge

Cuckmere River

Gutter Wood

Church Farm

Trolliloes Stream

Sheepwash Bridge

Trolliloes

Forge Meadow

Thorndean Farm

Trolliloes Farm

Heritage

BEMZELLS LA

Merrie Harriers (PH)

Beechcroft Farm

Bemzells Farm

Caterman's Gill

Cowbeech

Cattle Wood

Studdens Farm

Beard's

Cowbeech Farm

107
130

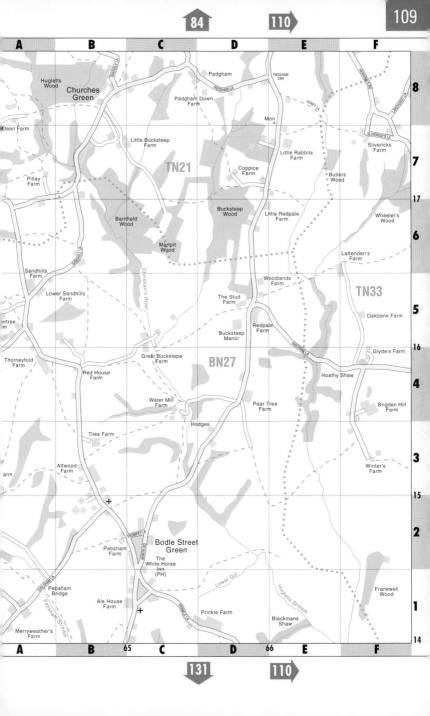

A B C D E F

8
7
17
6
5
16
4
3
15
2
1
14

Hugletts Wood
Churches Green
Padgham
PADGHAM LA
PADGHAM CNR
Dean Farm
Little Bucksteep Farm
Padgham Down Farm
Mon
HONEY LA
BESSING RD
LARKSHILL LA
Sliverick's LA
Slivericks Farm
TN21
Coppice Farm
Little Rabbits Farm
Butlers Wood
Pilley Farm
Bucksteep Wood
Little Redpale Farm
Wheeler's Wood
Barnfield Wood
Marlpit Wood
Lattenden's Farm
Sandhills Farm
Christian's River
Woodlands Farm
TN33
Lower Sandhills Farm
The Stud Farm
Oakbank Farm
rtree m
Redpale Farm
FARTHING LA
Thorneyfold Farm
Great Buckstepe Farm
BN27
Glyde's Farm
Bucksteep Manor
Red House Farm
Hoathy Shaw
Water Mill Farm
Pear Tree Farm
Brigden Hill Farm
Tiles Farm
Hodges
arm
Attwood Farm
Winter's Farm
+
TRUMPET LA
Bodle Street Green
Pebsham Farm
Frankwell Wood
CHURCH RD
Pebsham Bridge
The White Horse Inn (PH)
Lower Gill
Hugletts Stream
CHILSHAM LA
Pebsham Stream
Ale House Farm
+
Prinkle Farm
PRINKLE LA
Blackmans Shaw
Merryweather's Farm

65
66

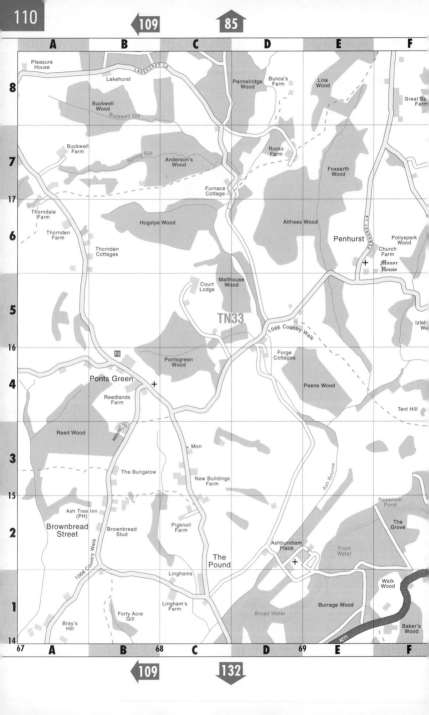

8

7

17

6

5

16

4

3

15

2

1

14

A   B   C   D   E   F

Pleasure House

Lakehurst

LAKEHURST LA

Buckwell Wood

Buckwell Gill

Buckwell Farm

Spring Gill

Anderson's Wood

Pannelridge Wood

Bunce's Farm

Link Wood

Great Sp Farm

Rocks Farm

Foxearth Wood

Thorndale Farm

Thornden Farm

Hogstye Wood

Thornden Cottages

Allfrees Wood

Penhurst

Pollyspark Wood

Church Farm

Manor House

PENHURST LA

Furnace Cottage

Court Lodge

Malthouse Wood

TN33

1066 Country Walk

Izleb West

Ponts Green

PO

Pontsgreen Wood

Forge Cottages

Peens Wood

Tent Hill

Reedlands Farm

A269 NING FIELD

Reed Wood

The Bungalow

Mon

New Buildings Farm

Ash Bourne

Reservoir Pond

The Grove

Ash Tree Inn (PH)

Brownbread Street

1066 Country Walk

Brownbread Stud

Pigknoll Farm

Ashburnham Place

Front Water

Walk Wood

Linghams

The Pound

Bray's Hill

Forty Acre Gill

Lingham's Farm

Broad Water

Burrage Wood

A271

Baker's Wood

67   A   B   68   C   D   69   E   F

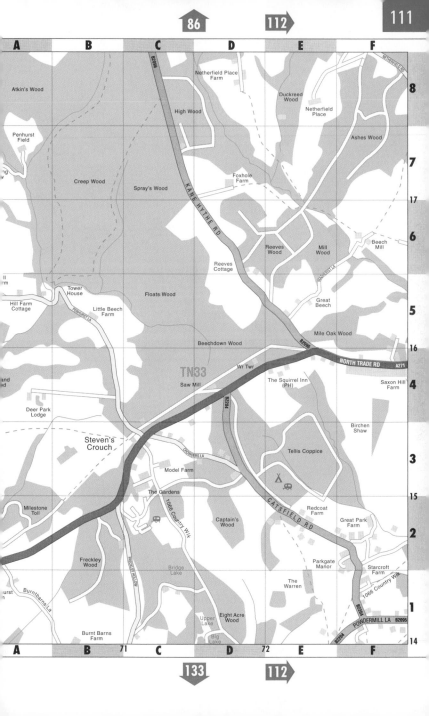

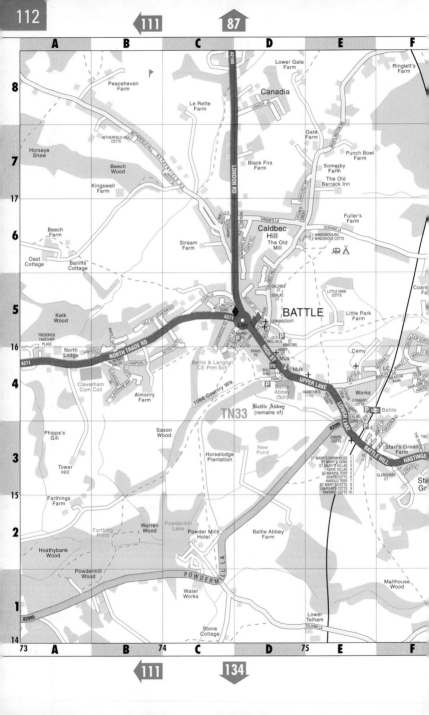

A | B | C | D | E | F

Riccards Wood
Queen's Head (PH)
Catt's Shaw

River Brede
Sedlescombe Bridge

THE BOWLINGS

Petley Wood
Lower Marley Farm
RIVERBRIDGE COTTS
Pestalozzi Children's Village

Felon Wood
Luff's Farm

RUTHERFORDS BSNS PK
Cold Spring Shaw
Magazine Farm
PAYGATE RD
B2244
COTTAGE LA

Horsmans Farm
Old Horsmans

Meadow View
Beanford Farm

Marley Farm
Marley House

WHYDOWN HILL
NEW ENGLAND LA

Battle Barn Stud Farm

Oak Wood

Woodland Walk
Whitefield Wood
Fir Wood

1066 Country Wlk
CH

TN33
Great Wood

KENT ST
Kent Street

riars
Norton's Farm

A21

Burnt Chimney Farm
Upper Morax Wood

Branshill Farm
Birchin Shaw
Duke's Wood
Screen Wood

Little Hemingfold Farm

LOOSE FARM COTTS
Mill Wood
Oak Wood
Bishop's Wood
Beauport Park

Loose Farm

Telham
HASTINGS RD
Alder Wood
Stonehouse

Bushy Wood
Blackhorse Hill
Hemingfold Farm
Ring Wood
TN38

Black Horse (PH)
Three Cedar Wood

A2100

A | B | 77 | C | D | 78 | E | F

8 | 7 | 17 | 6 | 5 | 16 | 4 | 3 | 15 | 2 | 1 | 14

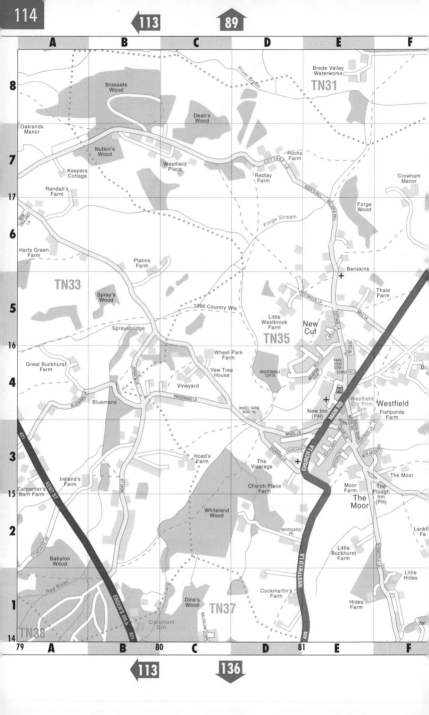

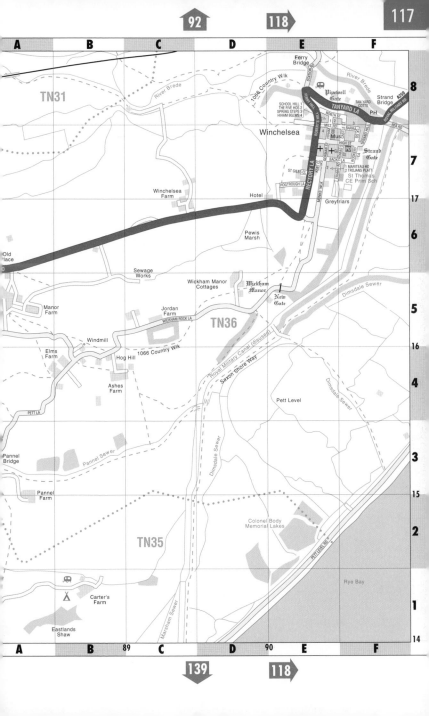

A B C D E F

8

River Brede
Farm

Sewage Wks

Nook Beach

The Nook

Saxon Shore Way

River Brede

Castle Farm

TN36

Nature Reserve

7

SUTTONS
IND PK

Watch
House

Nook Drain

17

WINDMILL WAY
GREYFRIARS

WINDMILL
CT

6

The Ship
(PH)

HARBOUR
BARN

WILLOW ST

THE RIDGE

Dimsdale Sewer

RD

5

Winchelsea
Beach

DOGS HILL RD

VUE
BRIS NEZ

16

DOALS WAY
WINDSOR WAY
CENTRAL WAY

Dogs Hill

4

PETT LEVEL RD

Rye Bay

3

15

2

1

14

ROYAL MILITARY RD

A259

A   B   C   D   E   F

Wolstonbury

Wolstonbury Hill

Wellcombe Bottom

Clayton

UNDERHILL LA

8

Clayton Holt

Rockrose

Clayton Windmills

P   Jill

Jack

Chantry

MILL LA

7

BN6

13

DALE HILL   PYECOMBE

New Barn Farm

Pyecombe

South Downs Way

6

CH

Wayfield Farm

Rag Bottom

Cow Down

PH

CHURCH LA

Riding School

Haresdean

5

Middle Brow

12

BN45

A273   LONDON RD

4

Pangdean Farm

Holt Bottom

Pangdean Holt

Sussex Border Path

3

South Hill

War Meml

BN1

11

South Hill Cottages

Poor Brow

2

South Hill Farm

Deep Bottom

The Pylons

Hogtrough Bottom

Sussex Border Path

Scare Hill

1

combe

Ewebottom Hill

Ewe Bottom

10

A   B   29   C   D   30   E   F

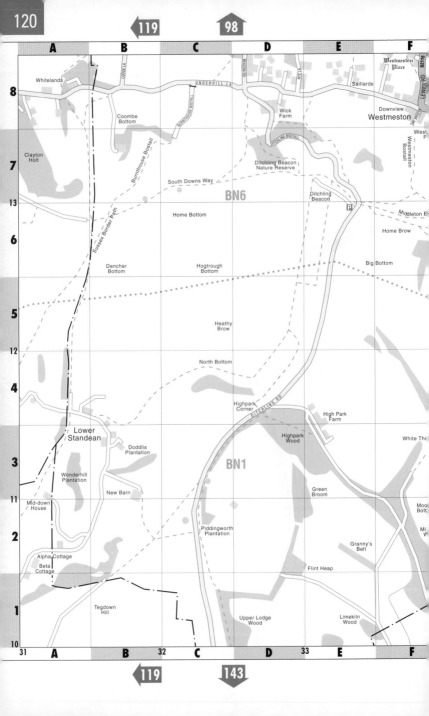

119
98

A **B** **C** **D** **E** **F**

Westmeston Place

Whitelands

UNDERHILL LA

Saillards

LEWES RD B2116

8

Coombe Bottom

Wick Farm

Downview

Westmeston

West F

Clayton Holt

BEACON RD

WYE LA

Westmeston Bostall

Burnhouse Bostall

7

Ditchling Beacon Nature Reserve

DITCHLING BOSTALL

South Downs Way

BN6

Ditchling Beacon

13

Middleton E

Sussex Border Path

Home Bottom

Home Brow

6

Dencher Bottom

Hogtrough Bottom

Big Bottom

5

Heathy Brow

12

North Bottom

4

Highpark Corner

DITCHLING RD

High Park Farm

Lower Standean

Doddlis Plantation

Highpark Wood

White Tho

3

Wonderhill Plantation

New Barn

BN1

Green Broom

Moo Bott

11

Mid-down House

2

Piddingworth Plantation

Granny's Belt

Mi V

Alpha Cottage

Beta Cottage

Flint Heap

1

Tegdown Hill

Upper Lodge Wood

Limekiln Wood

10

31 **A** **B** **32** **C** **D** **33** **E** **F**

119
143

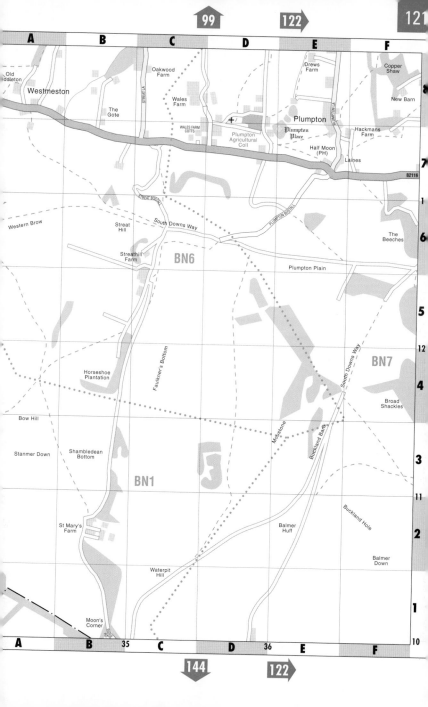

Warningore House

Warningore Farm

Allington Farm

Russet Shaw

Tulleyswells Farm

Lower Tulleyswells Farm

BEECHWOOD LA

BN8

Newstead Farmhouse

Watershoot Shaw

New Barn

B2116

B2116

Warningore Bostall

Courthouse Farm

Mount Harry House

Offham Farm

Offham House

Blackcap

Mount Harry

Coombe Place

Offham

Coombe Plantation

BN7

Ashcombe Bottom

Offham Hill

Training Gallop

Landport Bottom

Cuckoo Bottom

Training Gallop

South Downs Way

Balmer Down

Cook's Bridge

Cooksbridge
Hamsey Cty Prim Sch
Sewage Works

Cooksbridge

North End

Cowlease Farm

Bushy Island

Wellingham Farm

Copyhold Farm

Hamsey Manor

BN8

Hamsey

River Ouse

Hamsey House

Chalkham Farm

Sewage Works

Drove House

Hamsey Crossing

Hamseyplace Farm

Hamsey Place

Pay Gate Cottages

Upper Stoneham Farm

The Pells

Pellbrook Cut

Lower Stoneham Farm

Chalk Pit Inn (PH)

BN7

Landport Farm

Old Malling Farm

Malling House
(Sussex Pol HQ)

RUSSELL ROW 1
REED CT 2
MEALLA CL 3
PECKHAM CL 4.

Malling Hill

South Malling
CE Prim Sch

Landport

Pells CE Prim Sch

South Malling

The Brooks

Superstore

Wallands Cty Prim Sch

Wallands Park

Ind Est

LEWES

Obelisk

HQ

Cuilfail

HM Prison Lewes

St Anne's

Castle Mus

Library

Cliffe

WILLIE COTTS
THE MOORINGS

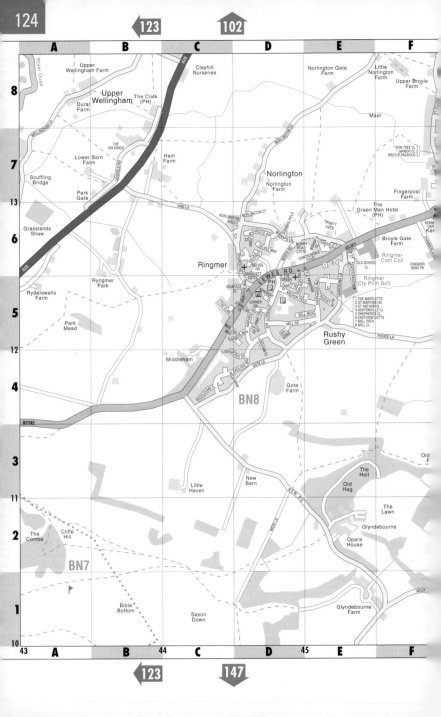

8
7
13
6
5
12
4
3
11
2
1
10

A   B   C   D   E   F

Upper Broyle
Farm

Longfield
Wood

Highfield
Farm

Plain
Barn

Broyle Mill
Farm

THE BROYLE

B2192

Turnpike
Farm

B2124

New
Barn

Lower Lodge
Farm

HALF MILE DRO

Broyle
Place

Paygate
Cottages

Colbrans
Farm

LAUGHTON RD

Barnfield
Farm

Sewage
Works

Decoy
Wood

Laughton Place
Farm House

Arches
Farm

Ashton
Green

Old
Barn

MOOR LA

MILES LA

New
Barn

BN8

Moorland
Farm

Laughton Place
(remains of)

Moor
House

Laughton
Place
Farm

Wakelands

Laughton
Level

Totts
Shaw

Lower
Wood

Glynde Reach

Cows
Wood

A   B   47   C   D   48   E   F

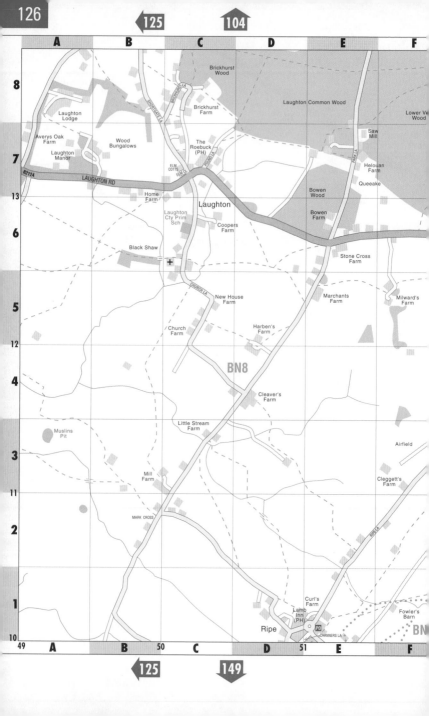

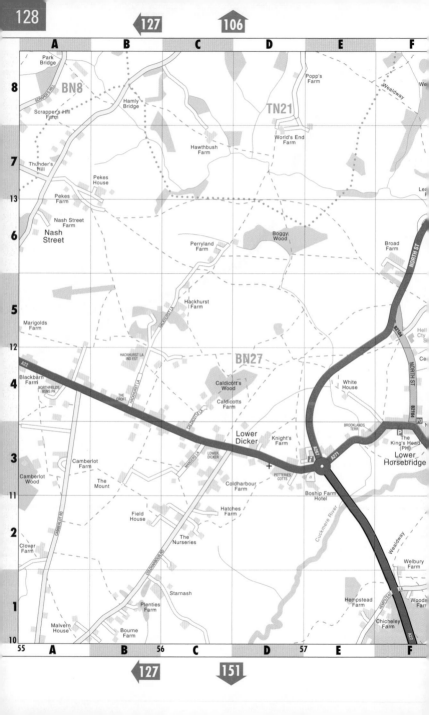

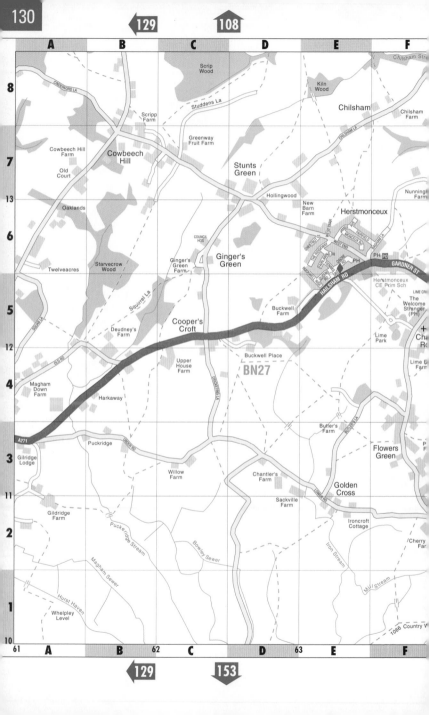

131
110

A B C D E F

8 | 1066 Country Wlk · ORCHARD RISE | Henley's Bridge | Hammer Wood | The Old Kennels | | Compass Wood | A271

Northland Wood | | | | | Combe Hill Farm

7 | | len Bourne | Spring Shaw | Wilding Wood | Luxford's Wood | Combe Hill

Wilson's Farm | Kitchenham Farm | | Combe Wood

13

6 | | | Ninfield Stream | | Lower Standard Hill Farm | STANDARD HILL CL 1 · COOKSTOWN CL 2 · HIGH ST

Gardners Farm | | | | Standard Hill House | Standard Hill

5 | 1066 Country Wlk | A269 | Little Standard Hill Farm | Works | Moor Hall Farm

Hazard's Green | TN33

12

Blackstock Bridge | Boreham Bridge

4 | BOREHAM HILL | | | Wet Wood | Re W

A271

3 | BN27 | | Hooe Level | | White's Wood

New Barn

11 | | Water's Haven | | | Tanyard Farm

2 | | | Waterol Stream | Sandhall Farm | Red Lion (PH) | Hooe Common | EL DOHAM HILL

School Farm

1 | Hogtrough Bridge | | | | B2095

10 | 67 | Bunts Barn | B2095 | Sadlers Farm | 69 | Longe Fa

A B 68 C D E F

131
155

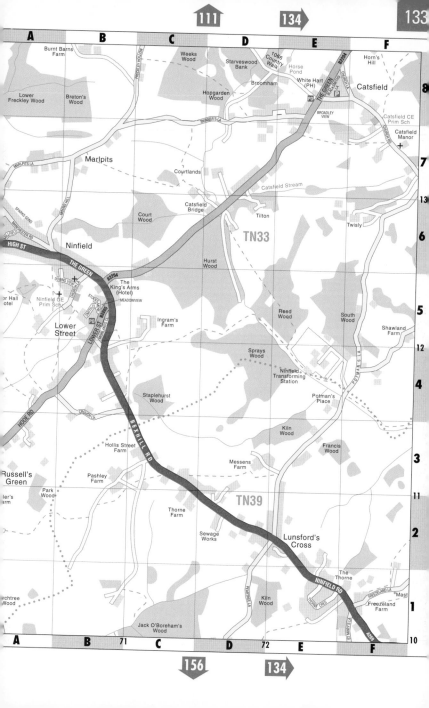

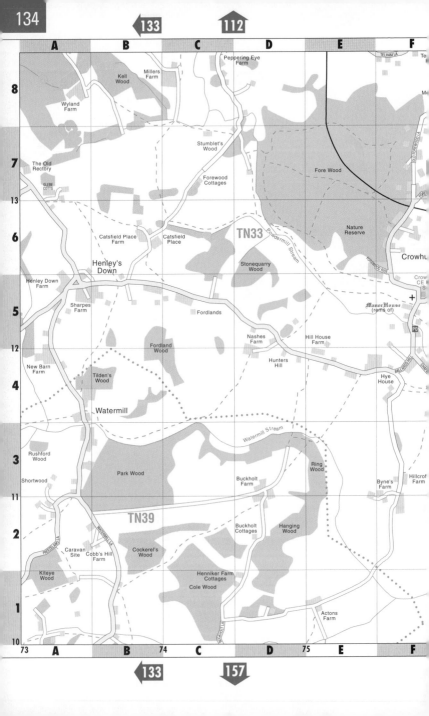

8

7

13

6

5

12

4

3

11

2

1

10

A B C D E F

Peppering Eye Farm

Kell Wood

Millers Farm

Wyland Farm

Stumblet's Wood

The Old Rectory

GLEBE COTTS

Forewood Cottages

Fore Wood

TN33

Nature Reserve

Catsfield Place Farm

Catsfield Place

Stonequarry Wood

Powdermill Stream

Crowhu

Henley's Down

Henley Down Farm

FOREWOOD RISE

Crow CE S

Sharpes Farm

Fordlands

Nashes Farm

Hill House Farm

Manor House (rems of)

PO

New Barn Farm

Fordland Wood

Hunters Hill

Hye House

Tilden's Wood

BALLARDS HILL

Watermill

Watermill Stream

Rushford Wood

Park Wood

Ring Wood

Byne's Farm

Hillcrof Farm

Shortwood

Buckholt Farm

TN39

PRETTE LANE

Caravan Site

Cobb's Hill Farm

Cockerel's Wood

Buckholt Cottages

Hanging Wood

Kiteye Wood

Henniker Farm Cottages

Cole Wood

Actons Farm

73 74 75

TELHAM LA

Te

Me

Crowhu

OLD DARWOOD LA

Lunsford

PETT RD

CHICK HILL

COASTGUARDS

Marsham Sewer

OLD
COASTGUARDS

IRB Sta
The Smuggler
(PH)

Old Marsham
Farm

CANAL BANK

PETT LEVEL RD

TN35

Cliff End

CLIFF END LA

Stumblet
Wood

Fairlight
(NT)

Saxon Shore Way

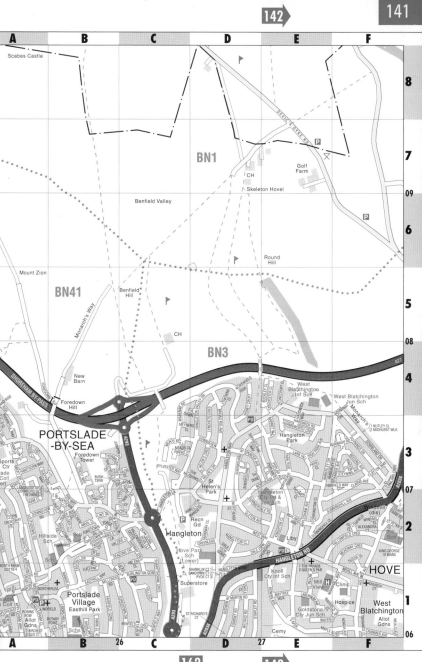

A B C D E F

8
7
09
6
5
08
4
3
07
2
06
1

Scabes Castle

BN1

Benfield Valley

CH
Skeleton Hovel

Golf
Farm

Mount Zion

BN41

Benfield
Hill

Round
Hill

Monarch's Way

CH

BN3

West
Blatchington
Inf Sch

West Blatchington
Jun Sch

SHOREHAM BY-PASS

New
Barn

Foredown
Hill

PORTSLADE
-BY-SEA

Foredown
Tower

Hangleton
Park

1 NUTLEY CL
2 MIDHURST WLK

Sports
Ctr
lade
Coll
er

BUSH
TERR

Monarch's Way

St Helen's
Park

The DENE

Windmill
(dis)

Hillside
Sch

Hangleton
Inf & Jun Sch

Liby

Alexandra

KING GEORGE
VI MANS

Hangleton

Recn
Gd

Hove Park
Sch
(Lower)

GREENLEAS

HANGLETON RD

HOVE

West
Blatchington

Superstore

Knoll
Cty Inf Sch

1 THE PARADE
2 QUEEN'S PAR

Mill
View

H Clinic

Hospice

NORTH FARM
COTTS

Portslade
Village
Easthill Park

Schs

ST RICHARD'S
CT

Goldstone
Cty Jun Sch

Cemy

Allot
Gdns

A B 26 C D 27 E F

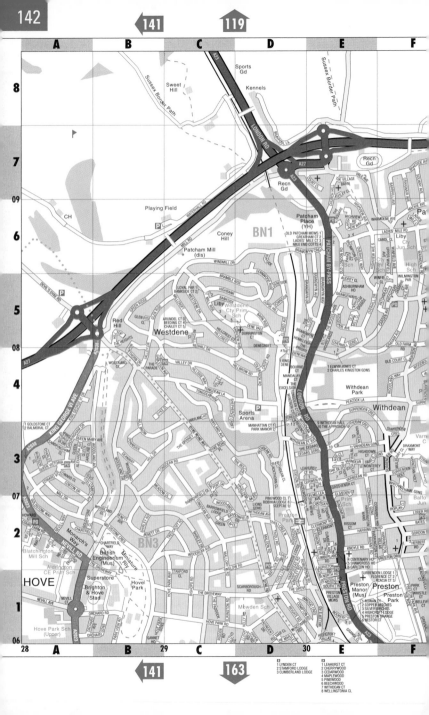

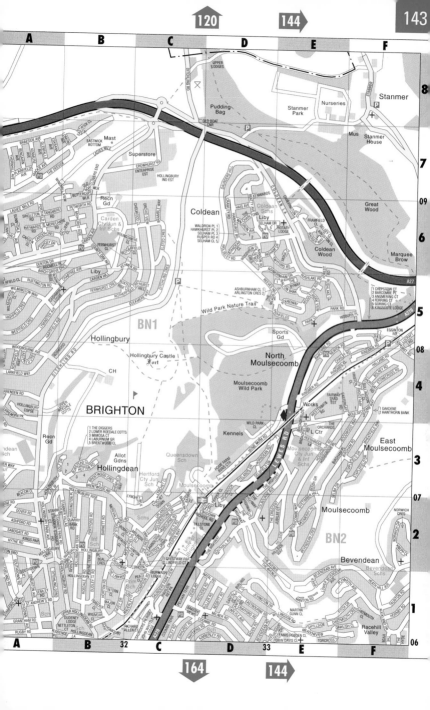

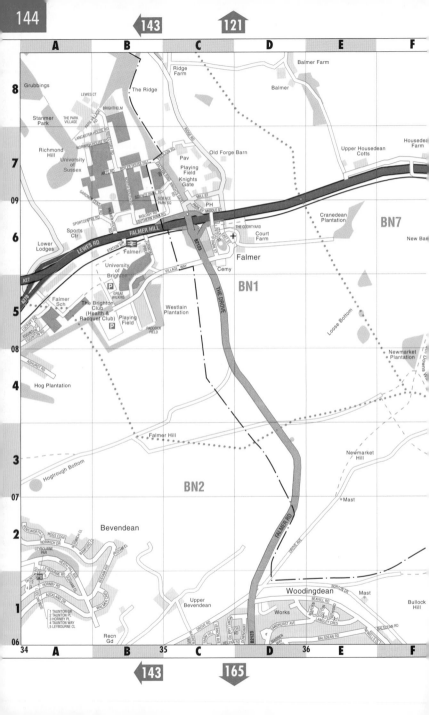

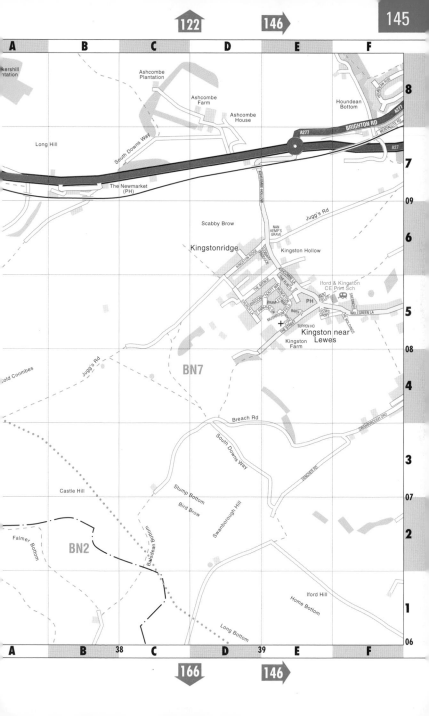

122
146

A B C D E F

8

Ashcombe
Plantation

Ashcombe
Farm

Ashcombe
House

Houndean
Bottom

ckershill
antation

Long Hill

South Downs Way

A277 BRIGHTON RD

A277

A27

7

09

The Newmarket
(PH)

Scabby Brow

Jugg's Rd

NAN
KEMP'S
GRAVE

6

Kingstonridge

Kingston Hollow

Iford & Kingston
CE Prim Sch

THE AVENUE

PH

WELLGREEN LA

5

Tuppen Ho

Kingston near
Lewes

Kingston
Farm

08

old Coombes

Jugg's Rd

BN7

SWANBOROUGH DRO

4

Breach Rd

South Downs Way

3

07

Castle Hill

Stump Bottom

Bird Brow

Swanborough Hill

2

Falmer
Bottom

BN2

Blacken Bottom

Iford Hill

Home Bottom

1

Long Bottom

06

A B 38 C D 39 E F

166
146

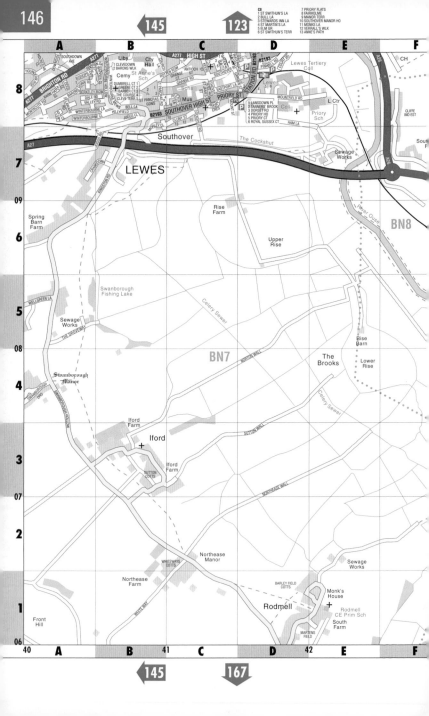

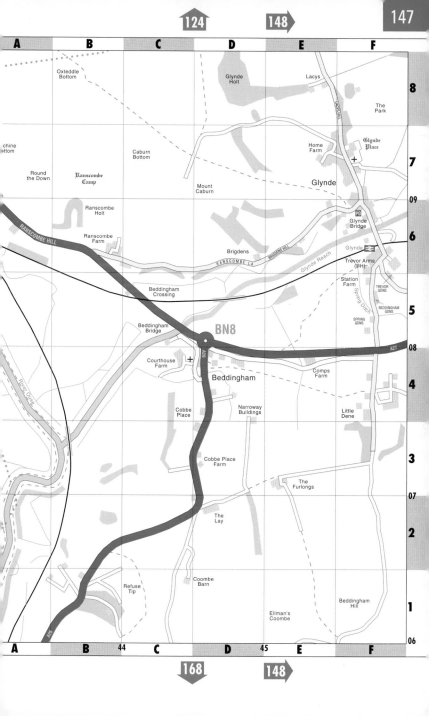

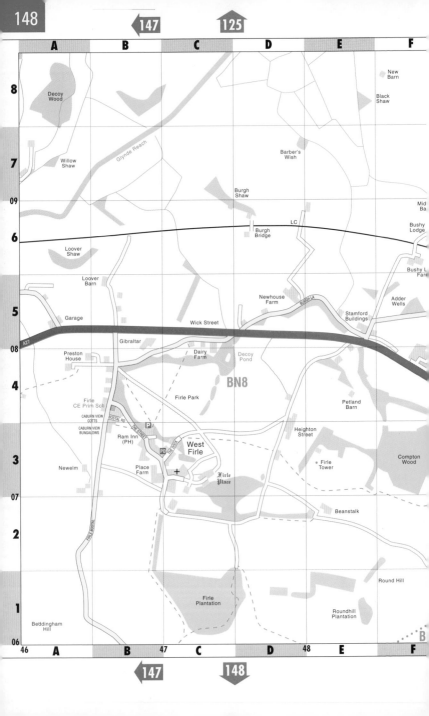

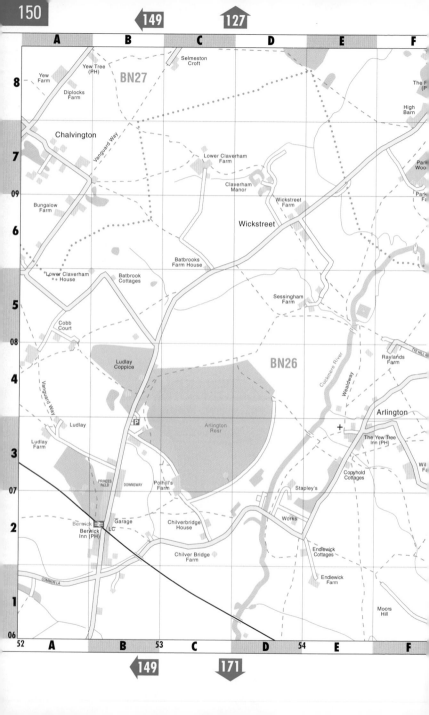

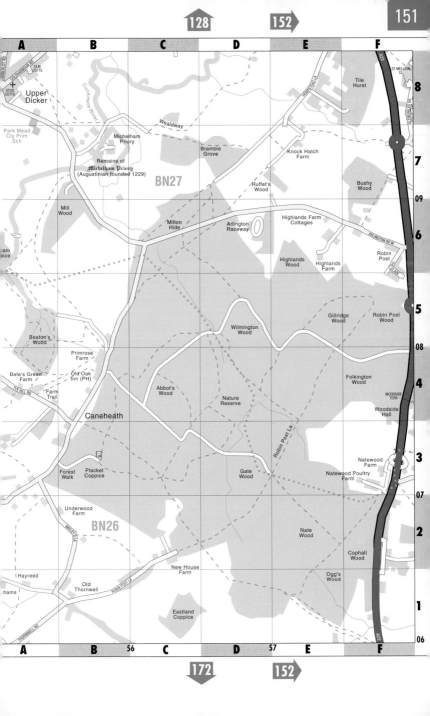

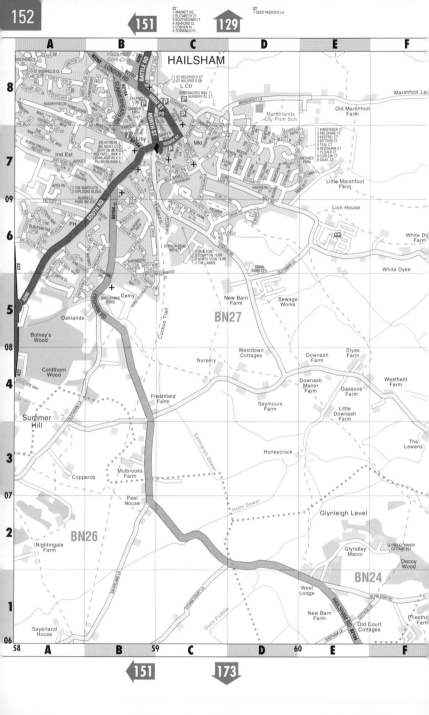

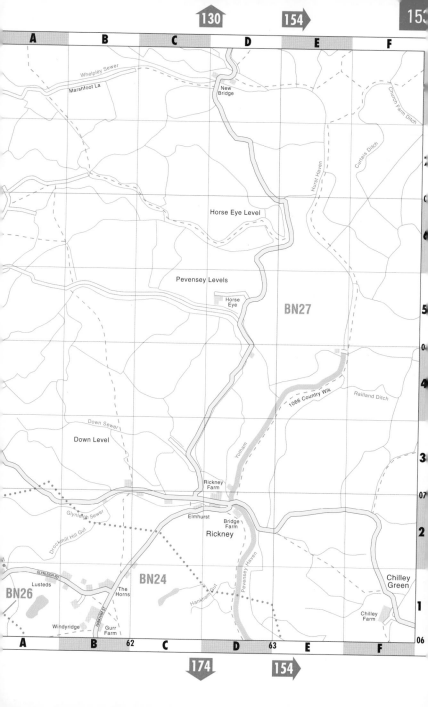

A B C D E F

Whelpley Sewer

Marshfoot La

New
Bridge

Church Farm Ditch

Curteis Ditch

Horse Eye Level

Hurst Haven

Pevensey Levels

Horse
Eye

BN27

1066 Country Wlk

Railland Ditch

Down Sewer

Down Level

Yotham

Rickney
Farm

Glynleigh Sewer

Elmhurst

Bridge
Farm

Rickney

Orockmill Hill Gut

GLYNLEIGH RD

BN24

Pevensey Haven

Chilley
Green

BN26

Lusteds

The
Horns

Hankham Gut

Windyridge

Gurr
Farm

Chilley
Farm

A B 62 C D 63 E F

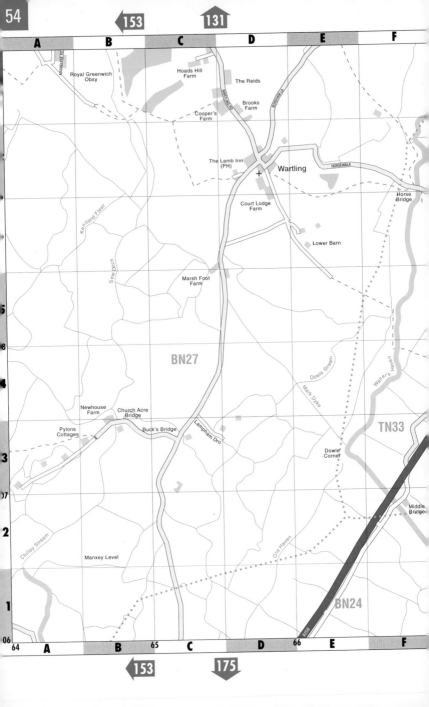

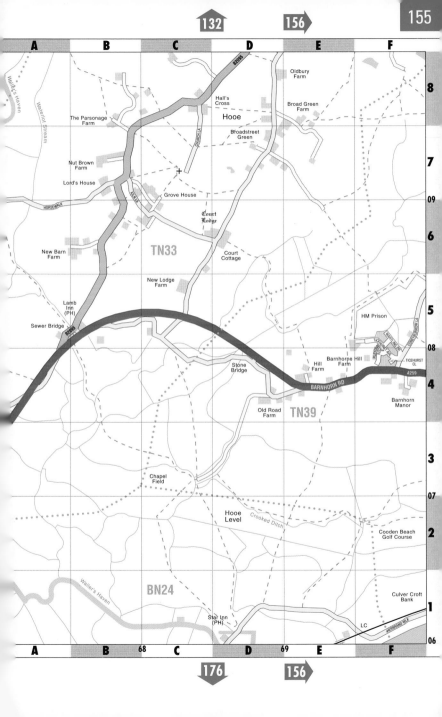

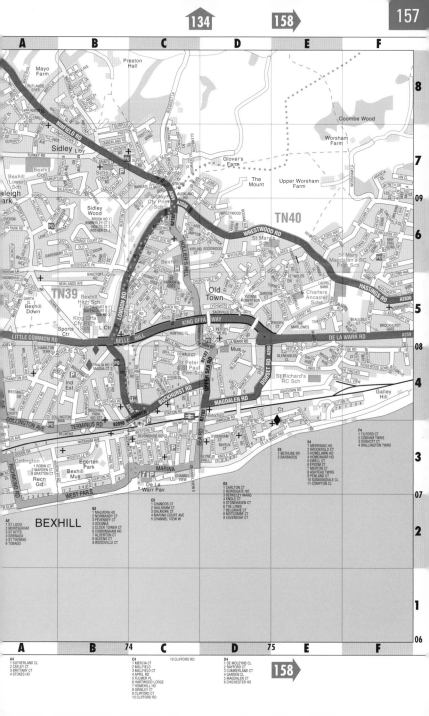

Nature Reserve

Combe Haven

TN38

Harley
Shute

HARLEY SHUTE RD

West
St Leonards
City Prim
Sch

Saxon
Mount Sqh

CARNOUSTIE CL

Pebsham
Wood

West
St Leonards

FILSHAM RD

TN40

1 IAN CL
2 GWYNETH GR
3 CHRISTINE CL

TOP CROSS RD

PEBSHAM DR

Pebsham
Farm

PEBSHAM LA

Refuse Tip

CONQUEROR RD

West/St Leonards
Prim Sch

St Vincent's
FINLEY Sch

PENHURST
DR

Nursery

Pebsham

Playing Fields

HARLEY WAY

GROSVENOR

SEABOURNE RD

PEBSHAM LA

Bulverhythe

BEXHILL RD

CLIFTONVILLE
WAY

BULVERHYTHE RD

ANNBURY
MEWS

CLIFTONVILLE RD

TA
Ctr

SEADUE RD

1 SEASIDE W
2 KEATS CL
3 WEST HILB
4 FLORIDA C

MARTYNS WAY

West Ma

HASTINGS RD

A2036

Schs

CLAYTON

GLOUCESTER
AVE

ASHLEY WAY

**Glyne
Gap**

HYTHE
AVE

DE LA WARR RD

A259

RAVENSIDE
RET & L PK

136

160

C7
1 STAINSBY ST
2 NORFOLK HO
3 ST RICHARDS HO
4 ROYAL TERR
5 EVERSFIELD MEWS N
6 ALAN CT

7 ASHLEY CT
8 ST MARY'S CT
9 CAVENDISH HO
10 DECIMUS BURTON WAY
11 UNION ST

F8
1 WATERWORKS COTTS
2 STONEFIELD PL
3 ELFORD ST
4 WALDEGRAVE ST
5 CORNWALLIS ST
6 ST ANDREW'S SQ

F8
7 ROBERT TRESSELL WKSHPS
8 SUSSEX CHAMBERS
9 MIDDLE ST
10 KINGS WLK
11 PORTLAND COTTS
12 STONE ST

13 PORTLAND PL
14 WELLINGTON TERR
15 PORTLAND TERR
16 PORTLAND VILLAS
17 WELLINGTON PL

B6
1 CRABTREE HO
2 HIGHLANDS MEWS
3 ARCHERY CT
4 WEST HILL CT
5 COURTLANDS
6 SADDLER'S CT
7 ARCHIE CT
8 GREERA CT
9 CONWAY CT

C6
1 STANHOPE PL
2 HAROLD MEWS
3 SHEPHERD ST
4 MARINE CT
5 ST CLEMENTS PL
6 MOUNT PLEASANT
7 UNDERCLIFF TERR
8 MARKET TERR
9 MARKET PAS
10 GRAND CT

D6
1 PRINCE'S RD
2 WARRIOR CT
3 EVERSFIELD CT
4 THE ALEXANDRA

E7
1 HOLMEBURY HO
2 TRINITY VILLAS
3 TRINITY MEWS
4 WAVERLEY CT
5 SCHWERTE WAY
6 NORMAN CT
7 WHITE ROCK GDNS
8 ST MICHAEL'S PL
9 CLAREMONT
10 TRINITY ST
11 PALACE CT

F7
1 ROBERTSON TERR
2 ALBANY CT
3 QUEEN'S AVE
4 YORK GDNS
5 YORK BLDGS
6 WELLINGTON PL
7 HOMEDANE HO
8 CASTLE ST
9 CASTLE GDNS

St Leonards

TN37

TN34

TN38

HASTINGS

Hastings

Pier

White Rock
Pleasure
Grounds

160 | 159 | 137

HASTINGS

159

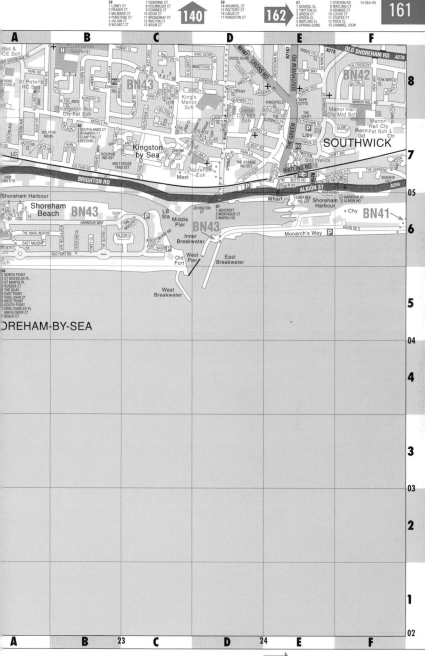

161

140 →

162 →

C8		C8		E7		7 STATION RD	14 SEA HO
1 LONEY CT	7 OSBORNE CT	14 ARUNDEL CT	1 SCHOOL CL	7 STATION RD	8 WATLING CT	
2 FRASER CT	8 HOLMBUSH CT	15 RECTORY CT	2 TWITTEN CL	9 GRANGE CT	
3 MILWARD CT	9 DOWNES CT	16 CAIUS CT	3 GREEN CT	10 LOCKS CT	
4 PENSTONE CT	10 ADUR CT	17 KINGSTON CT	4 GREEN CL	11 COATES CT	
5 JULIAN CT	11 BROADWAY CT		5 WATLING CL	12 ROOK CL	
6 WILMOT CT	12 WISTON CT		6 SPRING GDNS	13 CHANNEL VIEW	
	13 ARUN CT				

7 STEYNING CT
8 BRAMBER CT
9 EATON CT
10 GRANVILLE CT
11 HADDINGTON ST
12 MALVERN ST
13 MONMOUTH ST

C7
1 DEVONSHIRE CT
2 CORNWALL CT
3 SOMERSET CT
4 JANESTON CT
5 STIRLING CT
6 BRECON CT

7 ELIZABETH CT
8 PHILIP CT
9 GAINSBOROUGH HO
10 DRIVE LODGE
11 EATON MANOR
12 VERIC
13 VALVERDE HO

14 VALENTINE CT
15 HEREFORD CT
16 GAINSBOROUGH HO
17 EATON GATE
18 CHARIS CT
19 EATON HALL
20 EATON GDNS MANS

142

C7
21 VANBRUGH CT
D7
1 COWDRAY CT
2 GOODWOOD CT
3 CROMWELL CT
4 WILLOW CT

164

D7
5 KINSALE CT
6 PALMEIRA HO
7 BELL MEAD
8 AMBER CT
9 CONISTON CT
10 SOMERHILL CT

11 BERESFORD CT
12 PARHAM HO
13 PETWORTH HO

HOVE
BN3
Sussex Cty Cricket Gd
BRIGHTON
West Pier (dis)
189

B5
1 VICTORIA TERR
2 VICTORIA COTTS
3 BENHAM CT
4 SPA CT
5 THE PRIORY
6 ST CATHERINE'S TERR
7 COURTENAY TERR
8 HAMILTON MANS
9 OLIVER HO

B6
1 GROSVENOR MANS
2 LORRAINE CT
3 PARNELL CT
4 DURHAM CT
5 WINDSOR LODGE

C6
1 MARLBOROUGH CT
2 COPTHORNE CT
3 NORMANDY HO
4 GRAND AVENUE MANS
5 COOMBE LEA
6 VICTORIA CT
7 VICTORIA GR
8 HAREWOOD CT
9 WILBURY GRANGE
10 THE AMBASSADORS
11 BOWEN CT
12 GROVE CT
13 WILBURY LODGE
14 ASHDOWN
15 SUSSEX CT
16 THE ATHENAEUM
17 SANDRINGHAM LODGE
18 HATFIELD CT
19 AMBER CT
20 AVENUE CT
21 PALMEIRA MANS
22 ST JOHN'S PL

D5
1 LANSDOWNE SQ
2 ALICE CL
3 BRUNSWICK MEWS
4 DONKEY MEWS
5 UPPER MARKET ST
6 LOWER MARKET ST
7 KERRISON MEWS
8 CHAPEL MEWS
9 WATERLOO HO
10 EMBASSY CT
11 GOLDEN LA
12 CAVANDISH MEWS
13 IVY MEWS
14 CROSS ST
15 FARMAN ST

D6
1 CROWN CL
2 PALM CT
3 GWYDYR MANS
4 ROCHESTER CT
5 ROCHESTER CL
6 ST ARIES WELL, HO
7 LANSDOWNE MEWS
8 THE COURTYARD

E5
1 LITTLE WESTERN ST
2 DORCHESTER CT
3 NORFOLK ST
4 NORFOLK CT
5 NORFOLK BLDGS
6 NORFOLK MEWS
7 KINGSLEY CT
8 CAVENISH HO
9 BEDFORD TWRS
10 ASTRA HO
11 ABBOTTS
12 METROPOLE CT
13 SUSSEX HTS
14 RUSSELL MEWS
15 REGENCY MEWS
16 FRED EMERY CT
17 SILWOOD PL
18 OSPREY HO
19 SILWOOD CT
20 SILWOOD HALL
21 WESTERN TERR
22 SILWOOD TERR
23 MITRE HO
24 HAMPTON ST

E6
1 WORCESTER CT
2 KENYA CT
3 VERNON CT
4 VERNON GDNS
5 BELVEDERE MEWS
6 VICTORIA PL
7 HAMPTON TERR
8 HEATHER CT
9 MONTPELLIER LODGE
10 BOUNDARY PAS
11 BRAEMAR HO

E7
1 WESTCOMBE
2 PRESTONVILLE CT
3 CADOGAN CT
4 BELMONT CT
5 ST ARINS MANS
6 BERKELEY CT
7 DERBY CT
8 WARWICK CT
9 RICHMOND CT
10 MARSTON CT
11 LORRAINE CT
12 CHESTER CT
13 YORK CT
14 WINDLESHAM CT
15 PAVILION CT
16 WESTMORLAND CT

164
For full street detail of the highlighted area see page 189.

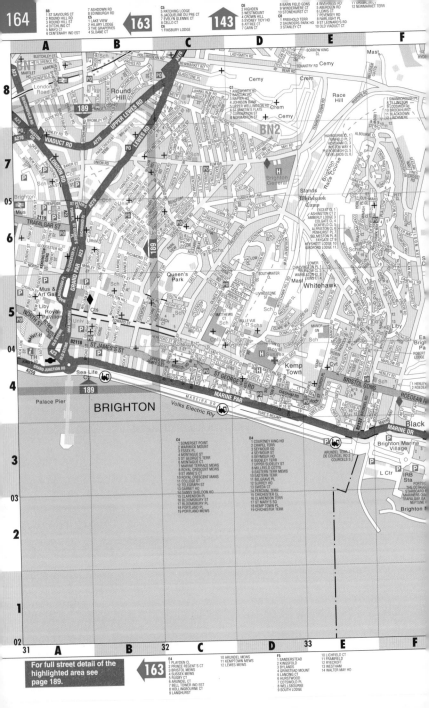

For full street detail of the highlighted area see page 189.

163

165 145

165 177

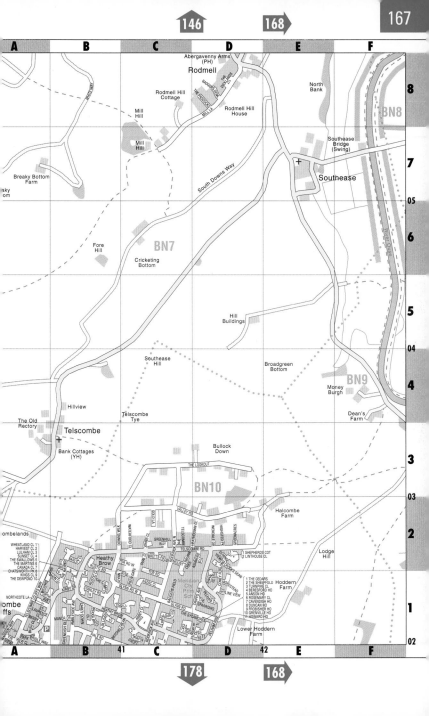

A   B   C   D   E   F

8

Abergavenny Arms (PH)
Rodmell
Rodmell Hill Cottage
Rodmell Hill House
North Bank
BN8

Mill Hill
Mill Hill

7

South Downs Way
Southease Bridge (Swing)
Southease

Breaky Bottom Farm
aky om

05

BN7

6

Fore Hill
Cricketing Bottom

River Ouse

5

Hill Buildings

04

Southease Hill
Broadgreen Bottom
BN9

4

Money Burgh

Hillview
Telscombe Tye
Dean's Farm

The Old Rectory
Telscombe
Bank Cottages (YH)
Bullock Down

3

THE LOOKOUT
BN10

03

ombelands

Halcombe Farm

2

WHEATLAND CL 1
HARVEST CL 2
LULHAM CL 3
SUNSET CL 4
THE SWALLOWS 5
THE MARTINS 6
CANADA CL 7
CHATSWORTH PK 8
KINGS CL 9
THE DEWPOND 10.
Heathy Brow
VALLEY RD
GREENHILL WAY
TELSCOMBE RD
1 SHEPHERDS COT
2 LINTHOUSE CL
Lodge Hill
Hoddern Farm

NORTHCOTE LA
ombe
ffs
Meridian City Prim Sch
THE SPARROWS
1 THE CEDARS
2 THE SHEEPFOLD
3 TURNPIKE CL
4 BERESFORD HO
5 ANSON HO
6 ROSEMARY CL
7 CAVENDISH HO
8 DUNCAN HO
9 FROBISHER HO
10 GRENVILLE HO
11 HOWARD HO

1

THE SYCAMORES
Lower Hoddern Farm

PARK BRIDLE WAY
P

02

A   B   41   C   D   42   E   F

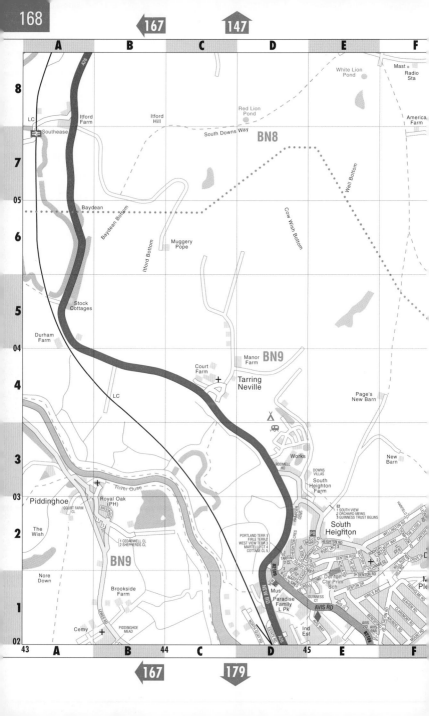

A   B   C   D   E   F

8
7
05
6
5
04
4
3
03
2
1
02

A26

LC
Southease

Itford Farm

Itford Hill

White Lion Pond

Mast
Radio Sta

Red Lion Pond

South Downs Way

BN8

America Farm

Baydean

Baydean Bottom

Itford Bottom

Muggery Pope

Well Bottom

Cow Wish Bottom

Stock Cottages

Durham Farm

LC

Manor Farm   BN9

Court Farm

Tarring Neville

Page's New Barn

Works

RODMELL HO

DOWNS VILLAS

South Heighton Farm

New Barn

Piddinghoe

COURT FARM CL

Royal Oak (PH)

River Ouse

The Wish

1 CEDARWELL CL
2 SHEPPERDS CL

BN9

South Heighton

E2
1 SOUTH VIEW
2 ORCHARD MEWS
3 GUINNESS TRUST BGLWS

HAREFIELD RD

PORT RD

WELLINGTON RD

PROSPERITY WAY

PORTLAND TERR 1
FIRLE TERR 2
WEST VIEW TERR 3
MARTELLO CT 4
COTTAGE CL 5

HEIGHTON RD

DENTON RISE

DENTON RD

VICARAGE CL

HILLSIDE

THE CLOSE

CANTICLE

Nore Down

Brookside Farm

PIDDINGHOE MEAD

Cemy

NEW RD

TARRING CL

ST MARTINS

Mus

Paradise Family L Pk

AVIS RD

GUINNESS CT

Denton Cty Prim Sch

KINGS AVE

ARUNDEL RD

BERESFORD RD

AVIS WAY

AVIS CLOSE
AVIS PAR

Ple

Ind Est

A26

B2109

43   A   B   44   C   D   45   E   F

167   179

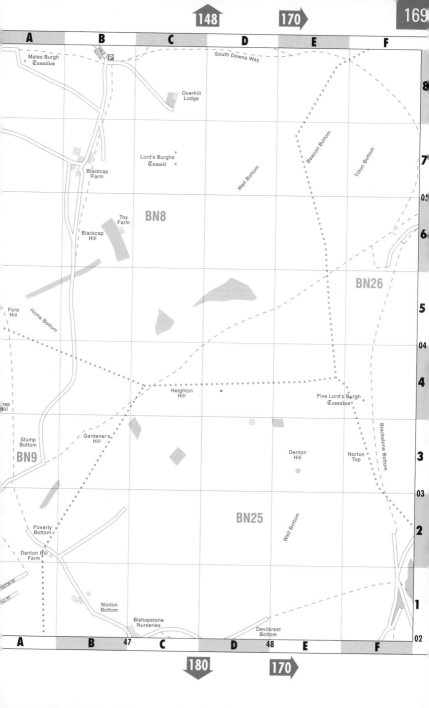

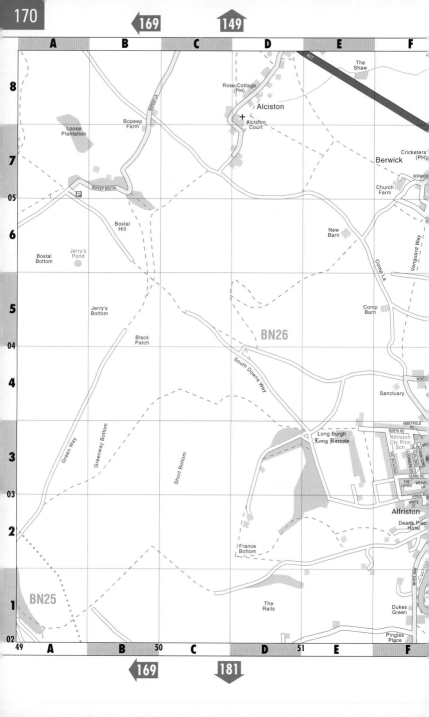

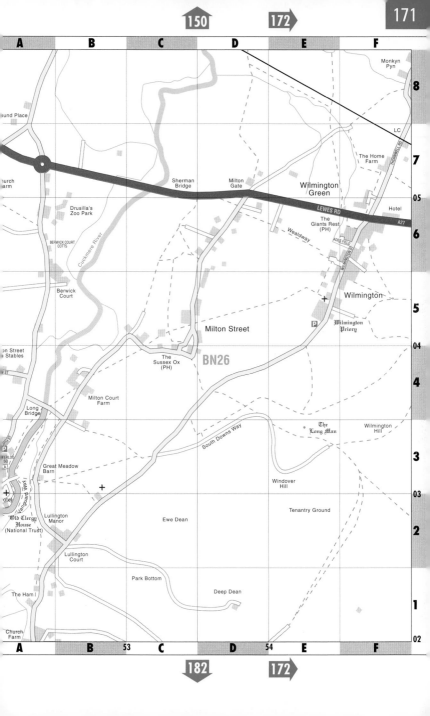

| A | B | C | D | E | F |

BORRELL RD

Warren
Farm

Monkyn
Pyn

Hide
Farm

Cophall
Farm

Cop Hall

Road und
constructio

Newbarn
Farm

Wootton
Manor

ST LEONARDS
TERR

GRAND PAR 1
THE BERNHARD BARON COTTAGE HOMES 2

A27 HAILSHAM

POLEGATE BY-PASS

A27

LEWES RD

The Flint
House
Farm

HYPERION AVE

SUNSTAR LA

GOLDEN MILLER LA

The Stud
Farm

Puddingham
Wood

Folkington
Manor Farm

The
Rough

The
Links

FOLKINGTON RD

Wannock
Coppice

OUTHFIELD

GROSVENOR C

The
Holt

Folkington
Manor

MAYFAIR RD

Wannock

Willingdon
Sch

Folkington

+

BN26

MILL GDNS

MILL RD

WANNOCK AVE

Folkington Bottom

Middle Brow

Cranesdown Bottom

Crane
Down

JEVINGTON RD

WISTON LANE DR

Folkington
Hill

Ash
Farm

WEALDWAY

JEVINGTON RD

Filching

WANNOCK GDNS

Filching Manor
Motor Mus

Hanging
Hill

Willingdon
Links

Hill
Barn

Teddard's
Bottom

Dean
Wood

BN20

South Downs Way

Helling Down

The Combe

A1066 Countr

Hayward's
Bottom

Jevington Holt

Holt
Bottom

GREEN LA

Combe
Hill

Wealdway

Holt
Brow

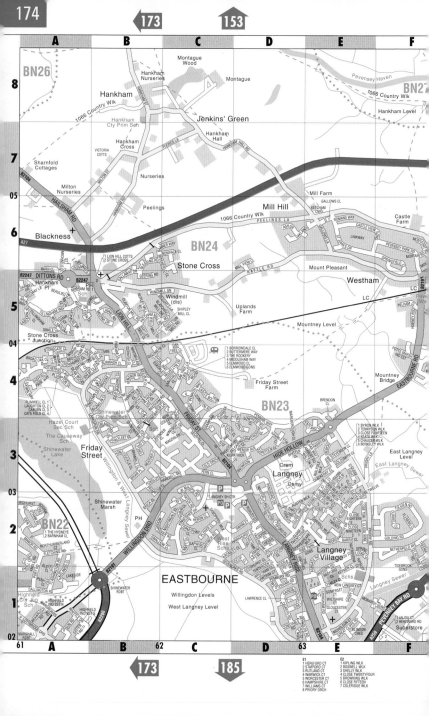

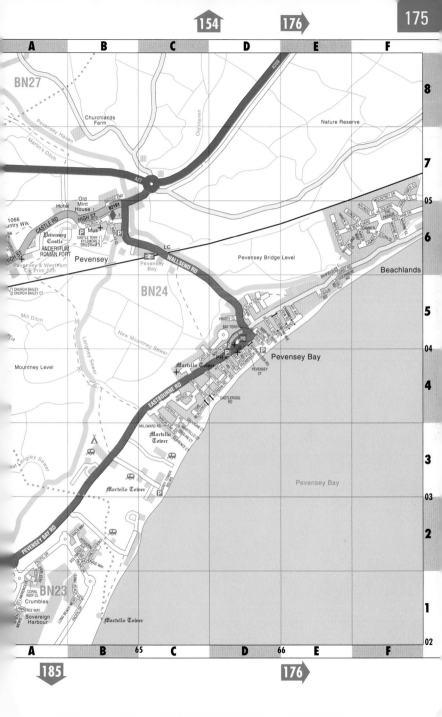

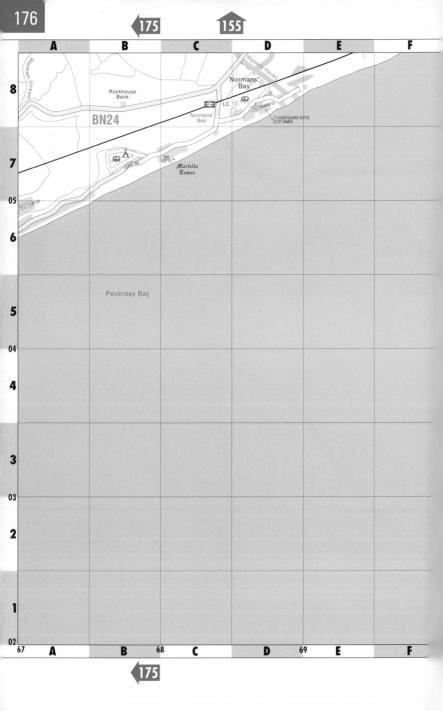

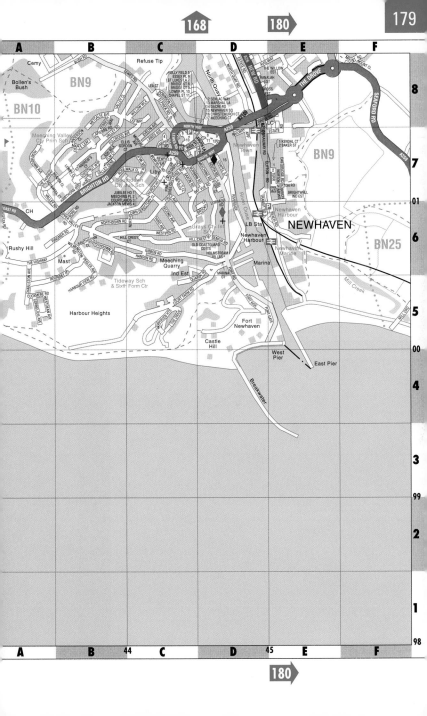

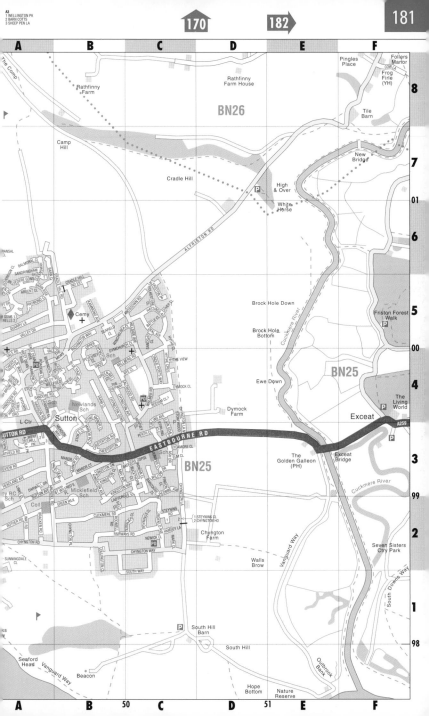

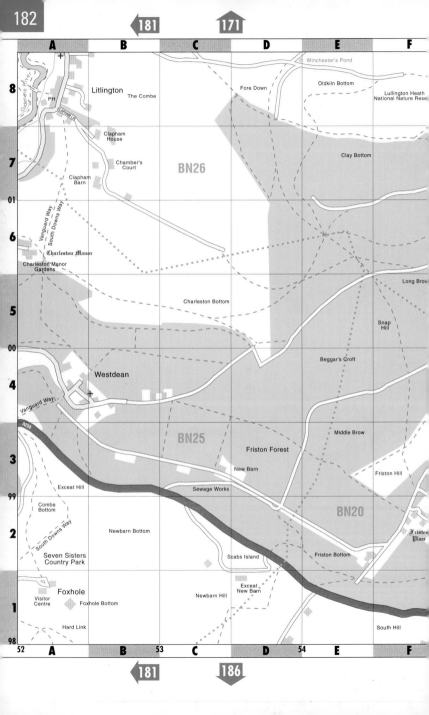

181
171

A **B** **C** **D** **E** **F**

8

Winchester's Pond

Litlington
The Combe

Fore Down

Oldkiln Bottom

Lullington Heath
National Nature Rese

Clapham
House

7

Clapham
Court
Chamber's

BN26

Clay Bottom

Clapham
Barn

01

Vanguard Way /
South Downs Way

6

Charleston Manor

Charleston Manor
Gardens

Long Brov

5

Charleston Bottom

Snap
Hill

00

Beggar's Croft

Westdean

4

Vanguard Way

A259

BN25

Middle Brow

Friston Forest

3

New Barn

Friston Hill

Exceat Hill

Sewage Works

99

Combe
Bottom

BN20

Newbarn Bottom

2

South Downs Way

Scabs Island

Friston
Place

Seven Sisters
Country Park

Friston Bottom

Exceat
New Barn

Foxhole

1

Visitor
Centre

Foxhole Bottom

Newbarn Hill

Hard Link

South Hill

98

52 **A** **B** 53 **C** **D** 54 **E** **F**

181
186

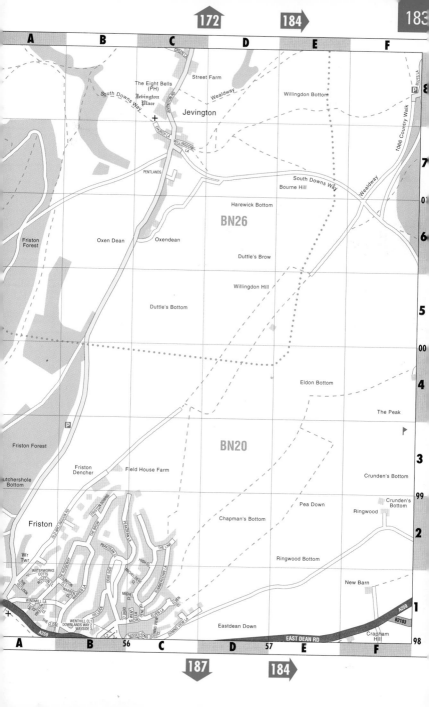

A2
1 CONNAUGHT RD
2 VALENTINE CT
3 PEARL CT
4 WESTDOWN HO
5 GANNET HO
6 SUSSEX HO
7 HARTINGTON MANSIONS
8 TAVISTOCK
9 VERNON LODGE
10 PARK LODGE
11 CORNFIELD TERR
12 MERLYNN
13 ASHBOURNE CT
14 THE LODGE
15 WEST HO
16 PARK GATES
17 BARCHESTER PL

A3
1 HOMELAND HO
2 GABLES CT
3 ETON MEWS
4 GLENMORE MEWS
5 THE OLD FIRE STATION
6 KILBURN TERR
7 WELLESLEY RD
8 STATION ST
9 STABLES LA

A4
1 BUCKINGHAM HEIGHTS
2 BEDFORDWELL CT
3 PERTH CT
4 KINROSS CT
5 OAKLANDS
6 CAREW CT
7 COMMERCIAL MEWS N

B3
1 BERWICK CT
2 CROFT CT
3 SALLY CT
4 RUSH CT
5 THORNTON CT
6 DORSET CT
7 WILLOWFIELD SQ
8 WINDSOR CT
9 PHOENIX CT

C
10 LEAF HALL RD
11 METROPOLE CT
12 BOURNESIDE CT
13 COLONNADE GDNS
14 COLONNADE RD
15 MARINE PARADE RD
16 LANCASTER CT
17 LINDSA CT
18 RENASCENT HO

B4
1 KILDA RD
2 STANLEY RD
3 NEVILLE RD
4 MIDDLESEX CT
5 LEICESTER CT
6 CHESHIRE CT
7 BERKSHIRE CT
8 OXFORD RD
9 BRADFORD CT

10 RIVERBOURNE HO

C4
1 TADDINGTON RD
2 TADDINGTON HO
3 COASTGUARD SQ
4 NORFOLK CT
5 SUFFOLK CT
6 WARRIOR SQ
7 GWENT CT
8 HAMPDEN TERR

9 TRAFALGAR MEWS

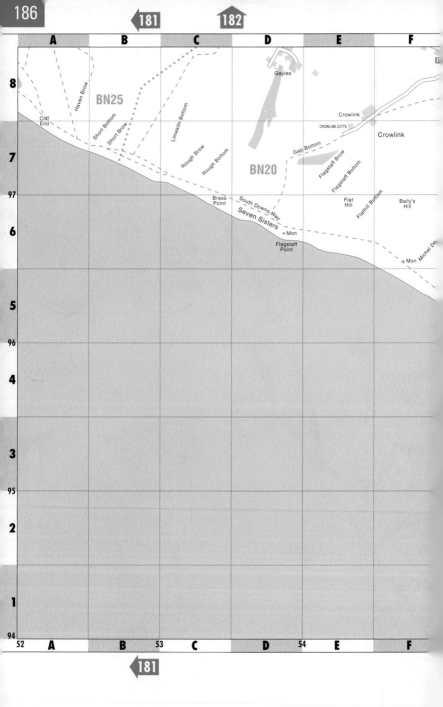

BN25

Haven Brow

Cliff
End

Short Bottom

Short Brow

Limekiln Bottom

Rough Brow

Rough Bottom

Brass
Point

South Downs Way

Seven Sisters

Gayles

Crowlink

CROWLINK COTTS

Crowlink

Gap Bottom

Flagstaff Brow

Flagstaff Bottom

BN20

Flat
Hill

Flathill Bottom

Baily's
Hill

Mon

Flagstaff
Point

Mon Michel Dn

A	B	C	D	E	F

EAST DEAN RD A259

Hobb's Eares

A259

The Tiger Inn (PH)

WENTHILL CL

DOWNS VIEW LA

Eastdean Down

East Dean

CHURCHFIELD

Crapham Hill

Crapham Barn

8

Mill Down

THE FRIDAYS

East Dean

New Barn

Bramble Bottom

Crapham Down

7

97

Birling Farm

Sheep Ctr

Went Hill

Wigden's Bottom

East Hale Bottom

Long Down

6

BN20

Kiln Combe

The Wish

Cornish Farm

BIRLING GAP RD

Sewage Works

5

Bulling Dean

Birling Gap

Frost Hill

96

Birling Gap Hotel

P

P

GRANDOWN COTTS

Horseshoe Plantation

Hodcombe Farm

4

BEACHY HEAD RD

Hod Combe

South Downs Way

Belle Tout

Shooters' Bottom

3

95

2

1

94

A	B	56	C	D	57	E	F

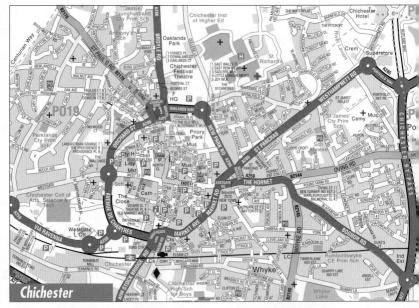

Chichester

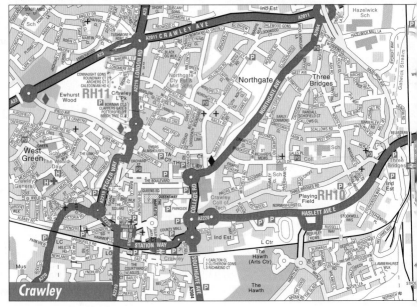

Crawley

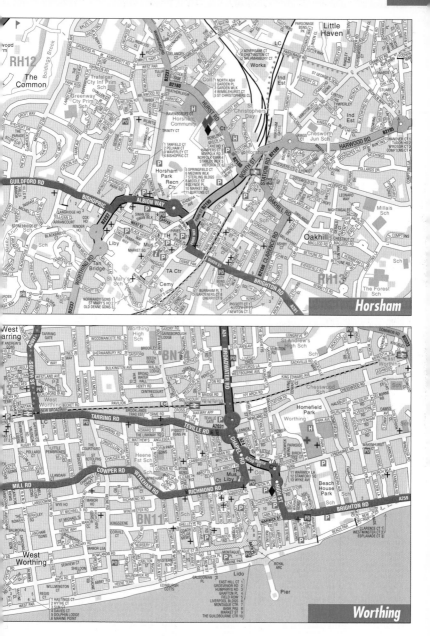

RH12

The Common

Horsham

RH13

Worthing

BN14

BN11

West Worthing

West Tarring

Index

Street names are listed alphabetically and show the locality, the Postcode District, the page number and a reference to the square in which the name falls on the map page

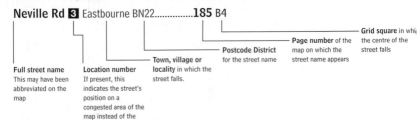

Neville Rd 🔳 Eastbourne BN22.............**185** B4

Full street name
This may have been abbreviated on the map

Location number
If present, this indicates the street's position on a congested area of the map instead of the name

Town, village or locality in which the street falls.

Postcode District
for the street name

Page number of the map on which the street name appears

Grid square in whi the centre of the street falls

Abbreviations used in the index

App	Approach	Cl	Close	Espl	Esplanade	N	North	S	South
Arc	Arcade	Comm	Common	Est	Estate	Orch	Orchard	Sq	Square
Ave	Avenue	Cnr	Corner	Gdns	Gardens	Par	Parade	Strs	Stairs
Bvd	Boulevard	Cotts	Cottages	Gn	Green	Pk	Park	Stps	Steps
Bldgs	Buildings	Ct	Court	Gr	Grove	Pas	Passage	St	Street, Saint
Bsns Pk	Business Park	Ctyd	Courtyard	Hts	Heights	Pl	Place	Terr	Terrace
Bsns Ctr	Business Centre	Cres	Crescent	Ind Est	Industrial	Prec	Precinct	Trad	Trading Est
Bglws	Bungalows	Dr	Drive		Estate	Prom	Promenade	Wlk	Walk
Cswy	Causeway	Dro	Drove	Intc	Interchange	Ret Pk	Retail Park	W	West
Ctr	Centre	E	East	Junc	Junction	Rd	Road	Yd	Yard
Cir	Circus	Emb	Embankment	La	Lane	Rdbt	Roundabout		

Town and village index

Alfriston 170 F2
Argos Hill 39 E5
Ashton Green 125 A5
Ashurst Wood 11 E6
Barcombe 101 E2
Barcombe Cross 101 E4
Battle 112 D5
Beachlands 175 E6
Beachy Head 188 B3
Beacon Down 81 A7
Beckley 68 A4
Beckley Furnace 90 D7
Beddingham 147 D4
Bells Yew Green 17 F5
Berner's Hill 32 A2
Berwick 170 F7
Bevendean 144 B2
Bewlbridge 20 D1
Bexhill 157 A2
Blackboys 80 A5
Blackness 26 A1
Boarshead 26 C6
Bodiam 65 E8
Bodle Street Green . . .109 C2
Brighton 189 B1
Brighton 164 B4
Broad Oak 59 F1
Broad Oak 90 C4
Broyle Side 125 A7
Burgess Hill 73 D2
Burwash 62 B6
Burwash Common 61 A4
Busted 56 B4
Cackle Street 90 A2
Cade Street 82 E6
Camber 94 F2
Catsfield 133 F8
Chailey 75 E4
Chapman's Town 83 B2
Chelwood Common . . .34 D6
Chelwood Gate 34 D8
Churches Green 109 B8
Cinder Hill 33 B8
Clayhill 67 D3
Clayton 119 E8
Cobbarn 15 E3
Cock Marling 92 A2
Coggins Mill 40 D4
Coleman's Hatch 23 E7
Cooksbridge 123 A8
Cousley Wood 30 C7
Cowden 4 A6
Cripp's Corner 88 D7
Cross-in-Hand 81 C7
Crowborough 26 C1

Crowhurst 134 F6
Crowlink 186 F7
Cuckfield 50 A6
Danehill 34 A4
Ditchling 98 D3
Dodd's Hill 35 D2
Dormans Park 1 E6
Dormans 2 B8
Durgates 29 E5
East Chiltington 100 A3
East Dean 187 B8
East Grinstead 1 E2
East Hoathly 105 B5
Eastbourne 185 B2
Etchingham 44 B1
Ewhurst Green 66 B5
Fairlight 138 C4
Fairlight Cove 138 F5
Fairwarp 36 B2
Falmer 144 D6
Felbridge 1 A6
Felcourt 1 C8
Five Ashes 58 B7
Flackley Ash 68 F3
Fletching 53 F4
Flimwell 32 C3
Flowers Green 130 F3
Fordcombe 6 B5
Forest Row 11 F3
Four Throws 46 D8
Framefield 79 B6
Frant 17 C3
Friston 183 A2
Ginger's Green 130 C6
Glynde 147 E7
Goatham Green 89 E5
Goddards' Green 72 A5
Golden Cross 130 E3
Green Street 135 B4
Groombridge 15 C7
Grove Hill 107 E1
Guestling Green 138 A8
Hadlow Down 57 C5
Hailsham 152 C8
Halland 104 C5
Hankham 174 B8
Hartfield 13 D4
Hassocks 97 E4
Hastings 159 F7
Haywards Heath 50 C3
Heathfield 82 B7
Hellingly 129 A5
Herstmonceux 130 E6
High Cross 39 C6
High Hurstwood 37 A1

Holtye 3 F3
Hooe 155 D8
Hooe Common 132 F2
Hook Green 19 C4
Horam 106 E7
Horsted Keynes 33 C6
Hove 163 B5
Hurst Green 45 B3
Hurst Wickham 97 C6
Hurstpierpoint 97 B6
Icklesham 116 C6
Iden 70 B4
Isfield 102 E7
Jevington 183 C8
John's Cross 87 C7
Keymer 98 B4
Kilndown 20 F3
Kingston near Lewes . .145 E5
Lamberhurst 20 B5
Langton Green 6 E3
Laughton 126 C6
Lewes 123 E1
Lidham Hill 115 E6
Lindfield 51 A7
Linkhill 47 E4
Lions Green 81 B1
Lower Cousley Wood . .30 E8
Lower Dicker 128 D3
Lower Horsebridge . . .128 F3
Lower Street 133 B5
Lower Willingdon 173 C6
Magham Down 129 F4
Mansfield 55 A5
Maresfield Park 55 A6
Mark Cross 28 A4
Marlpits 35 B8
Mayfield 40 A2
Maynard's Green 82 A1
Mill Corner 67 A3
Mount Pleasant 101 F6
Mountfield 87 A5
Newbury's 30 B8
Newenden 48 D3
Newhaven 179 B6
Newick 76 C8
Ninfield 133 B6
Normans' Bay 176 D8
North Chailey 75 E8
Northbridge Street 64 C6
Northiam 67 B6
Nutley 35 C4
Offham 122 F5
Old Heathfield 82 D5
Ovingdean 165 D3
Peacehaven 178 D7

Peacehaven Heights . . .178 F5
Peasmarsh 69 B2
Pembury 9 C6
Pett 138 E8
Pevensey 175 B6
Pevensey Bay 175 D4
Piddinghoe 168 A2
Plumpton Green 99 E6
Polegate 173 B5
Portslade Village 141 B1
Portslade-by-Sea 162 B5
Potman's Heath 49 E4
Poundfield 26 B2
Poundgate 37 A6
Poundsbridge 6 D8
Punnett's Town 83 C5
Pyecombe 119 B6
Ringmer 124 C6
Ripe 126 D1
Robertsbridge 64 A4
Rockrobin 29 D6
Rodmell 167 D8
Romford 9 F7
Roser's Cross 80 F6
Rotherfield 39 B7
Rottingdean 177 A6
Royal Tunbridge Wells . .8 D3
Rushlake Green 83 D2
Rusthall 7 C4
Rye 93 B6
Rye Foreign 69 E1
Rye Harbour 93 F2
St John's Common 72 E4
St Leonards 159 A7
Saint's Hill 6 A8
Saltdean 177 D6
Sandhurst 47 C6
Sandhurst Cross 46 F4
Scaynes Hill 51 E3
Seaford 180 D2
Sedlescombe 88 D1
Selmeston 149 D2
Sharpthorne 21 A6
Shellies Green 138 C8
Shoreham-by-Sea 161 A5
Shortgate 104 A3
South Chailey 100 D7
South Heighton 168 E2
South Street 75 E1
Southwick 161 F7
Sparrow's Green 29 F5
Speldhurst 7 B8
Standard Hill 132 E6
Standen Street 47 D8
Staplecross 65 E2

Steel Cross 26
Stone Cross 6
Stone Cross 174
Stonecrouch 31
Stonegate 42
Telscombe 167
Telscombe Cliffs 167
The Moor 45
Ticehurst 31
Town Row 29
Turner's Green 29
Uckfield 78
Union Street 32
Upper Wellingham . . .124
Wadhurst 30
Waldron 81
Waldron Down 80
Wannock 172
Warbleton 83
Wartling 154
Watermill 134
Wellbrook 82
West Firle 148
Westfield 114
Westham 174
Westmeston 120
Whatlington 88
White Post 5
Whitehill 37
Whitesmith 127
Willingdon 173
Winchelsea 117
Winchelsea Beach . . .118
Windmill Hill 131
Withyham 14
Wivelsfield 74
Wivelsfield Green 74
Wood's Corner 84
Woodingdean 165
Woolbridge 39

A

Abberton Field BN6 ... 97 B5
Abbey Cl BN10 ... 167 C1
Abbey Ct TN33 ... 112 D4
Abbey Dr TN38 ... 158 B5
Abbey Mews TN32 ... 64 B4
Abbey Path BN27 ... 129 C2
Abbey Rd Brighton BN2 ... 164 D4
Eastbourne BN20 ... 184 B5
Abbey View TN40 ... 157 D6
Abbey Way TN33 ... 112 D5
Abbeyfield Ho BN26 ... 170 F3
Abbot's Lodge 4 BN21 ... 184 F4
Abbots Cl Battle TN33 ... 112 F3
Hassocks BN6 ... 97 E4
Abbotsbury Cl BN2 ... 177 B5
Abbotsfield Cl TN34 ... 136 F3
Abbotsford Sch RH15 ... 72 E6
Abbotts 11 BN1 ... 163 E5
Aberdale Rd BN26 ... 173 C6
Aberdeen Rd 5 BN2 ... 164 C8
Abergavenny Rd BN7 ... 123 B1
Abigail Ho 10 RH16 ... 50 E4
Abinger Pl BN7 ... 123 C1
Abinger Rd
Portslade-by-Sea BN41 ... 162 B8
Woodingdean BN2 ... 165 E6
Acacia Ave BN3 ... 141 F1
Acacia Ct BN1 ... 142 F2
Acacia Rd
Eastbourne BN22 ... 173 D2
Newhaven BN9 ... 168 E2
Acer Ave TN2 ... 17 C8
Acorn Cl
East Grinstead RH19 ... 10 E8
St Leonards TN37 ... 136 C4
Acorn Gn 3 BN27 ... 129 B1
Acorn Way TN19 ... 45 A3
Acorns The
Burgess Hill RH15 ... 72 D4
Hailsham BN27 ... 152 D7
Stonegate TN5 ... 42 F6
Acre Cl RH16 ... 50 D2
Acres Rise TN5 ... 31 E1
Adam Cl Crowborough TN6 ... 38 A6
St Leonards TN38 ... 135 F4
Adams Cl BN1 ... 143 B2
Adams La TN31 ... 66 D2
Adastra Ave BN6 ... 98 A4
Addingham Rd BN22 ... 185 C4
Addington Cl TN38 ... 158 F7
Addison Rd BN1, BN3 ... 163 E7
Adelaide Cl BN25 ... 180 E5
Adelaide Cres BN3 ... 163 C5
Adelaide Rd TN38 ... 136 B3
Adelaide Sq BN43 ... 161 B7
Ades Field BN26 ... 171 F6
Admiral's Bridge La RH19 ... 10 C2
Adur Ct 10 BN43 ... 161 C8
Adur Dr
Shoreham-by-Sea BN43 ... 161 A7
Stone Cross BN24 ... 174 A5
Adur Rd RH15 ... 73 C4
gincourt Cl TN37 ... 135 F7
gnes St BN2 ... 164 C7
insworth Ave BN2 ... 165 D3
insworth Cl BN2 ... 165 D3
insworth Ho 1 BN2 ... 164 C7
ir St BN1 ... 189 A2
iry Rd BN27 ... 131 B2
kehurst Field TN33 ... 110 B3
lan Ct 6 TN37 ... 159 C7
lan Way BN2 ... 164 F5
lbany Ct 2 TN34 ... 159 F7
lbany Hill TN2 ... 8 C5
lbany Mans TN38 ... 159 B8
lbany Mews BN3 ... 163 B6
lbany Rd Bexhill TN40 ... 157 C3
Seaford BN25 ... 180 C3
St Leonards TN38 ... 159 B7
lbany Villas
Cuckfield RH17 ... 50 A6
Hove BN3 ... 163 B6
bert Cl RH16 ... 51 A4
bert Cotts TN1 ... 8 B4
bert Dr RH15 ... 72 E2
bert Mews BN3 ... 163 C6
bert Par BN21 ... 184 C4
bert Pl BN26 ... 173 A7
bert Rd Bexhill TN40 ... 157 C3
righton BN1 ... 189 A3
astings TN34 ... 159 F7
olegate BN26 ... 173 A7
outhwick BN42 ... 161 D7
ckfield TN22 ... 78 D6
bert St TN1 ... 8 B4
bert Terr BN21 ... 184 C5
bion Ct RH15 ... 72 F2
bion Hill BN2 ... 189 C3
bion Ho 3 Brighton BN2 ... 189 C3
outhwick BN42 ... 161 F7
bion La 4 TN34 ... 160 A3
bion Rd
astbourne BN22 ... 185 B4
oyal Tunbridge Wells TN1 ... 8 C5
bion St Brighton BN2 ... 189 C3
Lewes BN7 ... 123 D1
ortslade-by-Sea BN41 ... 162 B7
uthwick BN42 ... 161 E7
ourne Cl Brighton BN2 ... 164 F7
Leonards TN38 ... 158 F8
es Pl BN25 ... 180 E5
borough Rd TN37 ... 136 C1
er Cl Eastbourne BN23 ... 185 C8
eathfield TN21 ... 82 A5
Leonards TN37 ... 136 C5
Alderbrook Cl TN6 ... 38 A6
Alderbrook Cotts TN6 ... 38 A7
Alderbrook Path TN6 ... 38 A6
Alderbrook Way TN6 ... 38 A6
Alders Ave RH19 ... 1 E3
Alders View Dr RH19 ... 1 E3
Alderton Ct 7 TN39 ... 157 B3
Aldervale Cotts TN6 ... 38 A7
Aldrich Cl BN2 ... 164 F6
Aldrington Ave BN3 ... 163 A8
Aldrington CE Fst Sch
BN3 ... 162 F7
Aldrington CE Prim Sch
BN3 ... 142 A2
Aldrington Cl BN3 ... 162 D7
Aldrington House (Hospl)
BN3 ... 162 F6
Aldrington Pl BN3 ... 162 D8
Aldrington Sta BN3 ... 163 A8
Alexander Dr TN39 ... 156 E4
Alexandra Cl BN25 ... 180 E5
Alexandra Ct Hove BN3 ... 141 F2
St Leonards TN37 ... 136 C2
Alexandra Par TN34 ... 136 D3
Alexandra Rd
Burgess Hill RH15 ... 73 C2
Eastbourne BN22 ... 185 D6
Heathfield TN21 ... 82 B6
Mayfield TN20 ... 40 C3
St Leonards TN37 ... 159 C8
Uckfield TN22 ... 78 D6
Alexandra Terr TN20 ... 40 C3
Alexandra The TN37 ... 159 D7
Alexandra Villas BN1 ... 189 A3
Alford Way TN40 ... 157 E6
Alfray Rd TN40 ... 158 A5
Alfred Rd Brighton BN1 ... 189 A3
2 Eastbourne BN23 ... 185 F8
Hastings TN35 ... 137 D3
Alfred St TN38 ... 159 C7
Alfriston Cl Bexhill TN39 ... 156 C6
Brighton BN2 ... 164 F6
Eastbourne BN20 ... 184 C2
Alfriston Cty Prim Sch
BN26 ... 170 F4
Alfriston Pk BN25 ... 181 C5
Alfriston Rd BN25, BN26 ... 181 D6
Alice Bright La TN6 ... 37 F7
Alice Cl 2 BN3 ... 163 D5
Alice St BN3 ... 163 D5
All Saints CE Prim Sch
TN39 ... 157 B7
All Saints Gdns TN21 ... 81 F7
All Saints Jun Sch TN35 ... 160 C6
All Saints La TN39 ... 157 B7
All Saints Rd TN4 ... 8 B6
All Saints Rise TN4 ... 8 A6
All Saints' Cres TN35 ... 160 B4
All Saints' Hospl BN20 ... 188 E7
All Saints' St TN34 ... 160 B4
Allan Cl TN4 ... 7 C4
Allandale Rd TN2 ... 8 D7
Allards TN35 ... 138 C8
Allegria Ct TN38 ... 159 B7
Allen Rd RH16 ... 51 A4
Allen Way TN40 ... 157 F7
Allen's Cl RH19 ... 11 D6
Allfrey Rd BN22 ... 185 D6
Allfreys La TN6 ... 37 D6
Allington Cres BN8 ... 76 C7
Allington La BN7 ... 122 D7
Allington Rd BN8 ... 76 C6
Allwood Cres RH17 ... 74 C4
Alma Rd RH16 ... 51 B8
Alma Terr TN37 ... 136 C2
Alma Villas TN37 ... 136 C2
Almonry Fields TN33 ... 112 B4
Alpine Rd Hastings TN34 ... 160 A4
Hove BN3 ... 162 F8
Alverstone Cl BN23 ... 174 B4
Amanda Cl TN40 ... 157 F7
Ambassadors The 10
BN3 ... 163 C6
Amber Ct 19 Hove BN3 ... 163 C6
8 Hove BN3 ... 163 D7
Amberleaze Dr TN2 ... 9 D6
Amberley Cl
Burgess Hill RH15 ... 73 A4
Haywards Heath RH16 ... 50 D4
Hove BN3 ... 141 E3
Amberley Ct TN4 ... 8 C8
Amberley Dr BN3 ... 141 E3
Amberley Lodge BN2 ... 189 B4
Amberley Rd BN22 ... 173 C1
Amberly Lodge BN2 ... 164 F6
Ambermarle The BN2 ... 189 B1
Amberstone BN27 ... 129 E3
Amberstone Cl TN34 ... 137 A4
Amberstone Hospl BN27 ... 129 E4
Amberstone View BN27 ... 129 C2
Ambleside Ave BN10 ... 178 A8
Ambleside Ct BN10 ... 178 A7
America La RH16 ... 51 A5
Amesbury Cres BN3 ... 162 E7
Amherst Cl TN34 ... 136 D1
Amherst Cres BN3 ... 162 F8
Amherst Gdns TN34 ... 136 D1
Amherst Rd Bexhill TN40 ... 157 C4
Hastings TN34 ... 136 D1
Royal Tunbridge Wells TN4 ... 8 A5
Amhurst Rd BN10 ... 177 F3
Anchor Field BN8 ... 124 D5
Anchor Hill RH17 ... 52 A2
Anchor La BN8 ... 102 B5
Anchorage Way BN23 ... 175 B2
Anderida Ct TN39 ... 156 C4
Anderida Rd BN22 ... 173 C3
Anderson Cl BN9 ... 179 B7
Andrew Rd TN4 ... 8 C8
Andrews Cl
Northbridge Street TN32 ... 64 C5
Royal Tunbridge Wells TN2 ... 8 D5
Andros Cl BN8 ... 100 E6
Andwell Ct BN21 ... 185 B2
Angel Row TN18 ... 47 B5
Angel Terr TN18 ... 47 B6
Angela Cl TN40 ... 157 F7
Anglesea Mans TN38 ... 159 B8
Anglesea Terr
TN37, TN38 ... 159 C8
Anglesey Ave BN27 ... 129 A2
Angmering Ct BN1 ... 143 F5
Angrove Ho TN6 ... 25 D2
Angus Cl BN20 ... 173 B1
Anjou Ct BN23 ... 174 F1
Ann Cl BN6 ... 98 A5
Ann St Brighton BN1 ... 189 B4
Hastings TN34 ... 160 C6
Anne's Path 13 BN7 ... 146 C8
Annecy RC Prim Sch
BN25 ... 181 A2
Annington Rd BN22 ... 185 B5
Anscombe 5 RH16 ... 50 D6
Anson Cl BN23 ... 185 E7
Anson Ho BN10 ... 167 C1
Ansty Cl BN2 ... 164 E5
Antares Path BN27 ... 152 E7
Antioch St BN7 ... 146 C8
Antony Cl BN25 ... 180 B6
Antrim Ct BN23 ... 174 D1
Antrona Cl TN39 ... 156 C3
Anvil Cl
Portslade-by-Sea BN41 ... 141 B2
Uckfield TN22 ... 78 B6
Anvil Ct TN37 ... 136 C5
Anzac Cl BN10 ... 167 C1
Apex Pk BN27 ... 152 A7
Apple Tree La TN2 ... 8 D8
Appledene Cnr BN8 ... 100 E7
Appledore Cl BN23 ... 174 D2
Appledore Ct RH16 ... 51 A7
Appledore Gdns RH16 ... 51 A6
Appledore Rd BN2 ... 143 F4
Applesham Ave BN3 ... 141 E2
Applesham Way BN41 ... 141 A1
Applewood Cl TN37 ... 136 B5
Approach The
Brighton BN1 ... 142 E3
Dormans Park RH19 ... 1 F6
April Pl 4 TN40 ... 157 C4
Apsley St TN4 ... 7 D4
Aqua Ct BN10 ... 177 F3
Aquarius Cl BN10 ... 178 C6
Aquila Pk BN25 ... 181 A3
Arbor Ct RH16 ... 50 E5
Arbourvale TN38 ... 136 A1
Archer Ct RH15 ... 73 A3
Archers Ct TN35 ... 136 F6
Archery Ct
Eastbourne BN22 ... 185 C6
3 St Leonards TN38 ... 159 B6
Archery Rd TN38 ... 159 B7
Archery Wlk BN27 ... 152 C6
Archie Ct 7 TN38 ... 159 B6
Ardingly Ct 10 BN2 ... 189 C2
Ardingly Rd BN2 ... 177 D4
Ardingly St BN2 ... 189 C2
Argent Cl BN25 ... 181 A5
Argos Hill Rd TN20,TN6 ... 39 D4
Argyle Rd BN1 ... 189 A5
Argyll Ct BN22 ... 173 E2
Arkendale RH19 ... 1 A4
Arkwright Rd BN23 ... 174 A1
Arlington Cres BN1 ... 143 E5
Arlington Ct RH16 ... 50 E5
Arlington Gdns BN2 ... 177 D6
Arlington Ho 5 BN21 ... 184 D4
Arlington Rd BN21 ... 184 F3
Arlington Rd E BN27 ... 152 A6
Arlington Rd W BN27 ... 151 F6
Arlington Resr BN26 ... 150 C3
Armstrong Cl TN38 ... 135 E4
Arnbury Mews TN38 ... 158 E6
Arndale Ctr BN21 ... 185 A3
Arnold St BN2 ... 164 C7
Arnside Rd TN38 ... 158 E6
Arnworth Ct BN21 ... 184 F2
Arran Cl BN27 ... 129 A2
Arthur Bliss Ho RH16 ... 51 A8
Arthur Rd TN39 ... 157 B4
Arthur St BN3 ... 163 A8
Arts Rd BN1 ... 144 B7
Arun Ct 13 BN43 ... 161 C8
Arun Lodge BN21 ... 184 E3
Arun Path TN22 ... 55 E1
Arun Way BN24 ... 173 F5
Arundel Cl
Beachlands BN24 ... 175 F6
Hailsham BN27 ... 129 C2
Shoreham-by-Sea BN43 ... 161 C8
Arundel Ct
6 Brighton BN2 ... 164 E4
Burgess Hill RH15 ... 72 F4
Hove BN1 ... 142 C5
14 Shoreham-by-Sea BN43 ... 161 C8
Arundel Dr E BN2 ... 177 C5
Arundel Dr W BN2 ... 177 C5
Arundel Keep 8 BN21 ... 184 F4
Arundel Mews 10 BN2 ... 164 E4
Arundel Pl BN2 ... 164 E3
Arundel Rd Brighton BN2 ... 164 E4
Eastbourne BN21 ... 184 F4
Newhaven BN9 ... 168 F1
Peacehaven BN10 ... 178 D7
Royal Tunbridge Wells TN1 ... 8 B2
Seaford BN25 ... 181 A3
Arundel Rd W BN10 ... 178 B7
Arundel Road Central
BN10 ... 178 B7
Arundel St BN2 ... 164 E3
Arundel Terr BN2 ... 164 E3
Arundell Gn BN7 ... 123 B2
Ascham Pl BN20 ... 184 E1
Ascot Cl BN20 ... 188 F8
Ascot Mews TN38 ... 159 A8
Ash Cl Eastbourne BN22 ... 173 E3
Hove BN3 ... 142 C3
Royal Tunbridge Wells TN2 ... 17 D7
Ash Ct East Grinstead RH19 ... 1 E3
Hailsham BN27 ... 152 A7
Southwick BN42 ... 140 F1
Ash Dr BN25 ... 181 C3
Ash Gr
Haywards Heath RH16 ... 50 D2
Westham BN24 ... 174 D6
Ash Tree Cl TN21 ... 82 A7
Ash Wlk BN9 ... 179 B7
Ashbourne Ct
13 Eastbourne BN21 ... 185 A2
Rusthall TN4 ... 7 D4
Ashbrook Rd TN37 ... 136 B4
Ashburnham Cl BN1 ... 143 E5
Ashburnham Dr BN1 ... 143 E5
Ashburnham Gdns BN21 ... 184 E5
Ashburnham Ho BN1 ... 142 E5
Ashburnham Pl BN27 ... 129 A2
Ashburnham Rd
Eastbourne BN21 ... 184 E5
Hastings TN35 ... 160 C6
Ashby Cl TN39 ... 157 A8
Ashcombe Dr TN39 ... 156 D3
Ashcombe Hollow BN7 ... 145 D7
Ashcombe La BN7 ... 145 E5
Ashcroft 1 BN43 ... 161 D7
Ashcroft Cl Ringmer BN8 ... 124 D5
Shoreham-by-Sea BN43 ... 161 D8
Ashdown 14 BN3 ... 163 C6
Ashdown Ave BN2 ... 177 B5
Ashdown Chase TN22 ... 35 C5
Ashdown Cl
Forest Row RH18 ... 12 A2
Haywards Heath RH16 ... 51 B4
Royal Tunbridge Wells TN4 ... 7 F4
St Leonards TN38 ... 135 E2
Ashdown Ct
Crowborough TN6 ... 25 E2
Uckfield TN22 ... 78 D6
Ashdown Forest Riding Ctr
TN22 ... 36 B6
Ashdown Forest Visitors
Information Ctr RH18 ... 23 A5
Ashdown Gate RH19 ... 1 D2
Ashdown Llama Farm
RH18 ... 22 E4
Ashdown Nuffield Hospl
RH16 ... 50 D6
Ashdown Pl TN21 ... 82 B6
Ashdown Rd Bexhill TN40 ... 157 E4
7 Brighton BN2 ... 164 B8
Forest Row RH18 ... 11 F2
Ashdown View
East Grinstead RH19 ... 10 E7
Nutley TN22 ... 35 D6
Ashenden Ave TN31 ... 93 A5
Ashenden Wlk TN2 ... 8 E8
Ashenground Cl 5 RH16 ... 50 E3
Ashenground Rd RH16 ... 50 E3
Asher Reeds TN3 ... 7 A4
Ashford Cl 4 BN27 ... 152 C7
Ashford Rd Brighton BN1 ... 143 A2
Eastbourne BN21 ... 185 A3
Hastings TN34 ... 136 E2
Ashford Sq BN21 ... 185 A3
Ashford Way TN34 ... 136 E3
Ashgate Rd BN23 ... 174 E2
Ashington Ct BN2 ... 164 F6
Ashington Gdns BN10 ... 178 F6
Ashington Rd BN22 ... 174 A1
Ashlands TN6 ... 26 B1
Ashleigh Gdns TN6 ... 25 E4
Ashleigh Glegg Ho BN25 ... 180 D4
Ashley Cl BN1 ... 142 E7
Ashley Ct Hove BN3 ... 163 C5
7 St Leonards TN37 ... 159 C7
Ashley Gdns
Hailsham BN27 ... 129 C3
Mayfield TN20 ... 40 A2
Rusthall TN4 ... 7 C5
Ashley Park Cl TN4 ... 7 C5
Ashley Pk TN4 ... 7 C5
Ashley Rd TN6 ... 27 D1
Ashlings Way Hove BN3 ... 141 E2
Shoreham-by-Sea BN43 ... 140 B1
Ashmore Cl BN10 ... 167 D2
Ashtead Twrs 8 TN40 ... 157 E4
Ashton Lodge 14 BN2 ... 189 C3
Ashton Rise BN2 ... 189 C3
Ashtonville Cl BN8 ... 124 E5
Ashurst Ave BN2 ... 177 E5
Ashurst Hill TN3 ... 5 D2
Ashurst Rd Brighton BN2 ... 143 F5
Seaford BN25 ... 180 F2
Stone Cross TN3 ... 6 B2
Ashurst Sta TN3 ... 5 D2
Ashurstwood Abbey RH19 ... 11 E6
Ashurstwood Cty Prim Sch
RH19 ... 11 E6
Ashway RH15 ... 73 A2
Ashwyn Bsns Ctr RH15 ... 72 F5
Aspen Cl RH16 ... 51 B4
Aspen Rd BN22 ... 173 E2
Aspen Way TN39 ... 156 C4
Aspen Wlk
Haywards Heath RH16 ... 51 B4
Aspen Wlk *continued*
Heathfield TN21 ... 82 B5
Astaire Ave BN22 ... 185 B6
Asten Cl TN38 ... 158 E7
Asten Fields TN33 ... 112 C4
Astra Ho 10 BN1 ... 163 E5
Atfield Wlk BN22 ... 173 F3
Athelstan Cl 1 BN23 ... 185 F8
Athelstan Rd TN35 ... 160 D6
Athenaeum The 16 BN3 ... 163 C6
Atlantic Dr BN23 ... 185 F7
Atlingworth St BN2 ... 189 C1
Attree Ct 6 BN2 ... 164 C6
Attree Dr BN2 ... 164 C6
Auckland Dr BN2 ... 143 F1
Auckland Ho TN40 ... 157 C7
Auckland Rd TN1 ... 8 C5
Audrey Cl Brighton BN1 ... 142 E5
Seaford BN25 ... 180 D5
Audrey Sturley Ct TN4 ... 7 D4
Augustines Way RH16 ... 50 F4
Augustus Way TN37 ... 135 F6
Austen Cl RH19 ... 1 B1
Austen Way TN35 ... 137 D5
Austen Wlk BN23 ... 174 D2
Avard Cres BN20 ... 184 B6
Avards Cl TN18 ... 45 E8
Avenue Ct 20 BN3 ... 163 C6
Avenue La BN21 ... 184 F3
Avenue The Brighton BN2 ... 143 E1
Dormansland RH19 ... 2 B6
Eastbourne BN21 ... 184 F3
Fairlight Cove TN35 ... 138 F4
Hailsham BN27 ... 152 B6
Heathfield TN21 ... 82 B6
Horam TN21 ... 106 F8
Kingston near Lewes BN7 ... 145 D5
Lewes BN7 ... 123 C1
Mayfield TN20 ... 40 B2
Avery Cl BN41 ... 140 F4
Aviemore Rd TN6 ... 25 D2
Avis Cl BN9 ... 168 E1
Avis Par BN9 ... 168 E1
Avis Rd BN9 ... 168 E1
Avis Way BN9 ... 168 E1
Avocet BN27 ... 152 A7
Avocet Trad Est RH15 ... 72 F2
Avon St TN1 ... 8 C5
Avondale Rd
Eastbourne BN22 ... 185 B4
Hove BN3 ... 163 D7
Seaford BN25 ... 180 F3
St Leonards TN38 ... 136 A1
Avonhurst RH15 ... 73 B3
Avonmore BN20 ... 188 E8
Awbrook Cl RH17 ... 51 F3
Aylesbury BN3 ... 163 E6
Aylesbury Ave BN23 ... 185 E8
Aymer Ho 4 BN3 ... 163 A6
Aymer Rd BN3 ... 163 A6
Aynsley Ct BN3 ... 163 C8
Ayscue Cl BN23 ... 185 F7

B

Babylon Way BN20 ... 184 B8
Back La Cross-in-Hand TN21 ... 81 C6
Fairwarp TN22 ... 36 B2
Rushlake Green TN21 ... 83 D1
Winchelsea TN36 ... 117 E7
Back Rd TN18 ... 47 B5
Backwoods Cl RH16 ... 51 B6
Backwoods La RH16 ... 51 B6
Baden Rd BN2 ... 143 D1
Badens Cl BN8 ... 76 C6
Badger Cl BN41 ... 141 B2
Badger Dr RH16 ... 50 C5
Badger Gate TN31 ... 93 A5
Badger Way BN1 ... 143 E6
Badgers Brow BN20 ... 184 B8
Badgers Cl TN6 ... 25 E3
Badgers Copse BN25 ... 181 C3
Badgers Dene BN7 ... 167 D8
Badgers Field BN10 ... 167 C1
Badgers Holt TN2 ... 8 E5
Badgers Mount TN39 ... 156 E5
Badgers Way
East Grinstead RH19 ... 1 F2
Hastings TN34 ... 136 D5
Badgers Wlk RH15 ... 73 D2
Badlesmere Rd BN22 ... 185 B6
Bagham La BN27 ... 130 F6
Bahram Rd BN26 ... 172 F6
Bailey Cres BN22 ... 173 B3
Baillie Ave BN22 ... 185 C5
Bainbridge Cl BN25 ... 180 F3
Bainden Cl TN6 ... 27 D1
Baird Dr TN34 ... 136 E3
Baird Ho TN37 ... 159 C8
Baker Ct TN22 ... 78 C7
Baker St
Brighton BN1, BN2 ... 189 B4
Newhaven BN9 ... 179 E7
Uckfield TN22 ... 78 D6
Baker's Rd BN21 ... 184 D3
Bakery Mews BN1 ... 143 C1
Bakewell Rd BN21 ... 184 D4
Bal Edmund TN37 ... 136 B4
Balaclava La TN5 ... 30 A6
Balcombe Ct BN10 ... 178 C8
Balcombe Gn TN33 ... 88 E1
Balcombe La RH17, RH19 ... 21 E2
Balcombe Rd
Haywards Heath RH16 ... 50 D7

kdale TN1 . . . . .8 86
ken Rd TN2 . . . . .8 D6
ling Cl Brighton BN2 . . .143 D1
aford BN25 . . . . .181 A4
ling Dr TN2 . . . . .8 A1
ling Gap Rd BN20 . . . .187 B6
ling Park Ave TN2 . . . . .17 B8
ling Rd TN2 . . . . .17 B8
ling St BN21 . . . . .184 C4
ling Way TN22 . . . . .78 E8
scay Ave BN23 . . . . . . .174 E1
shop Bell CE Sch BN23 .174 E1
shop's 8
urstpierpoint BN6 . . . . . . .97 A7
homer BN8 . . . . .124 E6
shop's Down 7 F3
shop's Down Cty Prim Sch
. . . . .7 E5
shop's Down Park Rd
. . . . .7 F3
shop's La Ringmer BN8 .124 D6
shop's Wlk TN40 . . . . .157 F6
shops Cl BN25 . . . . . .180 C4
shops Ct TN4 . . . . .7 F3
shops Dr BN7 . . . . .146 A8
shops Rd BN3 . . . . .142 C1
shopstone Dr BN2 . . . .177 B6
shopstone La BN6,H17 . .72 A7
shopstone Rd BN25 . . .180 A4
shopstone Sta BN25 . . .180 B4
stern Ct BN27 . . . . .152 D7
ley La TN31 . . . . .68 B2
ack Hill RH16 . . . . .51 A7
ack Lion St BN1 . . . . . .189 B1
ack Path BN26 . . . . .173 A6
ackberry La RH7 . . . . . . .1 E8
ackberry Rd RH19,RH7 . . .1 E8
ackbird Cl RH15 . . . . . . .72 D2
ackboys CE Prim Sch
. . . . .80 A6
ackboys YH TN22 . . . . . .80 A8
ackbrook La BN8,RH17 .52 E2
ackdon Hill TN2 . . . . . . .27 B6
ackdown BN2 . . . . .164 F7
ackdown Rd TN21 . . . . .83 D6
ackfields Ave TN39 . . .156 F5
ackhouse La RH15 . . . . .73 B4
ackhurst La TN2 . . . . . . .8 F6
acklands TN33 . . . . . . .138 D5
acklands Cres RH18 . . . .11 F2
acklands Cty Prim Sch
TN34 . . . . .136 E2
acklands Dr TN34 . . . . .136 E2
ackman Ave TN38 . . . .136 A3
ackman St BN1 . . . . . .189 B3
ackmill Cl TN39 . . . . . .157 A8
ackmores 38 A8
ackness Villas TN6 . . . . .38 A8
ackness Way TN6 . . . . .38 A8
acksmith's Field TN33 .135 A4
acksmith's La TN5 . . . . .30 A5
acksmiths Copse TN27 .152 A6
acksmiths Field TN32 . .46 C1
acksmiths La TN33 . . . .133 E8
ackstone Way RH15 . . . .73 A5
ackthorn Cl
righton BN1 . . . . .142 D3
astbourne BN22 . . . . . .185 B5
ighton-by-Sea BN41 . . .141 B2
leonards TN37 . . . . . . .136 C4
ackthorn Way TN35 . . .138 F6
ackthorns RH16 . . . . . . .51 A7
ackthorns Ct RH16 . . . . .51 A6
ackthorns Cty Prim Sch
H16 . . . . .51 A6
ackthorns The RH15 . . .73 B5
ackwater Rd
N20, BN21 . . . . .184 F1
ackwell Cty Prim Sch
419 . . . . .1 E3
ackwell Farm Rd RH19 . .1 F3
ackwell Hollow RH19 . . .1 F2
ackwell Rd RH19 . . . . . .1 F2
ake Ct BN22 . . . . .189 C3
ake Way TN2 . . . . .8 D7
keney Ave BN10,BN9 . .179 C5
ker St BN21 . . . . .189 C2
akes Way BN23 . . . . . . .173 C2
atchington Cl BN25 . . .180 F4
atchington Hill BN25 . .180 F4
atchington Mill Dr
N24 . . . . .174 C5
atchington Mill Sch
N23 . . . . .141 F2
atchington Rd
yal Tunbridge Wells TN1 . .8 B1
aford BN25 . . . . .180 E3
enheim Cl RH19 . . . . . .2 A3
enheim Ct ■ Hove BN3 .163 A6
rightbridge TN32 . . . . . .64 B3
enheim Fields RH18 . . .11 E3
enheim Pl ■ BN1 . . . . .189 B3
enheim Way
immel TN5 . . . . .32 C3
legate BN26 . . . . .173 D6
itchingley La TN6 . . . . . .27 E1
tchley Ct BN1 . . . . .164 A8
nd La BN8 . . . . .76 E6
sis Rd BN7 . . . . .123 B2
mfield Rd TN37 . . . . . .159 D8
msbury Pl ▼ BN2 . . . .164 C4
enheim Ct ■ BN2 . . . .164 C4
ssom Wlk BN21 . . . . . .129 B1
unt Ave RH19 . . . . .1 C1
wers Hill Cowden TN8 . .4 D8

Blowers Hill continued
Speldhurst TN3 . . . . .7 B8
Blue Haze Ave BN25 . . .181 B4
Bluebell Cl
East Grinstead RH19 . . . . .1 B1
Haywards Heath RH16 . . .50 F4
Bluebell Rly
RH17,RH19,TN22 . . . . . . .21 A5
Bluebell Rly Mus TN22 . . .53 A4
Bluebell Way RH15 . . . . .72 D4
Bluebird Ct ■ BN3 . . . .163 A6
Bluemans La TN33 . . . .114 A4
Bluestone Ct TN38 . . . .135 F2
Blunts Wood Cres RH17 .50 E2
Blunts Wood Rd RH17 . . .50 C6
Blytons The RH19 . . . . . . .1 B1
Boarders La TN5 . . . . . . .31 C3
Boast La BN8 . . . . .101 F5
Bocking Cl TN5 . . . . .29 E4
Boddingtons La BN6 . . . .98 D3
Bodiam Ave
Bevendean BN2 . . . . . . .144 B1
Bexhill TN40 . . . . .157 D6
Bodiam Castle (NT) TN32 .65 F8
Bodiam CE Prim Sch TN32 .65 E8
Bodiam Cl Bevendean BN2 .144 B2
Seaford BN25 . . . . .181 C4
Bodiam Cres BN22 . . . .174 A2
Bodiam Ct RH16 . . . . . . .50 A8
Bodiam Dr TN38 . . . . . .135 D2
Bodiam Manor Sch TN32 .65 E8
Bodiam Rd TN18, TN32 . . .46 F3
Bodiam Sta TN32 . . . . . .65 E6
Bodle Cres TN39 . . . . . .157 F7
Bodmin Cl BN20 . . . . . .184 C3
Bohemia Rd TN34,TN37 .159 C8
Boiler House Hill BN1 . .144 B7
Bolding Way RH16 . . . . . .50 E2
Bolebrooke Rd TN40 . . .157 D3
Boleyn Ave BN10 . . . . . .178 C8
Bolney Ave BN10 . . . . . .178 C8
Bolney Rd BN2 . . . . . . .143 F4
Bolnore Rd RH16 . . . . . . .50 B4
Bolnore Rd RH16 . . . . . . .50 B4
Bolsover Ct BN20 . . . . .188 F8
Bolsover Rd
Eastbourne BN20 . . . . . .188 F8
Hove BN3 . . . . .162 E8
Bolton Cl TN22 . . . . .78 A6
Bolton Rd BN21 . . . . . .185 A2
Bolton Rd RH16 . . . . . . .50 D5
Bonchurch Rd BN2 . . . .164 C7
Bond St BN1 . . . . .189 B2
Bonfire La RH17 . . . . . . .33 D5
Boniface Cl BN24 . . . . .174 C6
Bonny Wood Rd BN6 . . .97 E3
Booker Cl TN6 . . . . .26 A1
Booth Mus
of Natural History BN1 . .163 E8
Bopeep Bostal BN26 . . .170 B7
Bopeep La BN26 . . . . . .170 B8
Border Ct RH10 . . . . .1 F4
Borders La TN19 . . . . . . .62 F7
Boreham Hill BN27,TN33 .132 A4
Boreham La BN27 . . . . .131 E2
Borodales TN39 . . . . . . .156 E4
Borough La BN20 . . . . .184 D3
Borough St BN1 . . . . . .163 E6
Borrow King Cl BN2 . . . .164 D8
Borrowdale Cl BN23 . . .174 C4
Boscawen Ct BN23 . . . .185 F7
Boscobel Ct TN38 . . . . .159 A7
Boscobel Lodge TN38 . .159 B7
Boscobel Rd TN38 . . . . .159 A7
Boscobel Rd N TN38 . . .159 A7
Boship Cl BN23 . . . . . . .174 A4
Bostal The BN8 . . . . . . .148 B4
Boston Cl BN23 . . . . . . .185 F7
Boston Rd RH16 . . . . . . .51 A5
Boston St BN1 . . . . .189 B4
Boswell Wlk ■ BN23 . . .174 F2
Bough Beeches RH15 . . .73 C1
Boughey Pl BN7 . . . . . .123 C3
Boulevard The BN24 . . .175 E6
Boundary Pas ■ BN3 . .163 E6
Boundary Rd Brighton BN2 .164 F4
Portslade-by-Sea
BN3, BN41 . . . . .162 C8
Royal Tunbridge Wells TN2 . .8 D1
Boundary The
Langton Green TN3, TN4 . . .7 B2
■ Seaford BN25 . . . . . .180 E2
Bourg-de-Peage Ave RH19 . .2 A1
Bourne Ct Brighton BN1 .142 D4
■ Hastings TN34 8
Bourne Cty Prim Sch
BN22 . . . . .185 B3
Bourne La TN32 . . . . . . .64 F7
Bourne Pas ■ TN34 . . .160 B4
Bourne Rd BN21 . . . . . .185 B3
Bourne The Hassocks BN6 . .97 E5
Bourneside Ct ■ BN22 .185 B3
Bowden House Sch BN25 .180 F6
Bowden Rise BN25 . . . .180 F6
Bowen Ct ■ BN1 . . . . . .163 C6
Bowen Rd TN4 . . . . .7 B4
Bower Cl TN37 . . . . .136 B4
Bower The RH16 . . . . . . .50 D5
Bowerhill Cotts RH19 . . .21 F6
Bowlers Town TN31 . . . .70 A2
Bowles Outdoor Ctr TN6 .26 E6
Bowley Rd RH27 . . . . . .159 C4
Bowlings The TN32 . . . .113 D8
Bowmans Dr TN33 . . . .112 D6
Bowood Ave BN22 . . . .185 B6
Bowrey Pl TN40 . . . . . . .157 C5
Bowring Way BN2 . . . . .164 D4

Bowsprit Mews TN38 . . .135 E7
Box La RH19 . . . . .11 E6
Box's La RH17 . . . . .34 C6
Boxes La RH17 . . . . .33 C5
Boxgrove Cl TN40 . . . . .157 F4
Boyce's St BN1 . . . . . . .189 A2
Boyne Pk TN4 . . . . .7 F4
Boyne Rd TN35 . . . . . . .160 C5
Bracken Cl
Crowborough TN6 . . . . . .26 C1
Royal Tunbridge Wells TN2 . .8 E5
Bracken Rd
Eastbourne BN20 . . . . . .184 B5
Royal Tunbridge Wells TN2 . . .8 E5
Seaford BN25 . . . . .181 A2
Bracken Way TN21 . . . . .59 E1
Brackenbury Cl BN41 . . .141 B2
Brackendale TN35 . . . . .160 D6
Brackenhill TN7 . . . . . . .13 A1
Brackerne Cl TN39 . . . .156 C2
Bradford Ct ■ BN2 . . . .185 B4
Bradford Rd BN7 . . . . . .123 B1
Bradford St BN7 . . . . . .184 D3
Brading Cl
Eastbourne BN23 . . . . . .174 B4
Hastings TN34 . . . . .136 E2
Brading Rd BN2 . . . . . . .164 C7
Bradley Rd Wartling BN21 .131 C1
White Post TN3 . . . . .5 D5
Braemar Ho ■ BN1 . . . .163 E6
Braemore Ct BN3 . . . . .162 E6
Braemore Rd BN3 . . . . .162 E6
Braeside Ave TN3 . . . . .143 A7
Bramber Ave Hove BN3 .141 F3
Peacehaven BN10 . . . . . .178 C8
Bramber Ave N BN10 . . .178 C8
Bramber Cl
Haywards Heath RH16 . . .50 D4
Peacehaven BN10 . . . . . .178 C8
Bramber Ct ■ Hove BN3 .163 B7
Bramber Rd BN25 . . . . .180 F2
Bramber Rd BN25 . . . . .180 F2
Bramber Way RH15 . . . . .73 A4
Bramble Cl BN23 . . . . . .174 B3
Bramble Croft TN6 . . . . .26 A2
Bramble Dr BN27 . . . . . .152 A7
Bramble Gdns RH15 . . . .72 D4
Bramble La BN23 . . . . . .142 C5
Bramble Twitten BN21 . . . .2 A1
Bramble Way
Brighton BN1 . . . . .143 C6
Fairlight Cove TN35 . . . .138 F4
Bramble Wlk TN2 . . . . . . .8 D7
Brambledean Rd BN41 . .162 B7
Brambles BN6 . . . . .97 F5
Brambles The RH17 . . . . .50 A6
Bramble Wlk TN2 . . . . . . .8 D7
Bramblesham Sch RH19 . .11 C5
Brambletye Ave TN27 . . .177 D5
Brambletye Sch RH19 . .11 C5
Brambletyne Ave BN2 . .177 D5
Bramley Rd BN26 . . . . .173 D6
Bramleys BN27 . . . . . . .145 E5
Brampton Cl TN29 . . . . .156 F4
Brampton Ct TN39 . . . . .156 F4
Brampton Rd BN22 . . . .184 F8
Brampton Road Trad Est
. . . . .185 A8
Brand Rd BN22 . . . . . . .173 E1
Brands Cl BN9 . . . . .168 E2
Brangwyn Ave BN1 . . . .142 E5
Brangwyn Cres BN1 . . .142 E5
Brangwyn Dr BN1 . . . . .142 E5
Brangwyn Way BN1 . . .142 E5
Branksome Rd TN38 . . .159 A8
Brassey Ave BN22 . . . . .173 D1
Brassey Ave BN2 . . . . . .173 D1
Brassey Par BN22 . . . . .173 F1
Brassey Rd TN40 . . . . . .157 C3
Brasslands Dr BN41 . . . .140 F1
Braybon Ave BN1 . . . . . .142 A4
Braybon Bsns Pk RH15 . .72 E2
Braybrooke Cl TN34 . . .159 E8
Braybrooke Rd TN34 . . .159 F8
Braybrooke Terr TN34 . .159 F8
Braypool La BN1 . . . . . .142 D7
Brazen Cl BN10 . . . . . . .179 B7
Bread St BN1 . . . . .189 B3
Breadsell La TN38 . . . . .135 D6
Brecon Cotts TN6 . . . . . .39 B3
Brecon Cl BN3 . . . . .163 C7
Brede Cl Brighton BN2 . .164 F5
Eastbourne BN22 . . . . . .185 D6
St Leonards TN37 . . . . .135 F7
Brede Cty Prim Sch TN31 .90 B4
Brede Hill TN31 . . . . . . .115 B8
Brede La Cackle Street TN31 .89 F2
Sedlescombe TN31,TN32 . .89 F1
Brede Valley View TN36 .116 C5
Breeds Pl TN34 . . . . . . .159 F7
Brendon Cl
Eastbourne BN23 . . . . . .174 E4
Royal Tunbridge Wells TN2 . .8 E5
Brendon Rise TN34 . . . .137 B3
Brentor Ct TN2 . . . . .8 D7
Brentwood Cl BN1 . . . . .143 B3
Brentwood Cres BN1 . . .143 B3
Brentwood Rd BN1 . . . .143 B3
Bretland Ct TN4 . . . . .7 D4
Bretland Rd TN4 . . . . . . .7 D4
Brett Dr BN27 . . . . .145 E5
Brett Dr TN40 . . . . .157 F4
Bretton RH15 . . . . .72 E5
Bretts Field BN10 . . . . .167 C2
Brewer St Brighton BN2 .189 C4
Lamberhurst TN3 . . . . . .39 B4
Brewers Gr BN20 . . . . . .40 B2

Brian Cres TN4 . . . . .8 B8
Briar Cl
Fairlight Cove TN35 . . . .139 A5
Woodingdean BN2 . . . . .165 D7
Briar Pl BN23 . . . . .174 B3
Briarcroft Rd BN2 . . . . .165 D7
Briary The TN40 . . . . . . .157 D5
Brick Kiln La TN20,TN22 . .57 E6
Brickfield TN31 . . . . .69 B2
Brickfields TN7 . . . . .9 E8
Brickhurst La BN8 . . . . .126 C8
Brickmead TN6 . . . . .26 A1
Bricky The BN10 . . . . . . .178 D8
Brickyard Cotts TN6 . . . .28 A4
Brickyard La
Mark Cross TN6 . . . . .27 E5
South Chailey BN8 . . . . .100 E7
Bridge Cl Burgess Hill RH15 .72 F4
Horam TN21 . . . . .107 A7
Bridge Ct BN7 . . . . .123 A2
Bridge End BN24 . . . . . .175 B7
Bridge Farm Rd TN22 . . .78 C6
Bridge Ho TN4 . . . . .8 B5
Bridge Rd TN31 . . . . .93 C6
Bridge Road Bsns Pk
RH16 . . . . .50 F7
Bridge St BN9 . . . . .179 D7
Bridge Way TN38 . . . . . .158 C6
Bridgelands BN8 . . . . . .101 D4
Bridgemere Rd BN22 . . .185 B6
Bridger Way TN35 . . . . .137 C4
Bridgersmill RH16 . . . . . .50 D6
Bridgewick Ct BN7 . . . .123 D3
Bridle Way BN10 . . . . . .178 C8
Briers Ave TN34 . . . . . . .136 C3
Briers Gdns TN34 . . . . .136 C3
Briers The TN37 . . . . . . .136 C4
Brigden St BN1 . . . . . . .189 A4
Brigdens Hill BN8 . . . . .147 E6
Bright Ridge TN4 . . . . . . .7 E8
Brighthelm BN1 . . . . . . .144 B8
Brightland Rd BN20 . . . .184 D3
Brightling Ave TN35 . . . .137 C4
Brighton & Hove High Sch
for Girls BN3 . . . . .163 E6
Brighton & Hove Stad
BN3 . . . . .142 B1
Brighton Coll BN2 . . . . .164 C5
Brighton Coll of Tech
Brighton BN1 . . . . .189 A5
Brighton BN1 . . . . .189 A5
Brighton BN2 . . . . .189 C4
Brighton College
Pre-Prep Sch BN2 . . . . .164 C5
Brighton Ctr The BN1 . .189 A2
Brighton Fishing Mus
BN1 . . . . .189 A1
Brighton General Hospl
BN2 . . . . .164 D7
Brighton Marina BN2 . . .164 F2
Brighton Marina Village
BN2 . . . . .164 F3
Brighton Mus & Art Gall
BN1 . . . . .189 B2
Brighton Pl BN1 . . . . . . .189 B2
Brighton Race Course
BN2 . . . . .165 A8
Brighton Rd Hassocks BN6 .97 A1
Lewes BN7 . . . . .146 A8
Newhaven BN9 . . . . . . .179 B7
Shoreham-by-Sea BN43 . .139 B5
Brighton Sea Life Ctr
BN2 . . . . .189 B1
Brighton Sq BN1 . . . . . .189 B2
Brighton Sta BN1 . . . . . .189 B3
Brighton Steiner Sch
BN2 . . . . .164 F7
Brighton, Hove & Sussex
Sixth Form Coll
BN3 . . . . .163 B8
Brightwell Ind Est BN9 .179 C7
Brills La BN1 . . . . .189 B1
Brincliffe TN6 . . . . .25 E3
Brinkers La TN5 . . . . .30 A7
Bristol Gate BN2 . . . . . .164 D4
Bristol Gdns BN2 . . . . . .164 E4
Bristol Mews ■ BN2 . . .164 E4
Bristol Pl BN2 . . . . .164 E4
Bristol Rd Brighton BN2 .164 C4
St Leonards TN38 . . . . .136 A3
Bristol St BN2 . . . . .164 E4
Britannia Ct BN2 . . . . . .165 A3
British Engineerium
(Mus) BN1 . . . . .142 B2
Britland Est BN22 . . . . .185 C6
Brittany Ct
■ Bexhill TN39 . . . . . . .157 A4
Hove BN3 . . . . .162 D7
Brittany Ho TN6 . . . . . . .37 D8
Brittany Mews TN39 . . .157 A4
Brittany Rd Hove BN3 . .162 D6
St Leonards TN37,TN38 .159 B8
Britten Cl BN23 . . . . . . .174 D3
Brittenden La TN7 . . . . . .80 E5
Britts Farm Rd TN22 . . . .56 C3
Britts Rd TN22 . . . . .56 C3
Broad Gn BN2 . . . . .165 E6
Broad Grave La BN26 . .173 B2
Broad La TN3 . . . . .39 B4
Broad Green Ave RH15 . .72 C2
Broad Oak Cl TN6 . . . . . .15 C6
Broad Oak Cl
Broad Oak TN31 . . . . . . .90 B5

Broad Oak Cl continued
Eastbourne BN23 . . . . . .174 A4
Royal Tunbridge Wells TN2 . .7 F1
Broad Oak Cty Prim Sch
TN21 . . . . .59 F2
Broad Rd BN20 . . . . . . .173 A4
Broad Rig Ave BN3 . . . .141 D3
Broad St Brighton BN2 . .189 B1
Cuckfield RH17 . . . . .50 A6
Icklesham TN36 . . . . . . .116 C6
Seaford BN25 . . . . .181 A2
Broad View Bexhill TN39 .156 F6
Broad Oak TN21 . . . . . . .59 E1
Broad Way TN35 . . . . . .138 C5
Broadcroft TN2 . . . . .16 F8
Broadfields BN2 . . . . . . .143 E3
Broadfields Rd BN2 . . . .143 E3
Broadhill Cl TN21 . . . . . .59 E1
Broadlands
Burgess Hill RH15 . . . . . .98 B8
Hastings TN35 . . . . .137 D2
Broadley View TN33 . . .133 E8
Broadmead TN2 . . . . . . .16 F8
Broadmead Ave TN38 . .16 F8
Broadoak La Buxted TN39 .156 E5
Bexhill TN39 . . . . .156 F5
Broads Cotts TN19 . . . . .62 B6
Broadstone RH14 . . . . . .12 A2
Broadview Cl BN20 . . . .172 F4
Broadwalk The TN39 . . .156 B4
Broadwater Down TN2 . .16 E8
Broadwater Down TN2 . .16 E8
Broadwater
Cty Prim Sch TN4 . . . . . .7 F1
Broadwater La
Royal Tunbridge Wells TN2 . .16 F8
Royal Tunbridge Wells
TN2, TN4 . . . . .7 F1
Broadwater Mews BN26 .172 E3
Broadwater Rise TN2 . . . .7 F1
Broadwater Way TN22 . .184 F8
Broadway The Bexhill TN39 .161 C8
Broadway The
Alfriston BN26 . . . . .170 F3
Crowborough TN6 . . . . . .25 F3
Eastbourne BN22 . . . . . .173 D1
Hastings TN35 . . . . .137 D4
Haywards Heath RH16 . .50 B5
Lamberhurst TN3 . . . . . .20 E5
Brockhurst BN2 . . . . . . .164 F7
Brockhurst Gate TN40 . .157 F5
Brockley Rd TN39 . . . . .157 A3
Brocks Gyhll BN20 . . . . .173 A3
Brodie Pl BN21 . . . . .184 D4
Brodrick Cl BN22 . . . . . .173 F1
Brodrick Rd BN22 . . . . .173 E2
Brokes Way TN4 . . . . .8 B8
Bromley Cl
Eastbourne BN23 . . . . . .174 C2
Keymer BN6 . . . . .98 A4
Bromley Rd Brighton BN2 .189 C5
Seaford BN25 . . . . .181 A4
Brompton Cl BN1 . . . . . .142 E6
Brontes The RH19 . . . . . .1 F3
Brook Ave BN6 . . . . .97 F3
Brook Cl Crowborough TN6 . .26 D1
East Grinstead RH19 . . . .2 B1
Brook Ho TN39 . . . . . . .157 A4
Brook La Beddingham BN8 .147 A6
Lindfield RH16 . . . . .50 F8
Brook Rd TN2 . . . . .8 D7
Brook St Hastings TN34 .159 F8
Lewes BN7 . . . . .123 C5
Polegate BN26 . . . . .172 F6
Brook Terr TN6 . . . . .25 D4
Brook View TN6 . . . . . . .25 D4
Brook Way TN35 . . . . . .137 B4
Brooker Pl BN3 . . . . . . .163 A7
Brooker St BN3 . . . . . . .163 A7
Brookfield TN18 . . . . . . .47 B5
Brookfield Rd TN40 . . . .157 E4
Brookfield Rd TN40 . . . .157 E4
Brookhouse Bottom TN34 .34 D4
Brookhouse Rd TN22 . . .79 A4
Brookland Cl
Beachlands BN24 . . . . . .175 E6
Hastings TN34 . . . . .136 F2
Brooklands TN6 . . . . .8 D7
Brooklands Ave TN6 . . . .37 F7
Brooklands Farm Cl TN3 . .6 A6
Brooklands Terr TN27 . .128 E3
Brooklands Way RH19 . .10 D8
Brooklyn Rd BN25 . . . . .180 E3
Brooks Cl BN22 . . . . . . .185 B5
Brooks Ct Lewes BN7 . .123 D2
Newhaven BN9 . . . . . . .179 D6
Brooks Gdns BN8 . . . . . .76 D6
Brooks Rd BN7 . . . . .123 D2
Brooks Rd BN7 . . . . .123 D2
Brookside Piddinghoe BN8 .168 B2
Uckfield TN22 . . . . .78 A6
Brookside Ave BN26 . . .172 F7
Brookway Burgess Hill RH15 .73 C3
Lindfield RH16 . . . . .51 B5
Broom Cl BN22 . . . . . . .173 D2
Broom La TN3 . . . . .6 E3
Broom Pk TN3 . . . . .6 E3
Broomans's Ct ■ BN7 . .123 C1
Broomans La BN7 . . . . .123 D1
Broomfield Ave BN10 . .177 A4
Broomfield Dr BN41 . . . .141 A3
Broomfield St
BN20, BN21 . . . . .184 C4
Broomgrove Rd TN34 . .160 B6

Broomham La BN8 ....127 B7
Broomham Sch TN35 ......116 A3
Broomhill Bank Sch TN3 ....7 C6
Broomhill Park Rd TN4 .....7 F8
Broomhill Rd TN3 ....7 D7
Bross Est BN9 ....179 D8
Brow The Burgess Hill RH15 ..73 A2
　Friston BN20 ....183 B2
　Woodingdean BN2 ....165 D8
Brown Jack Ave BN26 ....172 F6
Brown's La TN22 ....78 D8
Browning Rd 2 BN21 ......82 A7
Browning Wlk 3 BN23 ....174 E2
Brownings The 1 RH19 .....1 C1
Brownleaf Rd BN2 ....165 E6
Browns Cl TN2 ....78 D8
Browns La TN21 ....81 B6
Browns Wood RH19 ....1 E4
Broyle Cl BN8 ....125 A8
Broyle La BN8 ....124 F8
Broyle Paddock BN8 .....124 F7
Broyle Side BN8 ....125 A7
Broyle The BN8 ....125 B7
Bruce Cl RH16 ....50 E3
Brunel Rd TN38 ....135 E4
Brunswick Mews 3 BN3 ...163 D5
Brunswick Pl BN3 ....163 D6
Brunswick Rd BN3 ....163 D6
Brunswick Row BN1 ......189 B4
Brunswick Sq BN3 ....163 D5
Brunswick St E BN3 ......163 D5
Brunswick St W BN3 .....163 D5
Brunswick Terr
　Hove BN1, BN3 ....163 D5
　Royal Tunbridge Wells TN1 ..8 A2
Brushes La RH16 ....51 B8
Bryants Field TN6 ....25 E3
Brydges Cl BN22 ....185 C6
Buci Cres BN43 ....140 C1
Buckholt Ave TN40 ......158 A7
Buckholt La TN39 ....157 C8
Buckhurst Cl
　East Grinstead RH20 .....1 C3
　Eastbourne BN20 ....184 B8
　Lewes BN7 ....123 C3
Buckhurst La TN5 ....29 A6
Buckhurst Mead RH19 .....1 C4
Buckhurst Pl TN39 ......157 C4
Buckhurst Rd
　Bexhill TN40 ....157 C4
　Telscombe Cliffs BN10 ..177 F3
Buckhurst Way RH19 ......1 C2
Buckingham Cl
　4 Brighton BN1 ....189 A4
　Seaford BN25 ....180 F4
　Shoreham-by-Sea BN43 ..161 A8
Buckingham Dr BN15 ....159 A6
Buckingham Dr RH19 ....11 A8
Buckingham Heights 1
　BN22 ....185 A4
Buckingham Lodge BN1 ..189 A4
Buckingham Pl BN1 .....189 A4
Buckingham Rd
　Brighton BN1 ....189 A3
　Royal Tunbridge Wells TN3 ..7 B2
　St Leonards TN38 .....136 A4
Buckland Rd BN25 ......180 F5
Buckle By-Pass BN25 ...180 C4
Buckle Cl BN25 ....180 C4
Buckle Dr BN25 ....180 C4
Buckle Rise BN25 ......180 C4
Buckler St BN41 ....162 B8
Bucklers Cl TN2 ....8 C3
Buckley Cl BN41 ....162 A8
Buckswood Grange Sch
　TN22 ....78 B8
Buckthorn Cl BN25 .....181 C3
Buckwell Ct BN7 ....123 A3
Bugsell La TN32 ....63 F4
Bulbeck Cl RH15 ....72 E2
Bull La 2 BN7 ....146 C8
Bull Lane Cotts TN3 .....19 C4
Bull Ring TN33 ....112 D4
Buller Cl TN6 ....26 A1
Buller Rd BN2 ....143 D1
Bullfinch Gdns TN22 .....78 E4
Bullingstone Cotts TN3 ...6 F7
Bullingstone La TN3 ......6 F7
Bulls Pl TN2 ....9 D6
Bulrush Pl TN38 ....135 E1
Bulverhythe Rd TN38 ...158 D6
Bungalows The TN22 .....79 B5
Bunny La TN16 ....16 C5
Bunting Cl TN38 ....158 E8
Burchetts Cl RH16 ......50 E7
Burden Pl TN38 ....136 A3
Burdett Pl 2 TN34 .....160 A3
Burdett Rd
　Crowborough TN6 ......26 C1
　Rusthall TN4 ....7 B4
Burdocks Dr BN15 ....73 D1
Burfield Park Ind Est
　BN27 ....152 B6
Burfield Rd BN22 ......185 B3
Burgess Hill Sch RH15 ..73 B2
Burgess Hill Sta RH15 ..73 B2
Burgess Rd TN35 ......137 C5
Burgh Hill TN19 ....44 E2
Burgh La BN8 ....148 E5
Burgundy Ho 3 BN25 ...185 F8
Burhill Way TN38 ......135 F7
Burleigh Pl BN22 ......185 C6

Burlington Gdns BN41 ...141 C1
Burlington Pl BN21 ....185 A2
Burlington Rd BN21 ....185 B2
Burlington St BN2 ......164 C4
Burlow Cl Brighton BN2 ..164 E5
　Lower Willingdon BN22 ..173 C3
Burma Cl RH16 ....51 C4
Burners Cl RH15 ....73 D1
Burnham Cl BN2 ....165 F7
Burns Way RH19 ....1 C1
Burnside BN26 ....173 A6
Burnside Ct BN26 ......173 A6
Burnt House La TN3 ......7 A5
Burnt Lodge La TN5 .....31 B2
Burnt Oak Rd TN22, TN6 ..37 C2
Burnthouse Bostall BN6 ..120 C8
Burrell Rd RH16 ....50 D6
Burrells La TN22 ....55 A7
Burrells The BN43 .....161 B6
Burrow Down BN20 .....184 B5
Burrow Down Cl BN20 ..184 A4
Burrswood Villas TN3 ...15 B7
Burstead Cl BN1 ....143 B3
Burston Gdns BN21 ....184 E5
Burton Rd BN21 ....184 E5
Burton Villas BN3 .....163 D8
Burton Way TN38 ......159 B6
Burton Wlk BN27 ......152 B7
Burwash CE Prim Sch
　TN19 ....62 B6
Burwash Cl
　Eastbourne BN23 ......174 B4
　Hastings TN34 ....137 A5
Burwash Lodge BN1 ...143 C1
Burwash Rd
　Broad Oak TN21 ....82 C8
　Hove BN3 ....141 F3
Bush Cl
　Telscombe Cliffs BN10 ..167 A1
　Woodingdean BN2 .....165 D8
Bush Farm Dr BN41 ....141 C3
Bush Rd BN9 ....179 B8
Bushbury La TN22 ....80 A3
Busheyfields BN27 ....152 A8
Bushy Croft TN39 .....156 F5
Bushy Gill TN3 ....7 A3
Butcher's Cross TN7 ....13 B7
Butcher's La TN5 ......115 E2
Butcherfield La TN7 .....13 B6
Bute St BN2 ....164 C4
Butler's Green Ho RH16 ..50 B5
Butler's Green Rd RH16 ..50 C4
Butler's La BN27 ......130 E3
Butlers Way BN8 ......124 C5
Butterbox La RH17 ......52 D4
Buttercup Wlk BN1 ....143 B3
Butterfield RH19 ....1 B3
Butterfly Cl BN27 .....130 F4
Buttermere Way BN23 ..174 C4
Button Cl BN2 ....189 C4
Butts Field BN27 ......152 C6
Butts La BN8 ....173 A1
Butts Rd BN42 ....161 E7
Buttsfield La BN8 .....105 A5
Buxted CE Prim Sch TN22 ..55 F3
Buxted Cl TN22 ....56 C3
Buxted Rise TN40 .....148 B5
Buxted Sta TN22 ....56 B3
Buxted Wood La TN22 ..56 C5
Buxton Dr TN39 ....157 B6
Buxton Rd Brighton BN1 ..163 E7
　Eastbourne BN20 ......184 D8
By Sunte RH16 ....50 F8
Bydown BN25 ....181 A4
Bye-law Cotts BN8 ....101 E6
Byeway The Bexhill TN39 ..156 D5
　Hastings TN34 ....159 A8
Byeways The BN25 ....180 F4
Byfields Croft TN39 ...156 F5
Byland Cl BN22 ....173 E3
Bylands 3 BN2 ....164 F5
Byng Rd TN4 ....7 F5
Byre Cotts BN2 ....165 D4
Byron Cl 4 RH16 ....50 D5
Byron Gr 2 RH19 ....1 C2
Byron St BN3 ....163 A7
Byron Wlk BN23 ....174 E3
Byway The BN1 ....143 A5
Byways TN33 ....136 D6
Byworth Cl Bexhill TN39 ..156 D6
　Brighton BN2 ....164 F6

C

Cabbage Stalk La TN4 ....7 E2
Cabot Cl BN23 ....185 G7
Caburn Cl BN23 ....174 A4
Caburn Cres BN7 ......123 A2
Caburn Rd BN3 ....163 E7
Caburn View Bungalows
　BN8 ....148 B3
Caburn View Cotts BN8 ..148 B3
Caburn Way BN27 .....152 C6
Cackle St
　Cackle Street TN31 .....90 A2
　Nutley TN22 ....35 E2
Cacklebury Cl BN27 ...152 A6
Cadborough Cliff TN31 ..93 A4
Cade St BN22 ....173 F2
Cadogan St
　Pevensey Bay BN24 ...175 C4
　3 Brighton BN1 ......163 E7
Cadogan Gdns 6 TN1 ....8 B4
Cairngorm Cl BN23 ...174 D3

Cairo Ave BN10 ....178 A8
Cairo Ave S BN10 .....178 A7
Caister's Cl BN3 ......163 C8
Caius Ct 18 BN43 .....161 C8
Calbourne RH16 ....50 C5
Caldbec Cl TN31 ......112 D5
Caldbec Hill TN31 ....112 D5
Caldicotts La BN27 ...128 C4
Caledonian Rd BN2 ...189 C5
Caley Rd TN2 ....8 D7
Calgary Rd TN39 .....157 B7
Callums Wlk TN40 ....157 E5
Calvert Cl TN1 ....7 F1
Calverley Park Cres 1 TN1 ..8 B3
Calverley Park Gdns TN1 ..8 B3
Calverley Pk TN1 ....8 B3
Calverley Rd
　Eastbourne BN21 .....184 F2
　Royal Tunbridge Wells TN1 ..8 B3
Calverley St TN1 ....8 B4
Calverley Wlk BN21 ...184 F2
Calvert Rd Hastings TN34 ..160 A6
　Uckfield TN22 ....78 A7
Camber Cl
　Beachlands BN24 .....175 F6
　Bexhill TN40 ....157 F6
　Brighton BN2 ....164 F5
Camber Dr BN24 ......175 F6
Camber Rd TN31 ....94 B3
Camber Way BN24 ....175 F6
Camberlot Rd BN27 ...128 A2
Cambrian Rd TN4 ....8 C7
Cambridge Gdns
　Hastings TN34 ....159 E7
　Royal Tunbridge Wells TN2 ..8 B3
Cambridge Gr BN3 ....163 C7
Cambridge La TN21 ....81 C2
Cambridge Rd
　Bexhill TN40 ....157 C6
　Hastings TN34 ....159 E7
　Hove BN3 ....163 D6
Cambridge St TN2 ......8 B3
Cambridge Way TN22 ..55 C1
Camden Ave TN2 ....9 C6
Camden Ct Pembury TN2 ..9 D6
　Royal Tunbridge Wells TN1 ..8 B4
Camden Hill TN2 ....8 B3
Camden Pk TN2 ....8 B3
Camden Rd
　Eastbourne BN21 .....184 F2
　Royal Tunbridge Wells TN1 ..8 B4
Camden St BN41 ......162 C6
Camden Terr BN1 ......189 A3
Camdon Rd TN39 .....157 B7
Camelford St BN2 .....189 C1
Cameron Cl BN27 ....152 A8
Campbell Cl TN22 .....55 C1
Campbell Cres RH19 ....1 B1
Campbell Ct TN38 ....159 A8
Campbell Rd
　Brighton BN1 ....189 A5
　Royal Tunbridge Wells TN4 ..8 A6
Camperdown St TN39 ..157 B7
Canada Cl BN10 ......167 A1
Canada Way TN34 ....159 B7
Canadia Rd TN33 .....112 D8
Canal Bank TN35 .....139 B7
Canfield Cl BN2 ....143 D1
Canfield Rd BN2 ......143 D1
Canning St BN2 ......164 D5
Cannon Pl BN1 ....189 A2
Cansiron La
　Ashurst Wood RH19 ...11 C6
　Holtye TN7, TN8 ....3 E2
Cantelupe Mews 4 RH19 ..1 C1
Cantelupe Rd
　East Grinstead RH19 ...1 F1
Canterbury Cl BN22 ...173 C2
Canterbury Dr 8 BN2 ..189 C4
Canterbury Rd TN2 .....9 E6
Canterbury Rise TN34 ..136 E3
Cantercrow Hill BN9 ..168 F2
Canton 8 RH16 ....50 D6
Cants Cl RH15 ....73 C3
Cants La RH15 ....73 C3
Canute Cl BN23 ....185 F8
Canute Rd TN35 ......137 D3
Capel Ave BN10 ....178 D7
Capello Path BN27 ...152 D7
Capenors RH15 ....73 B1
Caple Ct TN38 ....159 B8
Caple Gdns TN38 .....159 B7
Card Hill RH18 ....11 F1
Carden Ave BN1 ......143 A6
Carden Cl BN1 ....143 A6
Carden Cty Inf Sch BN1 ..143 B6
Carden Cty Jun Sch
　BN1 ....143 B6
Carden Hill BN1 ......143 B5
Cardiff Rd TN38 ......159 C7
Cardinal Newman Sch
　BN3 ....163 D8
Cardinals Cl TN40 ....157 F6
Carew Cl 3 BN21 .....185 A4
Carew Lodge 1 BN21 ..184 F4
Carew Rd BN21 ......184 F4
Carew Views 2 BN21 ..184 F4
Carey Down BN10 ....167 B1
Carfax Cl TN39 ....156 F5
Carinus Gdns TN34 ...136 A6
Carisbrooke Cl BN23 ..174 B4
Carisbrooke Rd
　Brighton BN2 ....164 D7
　St Leonards TN38 .....159 C7
Carlisle Par TN34 ....159 F7

Carlisle Rd
　Eastbourne BN20, BN21 ..184 F1
　Hove BN3 ....162 F6
Carlton Cl BN25 ......180 E4
Carlton Cres 8 C4
Carlton Ct 1 Bexhill TN40 ..157 D3
　Portslade-by-Sea BN41 ..162 C8
Carlton Hill BN2 ......189 C2
Carlton Hill Cty Prim Sch
　BN2 ....189 C2
Carlton Ho BN1 ....142 E2
Carlton Ho 8 BN2 ....189 C2
Carlton Rd
　Eastbourne BN22 .....185 C4
　Royal Tunbridge Wells TN1 ..8 C4
　Seaford BN25 ....180 D4
Carlton Terr
　Portslade-by-Sea BN3, BN41 ..162 C8
　Whitehill TN6 ....37 F8
Carlyle Ave BN2 ......143 D1
Carlyle St BN2 ....164 C7
Carmel Cl TN39 ......156 D3
Carmen Ct BN20 .....173 B3
Carn Ct 1 BN2 ....164 C6
Carnoustie Cl TN38 ...158 F7
Carnoustie Cl 18 RH16 ..50 E4
Carol Cl BN1 ....142 F6
Caroline Cl BN25 .....180 D5
Carpenter Dr TN38 ...135 F4
Carpenters Croft BN8 ..105 A5
Carpenters Way BN27 ..152 A6
Carrier's Path BN27 ...152 B8
Carriers Pl TN3 ....5 B4
Carroll Wlk BN23 ....174 E2
Cashman Lodge BN1 ..143 A5
Caspian Cl 8 BN1 ....189 A4
Caspian Sq BN2 ......165 F1
Castle Banks 8 BN27 ..123 C1
Castle Bolton BN23 ...174 A4
Castle Cl BN7 ....123 D2
Castle Ditch La BN7 ...123 C1
Castle Dr BN24 ....175 C4
Castle Farm Cotts TN7 ..13 E4
Castle Gate 8 BN7 ...123 C1
Castle Gdns BN10 ....159 F7
Castle Hill TN6 ....39 A5
Castle Hill Pas BN7 ...159 F8
Castle Hill Rd TN34 ..159 F7
Castle Hurst TN22 ....165 B6
Castle Mount BN20 ..184 D1
Castle Prec 8 BN7 ....123 C1
Castle Rd Pevensey BN24 ..175 A6
　Royal Tunbridge Wells TN4 ..8 A3
Castle Rise 8 Lewes BN7 ..123 C1
　Uckfield TN22 ....78 A7
Castle Sq BN1 ....189 B2
Castle St Brighton BN1 ..163 E5
　8 Hastings TN34 .....159 F7
　8 Royal Tunbridge Wells TN1 ..8 A2
　Winchelsea TN36 .....117 F7
Castle Terr BN24 .....175 B6
Castle View Gdns TN38 ..184 E6
Castle Way TN22 ....78 D4
Castle Wlk TN6 ....39 D5
Castledean Sch BN1 ..143 C2
Castledown Ave TN34 ..160 A4
Castledown Cty Prim Sch
　TN34 ....160 A5
Castledown Terr 2 TN34 ..160 A4
Castlefields TN7 ....13 F7
Castleham Rd TN38 ...135 F5
Castleross BN24 ......175 C4
Cat St TN7 ....12 F1
Catherine Pl 2 TN1 ....8 B4
Catherine Vale BN2 ..165 E8
Catkin Way RH16 ......51 B4
Catley Ct 2 TN39 ....157 A4
Cats Field Cl BN23 ....173 F4
Catsfield CE Prim Sch
　TN33 ....133 F8
Catsfield Cl TN38 ....135 D2
Catsfield Rd TN33 ...111 E2
Catt's Corner Cotts TN6 ..27 E1
Catt's Hill TN6 ....27 E1
Causeway Sch TN38 ..174 A3
Causeway The
　Brighton BN2 ....164 D6
　7 Seaford BN25 .....180 E2
Cavalier Way RH19 ....10 F7
Cavalry Cres BN20 ....184 E6
Cavendish Mews 12 BN1 ..163 E5
Cavell Ave BN10 ......178 B7
Cavell Ave N BN10 ...178 C8
Cavendish Ave
　Eastbourne BN22 .....185 B4
　St Leonards TN38 .....159 A7
Cavendish Cl BN10 ...167 B1
Cavendish Ct 9 TN40 ..157 D3
Cavendish Dr BN8 ......8 B1
Cavendish Ho
　8 Brighton BN1 ......163 E5
　Peacehaven BN10 .....167 C1
　8 St Leonards TN37 ..159 C7
Cavendish Hse RH16 ...50 F7
Cavendish Pl
　Brighton BN1 ....163 E5
　Eastbourne BN21 .....185 B3
　4 Hastings TN34 .....159 C7
Cavendish Sch BN21 ..184 C5
Cavendish St BN21 ...185 A3
Caveridge La BN8 ....100 C8
Caverley Rd TN1 ....8 B3
Caves Rd TN38 ....159 A6
Cavix Field 1 TN31 ....67 B7
Caxton Way 15 RH16 ..50 E4
Cedar Cl 1 Burgess Hill RH15 ..73 B5
　Eastbourne BN22 .....173 D2
　St Leonards TN37 ....136 D5

Cedar Ct TN4 8
Cedar Lodge TN4 7
Cedar Ridge TN2 8
Cedar Way RH16 51
Cedars Cl TN22 78
Cedars Gdns BN1 142
Cedars The
　1 Brighton BN2 189
　Brighton, Withdean BN1 ..142
　Hailsham BN27 129
　Haywards Heath RH16 ...50
　Peacehaven BN10 167
　Uckfield TN22 78
Cedarwell Cl BN9 168
Cedarwood 3 BN1 ...142
Celandine Dr TN38 ...136
Centenary Ho BN1 ...142
Century Ind Est 6
　BN2 189
Central Ave
　Eastbourne BN20 184
　Polegate BN26 173
　Telscombe Cliffs BN10 ..179
Central Sta TN1 8
Centurion Rd BN1 189
Centurion Rise TN34 ..137
Ceylon Pl BN21,BN22 ..185
Ceylon Wlk TN39 156
Chadborn Cl BN2 164
Chaffinch Cl RH15 72
Chaffinch Rd BN23 ...174
Chaffinch Wlk TN22 ...78
Chafford Cotts TN3 5
Chafford La TN3 5
Chailey Ave BN2 177
Chailey Cl
　Eastbourne BN23 174
　Hastings TN34 136
Chailey Common
　Nature Reserve BN8 ...75
Chailey Cres BN2 177
Chailey Ct
　8 Haywards Heath RH16 ..5C
　Hove BN1 142
Chailey Cty Sec Sch BN8 ..100
Chailey Heritage Craft Sch
　& Hospl (New Heritage)
　BN8 52
Chailey Heritage Craft Sch
　& Hospl (Old Heritage)
　BN8 75
Chailey La BN8 76
Chailey Rd BN1 143
Chailey St Peter's
　CE Prim Sch BN8 75
Chailey Windmill
　Rural Life Mus BN8 ...75
Chain La TN33 112
Chalden Pl TN39 156
Chaldon BN27 152
Chalfont Dr BN3 142
Chalk Farm Cl BN20 ..173
Chalkers La BN6 97
Chalkland Rise BN2 ..165
Chalky Rd BN41 141
Challoners Cl BN2 ...177
Challoners Mews BN2 ..165
Challow Cl BN6 97
Chaloner Cl RH16 51
Chaloner Rd RH16 51
Chalvington Cl
　Brighton BN1 143
　St Leonards TN38 180
Chalvington Dr 8 BN27 ..136
Chalvington Rd BN22 ..184
Chamberlain Rd BN21 ..184
Chamberlaines La BN8 ..124
Chambers Cres TN36 ..135
Chambers Rd TN38 ...135
Champions Row BN3 ..163
Chancellor Ho TN4 7
Chancellors Pk BN6 ...97
Chanctonbury Dr TN37 ..136
Chanctonbury Rd
　Burgess Hill RH15 73
　Hove BN3 163
Chandler Rd TN39 ...157
Chandler's Mead BN8 ..123
Chandos Cl 1 TN40 ...157
Chandos Rd TN1 8
Channel View
　Bexhill TN40 157
　8 Southwick BN42 ...161
Channel View E TN34 ..160
Channel View Rd
　Eastbourne BN22 185
　Pevensey Bay BN24 ...175
Channel View W 9 TN31 ..167
Channel Way TN35 ...138
Channers La BN8 126
Chant La TN6 27
Chanters Cl TN33 113
Chanters Mead TN6 ...25
Chantry Ave TN40 ...157
Chantry Cty Inf Sch TN40 ..157
Chantry La TN40 157
Chantry The 8 BN21 ..184
Chapel Barn Cl BN27 ..152
Chapel Cl Burgess Hill RH15 ..73
　Seaford BN25 180
Chapel Cotts Battle TN33 ..112
　Mayfield TN20 ....
Chapel Field TN35 67
Chapel Gn TN6 27

Chapel Hill
Crowhurst TN33 ....134 F4
Lewes BN7 ....123 E1
Sedlescombe TN33 ....113 E7
Chapel La
Ashurst Wood RH19 ....11 D6
Blackboys TN22 ....80 B7
East Chiltington BN7 ....100 A3
Forest Row RH18 ....11 F2
Guestling Green TN35 ......138 A8
Horsted Keynes RH17 ....33 C5
Chapel Mews 🔢 BN3 ......163 D5
Chapel Park Rd TN37 ....159 C8
Chapel Pl
Portslade-by-Sea BN41 ....162 B7
🔢 Royal Tunbridge Wells TN1 ..8 A2
Ticehurst TN5 ....31 E1
Chapel Rd
Plumpton Green BN7 ....99 E7
Southwick BN41 ....162 A7
Chapel St Brighton BN2 ..189 C2
Newhaven BN9 ....179 D7
Chapel Terr 🔢 BN2 ......164 D4
Chapman Way TN2 ....8 C8
Chapman's La
East Grinstead RH19 ....1 B1
East Grinstead RH19 ....1 D1
Chapman's Town La TN21 ..83 B2
Charis Ct 🔢 BN3 ....163 C7
Charity Farm Way TN6 ......26 A3
Charles Ave RH15 ....72 D2
Charles Bennett Ct RH16 ..51 A4
Charles Cl Hove BN3 ......142 A3
Seaford BN25 ....180 D5
Charles Ct TN2 ....8 A5
Charles Moore Ct BN26 ...173 A7
Charles Rd TN38 ....159 C8
Charles Rd W TN38 ....159 B8
Charles St Brighton BN2 ..189 B1
Royal Tunbridge Wells TN4 ....8 A8
Charleston Farmhouse
BN8 ....149 A2
Charleston Manor Gdns
BN25 ....182 A6
Charleston Rd BN21 ....184 D4
Charlesworth Pk RH16 .....51 C4
Charlotte St BN2 ....189 C1
Charlston Ave BN9 ....179 A5
Charlton Gdns BN9 ....98 D3
Charlton's Way TN4 ....7 E1
Charltons The BN1 ....143 D6
Charlwood Gdns RH15 ......73 C5
Charlwood Rd RH15 ....73 D6
Charlwoods Bsns Ctr RH19 ..2 E2
Charlwoods Pl RH19 ....1 E3
Charlwoods Rd RH19 ....1 E3
Charters Ancaster Sch
TN40 ....157 F5
Charters Ancaster Sch
(Jun Dept) TN40 ....157 E5
Chartfield BN3 ....142 A2
Chartfield Way TN2 ....142 B2
Chartres TN40 ....157 D6
Chartwell Cl TN40 ....180 E6
Chartwell Ct BN1 ....189 A2
Charles Farm Ct BN2 .....189 C3
Chatfield Cres BN22 ......173 C1
Chatfield Rd RH17 ....50 A6
Chatham Pl Brighton BN1 ..189 A4
🔢 Seaford BN25 ....180 D5
Chatham Rd 🔢 TN37 ....136 B2
Chatsfield Ct TN38 ....135 F4
Chatsworth Ave BN10 .....167 A1
Chatsworth Cl BN1 ....178 A8
Chatsworth Ct BN11 ......188 C8
Chatsworth Gdns BN20 ....188 F8
Chatsworth Pk BN10 ......167 B1
Chatsworth Rd
Brighton BN1 ....163 E8
Hove BN3 ....163 D7
Chaucer Ave 🔢 RH19 ....1 C1
Chaucer Ct 🔢 BN26 ....50 D5
Chaucer Ind Est BN26 ....173 D6
Chaucer Wlk BN23 ....174 E3
Chawbrook Rd BN22 ....185 B4
Chaworth 🔢 BN43 ....161 A6
Cheapside BN1 ....189 B3
Cheeleys RH17 ....33 C5
Chelgates TN39 ....156 C2
Chelmsford St 🔢 BN2 ....184 F1
Chelsea Arc RH16 ....50 E4
Chelsea Cl TN40 ....157 D4
Chelston Ave BN22 ....162 D7
Cheltenham Pl BN1 ....189 B3
Chelwood Cl BN11 ....143 C6
Chelwood Ct RH15 ....73 A4
Chelwood Gate Rd
RH17,TN22 ....34 F7
Chelworth Rd BN22 ....173 D2
Chene Rd BN10 ....178 F6
Chenies Cl TN2 ....42 A6
Chepbourne Rd TN40 ......157 C4
Chepstow Ct BN1 ....143 F5
Chequer Grange RH18 .....11 E1
Chequer Mead Arts Ctr
19 ....1 E1
Chequer Rd RH19 ....1 E1
Chequers Cl TN6 ....26 A2
Chequers Way TN6 ....26 A2
Cherington TN6 ....97 B5
Cherith Cotts BN27 ....182 A6
Cheriton Cl BN20 ....184 C4
Cherry Cl RH15 ....72 E3
Cherry Clack TN21 ....82 A6
Cherry Cotts Fletching TN22 ..54 A4

Cherry Cotts *continued*
Hastings TN35 ....137 C3
Cherry Garden Rd BN20 ...184 B3
Cherry Gdns
Heathfield TN21 ....82 B5
High Hurstwood TN22 ....56 B8
Cherry Gdns BN27 ....152 A7
Cherry Tree Cl TN37 .....159 D8
Cherry Tree Ct TN21 .....106 F7
Cherry Tree Gdns TN40 ...157 F6
Cherry Tree Rd TN2 ....7 C3
Cherrywood 🔢 BN21 ......142 E3
Cherwell Cl BN24 ....173 F5
Cherwell Ct TN21 ....82 A8
Cherwell Rd TN21 ....82 A8
Chesham Pl BN2 ....164 D4
Chesham Rd BN2 ....164 D4
Chesham St BN2 ....164 D4
Cheshire Ct 🔢 BN22 ......185 B4
Chesnut Cl BN27 ....129 A1
Chester Ave TN40 ....163 E7
Chester Ct 🔢 BN3 ....163 E7
Chester Terr BN1 ....143 A1
Chesterfield Gdns BN20 ..188 E8
Chesterfield Rd BN20 ....188 E8
Chesterton Ave BN25 .....181 B3
Chesterton Cl RH19 ....10 F7
Chesterton Dr BN25 ......181 B3
Chestnut Ave TN4 ....8 B8
Chestnut Cl Broad Oak TN31 ..90 B5
Burgess Hill RH15 ....73 B5
East Grinstead RH19 ....1 F4
Eastbourne BN22 ....173 E2
Herstmonceux BN27 ....130 E6
Royal Tunbridge Wells TN4 ...8 A8
Chestnut Cotts
Fletching TN22 ....53 F3
🔢 Heathfield TN21 ....82 A7
Chestnut Dr BN26 ....173 A6
Chestnut Pl TN8 ....4 A5
Chestnut Way BN20 ....179 B7
Chestnut Wlk
Bexhill TN39 ....156 C5
Felcourt RH19 ....1 C8
Chestnuts Ct RH16 ....51 A7
Chestnuts The
Lindfield RH16 ....50 F7
The Moor TN18 ....45 F8
Chet Nole RH19 ....1 D2
Cheviot Cl BN23 ....174 C3
Cheviots The TN34 ....137 C4
Cheyne Ct BN43 ....161 A6
Chichester Cl Bexhill TN39 ..157 B6
🔢 Brighton BN2 ....164 D4
Eastbourne BN22 ....173 B2
Hove BN3 ....141 E4
Peacehaven BN10 ....178 F7
Saltdean BN2 ....177 C5
Seaford BN25 ....180 E3
Chichester Ct TN39 ....156 C3
Chichester Dr E BN2 .....177 C5
Chichester Dr W BN2 .....177 B5
Chichester Ho TN40 ......157 D4
Chichester Lodge BN20 ...188 E3
Chichester Pl BN2 ....164 D4
Chichester Rd
Seaford BN25 ....180 E3
St Leonards TN38 ....159 B6
Chichester Terr 🔢 BN2 ..164 D4
Chichester Way RH15 ......73 C5
Chick Hill TN35 ....139 B8
Chicks La TN17 ....20 F7
Chiddingley Cl BN2 ....164 F5
Chiddingly Cty Prim Sch
BN8 ....127 E7
Chieveley Cotts TN38 ....136 B1
Chieveley Dr TN2 ....42 A6
Chilcomb BN2 ....73 C1
Chilham Cl BN23 ....174 D2
Chillies La TN22,TN6 ....37 B3
Chilling St RH19 ....21 D3
Chillis Wood Rd RH16 .....50 C5
Chilsham La BN27 ....130 E7
Chiltcombe Rd TN31 ....89 E5
Chiltcombe Wlk TN34 .....137 A5
Chorley Ave BN2 ....177 B6
Chown's Hill TN35 ....137 A4
Chownes Mead La RH16 .....50 B4
Chrisdory Rd BN41 ....140 F3
Christ Church
CE Prim Sch TN37 ....136 C1
Christchurch Ct BN9 ......179 D7
Christie Ave BN20 ....124 D6
Christie Rd BN7 ....123 A2
Christies RH19 ....10 D8
Christine Cl TN40 ....158 A7
Christopher Rd RH19 ....1 B1
Church Ave
Haywards Heath RH16 ....50 E6
Hove BN3 ....175 A6
Church Bailey BN24 ......175 A5
Church Bailey Ct BN24 ...175 A5

Church Cl Brighton BN1 ..142 F5
Burgess Hill RH15 ....73 A3
Lower Willingdon BN20 .....173 A4
Church Ct
🔢 Haywards Heath RH16 ....50 E4
Hove BN3 ....141 F1
Church Farm Ct TN19 ......44 C1
Church on BN43 ....161 C7
Church Hill Bexhill TN39 ..156 D4
Brighton BN1 ....142 E7
Etchingham TN19 ....40 A8
Newhaven BN9 ....179 C7
Pyecombe BN45 ....119 C6
Ringmer BN8 ....124 D6
Church Hill Ave TN39 .....156 D4
Church House Cl BN27 ....140 F1
Church in the Wood La
TN38 ....135 F3
Church La Burgess Hill RH17 ..72 E4
Buxted TN22 ....56 C5
Catsfield TN33 ....133 E8
Clayhill TN31 ....91 C1
Danehill RH17 ....34 A3
Ditchling BN6 ....98 D3
East Grinstead RH19 ....1 F1
🔢 Eastbourne BN21 ....184 D3
Etchingham TN19 ....40 A8
Frant TN3 ....17 B4
Guestling Green TN35 ......116 B1
Hellingly BN27 ....129 A6
Hooe TN33 ....155 C7
Haywards Heath RH17 ....33 C5
Jevington BN26 ....183 C7
Kingston near Lewes BN7 ...145 D5
Laughton BN8 ....126 C5
Lewes, South Malling BN7 ..123 D3
Lewes, St Anne's BN7 ......146 B8
Ninfield TN33 ....133 B5
Northbridge Street TN32 ....64 C5
Northiam TN31 ....67 C6
Peasmarsh TN31 ....92 B8
Pevensey BN24 ....175 B6
Pyecombe BN45 ....119 C6
Ripe BN27,BN8 ....149 E8
Seaford BN25 ....180 E2
Southwick BN42 ....161 D7
Westfield TN35 ....114 D3
Church Marks La BN8 .....104 F5
Church Mead BN6 ....98 B3
Church Mews BN20 ....173 B1
Church Pas TN34 ....160 A4
Church Path BN27 ....129 A6
Church Pl BN2 ....164 F5
Church Rd Barcombe BN8 ..101 E2
Burgess Hill RH15 ....73 A3
Buxted TN22 ....56 B4
Catsfield TN33 ....133 F7
Crowborough TN6 ....26 F1
Flowers Green BN27 ....11 A1
Haywards Heath RH16 ....50 F4
Hove BN3 ....163 B6
Kildown TN17 ....20 F3
Lamberhurst TN3 ....20 C6
Lewes BN7 ....123 C1
Mountfield TN32 ....87 B5
Newick BN8 ....76 E6
Polegate BN26 ....173 A6
Portslade-by-Sea BN41 .....162 B7
Royal Tunbridge Wells TN1 ...8 A3
Sandhurst Cross TN18 ....46 F4
Scaynes Hill RH17 ....51 F3
St Leonards TN37 ....159 D7
Church Sq TN31 ....93 C5
Church St Bexhill TN40 ....157 D5
Brighton BN1 ....189 B2
Cowden TN8 ....4 B5
Eastbourne BN20,BN21 ......184 D3
Hartfield TN7 ....13 A6
Hastings TN33 ....137 C3
Old Heathfield TN21 ....82 D5
Portslade-by-Sea BN41 .....162 B7
Rotherfield TN6 ....39 A8
Seaford BN25 ....180 E2
Ticehurst TN5 ....31 D1
Uckfield TN22 ....78 C7
Willingdon BN20,BN22 ......173 C2
Church St Bexhill TN40 ....157 D5
Brighton BN2 ....189 B2
Church Twitten 🔢 BN7 ...123 D1
Church Vale Rd TN40 .....157 D5
Church View BN23 ....173 A4
Church Wlk RH15 ....73 A3
Church Wood
Cty Prim Sch TN38 ....135 F3
Church Wood Dr TN38 .....135 E4
Church Wood Way TN38 ...135 F2
Churchdale Ave BN22 .....185 C6
Churchdale Pl BN22 ......185 B6
Churchdale Rd BN22 ......185 C6
Churchfield
East Dean BN20 ....187 B8
Westfield TN35 ....114 D3
Churchfields TN22 ....35 C4
Churchill Ave TN35 ......137 D5
Churchill Cl TN38 ....136 B2
Churchill Ho BN20 ....141 E2
Churchill Rd
Heathfield TN21 ....82 B6
Lewes BN7 ....123 B3
Seaford BN25 ....180 C5
Churchill Sq BN1 ....73 C2
Churchland La TN33 ....88 E3
Churchsettle La TN5 ....42 B7
Churchyard Cotts TN3 ......7 A8
Chyngton Ave BN25 ....181 B4
Chyngton Ct BN23 ....174 A4
Chyngton Cty Prim Sch
BN25 ....181 B4

Chyngton Gdns BN25 ......181 B4
Chyngton Ho BN25 ....181 C2
Chyngton La BN25 ....181 C3
Chyngton La N BN25 ......181 C3
Chyngton Pl BN25 ....181 B2
Chyngton Rd BN25 ....181 B2
Chyngton Way BN25 ....181 C2
Cider House Wlk BN8 .....105 A5
Cinder Hill Chailey BN8 ....75 F3
Cinder Hill RH19 ....21 B1
Cinder Hill La BN27 ......129 F8
Cinque Ports St TN31 ......93 B5
Cinque Ports Way
Seaford BN25 ....181 C4
St Leonards TN38 ....158 E6
Cinquefoil BN10 ....178 C7
Circus Par BN1 ....189 B4
Circus St BN2 ....189 B2
Cissbury Ave BN10 ....178 E7
Cissbury Cres BN25 ......177 E5
Cissbury Rd
Burgess Hill RH15 ....72 E4
Hove BN3 ....163 E7
Civic App TN22 ....78 C7
Civic Way Burgess Hill RH15 ..73 A3
St Leonards TN38 ....158 A8
CJ Gallards Almshouses
TN4 ....8 A8
Clackhams La TN6 ....38 D7
Clair Ct RH16 ....50 E5
Clair Rd RH16 ....50 E5
Clanricarde Gdns 🔢 TN1 ..8 A3
Clanricarde Rd 🔢 TN1 .....8 A3
Clapham La BN26 ....182 A8
Clapham St TN32 ....64 B4
Clappers The TN32 ....64 A4
Clare Rd BN7 ....123 A2
Clare Wlk BN2 ....164 D5
Claremont 🔢 TN34 ....159 E7
Claremont 🔢 BN25 ....180 D3
Claremont Gdns TN2 ....8 B2
Claremont Rd
Bexhill TN39 ....157 B7
🔢 Royal Tunbridge Wells TN1 ..168 F1
Seaford BN25 ....180 D3
Claremont Rise TN22 ....55 C1
Claremont St TN33 ....114 B1
Clarence Dr RH19 ....10 F7
Clarence Rd
Eastbourne BN22 ....185 B4
Royal Tunbridge Wells TN1 ...8 A3
St Leonards TN37 ....136 C1
Clarence Row TN1 ....8 A3
Clarence Sq BN1 ....189 A2
Clarendon Cl TN37 ....136 B4
Clarendon Gdns BN25 .....181 A1
Clarendon Ho 🔢 BN3 .....163 B7
Clarendon Pl
🔢 Brighton BN2 ....164 C4
Portslade-by-Sea BN41 .....162 C6
Clarendon Rd Hove BN3 ...163 B7
Shoreham-by-Sea
BN42,BN43 ....161 D8
Clarendon Terr 🔢 BN2 ...164 D4
Clarendon Villas BN3 .....163 B7
Clarendon Way TN2 ....8 A1
Claridge TN1 ....8 B6
Clarke Ave BN3 ....141 F3
Clarke Rd BN2 ....189 A3
Clarks Ind Est BN23 ......163 B8
Claverham Cl TN33 ....112 B4
Claverham Com Coll
TN33 ....112 A4
Claverham Way TN33 ......112 B4
Clavering Wlk TN39 ....156 B2
Claxton Cl BN21 ....184 D5
Claxton Rd TN40 ....158 A5
Clay Corner BN6 ....101 F6
Clay Hill BN23 ....174 D2
Clayfields BN10 ....178 B7
Clays Cl RH19 ....10 E8
Clayton Ave BN6 ....97 F3
Clayton Dr RH15 ....72 F1
Clayton Hill BN6,BN45 ....119 D7
Clayton Mill Rd BN24 ....174 B5
Clayton Pk BN6 ....97 E4
Clayton Rd Brighton BN2 ..164 D7
Ditchling BN6 ....98 C3
Clayton Way BN3 ....141 F3
Clayton Windmills BN6 ....97 F3
Clayton's La TN3 ....9 E2
Clearwater La RH17 ....52 A3
Clearwaters La RH16 ....73 D8
Cleave Ave TN2 ....42 B7
Cleve Terr BN7 ....146 A8
Clevedon Rd TN39 ....157 A6
Clevedown BN7 ....146 A8
Cleveland BN2 ....8 D4
Cleveland Cl BN23 ....174 C3
Cleveland Gdns RH15 .....143 A1
Cleveland Rd BN1 ....163 E7
Clevelands RH16 ....50 E6
Cliff App BN2 ....164 F4

Cliff Ave BN10 ....178 E5
Cliff Cl BN25 ....180 F1
Cliff Ct TN38 ....158 D6
Cliff End La TN35 ....139 B7
Cliff Gdns Seaford BN25 ..180 F1
Telscombe Cliffs TN40 .....177 F4
Cliff Park Cl BN10 ....178 F7
Cliff Rd Brighton BN2 .....164 E4
Cliff The 164 F4
Cliff Way TN35 ....138 F5
Cliff High St BN7 ....123 D1
Cliffe Ind Est BN7 ....123 E2
Clifford Ave BN21 ....184 C4
Clifford Cl 🔢 Bexhill TN40 ..157 C4
Crowborough TN6 ....25 F2
Clifford Rd 🔢 TN40 ......157 C4
Clifton Cl BN22 ....184 D8
Clifton Cotts TN2 ....8 D8
Clifton Ct TN34 ....159 E8
Clifton Hill BN1 ....189 A3
Clifton Ho BN20 ....184 D8
Clifton Mews BN1 ....189 A3
Clifton Pl Brighton BN1 ..189 A3
Newhaven BN9 ....179 D7
Royal Tunbridge Wells TN1 ...8 C7
Clifton Rise TN40 ....157 F5
Clifton Rd Brighton BN1 ..189 A3
Burgess Hill RH15 ....72 D5
Hastings TN35 ....159 E8
Newhaven BN9 ....179 D7
Royal Tunbridge Wells TN1 ...8 C7
Clifton St BN1 ....189 A4
Clifton Terr BN1 ....189 A3
Clifton Way BN10 ....178 A8
Cliftonville Ct 🔢 BN3 ...163 B7
Cliftonville Rd TN38 .....158 D6
Cliftonville Way TN38 ....158 D6
Climping Ave TN35 ....50 D3
Clinch Green Ave TN39 ...156 B1
Clinton Cres TN38 ....136 B1
Clinton Hill RH7 ....2 A8
Clinton La BN25 ....180 E3
Clinton Pl BN25 ....180 E3
Clinton Way TN35 ....139 B8
Clive Ave TN35 ....160 C6
Clive Villas TN33 ....112 E3
Clock Tower La TN22 ......35 C4
Clock Tower Ct 🔢 TN39 ..157 B3
Clockhouse TN2 ....8 F6
Cloisters BN19 ....179 C7
Cloisters The Battle TN33 ..112 C6
Eastbourne BN22 ....173 C2
St Leonards TN38 ....159 B6
Close Eight BN23 ....174 E3
Close Eighteen BN23 ......174 E2
Close Eleven BN23 ....174 E3
Close Fifteen 🔢 BN23 ....174 E2
Close Five BN23 ....174 E3
Close Four BN23 ....174 E2
Close Fourteen BN23 ......174 E3
Close Nine BN23 ....174 E3
Close Nineteen BN23 ......174 E2
Close Seven BN23 ....174 E3
Close Seventeen BN23 .....174 E3
Close Six BN23 ....174 E3
Close Sixteen BN23 ....174 E2
Close Ten BN23 ....174 E2
Close The Blackboys TN22 ..80 B6
Brighton BN1 ....142 E5
Burgess Hill RH15 ....73 C4
Crowborough TN6 ....25 E3
East Grinstead RH19 ....10 D8
Eastbourne BN20 ....184 B8
Fairlight TN35 ....138 C4
Friston BN20 ....183 A1
Groombridge TN3 ....15 C6
Hassocks BN6 ....97 F4
Lower Willingdon BN20 ......5 C8
Newhaven BN9 ....168 F2
Royal Tunbridge Wells TN3 ...8 C8
Rye TN31 ....93 A6
Seaford BN25 ....180 F2
Close Three BN23 ....174 E2
Close Twelve BN23 ....174 E2
Close Twenty BN23 ....174 E2
Close Twentyfive BN23 ...174 E3
Close Twentyfour 🔢 174 E2
Close Two BN23 ....174 E2
Cloudesley Rd TN37 ....159 C8
Clovelly Ho BN26 ....173 A7
Clover Ct 🔢 RH16 ....50 E4
Clover Way BN41 ....141 B2
Clovers The BN27 ....152 C7
Clovers End BN1 ....143 B7
Cluny St BN7 ....146 C8
Clyde Pk BN27 ....152 C7
Clyde Rd Brighton BN2 ....163 E7
St Leonards TN37,TN38 .....157 D8
Coach & Horses La RH7 ....3 A6
Coach & Horses Pas 🔢 TN38 ..A2
Coach House Cotts TN3 ....94 F7
Coach Rd TN37 ....34 C6
Coach Rd TN4 ....7 C3
Coastal Counties Ho 🔢
BN2 ....189 C3
Coastguard Cl BN24 ......176 D8
Coastguard Cotts
Camber TN31 ....94 D2
Norman's Bay BN24 ....176 D8
Coastguard La TN35 ......138 C4

Coastguard Sq
 3 Eastbourne BN22 .....185 C4
Rye Harbour TN31 ....94 A3
Coastguards TN35 ....139 C8
Coates Ct **11** BN42 .....161 E7
Cobald Rd BN24 ....175 E5
Cobbett's Ride TN7 ....7 B1
Cobbetts Mead RH16 ....51 B3
Cobblers Field TN19 ......61 A3
Cobbold Ave BN21 ....184 C5
Cobden Pl **5** BN27 .....152 C7
Cobden Rd BN21 ....164 C7
Cobdown La TN22 ....55 C5
Cobham Twn **2** TN40 ...157 F4
Cobhams TN31 ....7 A8
Cobourg Pl **6** TN34 ....160 A4
Cobton Dr BN3 ....142 A3
Coburn Ct **12** BN7 .....123 D1
Cochrane Cl BN23 ....185 E7
Cockcrow Wood TN37 ......136 D5
Cockfield La BN8 ....76 B3
Cockhaise Cotts RH16 .....52 A8
Cockmount La TN5 ....29 F5
Cockshut Rd BN7 ....146 C8
Cogger's Cross TN21 .....106 F3
Cogger's La TN21 ....106 F4
Coggins Mill La TN20 .....40 D4
Coghurst Rd TN35 ....137 C4
Colbourne Dr BN3 ....143 D2
Colbourne Rd BN3 ....143 E2
Colchester Vale RH18 .....11 E2
Colchins RH15 ....72 F1
Coldean Cty Inf Sch BN1 ..143 D6
Coldean Cty Jun Sch
 BN1 ....143 D6
Coldean La BN1 ....143 E6
Coldharbour Cl TN6 ....26 A1
Coldharbour La
 Newick BN8 ....76 A7
 Rye Foreign TN31 ....69 E3
Coldharbour Rd
 Lower Dicker BN27 ......128 B2
 White Post TN8, TN11 ....15 E8
Coldthorn La BN26,BN27 ..152 A4
Coldthorn La RH15 ....73 D2
Colebrook Rd
 Brighton BN1 ....142 D4
 Royal Tunbridge Wells TN4 .8 C8
 Southwick BN42 ....161 F7
Colebrooke Rd TN39 ......157 A4
Coleman Ave BN3 ....160 E7
Coleman St BN2 ....189 C4
Colemans Hatch Rd
 RH18,TN7 ....2 C6
Coleridge St BN3 ....163 A3
Coleridge Wlk **7** BN23 .174 E2
Coles Ct TN2 ....8 C3
Colgate Cl BN27 ....164 F6
Coll of the Holy Child
 Jesus TN37 ....159 D7
College Cl
 East Grinstead RH19 ......1 F1
 Portslade-by-Sea BN41 ...140 F3
College Dr TN2 ....8 D4
College Gdns BN24 ....164 C4
College La BN21 ....184 E4
College La
 East Grinstead RH19 ......1 F1
 Hurst Wickham BN6 ....97 C6
College Pl Brighton BN2 ..164 C4
 Hurst Wickham BN6 ....97 C6
College Rd Bexhill TN40 ..157 F1
 Brighton BN2 ....164 C4
 Eastbourne BN21 ....184 F2
 Haywards Heath RH16 .....50 E7
 Seaford BN25 ....180 F2
College St **1** BN2 .....164 C4
College Terr BN21 ....164 D5
Collett Cl TN38 ....135 F5
Collier Cl BN27 ....185 B7
Collier Rd Hastings TN34 ..160 A5
 Pevensey Bay BN24 ....175 D4
Collier's Gn TN21 ....83 F3
Collingford La RH17 ......34 B4
Collington Ave TN39 .....156 F3
Collington Cl BN20 ....184 E1
Collington Gr TN39 ......156 E4
Collington La E TN39 .....156 F4
Collington La W TN39 ....156 D3
Collington Man TN39 .....157 B3
Collington Park Cres TN39 156 E4
Collington Rise TN39 ....156 E4
Collington Sta TN39 .....157 A3
Collingwood Ave TN21 ....32 B7
Collingwood Cl **4**
 East Grinstead RH19 ......2 E7
 Eastbourne BN23 ....185 E6
 Peacehaven BN10 ....167 D1
Collingwood Ct BN1 ......163 E5
Collingwood Rise TN21 ...82 A7
Collinstone Rd TN38 .....159 F7
Collinswood Dr TN38 .....159 D7
Colmer Cl RH15 ....72 E3
Colmer Pl RH15 ....72 E3
Colonnade Gdns **13** BN21 185 B3
Colonnade Rd **14** BN21 .185 B3
Coltstocks Rd BN20 ......186 D3
Columbus Dr BN23 ....185 G7
Colville Ct **2** BN21 ...184 E4
Colwell Cl RH16 ....50 F3
Colwell Gdns RH16 ....50 F3
Colwell La
 Haywards Heath RH17 .....51 B3
 Haywards Heath, Fox Hill
  RH16, RH17 ....50 F1

Colwell Rd RH16 ....50 F2
Colwood Cres BN20 ....184 B6
Colwood Hospl RH17 ......51 A3
Combe End TN6 ....37 E8
Combe La
 Eastbourne BN20 ....188 D7
 Ninfield TN33 ....132 E6
Combe Rise BN20 ....173 A2
Combe The BN20 ....184 A7
Combermere Rd TN38 .....136 B1
Command Rd BN20 ....184 B5
Commanders Wlk TN35 ...138 E4
Commercial Mews N **7**
 BN21 ....185 A4
Commercial Rd
 Burgess Hill RH15 ....72 F3
 Eastbourne BN21 ....185 A3
 Royal Tunbridge Wells TN1 ..8 B5
Commercial Sq RH15 ......50 D3
Common La Ditchling BN6 ..98 D6
 Selmeston BN26 ....149 E1
Common View TN6 ....7 C4
Common Wood Rise TN6 ...25 F4
Compass Ct BN41 ....140 E3
Compasses La TN32 ....88 C6
Comphurst La BN27 ......131 B4
Compton Ave BN1 ....189 A4
Compton Cl **11** TN40 ..157 E4
Compton Dr BN20 ....184 C2
Compton Lodge BN21 .....184 E2
Compton Place Rd
 BN20,BN21 ....184 E2
Compton Rd Brighton BN1 .142 D1
 Lindfield RH16 ....51 B8
Compton St BN21 ....185 A1
Compton Terr BN27 ......152 C6
Compts The BN10 ....167 B1
Conan Doyle Ct TN6 ......25 E2
Concord Cl TN2 ....8 C3
Concorde Cl TN39 ....156 F6
Condor Way RH15 ....72 E3
Conduit Hill TN31 ....93 C6
Coney Furlong BN10 .....167 D1
Coneyburrow Gdns TN38 .3 59 E4
Coneyburrow La TN39 ....155 F5
Coneyburrow Rd TN2 .....9 B5
Conghurst La TN18 ....46 B6
Conifer Cl TN34 ....160 A4
Conifers The BN21 ......184 F4
Coniston Ave TN4 ....7 E5
Coniston Rd **9** BN3 ....163 D7
Coniston Rd BN23 ....174 C4
Connaught Ctr Brighton
 Coll of Tech & F Ed
  BN3 ....163 A3
Connaught Rd
 1 Eastbourne BN21 ....185 A2
 Hove BN3 ....163 A6
 Seaford BN25 ....180 C3
Connaught Terr BN3 ......163 B7
Connaught Way TN2 ......7 F5
Connell Dr BN2 ....165 E7
Conqueror Rd BN27 ......135 F6
Conqueror Rd TN38 .....135 F7
Conqueror Terr TN33 .....88 F1
Conquest Hospl TN37 ....136 D6
Consort Way RH15 ....72 E2
Constable Rd BN23 ......174 D1
Constable Way TN40 .....157 F1
Convent of The Holy
 Child Jesus TN37 ....40 A3
Conway Ct
 1 Hove BN3 ....163 B7
 3 St Leonards TN38 ...159 B6
Conway Pl BN3 ....163 A8
Conway St BN3 ....163 B8
Cooden Beach Sta TN39 ..156 C3
Cooden Cl TN39 ....156 C3
Cooden Dr TN39 ....156 C3
Cooden Sea Rd
 Bexhill TN39 ....156 B2
 Bexhill TN39 ....156 C2
Cook Ave BN23 ....185 E6
Cookham Dene TN40 .....157 E2
Cooksbridge Rd BN2 .....164 E6
Cooksbridge Sta BN8 ....123 A7
Cookson Gdns TN35 .....138 C5
Cookstown Cl TN33 ......132 F6
Coolham Dr BN2 ....164 E7
Coombe Cl BN27 ....131 B5
Coombe Hall Sch RH19 ...10 D6
Coombe Hill Rd RH19 ....10 D6
Coombe La TN5 ....41 C7
Coombe Lea BN3 ....163 C6
Coombe Mdw BN27 ......166 E3
Coombe Rd
 Brighton BN2 ....143 D1
 Eastbourne BN20 ....184 C4
 Lewes BN7 ....123 D2
Coombe Rise BN20 ....166 D3
Coombe Road
 Cty Prim Sch BN2 ....143 D1
Coombe Shaw TN31 .....133 A6
Coombe Terr BN2 ....143 C1
Coombe Vale Vale BN2 ...166 D3
Coombers La RH16 ....51 B5
Coombs Cl TN31 ....68 C5
Coombs Cotts TN31 ......68 C5
Cooper Dr TN39 ....157 B8
Cooper Rd TN31 ....93 A5
Cooper Rise TN37 ....136 A5
Coopers Cl RH15 ....73 B5
Coopers Hill BN20 ....173 B2
Coopers La
 Crowborough TN6 ....25 D4
 Poundsbridge TN11,TN3 ..6 C7
Coopers Row TN22 ....55 D4
Coopers Way BN27 ......152 A6

Coopers Wood TN6 ....25 D4
Copestake Dr RH15 ......73 D3
Coplands Plot **3** TN31 ..67 B7
Coplands Rise TN31 ......67 B7
Coppards Cl RH17 ....74 C4
Coppards La TN31 ....67 C8
Copper Beeches
 Hove BN1 ....142 E1
 St Leonards TN37 ....136 C4
Copper Cl RH15 ....72 C4
Copper's Hill TN19 ....61 C4
Coppice Ave BN20 ......173 A4
Coppice Cl BN20 ....173 A4
Coppice The Battle TN33 .113 A3
 Hastings TN34 ....136 E1
 Pembury TN2 ....9 D7
Coppice View TN21 ......82 B6
Coppice Way RH16 ....50 D3
Copse Cl East Grinstead RH19 .2 A3
 St Leonards TN38 ....135 D3
Copse Hill BN1 ....142 D6
Copse Rd TN39 ....156 E4
Copse The RH16 ....51 B5
Copt Hall TN18 ....48 D3
Copthorne Ct **2** BN3 ..163 C6
Copthorne Rd RH10 ......1 F1
Copwood Ave TN22 ......78 B7
Copyhold La RH17 ....50 A4
Copyhold Rd RH19 ......10 D8
Copythorne Ho RH16 ....50 E6
Coral Reef Cl BN25 ......179 B4
Corbyn Cres BN43 ....161 A7
Cordons BN7 ....145 D5
Cormorant Cl BN23 ......174 C2
Cornelius Ave BN9 ....179 A5
Corner Gn BN8 ....102 A4
Cornfield Cl BN25 ....180 F3
Cornfield Ct BN21 ....185 A2
Cornfield La
 Eastbourne BN21 ....185 A2
 St Leonards TN37 ....136 C1
Cornford Cl
 Burgess Hill RH15 ....72 E5
 Crowborough TN6 ....26 A1
 Pembury TN2 ....9 B5
Cornford Pk TN2 ....9 C6
Cornish Cl BN23 ....174 B4
Cornwall Ave BN10 ......178 A6
Cornwall Cl
 Eastbourne BN20 ....184 C5
 3 Hove BN3 ....163 C7
Cornwall Gdns
 Brighton BN1 ....142 E2
 8 East Grinstead RH19 .10 F8
Cornwall Rd BN10 ....157 B2
Cornwall Rd TN39 ......157 B3
Cornwallis Gdns TN34 ...159 B8
Cornwallis St **5** TN34 ..159 B8
Cornwallis Terr **1** TN34 159 B8
Coronation Cotts
 Berner's Hill TN5 ....31 F2
 Burwash TN19 ....62 A6
 Northbridge Street TN32 ..64 C5
Coronation Gdns
 Battle TN33 ....112 F5
 Hurst Green TN19 ....44 F7
Coronation Rd RH19 .....10 C7
Coronation St **7** BN2 ..189 B4
Corseley Rd TN5 ....18 B5
Corsica Cl BN25 ....180 F3
Corsica Rd BN25 ....180 F1
Costells Edge RH17 ......51 F3
Costume Mus TN40 ......157 D4
Cotchford Hill TN7 ......13 D1
Cotchford La TN7 ....13 C1
Cotswold Cl
 Eastbourne BN23 ....174 C4
 Hastings TN34 ....137 B4
Cotswold Pl **2** BN22 ..164 F5
Cotswolds The BN42 ....161 E7
Cottage Bush Cl BN22 ..141 C2
Cottage Cl BN9 ....168 D2
Cottage Homes BN6 .....98 E6
Cottage La Hankham BN24 152 E1
 Westfield TN33, TN35 ...114 F7
Cottenden Rd TN5 ....43 A6
Cottesmore St Mary's
 RC Prim Sch BN3 ....163 D8
Coulstock Rd RH15 ....72 C3
Council Cotts
 Crowborough TN6 ....38 A8
 Robertsbridge TN32 .....63 F3
Council Hos
 Ginger's Green BN27 ....130 C6
 Rushlake Green TN21 ....83 D1
Countess of Thanet's
 Almshouses **1** TN34 ...3 F3
County Oak Ave BN1 .....143 B6
Courcels BN2 ....164 E3
Course The BN7 ....146 B8
Court Cl Brighton BN1 ...142 E7
 East Grinstead RH19 .....1 F1
Court Cres RH19 ....1 F1
Court Farm Cl BN7 ......168 A2
Court Farm Rd Hove BN3 .142 A2
 Newhaven BN9 ....179 C5
 Rottingdean BN2 ....164 C4
Court House Mus The
 BN24 ....175 B6

Crest Rd BN9 ....168 F1
Crest Way BN41 ....141 B3
Cresta Cl BN26 ....173 A7
Cresta Rd BN9 ....179 A6
Crestway Par BN1 ....143 C2
Crestway The BN1 ......143 C2
Cricket Ct RH19 ....1 E1
Cricketers Cl TN33 ......18 A5
Cricketers Field TN32 ...65 E1
Cricketfield BN6 ....76 D8
Cricketfield Ct **8** BN25 .180 F2
Cricketfield Rd BN25 ....180 F2
Cricketing La BN27 .....130 C4
Criers La TN20,TN22 ....57 F7
Crink Hill BN8 ....101 F3
Cripland Cl RH16 ....51 B6
Cripps Ave BN10 ....167 D1
Crisp Rd BN7 ....123 A3
Crittle's Ct TN5 ....29 F4
Crockers Hatch Cnr TN3 ..6 D2
Crockers La TN31 ....67 B8
Crocks Dean BN10 ......167 D2
Croft Ave BN42 ....161 F7
Croft Cl BN26 ....173 A4
Croft Ct
 2 Eastbourne BN21 ...185 B3
 3 Seaford BN25 ......180 E3
Croft Dr BN41 ....141 A3
Croft La BN25 ....180 E3
Croft Rd Brighton BN1 ..142 D4
 Crowborough TN6 ....25 F2
 Hastings TN34 ....160 A4
Croft The Bexhill TN39 ..157 A4
 Hassocks BN6 ....97 F5
 Hastings TN34 ....128 A4
 Lower Dicker BN27 .....128 B4
 Southwick BN42 ....161 E8
 Willingdon BN20 ....173 B1
Crofts Works BN27 ......152 B7
Crofton Park Ave TN39 ..156 E3
Croham Rd TN6 ....25 F3
Cromarty Wlk **3** BN23 .185 F8
Cromer Way BN27 ......129 A1
Cromer Wlk **3** TN34 ..136 F1
Cromleigh Way BN42 ....140 E2
Cromwell Cl **3** BN21 ..163 D7
Cromwell Pl **1** RH19 ..10 C7
Cromwell Rd
 Burgess Hill RH15 ....72 F3
 Hove BN3 ....163 C7
 Royal Tunbridge Wells TN1 ..8 C3
Cromwell St BN2 ....164 C7
Crooked La BN25 ....180 F2
Cross La TN5 ....31 D2
Cross Lane Gdns TN5 ....31 D1
Cross Levels Way
 BN21 ....184 E2
Cross Rd BN42 ....161 E8
Cross St Brighton BN1 ..189 B4
 1 Hove BN1, BN3 ......163 D7
 Polegate BN26 ....173 A6
 St Leonards TN37 ......159 C7
Cross Way BN7 ....123 A4
Cross-in-Hand
 CE Prim Sch TN21 ......81 F7
Crossbush Rd BN2 ......164 E7
Crossroad Cl BN42 .....161 D7
Crossway The
 Brighton BN1 ....143 E7
 Portslade-by-Sea BN41 ..141 A3
 Royal Tunbridge Wells TN4 ..7 D8
Crossways Ave RH19 ....1 C8
Crossways The
 Broad Oak TN31 ....90 B7
 Hassocks BN6 ....97 C7
 Stone Cross BN24 ......174 A3
Crouch Cl BN24 ....173 B1
Crouch La Linstead TN18 ..33 A3
 Lower Street TN33 ......133 D5
 Seaford BN25 ....180 E4
Crouchfield Cl **2** BN25 .180 F2
Crowborough Hill TN6 ...26 C3
Crowborough Mews TN6 ..25 E3
Crowborough Rd
 Hastings TN35 ....137 B3
 Marlpits TN22 ....37 A2
 Saltdean BN2 ....177 A3
Crowders La TN33 ....131 C5
Crowhurst CE Prim Sch
 TN33 ....134 B4
Crowhurst Cl BN23 .....174 C2
Crowhurst La TN39 .....157 A6
Crowhurst Rd
 Brighton BN1 ....143 B6
 Green Street TN38 .....135 E7
 St Leonards TN33 ......135 D7
Crowhurst Sta TN33 ....135 A3
Crowlink Cotts BN20 ...186 D3
Crowmere Ave TN40 ....157 F3
Crowmere Terr TN40 ....157 F3
Crown Cl Hailsham BN27 .152 B7
 1 Hove BN3 ....163 B7
 Uckfield TN22 ....78 B8
Crown Ct **2** TN33 .....88 F1
Crown Gdns BN1 ....189 A4
Crown Hill
 4 Brighton BN2 ......164 F5
 Seaford BN25 ....180 E3
Crown La TN34 ....160 C1
Crown Point Ho BN1 ....163 E5
Crown Rd
 Portslade-by-Sea BN41 ..162 B8
 Shoreham-by-Sea BN43 ..161 D2
Crown St Brighton BN1 ..189 A4
 1 Eastbourne BN21 ...185 A2
Crowne Ho **8** BN21 ....185 A2
Croxden Way BN22 ......174 C2

...xton La RH16 ....51 B6
...amp's Cnr TN22 ....103 D6
...anden Rd BN20 ....184 C4
...oitt Way TN38 ....135 E4
...ckfield Ct TN40 ....158 A5
...urgess Hill RH15 ....72 E7
...ddards' Green BN6,RH17 .72 A4
...ckmere Dr BN26 ....170 F3
...ckmere Cl BN24 ....173 F5
...ckmere Ho BN24 ....175 E5
...ckmere House Sch
...25 ....181 C3
...ckmere Path TN22 ....55 E1
...ckmere Rd
...whaven BN9 ....179 A5
...anden BN25 ....181 B2
...ckmere Rise TN21 ....82 B8
...ckmere Way BN1 ....143 C5
...ckmere Rd BN22 ....173 D1
...koo Dr TN21 ....82 A6
...pepper RH15 ....72 E4
...pepper Dr BN21 ....143 D2
...ross Ave RH16 ....50 D5
...verden Ave TN4 ....8 A6
...verden Down TN4 ....7 F5
...verden Park Rd TN4 ....7 F5
...verden Pk TN4 ....7 F5
...verden St TN4 ....8 A5
...verden St TN1 ....8 A4
...mballa Ct BN20 ....188 F8
...mberland Ct
...Bexhill TN39 ....157 D4
...stbourne BN20 ....184 B6
...mberland Rd BN1 ....142 E2
...mberland Gdns
...Royal Tunbridge Wells TN1 ..8 A2
...Leonards TN38 ....159 B8
...mberland Lodge
...1 ....142 E2
...mberland Mews TN1 ..8 A2
...mberland Rd
...xhill TN39 ....157 B7
...ighton BN1 ....142 E2
...mberland Wlk TN1 ....8 A2
...mberland Yd TN1 ....8 A2
...nnor House Sch RH17 ..34 B5
...nningham Cl TN4 ....8 B8
...nningham Ct BN26 ....185 E7
...nningham Gr BN23 ....185 E7
...nningham Ho BN3 ....157 B3
...nningham Rd TN4 ....8 A7
...slew Ct Hailsham BN27 ..152 D7
...Leonards TN38 ....135 E3
...lews The BN43 ....161 A8
...rie Rd TN4 ....8 A5
...wen Pl BN1 ....142 E3
...zon Ho BN20 ....177 C4
...hbert Dr TN9 ....157 A7
...hbert Rd BN2 ....164 C5
...ess Ct TN34 ....160 A3
...ess Cl
...oreham-by-Sea BN43 ..140 A1
...ess Gr TN2 ....17 C8
...rus Mews RH15 ....73 B3
...rus Pl TN1 ....93 B5
...rus Rd RH15 ....73 A3

...ubigny Rd BN2 ....164 B8
...re Pk BN22 ....152 D7
...re Rd
...stbourne BN20, BN21 ..184 C4
...rstroncaux BN27 ....130 E6
...whaven BN9 ....179 D7
...re La TN22 ....65 F5
...ins The RH19 ....10 E8
...e Ave Brighton BN1 ..142 F5
...meney BN3 ....98 A3
...rus Cres BN1 ....142 F6
...e Dr BN1 ....143 A6
...e Hill BN45 ....119 A6
...e Rd Forest Row RH18 ..11 F1
...e Rd BN7 ....146 A8
...e St TN1 ....3 B1
...e View BN3 ....141 D2
...e View Gdns BN3 ..141 D2
...ehurst TN6 ....38 C7
...ehurst Rd TN39 ....157 C3
...es Cl BN27 ....131 B5
...ewood Gdns RH15 ..73 C2
...as La BN8 ....101 F6
...away Dr BN24 ....174 B5
...away Gdns RH19 ....1 E1

...................83 D3
...ington Cl TN40 ....158 A6
...e BN2
...stbourne BN22 ....174 A1
...e View BN3 ....162 F8
...meny Rd TN39 ....157 A5
...more Ct TN40 ....157 C3
...ton Rd BN20 ....188 E8
...rian Way BN6 ....98 B4
...ton Cl BN10 ....178 C2
...e Lodge BN12 ....178 A7
...e Cl BN25 ....180 D2
...e Court TN39 ....157 B6
...ets TN25 ....180 E2
...e Rd Seaford BN25 ..180 D2
...Leonards TN38 ....159 B8
...ehill CE Prim Sch

...................34 A4
...ehill La RH17 ....33 E5

Danehill Rd BN2 ....164 F5
Daniel Way TN31 ....94 F2
Dannfields Ho TN31 ....94 F3
Danny Sheldon Ho
BN2 ....164 C4
Danum Cl BN21 ....129 C3
Danworth La BN6 ....72 B2
Darby's La TN5 ....30 B2
Darcey Dr BN1 ....143 A6
Darent Cl BN19 ....173 F5
Daresbury Cl TN39 ....157 B6
Darley Rd BN20 ....188 D2
Dart Cl RH19 ....2 A3
Dartmouth Cl BN2 ....143 F1
Dartmouth Cres BN2 ..143 F1
Darvel Down TN33 ....86 B2
Darwall Dr BN25 ....181 A3
Darwell Cl
Robertsbridge TN32 ....64 B3
Eastbourne BN24 ....174 A5
Davey Dr BN1 ....143 B1
Davey's La BN7 ....123 E2
David Lloyd Club The
BN2 ....184 F8
David Saloman's Ho TN3 ..7 D8
Davids Hts BN21 ....184 E5
Davigdor Cty Inf Sch
BN3 ....163 D6
Davigdor Rd BN3 ....163 E7
Davis Cl TN39 ....157 B6
Dawber Bldgs BN27 ....152 B7
Dawlish Cl BN2 ....143 F1
Dawson Terr BN2 ....164 C6
Daynes Way RH15 ....72 E1
De Cham Ave TN37 ....159 C6
De Cham Rd TN37 ....159 C6
De Chardin Dr TN34 ....137 A5
De Courcel Rd BN2 ....164 E3
De Grey Cl BN7 ....123 D2
De La Warr Gn BN7 ....123 E3
De La Warr Par TN40 ..157 E3
De La Warr Rd TN40 ..157 C3
De La Warr Rd
Bexhill TN40 ....157 C5
East Grinstead RH19 ....1 F1
De Moleyns Cl TN40 ..157 F4
De Montfort Rd
Brighton BN2 ....164 C7
Lewes BN7 ....123 B1
De Roos Rd BN21 ....184 C4
De Walden Mews BN20 ..188 E8
De Warrenne Rd BN7 ..123 B1
Deacons Dr BN41 ....141 C2
Deadman's Cross TN31 ..83 B5
Deadmans La TN31 ....93 C6
Deadmantree Hill BN8 ..101 B3
Deal Ave BN25 ....181 C5
Deals The BN3 ....93 B5
Dean Cl BN41 ....141 C2
Dean Court Rd TN34 ..177 A6
Dean Gdns BN41 ....141 C2
Dean Rd BN25 ....180 F2
Dean St BN1 ....163 E5
Dean Wood Cl BN23 ..174 A4
Deanery Cl BN1 ....123 D3
Deans Cl Bexhill TN39 ..157 B6
Woodingdean BN2 ....165 E8
Deans Dr TN39 ....157 A6
Deans Rd BN26 ....170 F3
Deanway BN3 ....142 B3
Decimus Burton Way
TN37 ....159 C7
Decoy Dr TN31 ....173 D1
Deepdene TN5 ....30 A6
Deepdene Gdns TN35 ..137 C3
Deepdene Sch TN32 ..162 D7
Deer Paddock La
BN27 ....152 C7
Deerswood La TN39 ..156 E5
Deeside The BN1 ....143 A7
Delaval Wlk BN23 ....185 F6
Delaware Cl TN22 ....135 F6
Delaware Rd BN7 ....146 A8
Delfryn BN41 ....140 F3
Dell Cl TN38 ....123 A1
Dell The East Grinstead RH19 ..2 B1
Haywards Heath RH16 ..50 C5
Dellney Ave RH16 ....50 F7
Dellsfoot Cotts TN6 ....28 A3
Delmonden Rd TN18 ..31 C4
Delves Ave TN2 ....8 C1
Delves Cl BN26 ....124 D6
Delves Ho BN27 ....124 D6
Delves Way BN8 ....124 D6
Den Hill BN20 ....184 A4
Denbigh Cl TN39 ....156 A4
Denbigh Rd TN4 ....8 C7
Dencher Rd BN3 ....145 E3
Dene Cl BN20 ....183 B1
Dene Dr BN22 ....173 C1
Dene Path TN22 ....55 D1
Dene Side BN20 ....183 B1
Dene The Hastings TN35 ..137 A5
Hove BN3 ....141 D3
Lower Willingdon BN20 ..173 A3
Uckfield TN22 ....55 D1
Dene Vale BN1 ....142 D5
Dene Way TN3 ....7 A7
Denecroft BN1 ....142 D5
Denehurst Gdns TN35 ..137 A5
Deneside BN1 ....142 D6
Deneway The BN1 ....142 D4
Denham Cl TN38 ....135 F4
Denham Dr BN11 ....72 D3
Denham Rd RH15 ....72 D3

Denham Way TN31 ....94 E2
Denman's Cl RH16 ....51 A8
Denman's La Lindfield RH16 .51 A7
Lindfield RH16 ....51 B7
Denmark Pl TN34 ....159 F7
Denmark Rd BN41 ....162 C7
Denmark Terr BN1 ....163 E6
Denmark Villas BN3 ....163 B7
Dennis Hobden Cl BN2 ..143 E1
Denton Cl TN31 ....93 A6
Denton Cty Prim Sch
BN9 ....168 E1
Denton Dr Brighton BN1 ..143 A6
Newhaven BN9 ....168 E1
Denton Rd
Eastbourne BN20 ....188 D8
Newhaven BN9 ....168 E1
Denton Rise BN9 ....168 E2
Dentons The BN20 ....188 D8
Denys Rd BN20 ....173 A2
Derby Cl TN39 ....157 B6
Derby Pl BN2 ....189 C2
Derek Ave BN3 ....162 D6
Derek Ho BN3 ....162 F6
Dern La TN21 ....106 B7
Dervia Ho BN3 ....163 C7
Derwent Cl BN27 ....129 A1
Derwent Dr BN13 ....189 A3
Derwent Lodge Sch TN1 ..8 B4
Derwent Rd BN20 ....188 E8
Desmond Rd BN22 ....173 A2
Desmond Way BN22 ..164 F6
Devil's Dyke Rd BN1,BN3 ..141 E7
Devon Villas RH16 ....50 F4
Devonian Ct BN2 ....189 C4
Devonport Ho TN31 ....93 C6
Devonshire Cl TN40 ..157 F4
Devonshire Ct BN3 ....163 C7
Devonshire Lodge
BN22 ....185 C5
Devonshire Pl
Brighton BN2 ....189 C4
Eastbourne BN21 ....185 A2
Devonshire Rd
Bexhill TN40 ....157 C3
Hastings TN34 ....159 F8
Devonshire Sq TN40 ..157 F4
Dew La TN21 ....92 A8
Dewe Rd BN2 ....143 C1
Dewhurst Cotts TN5 ..29 A7
Dewlands Hill TN5 ....29 B8
Dewlands Rd BN22 ....173 A2
Devpond The BN10 ..167 B1
Dexter Dr RH19 ....10 E8
Diamond Cotts RH17 ..74 A5
Diana Cl TN40 ....158 A6
Dickens Cl RH19 ....1 C1
Dickens Way BN23 ....174 E3
Dicklands The BN7 ....167 D8
Diggers The BN1 ....143 B3
Dillingham Rd BN20 ..184 C4
Dillon Way TN2 ....16 E8
Dinapore Ho BN2 ....189 C3
Diplock Cl BN25 ....172 F6
Diplocks Bldgs BN27 ..152 A7
Diplocks Way BN27 ..152 A8
Diplocks Wlk BN27 ..152 A8
Dirty La RH19 ....1 C8
Ditchling Beacon
Nature Reserve BN6 ..120 D3
Ditchling Bostall BN6 ..120 D7
Ditchling Cl BN23 ....173 F4
Ditchling Common
Ctry Pk BN6 ....73 F1
Ditchling Cres BN1 ....143 C5
Ditchling Ct BN1 ....168 B8
Ditchling Dr TN35 ....137 D4
Ditchling Gdns BN1 ..143 B1
Ditchling Mus BN6 ....98 C3
Ditchling Rd
Brighton BN1 ....143 B4
Westmeston BN1,BN6 ..120 C6
Ditchling Rise BN1 ..163 E6
Ditchling Way BN27 ..152 B6
Ditton's Cnr BN26 ....173 C6
Ditton's Rd BN26 ....173 C6
Dittons BN26 ....173 C6
Dittons Mews TN36 ..135 E2
Dittons Rd BN21 ....184 E3
Dixter La TN31 ....67 B8
Dixter Rd TN31 ....67 A6
Dock The BN8 ....124 A1
Dodshill TN6 ....26 A1
Dog Cotts RH19 ....3 B1
Dog Kennel La TN22 ..57 F6
Dogs Hill Rd TN36 ....118 B5
Doleham Gdns TN35 ..115 C5
Doleham Hill TN35 ....115 C5
Doleham La TN35 ....115 B6
Doleham Sta TN35 ....115 C5
Dolphin Ct
Eastbourne BN20 ....188 E7
Hove BN3 ....163 A6
Dolphin Ind Est BN43 ..161 B2
Dolphin L Ctr The RH16 .50 D6
Dolphin Mews BN41 ..161 A7
Dolphin Rd
Haywards Heath RH16 ..50 D4
Shoreham-by-Sea BN43 ..161 B7
Dolphin Way BN43 ..161 B7
Donald Hall Rd BN2 ..164 D5
Donald Way TN36 ....118 A5
Doney Mews BN20 ..163 D5
Donnington Rd BN2 ..165 D6
Dorchester Ct TN1 ....8 B6
Dorchester Ct
Brighton BN1 ....163 E5

Dorchester Ct continued
Eastbourne BN21 ....184 E4
Dordrecht Way TN34 ..136 E1
Dorin Ct TN2 ....8 C3
Dorking Rd TN1 ....8 C6
Dorman's Cl RH17 ....2 A8
Dorman's Ct RH7 ....2 A8
Dormans Gdns RH19 ..1 E6
Dormans High St RH7 ..2 A8
Dormans Park Rd
East Grinstead RH19 ..1 E6
East Grinstead RH19 ..1 D3
Dormans Sta RH7 ....1 F8
Dormans Station Rd RH7 .1 F7
Dormansland Prim Sch
RH7 ....2 A8
Dornden Dr TN3 ....7 A4
Dorothy Ave BN10 ....178 C2
Dorothy Ave N BN10 ..178 C8
Dorothy Rd BN3 ....162 D8
Dorothy Stringer Sch
BN1 ....142 F3
Dorset Ave RH19 ....1 C3
Dorset Ct TN7 ....14 B4
Dorset
Cl Eastbourne BN20 ..185 B3
Hove BN3 ....162 F6
Dorset Gdns Brighton BN2 .189 C2
East Grinstead RH19 ..1 C3
Dorset Mews BN2 ....189 B2
Dorset Pl Brighton BN2 ..189 C2
Hastings TN34 ....159 F8
Dorset Rd Bexhill TN40 ..157 D4
Lewes BN7 ....146 D8
Dorset St BN2 ....189 B2
Dorset Rd S TN40 ....157 D4
Doubledays BN8 ....73 B2
Doucegrove TN38 ....136 A1
Douglas Cl BN27 ....129 B2
Douglas Rd TN6 ....27 D1
Dover Stables TN4 ....7 A8
Dove Ct TN22 ....78 C8
Dovedale Gdns BN22 ..173 F2
Dover Cl BN25 ....181 C5
Dover Rd Brighton BN1 ..143 A2
Polegate BN26 ....173 B7
Dover Cl BN2 ....165 D3
Down Ave TN3 ....20 A4
Down La TN3 ....28 C8
Down Rd TN39 ....157 A5
Down St TN22 ....54 C5
Down Terr BN2 ....164 C6
Down The BN3 ....141 D4
Downash Cl BN2 ....164 E6
Downash Ho TN5 ....32 A3
Downash Rd TN5 ....32 A3
Downey Cl TN37 ....136 B6
Downland Ave
Eastbourne BN20 ....178 E6
Southwick BN42 ....140 D1
Downland Cl
Southwick BN42 ....140 D1
Woodingdean BN2 ....165 B8
Downland Copse TN22 ..55 E7
Downland Cres BN3 ..141 F3
Downland Dr BN3 ....141 A2
Downland Rd BN26 ..165 B8
Dormans Park Rd BN11 ..157 A8
Downlands Ave BN11 ..157 A8
Downlands Cl TN39 ..157 A7
Downlands Way RH15 ..97 F3
Downline TN21 ....106 F7
Downs Ave BN20 ....184 B6
Downs Cl BN7 ....146 E3
Downs Cty Inf Sch BN1 .168 B8
Downs Cty Jun Sch BN1 .143 A1
Downs Park Sch BN41 ..141 B2
Downs Rd Burgess Hill RH15 .72 E4
Seaford BN25 ....181 B3
Downs Sch The BN4 ..184 B4
Downs Valley Rd BN2 ..165 E8
Downs View Nnfield TN33 ..133 B5
North Chailey BN8 ....75 C7
Peacehaven BN10 ....167 D2
Downs View Cl
East Dean BN20 ....183 C1
North Chailey BN8 ....75 E7
Downs View La BN20 ..183 C1
Downs View Rd BN9 ..97 F3
Downs View Sch BN20 ..173 A2
Downs Villas BN9 ....168 E3
Downs Wlk BN10 ....167 B2
Downscroft RH15 ....73 D6
Downside Brighton BN1 ..142 D5
Hove BN3 ....142 B3
Lewes BN7 ....146 A8
Shoreham-by-Sea BN43 ..140 A1
Downside Cl
Eastbourne BN20 ....184 C3
Shoreham-by-Sea BN43 ..140 A1
Downsmeade BN24 ....184 E3
Downsvalley Rd BN20 ..173 A4
Downsview Heathfield TN21 ..82 B8
Lower Willingdon BN20 ..173 A3
Downsview Ave BN2 ..165 C8
Downsview Cotts BN8 ..123 A7
Downsview Cres TN22 ..78 C8
Downsview Dr TN37 ..74 C4
Downsview Rd
Lower Willingdon BN20 ..173 A3
Portslade-by-Sea BN41 ..141 A2

Downsview Rd continued
Seaford BN25 ....181 A3
Downsview Way TN7 ..152 B7
Downsway Berwick BN26 ..150 B3
Woodingdean BN2 ....144 D1
Draffin La TN31 ....94 D3
Drake Ave BN23 ....185 E7
Drake Cl BN25 ....180 E2
Drake Ho TN9 ....156 E4
Drapers Way TN38 ....136 B2
Draxmont Way BN1 ....142 F6
Drayton Rise TN39 ....156 D4
Drive Lodge BN3 ....163 C7
Drive The Burgess Hill RH15 ..73 B4
Crowborough TN6 ....25 D3
Hailsham BN27 ....152 B6
Hove BN3 ....163 C6
Maresfield TN22 ....55 A5
Maresfield TN22 ....55 A7
Newhaven BN9 ....179 C5
Royal Tunbridge Wells TN1 ..8 B1
Southwick BN42 ....140 E1
St Leonards TN38 ....158 F8
Uckfield TN22 ....78 C8
Drockmill Cl BN26 ....173 C6
Drove Ave BN2 ....144 D2
Drove Cres BN41 ....141 A2
Drove Rd Newhaven BN9 ..179 D8
Portslade-by-Sea BN41 ..141 A1
Woodingdean BN2 ....165 B8
Drove The Brighton BN1 ..142 D1
Falmer BN1 ....144 B8
Newhaven BN9 ....179 E8
Offham BN7,BN8 ....123 A5
Drovers Cl BN41 ....141 C2
Drovers Way BN15 ....73 C1
Droveway The
Haywards Heath RH16 ..50 C6
Hove BN3 ....142 B2
Lewes BN7 ....142 C1
Lewes BN7 ....146 A5
Drummond Cl RH16 ....50 D4
Drummond Ct BN10 ....167 C8
Drury La TN38 ....136 A2
Drusilla's Zoo Park BN26 ..171 B6
Dryden Wlk BN23 ....174 E3
Duchess Dr BN25 ....180 E6
Dudeney Lodge BN1 ..143 B1
Dudley Int Sch TN35 ..160 C5
Dudley Lodge TN2 ....8 C4
Dudley Rd Brighton BN1 ..143 B1
Eastbourne BN23 ....185 B4
Hastings TN35 ....160 C5
Royal Tunbridge Wells TN1 ..8 C5
Dudwell Rd BN2 ....165 E7
Duke Bernard Ct
BN22 ....185 C5
Duke Mews BN3 TN37 ..136 B2
Duke Rd TN37 ....136 B2
Duke St Bexhill TN35 ..156 F5
Brighton BN1 ....189 A2
St Leonards TN37 ....136 B2
Duke Terr TN37 ....136 B2
Duke's Dr BN20 ....188 F7
Duke's Mound BN2 ....164 D4
Dukes Barn Ct RH16 ....51 B7
Dukes Cl BN25 ....180 D5
Dukes Hill TN33 ....112 D6
Dukes La BN1 ....189 A2
Dukes Rd Lindfield RH16 .51 B8
Royal Tunbridge Wells TN1 ..8 C5
Dulwich Cl BN25 ....181 B4
Dumb Woman's La TN31 ..92 D3
Dumbrell Cl BN7 ....146 B8
Dumbrells Court Rd BN6 .98 D4
Dumbrells Ct BN6 ....98 D4
Dumbrills Cl RH15 ....73 A5
Dunbar Dr BN27 ....129 A1
Duncan Ho BN10 ....167 D1
Dunclutha Rd TN34 ....136 F4
Duncton Cl RH16 ....50 D4
Duncton Ho BN20 ....97 E4
Dundale Rd TN3 ....9 E1
Dunes Ave TN31 ....94 F2
Dunning's Rd RH19 ..10 E7
Dunnings Mill Complex
RH19 ....10 E6
Dunorlan Farm Cotts TN2 ..8 E4
Dunstall Ave RH15 ....72 E4
Dunstall Farm Rd RH15 ..72 E4
Dunstan Gr TN4 ....8 B6
Dunstan Rd TN4 ....8 B6
Dunstans Croft TN20 ..40 C3
Dunster Cl BN1 ....143 B1
Dunwan Cl BN7 ....123 C3
Durham Cl BN7 ....144 A1
Durham Ct
Hove BN3 ....184 B6
Hove BN3 ....163 B6
Durkins Rd RH19 ....1 D3
Durrell Cl BN23 ....174 F2
Durrington Cl BN1 ....142 D5
Dursley Rd BN22 ....185 A4
Dutchells Way BN22 ..173 E4
Dyall Cl RH15 ....72 D3
Dyke Cl BN3 ....142 B4
Dyke Rd BN1, BN3 ....163 E7
Dyke Rd Ave BN1, BN3 ..142 B3
Dyke Rd Dr BN1 ....163 F8
Dyke Rd Mews BN1 ..189 A4
Dyke Rd Pl BN1 ....142 C3
Dymchurch Cl
Polegate BN26 ....173 C7
Seaford BN25 ....181 C5

Dymock Ct BN25 ....181 C4
Dymock's The BN6 ....98 D3
Dymond Rd TN18 ....136 A3
Dynevor Rd TN4 ....8 C7

E

Eagle Cl TN22 ....78 E5
Eagle Rd TN31 ....93 C6
Earl St TN34 ....159 F8
Earl's Rd TN4 ....7 F4
Earls Cl TN35 ....180 C5
Earls Gdn 5 BN7 ....123 D1
Earwig Cnr BN8 ....180 F3
East Albany Rd BN25 ....180 F3
East Ascent TN38 ....159 C6
East Beach St TN34 ....160 A6
East Beeches Rd TN6 ....26 B2
East Bourne St 22 TN34 .....160 B4
East Brighton College
of Media Arts (Sch) BN2 .164 F5
East Cl BN26 ....173 A6
East Cliff TN31 ....93 C6
East Cliff Rd TN4 ....8 A6
East Dean Rd BN20 ....184 B2
East Dean Rise BN25 ....181 A4
East Dr BN2 ....109 D2
East Gdns BN6 ....98 D3
East Grinstead Sta RH19 .....1 D1
East Grinstead Town Mus
RH19 ....1 F2
East Hill RH19 ....1 F2
East Hill Cliff Rly TN34 .....160 B4
East Hill Pas 22 TN34 ....160 B4
East Hoathly CE Prim Sch
BN8 ....104 F5
East Mascalls Rd TN6 ....51 E6
East Meadway BN43 ....161 A6
East Par TN34 ....160 A3
East Point 8 BN43 ....184 E2
East St Brighton BN1 ....189 B1
Coggins Mill TN20 ....40 C3
Falmer BN1 ....144 C6
Hastings TN34 ....160 A4
Lewes BN7 ....123 D1
Portslade-by-Sea BN41 ....162 C7
Rye TN31 ....93 C5
Seaford BN25 ....180 E3
East Sussex F HQ BN7 ......123 B2
East Sussex Music Sch
BN7 ....146 C8
East Sussex Music Sch
(Annexe) BN7 ....123 D1
East Sussex
National Golf Club TN22 .103 C7
East View TN21 ....82 B6
East View Fields BN27 ....99 E5
East View TN33 ....88 F1
East Way BN7 ....122 F2
East Wick RH16 ....51 C7
Eastbank BN27 ....140 F1
Eastbourne Ave BN24 .....175 D5
Eastbourne Coll BN21 .....184 E3
Eastbourne Coll of Arts
& Tech Eastbourne BN21 ..184 E7
Eastbourne, Upperton BN21 184 C4
Eastbourne Coll
of Food & Fashion BN20 .185 A1
Eastbourne District
General Hospl BN21 ....184 E7
Eastbourne Miniature
Steam Rly FK BN23 ....185 A7
Eastbourne Rd
Brighton BN2 ....143 D1
Felbridge RH19 ....1 A5
Halland BN8 ....130 C4
Lower Willingdon BN20 ....173 B4
Pevensey Bay BN24 ....175 C4
Seaford BN25 ....181 C3
Uckfield TN22 ....78 F3
Westham BN23,BN24 ....184 F3
Eastfield Cres BN1 ....143 A4
Eastgate St BN7 ....123 D1
Eastgate Wharf 9 BN7 .....123 D1
Eastgate Rd BN7 ....143 F4
Eastern Ave
Polegate BN26 ....173 B7
Shoreham-by-Sea BN43 ....161 A7
Eastern Cl BN41 ....161 A7
Eastern Cotts RH16 ....51 B7
Eastern Pl BN2 ....164 E4
Eastern Rd Brighton BN2 ...164 D4
Haywards Heath RH16 ....50 F3
Lindfield RH16 ....51 C7
Wivelsfield RH17 ....74 B4
Eastern Ring Rd BN1 ....144 C2
Eastern Terr 10 BN2 ....164 D4
Eastern Terrace Mews
BN2 ....164 D4
Eastgate St BN7 ....123 D1
Eastgate Wharf BN7 ....123 D1
Easthill Dr BN41 ....141 F1
Easthill Way BN41 ....141 B1
Eastlands Cl TN4 ....18 E8
Eastlands Rd TN4 ....7 E1
Eastport La BN7 ....146 C8
Eastview Cotts BN8 ....124 E5
Eastway TN39 ....156 D4
Eastwell Pl BN27 ....152 B8
Eastwell Bottom BN1 ....143 B7
Eastwick Cl BN1 ....143 B7
Eastwood Rd TN39 ....157 A4
Eatenden La TN32,TN33 .....87 B3
Eaton Ct 9 BN2 ....163 C7
Eaton Gardens Mans 20
BN3 ....163 C7
Eaton Gate 17 BN3 ....163 C7
Eaton Gdns BN3 ....163 C7
Eaton Gr BN3 ....163 C7
Eaton Hall 19 BN3 ....163 C7
Eaton Manor 11 BN3 ....163 C7
Eaton Pl BN2 ....164 D4
Eaton Rd BN3 ....163 C7
Eaton Villas BN3 ....163 B7
Eaton Wlk TN33 ....136 B8
Ebden's Hill TN37 ....140 F2
Ebenezer Rd TN34 ....160 B4
Ecclesden 6 BN2 ....189 C3
Ecmod Rd BN22 ....185 C6
Edburton Ave BN1 ....144 A5
Eden Cl BN24 ....174 A5
Eden Dr TN35 ....156 F4
Eden Rd TN1 ....8 A2
Eden Vale
Dormans Park RH19 ....1 F5
Edenbridge Rd TN7 ....13 E8
Edensor Rd BN20 ....188 D7
Edgar Rd TN35 ....160 C6
Edgehill Cl TN21 ....81 F7
Edgehill Way TN40 ....140 F2
Egdeland Terr BN22 ....173 F1
Edinburgh Ct
Eastbourne BN20 ....184 C5
Seaford BN25 ....180 D3
Edinburgh Rd
Bexhill TN40 ....157 C5
1 Brighton BN2 ....164 B8
Seaford BN25 ....180 D3
St Leonards TN38 ....158 E2
Edinburgh Way RH19 ....10 E7
Edison Rd BN23 ....174 A1
Edith Ave BN13 ....178 D3
Edith Ave N BN10 ....178 C8
Edmond Cl BN23 ....185 E8
Edmonton Rd TN35 ....157 B7
Edmund Rd TN35 ....160 C5
Edward Ave TN4 ....72 B8
Edward Cl Hove BN3 ....142 A3
Saltdean BN2 ....166 D3
Edward Ct Hove BN3 ....142 A3
Saltdean BN2 ....180 A6
Edward Ho BN3 ....143 A4
Edward Rd
Haywards Heath RH16 ....50 E2
St Leonards TN37 ....159 D7
Edward St Brighton BN2 ...189 C3
6 Lewes BN7 ....123 D1
Royal Tunbridge Wells TN4 ..7 F8
Rusthall TN4 ....7 C4
Edward Terr TN34 ....136 A4
Edward Way RH15 ....72 D2
Edwin Rd TN35 ....160 C6
Effingham Ct BN2 ....177 C6
Effingham Dr TN39 ....156 D3
Egbert Cl BN23 ....185 E8
Egerton Rd BN20 ....188 B8
Egerton Rd TN37 ....157 B3
Egginton Cl BN1 ....144 A5
Egginton Rd BN1 ....144 A5
Egles Gr TN22 ....78 B8
Egmont Rd BN3 ....142 A1
Egremont Pl Brighton BN2 189 C2
Hastings TN34 ....160 B6
Eight Acre La TN35 ....115 D1
Eight Bells Cl TN22 ....56 C4
Eileen Ave BN2 ....177 B5
Eisenhower Dr TN37 ....135 F6
Elder Cl BN41 ....141 B2
Elder Pl BN1 ....189 B4
Elderwood Cl
Bexhill TN39 ....157 C7
Eastbourne BN22 ....173 D2
Eldon Rd BN21 ....184 C5
Eldred Ave BN1 ....142 D5
Eleanor Cl Lewes BN7 .....123 B2
Seaford BN25 ....180 D5
Eleanor Terr TN35 ....137 D4
Eley Cres BN2 ....165 E3
Eley Rd BN2 ....165 E3
Elford St 3 TN34 ....159 F8
Elgar Way BN23 ....174 E3
Elgin Gdns BN25 ....181 D6
Elim Court Gdns TN6 ....25 E4
Elim Wlk TN34 ....136 F2
Eliot Ho 4 RH16 ....50 E3
Elizabeth Ave BN3 ....142 A3
Elizabeth Cl Hove BN3 .....142 A3
Eastbourne BN23 ....180 A6
Elizabeth Cres BN1 ....142 D3
Elizabeth Ct
Eastbourne BN20 ....184 C5
2 Haywards Heath RH16 ....50 D3
4 Hailsham BN27 ....151 C4
Polegate BN26 ....173 A6
Elizabeth Garlick Ct TN1 ....8 B4
Elizabeth Rd
Shoreham-by-Sea BN43 ....161 C8
St Leonards TN38 ....136 A2
Elizabethan Cl TN33 ....132 F2
Ellen Ho BN1 ....163 D7
Ellen St TN38 ....163 B7
Ellenslea Rd TN37 ....159 C7
Ellenwhorne La TN32 ....89 A7
Ellerslie La TN39 ....156 F6
Elliots Way TN21 ....82 A8
Ellis Cl TN34 ....159 F7
Ellis Gordon Ct 1 BN9 ....179 B7
Ellis Way TN22 ....78 A7
Ellison Cl TN6 ....25 E4
Elm Cl Hove BN3 ....142 C2
Laughton BN8 ....126 C7
Seaford BN25 ....181 C3
Elm Cotts Hailsham BN27 ..151 A8
Laughton BN8 ....126 C7
Elm Ct Brighton BN1 ....163 D7
4 East Grinstead RH19 ......1 D2
Newhaven BN9 ....179 B7
Polegate BN26 ....173 A6
Portslade-by-Sea BN41 .....2 A1
Elm Dr East Grinstead RH19 ..2 A1
Elm Gn 6 BN21 ....129 B1
Elm Gr Brighton BN2 ....164 C7
Eastbourne BN22 ....173 F1
5 Lewes BN7 ....123 D1
Elm Grove Cty Prim Sch
BN2 ....164 C7
Elm Rd BN41 ....162 B8
Elm Way TN21 ....82 B6
Elmhurst Ave TN2 ....9 D1
Elmore Rd BN2 ....189 C3
Elms Ave BN21 ....185 B2
Elms La TN35 ....116 F1
Elms Lea Ave BN1 ....142 E3
Elms Rd BN21 ....185 B2
Elms The BN8 ....124 C5
Elmstone Pl BN27 ....152 C7
Elmstead TN31 ....70 B4
Elmsted RH19 ....10 E8
Elmstead Rd TN40 ....157 E5
Elmwood Cl BN22 ....174 C4
Elmwood Ct BN23 ....174 C4
Elmwood Gdns BN23 ......174 C4
Elphick Pl TN6 ....25 F3
Elphick Rd BN9 ....179 B7
Broyle Side BN8 ....124 F7
Elphick's Pl TN6 ....17 B8
Elphinstone Ave TN34 .....136 F2
Elphinstone Cty Prim Sch
TN34 ....160 A6
Elphinstone Gdns TN34 ...160 A6
Elphinstone Inf Sch TN34 .136 F2
Elphinstone Rd TN34 ......136 F2
Elrington Rd BN3 ....142 C1
Elsted Cl BN22 ....174 A1
Elsted Cres BN1 ....143 C6
Elsted Rd TN6 ....25 F3
Elven Cl BN20 ....183 C1
Elven Rd BN20 ....183 C1
Elvin Cres BN2 ....165 E4
Elwood Cl RH15 ....72 F1
Elwyn Jones Ct BN1 ......142 E4
Ely Ct TN1 ....8 B4
Embassy Ct
10 Brighton BN1 ....163 D5
Haywards Heath RH16 ......50 E6
Emerald Quay BN43 ....161 A6
Emerson Coll RH18 ....12 B3
Emmanuel Rd RH16 ....160 A5
Encore Ho TN21 ....82 A8
Endcliffe Cl BN20 ....188 E8
English Cl BN3 ....162 B8
English's Pas 10 BN7 ......123 D1
Engakee RH19 ....1 C2
Enterprise Est BN1 ....142 A4
Enys Rd BN21 ....184 F4
Epsom Cl TN38 ....159 A8
Epsom Ct 6 BN40 ....157 E4
Erica Cl BN23 ....174 B2
Eridge Cl TN39 ....157 A4
Eridge Dr TN6 ....26 A3
Eridge Gdns TN6 ....26 A3
Eridge Gn BN7 ....123 B2
Eridge La TN3,TN6 ....27 B2
Eridge Rd
Boarshead TN3,TN6 ....26 D7
Crowborough TN6 ....26 A3
Eastbourne BN21 ....184 D7
Hove BN3 ....142 A2
Royal Tunbridge Wells
TN2,TN4 ....7 E1
Steel Cross TN6 ....26 C4
Eridge Sta TN3 ....15 E2
Erin Way RH15 ....72 E3
Erroll Rd BN3 ....162 C6
Ersham Rd BN27 ....152 B6
Ersham Way BN27 ....152 B6
Erskine Park Rd TN4 ....7 C4
Esher Cl BN25 ....180 F4
Eshton Rd BN22 ....185 C5
Esbank Ave BN1 ....174 C4
Esdale Cl BN20 ....180 E2
Esplanade BN10 ....180 E2
Esplanade
Mews 6 BN10 ....180 E2
Esplanade The BN10 ....177 E3
Essenden Rd TN38 ....159 A7
Essex Cl TN2 ....26 D1
Essex Pl 3 BN2 ....184 B6
Essex Pl 3 Brighton BN2 .164 C4
Newhaven BN9 ....179 C7
Essex Rd TN38 ....159 A7
Essex St BN2 ....164 C4
Estate Rd BN9 ....179 D7
Estcots Cty Prim Sch RH19 ..2 A1
Estcots Dr RH19 ....2 A1
Etchingham CE Prim Sch
TN19 ....44 D1
Etchingham Rd BN3 ....174 E1
Etchingham Sta TN19 ......44 C1
Ethel St BN3 ....163 D7
Ethelred Cl BN13 ....185 E8
Etherington Hill TN3 ....7 C8
Etherton Way BN25 ....181 A4
Etherton Way BN25 ....181 A4
Ethnam La TN18 ....137 A2
Eton Cl BN25 ....181 A4
Eton Mews 3 BN1 ....185 A3
Eurythmy Sch RH19 ....10 E5
Evelyn Ave BN9 ....179 C7
Evelyn Ct BN41 ....162 A8
Evelyn Glennie Ct 7
BN2 ....164 C5
Evelyn Rd BN22 ....123 B2
Evelyn Terr BN2 ....164 C7
Everest Ho BN2 ....162 F7
Eversfield Cl TN37 ....159 D7
Eversfield Hospl TN38 .....159 C6
Eversfield Mews N 5
TN37 ....159 C7
Eversfield Pl TN37 ....159 D7
Evershed Rd BN21 ....184 F4
Evershed Way BN41 ....161 B7
Eversley Cl TN37 ....136 C2
Eversley Cres BN27 ....157 C3
Eversley Cres BN27 ....157 C3
Eversley Rd Bexhill TN40 ..157 C3
Eversley Rd TN37 ....136 C2
Everton Cotts TN19 ....62 B6
Evesham Cl BN13 ....136 A3
Ewart St BN2 ....189 C3
Ewbank Ho BN3 ....163 C6
Ewehurst La TN3 ....6 F6
Ewell Cl TN40 ....157 E4
Ewhurst Cl TN34 ....136 F4
Ewhurst La TN31 ....66 F4
Ewhurst Rd BN2 ....143 C1
Excelsior The BN1 ....142 D4
Exeat Cl Brighton BN2 .....164 E6
Eastbourne BN24 ....174 B4
Exeter St BN22 ....173 B2
Exeter St BN1 ....163 E8
Exmouth Pl TN34 ....160 A4

Factory La BN27 ....152 A6
Fair Isle Cl BN23 ....185 E8
Fair La Robertsbridge TN32 ..64 C4
Robertsbridge TN32 ....64 C4
Fair Mdw TN31 ....93 C5
Fair Oak Cl TN21 ....82 A8
Fair View TN5 ....30 A6
Fairbairns RH15 ....50 E4
Fairbridge Way RH15 ....72 F5
Faircroach La TN3 ....29 B5
Fairdene BN42 ....140 F1
Fairfax Ave TN37 ....135 F7
Fairfax
Herstmonceux BN27 ....130 E6
Peacehaven BN10 ....178 A7
Fairfield Ave TN2 ....26 E4
Fairfield Cl
Burgess Hill RH15 ....72 F4
Shoreham-by-Sea BN43 ...140 C1
Fairfield Cotts BN20 ....149 D2
Fairfield Cres BN6 ....97 A6
Fairfield Gdns
Burgess Hill RH15 ....72 F4
Portslade-by-Sea BN41 ....141 B1
Fairfield Lodge BN20 ......188 E8
Fairfield Rd
Burgess Hill RH15 ....72 F4
East Grinstead RH19 ....10 E8
Eastbourne BN20 ....184 E1
St Leonards BN7 ....123 B2
Fairfield Way RH16 ....50 D8
Fairglen Cotts TN5 ....29 B3
Fairglen Rd TN5 ....29 B4
Fairhaven RH17 ....99 E1
Fairholme BN10 ....158 E5
Fairholme Cl TN6 ....25 F1
Fairholme Ct TN6 ....25 F1
Fairhurst BN10 ....168 F1
Fairisle Cl BN27 ....177 F3
Fairisle Rd BN12 ....129 A2
Fairlawn 1 RH16 ....50 E4
Fairlawn Cres RH19 ....1 B2
Fairlawn Dr RH19 ....1 B2
Fairlawns 3 Hove BN3 ....163 A6
Shoreham-by-Sea BN43 ...161 A8
Fairlawns Dr BN22 ....173 F2
Fairlea Cl RH15 ....72 F4
Fairlie Gdns BN1 ....142 E3
Fairlight TN22 ....55 E1
Fairlight
Hastings TN35 ....137 D3
Telscombe Cliffs BN10 .....177 F3
Fairlight Cl Bexhill TN40 ...158 A5
Polegate BN26 ....173 A6
Fairlight Ct BN10 ....179 B7
Fairlight Cty Prim Sch
BN2 ....164 C8
Fairlight Field BN26 ....124 D5
Fairlight Gdns TN35 ....138 F4
Fairlight Pl 8 BN2 ....164 C8
Fairlight Rd
Eastbourne BN22 ....185 C5
Fairlight TN35 ....138 A4
Fairmile Rd TN6 ....8 E5
Fairmount Rd TN40 ....157 D5
Fairoak Rd BN26 ....173 C6
Fairplace RH17 ....74 A4
Fairstone Cl TN35 ....137 E4
Fairview Cotts TN6 ....25 E4
Fairview Rise BN1 ....142 D5
Fairway Cl BN20 ....184 C2
Fairway Cres BN41 ....141 C2
Fairway The Bexhill TN39 .156 F6
Newhaven BN9 ....158 F8
Fairway Trad Est BN22 ....143 E4
Fairways BN1 ....163 E8
Fairways Cl BN25 ....181 C2
Fairways Rd BN25 ....181 B2
Fairways The TN4 ....8 A7
Falaise Rd Hastings TN34 .159 D7
Newhaven BN9 ....168 F1
Falcon Cl BN43 ....161 C6
Falcon Way BN27 ....156 D3
Falconbury Dr TN39 ....156 D3
Falconer Dr TN33 ....112 F4
Fallowfield Cl BN13 ....141 F2
Fallowfield Cres BN1 ....141 F2
Falmer Ave BN2 ....164 D2
Falmer Rd BN2 ....184 B7
Falmer Gdns BN2 ....165 D8
Falmer Hill BN1 ....144 B6
Falmer House Rd BN1 .....144 B6
Falmer Rd BN2 ....165 E5
Falmer Rd BN2 ....144 A5
Falmer Sta BN1 ....144 B6
Falmouth Cl BN23 ....185 F8
Faraday Ave RH19 ....10 F6
Faraday Cl BN22 ....173 F1
Faraday Lodge TN2 ....184 C6
Farlaine Rd BN21 ....184 C6
Farley Bank TN35 ....160 B6
Farley Way TN35 ....138 E5
Farleys Way TN31 ....69 B2
Farm Cl BN43 ....50 F5
Farm Hill BN2 ....165 D8
Farm Cl East Grinstead RH19 .11 B8
Hassocks BN6 ....97 E4
Portslade-by-Sea BN41 ....141 A2
Farm Gdns TN3 ....6 D5
Farm Hill BN2 ....165 C8
Farm La Camber TN31 ......94 D2
Ditchling BN6 ....98 E3
Farm Mews BN3 ....163 D6
Farm Rd BN3 ....163 D6
Farm Trail BN6 ....151 A4
Farm Way
Burgess Hill RH15 ....73 D1
Southwick BN42 ....162 A7
Farman St 30 BN3 ....163 D5
Farncombe Cl TN2 ....8 B2
Farncombe La TN2 ....8 B2
Farmet Ct RH19 ....1 C3
Farmcombe Rd TN2 ....8 B2
Farmlands Ave BN27 ......129 C3
Farmlands Cl
Lower Willingdon BN26 ...173 A4
St Leonards TN37 ....136 C5
Farmlands Cl BN26 ....173 A4
Farmlands Cl BN26 ....172 F5
Farmway Cl BN3 ....141 D2
Farncombe Cl RH17 ....74 D4
Farncombe Rd 6 BN7 .....123 E1
Farne Ct TN22 ....129 A2
Farnham Ave BN1 ....98 A8
Farnham Beeches TN3 ......7 A
Farnham La TN3 ....7 A
Farnham Pl TN3 ....7 A
Farningham Rd TN6 ....38 C3
Farnol Rd BN2 ....184 D3
Farrance Ct TN1 ....8 B
Farriers Way TN22 ....31 E6
Farthing Hill TN5 ....31 E6
Farthing La BN27,TN33 ....109 E3
Farthings The TN6 ....25 F1
Fastnet Cl BN23 ....185 E8
Faulkners Way RH15 ....74 A4
Faversham Rd BN23 ......174 E3
Fayette Cl TN39 ....157 E5
Faygate Cl BN1 ....142 A6
Faygate Rd BN2 ....173 F4
Fayre Mdw TN32 ....64 C4
Fazan Ct TN5 ....29 F4
Fearon Rd TN34 ....136 F1
Felbridge Ct RH19 ....1 C3
Felbridge Rd RH19 ....1 C3
Felbridge Ctr The RH19 ....1 C3
Felbridge Pl RH10 ....1 C3
Felcourt Cotts RH19 ....1 C3
Felcourt La RH19, RH7 ......1 C3
Felcourt Rd RH19, RH7 ......1 C3
Feld The RH19 ....1 C3
Fellows Rd TN34 ....137 B3
Felride RH16 ....50 C4
Felvater Ct RH19 ....1 C3
Fen Ct TN38 ....135 F7
Fennel Wlk BN43 ....140 C1
Fennell's Cl BN21 ....184 D6
Ferbies TN3 ....7 A
Ferbies Cl TN3 ....7 A
Ferdinand Terr TN3 ....7 A
Ferguson Rd TN29 ....96 A5
Fermor Rd TN6 ....39 B8
Fermor Row TN6 ....38 F8
Fermor Way TN6 ....38 F8
Fern Cl BN23 ....174 C4
Fern Gn 1 BN27 ....129 C3
Fern Rd TN38 ....158 E5
Fernbank Sh Ctr TN6 ....25 F4
Ferndale TN2 ....9 A
Ferndale Cl TN2 ....9 A
Ferndale Point TN2 ....9 A
Ferndale Rd
Burgess Hill RH15 ....73 D1
Hove BN3 ....163 A6

hurst BN1 ....143 B6
hurst Cres BN1 ....143 B5
len Cl TN35 ....114 E4
es The TN1 ....8 D6
side 🖪 RH19 ....1 D2
side Ave TN38 ....135 F1
wood Rise BN3 ....142 D5
ers Rd BN7 ....123 B1
ng Cl TN31 ....93 A6
ng Ct BN1 ....143 F5
ngham TN4 ....7 F4
y Hill TN36 ....117 E8
s Rd TN31 ....93 B5
val Gdns TN30 ....157 C7
rsham Cl BN43 ....161 B6
Cl Burgess Hill RH15 ..72 E4
sport BN25 ....181 B2
Cotts RH15 ....73 B4
ield TN22 ....92 E3
Way TN38 ....158 E8
en La TN6 ....25 D1
en Rd TN6 ....25 D2
fare Ct BN27 ....152 D7
es End Cl RH16 ....50 F4
way Broad Oak TN21 ...90 C5
ing Manor 98 D3
or Mus BN26 ....172 D2
ield RH16 ....50 F8
nes Rd BN27 ....152 B7
nesLa TN6 ....37 F8
ing Ct BN26 ....172 E3
ing Ct BN20 ....184 B5
ing Manor
eham-by-Sea BN43 .....141 F6
st Leonards TN38 .....136 A5
en Ave BN7 ....177 E6
on Cl Bexhill TN39 ...156 E3
BN3 ....141 F3
on Ct BN25 ....181 C3
on Rd BN2 ....169 E3
ere Ave BN23 ....185 E8
ere Cl TN38 ....158 F6
ere Cl BN25 ....185 C6
ere Ct BN2 ....185 C6
bury Lodge 🖪 BN2 ....164 C6
bury Rd BN2 ....164 C6
BN7 ....165 F7
rove Rd TN21 ....81 B6
oll Cl TN20 ....39 C2
oll Rd Woolbridge TN20 .39 C2
bridge TN20 ....39 E2
ere Cl Bexhill TN39 ..156 C3
sport BN27 ....129 C2
Cres BN7 ....122 F2
Gn TN20 ....55 E1
Grange BN25 ....180 E5
Place BN8 ....148 C3
Rd Bexhill TN39 .....156 D4
hton BN2 ....164 D6
bourne BN22 ....185 B4
ohaven BN10 ....178 C8
ord BN25 ....180 E6
Terr BN7 ....168 D2
Ct TN4 ....7 F6
The TN35 ....156 C8
Ave Bexhill TN40 .....157 F5
ber TN31 ....94 F2
BN3 ....163 C6
haven BN9 ....179 C7
St TN3 ....6 F3
Ct RH15 ....73 B3
ee Rd TN4 ....160 A6
ood Cl
bourne BN22 ....173 E1
ithfield TN21 ....82 A8
ood Rise TN21 ....82 A8
er Cl BN23 ....185 F7
er St BN7 ....123 D1
er's Gate Cotts TN ...14 A1
ermans's Mus TN14 ...160 B3
ersgate Cl BN41 .....162 A7
ersgate Cty Fst Sch
TN1 ....162 A7
ersgate Sta BN41 ....162 B7
ersgate Terr BN41 ...162 A7
market Rd TN31 ......93 C6
onds La TN35 ....114 E3
Ct BN3 ....143 F1
alan Ho 🖪 BN21 ......184 F4
erald Ave BN25 ......180 F2
erald Cl BN20 ....184 F1
erald Ho 🖪 BN25 .....180 E3
erald Pk BN25 ....180 F2
erald Rd BN7 ....123 D3
erbert Dr BN2 ....164 D8
er St BN6 ....97 F3

Fitzjohns Rd BN7 .....123 B2
Fitzmaurice Ave BN22 .185 B5
Fitzroy Rd BN7 ....123 B2
Five Acre Wlk TN34 ...136 E1
Five Ashes CE Prim Sch
TN20 ....58 B6
Five Chys La TN22 ....57 A6
Five Hos The TN36 ...117 E8
Five Villages Ho TN36 116 F6
Fiveways TN1 ....8 A4
Flag Ct BN3 ....163 B5
Flamsteed Rd BN27 ...131 A1
Fleetway Cl TN1 ......94 F2
Fleming Cl BN22 .....174 F2
Fletcher Ave TN37 ...135 F7
Fletching CE Prim Sch
TN22 ....53 F3
Fletching Cl BN21 ...164 F6
Fletching Rd BN22 ...174 E2
Fletching St TN20 ...40 B3
Flimwell Bird Pk TN5 .32 E2
Flimwell CI Brighton BN2 .164 E5
Eastbourne BN23 .....174 A4
Flimwell TN5 ....32 D4
Flint CI
Portslade-by-Sea BN41 141 B2
Seaford BN25 ....180 E6
Flints The TN5 ....145 E5
Flitterbrook La TN13 .83 C4
Florance La TN3 .....15 B6
Florence Ave BN3 ...162 D8
Florence Cl BN1 .....142 F2
Florence Pl BN1 .....143 B1
Florence Rd BN1 .....164 A8
Florida Ct TN38 .....156 F6
Fold Sch The BN3 ...162 D7
Folders CI RH15 .....73 D1
Folders La RH15 .....73 D1
Foley CI BN23 ....185 E7
Folkestone Cl BN25 .181 C5
Folkestone Rd BN31 ..93 F8
Folkington Gdns TN37 136 C5
Folkington Rd BN26 .172 D5
Follett Holt Ho BN8 .148 F7
Folly Field BN9 .....179 C7
Fonthill Rd BN3 .....168 B8
Fontridge La TN19 ...62 E3
Fontwell Ave TN39 ...156 C5
Foords La BN24 .....174 C7
Foot's La TN5 ....49 A3
Ford Rd TN38 ....135 F2
Fordbrook Hill TN6 ..37 F2
Fordcombe CE Prim Sch
TN3 ....6 B5
Fordcombe Rd TN6 ...6 C4
Foredown CI
Eastbourne BN22 .....184 C2
Portslade-by-Sea BN41 141 B2
Foredown Dr BN41 ...141 C1
Foredown Rd
Portslade-by-Sea BN41 141 B4
Portslade-by-Sea BN41 141 B2
Forest Dene
Crowborough TN6 .....26 D1
Royal Tunbridge Wells TN2 .8 B2
Forest Fold Cotts TN6 25 D5
Forest La TN21 ......83 D6
Forest Lodge
Crowborough Warren TN6 37 D8
🖪 Royal Tunbridge Wells RH19 10 F8
Forest Pk Crowborough TN6 25 D2
Maresfield TN22 .....54 F5
Forest PI TN21 ......80 F6
Forest Rd Brighton BN1 143 E6
Forest Row RH18 ....12 B2
Royal Tunbridge Wells TN2 .8 D1
Forest Ridge RH19 ..21 A5
Forest Rise TN6 .....26 D1
Forest Row Bsns Pk RH18 11 F4
Forest Row CE Inf Sch
RH18 ....11 F2
Forest View
Hailsham BN27 ......152 A8
Nutley TN22 ....35 C3
Forest View Rd RH19 10 E6
Forest Way Hastings TN34 136 E1
Pembury TN2 ....9 D8
Royal Tunbridge Wells TN2 .8 D1
Forewood La TN33 ...135 A7
Forewood Rise TN33 .134 F6
Forge Cl
Portslade-by-Sea BN41 141 B2
Staplecross TN32 ....65 E3
Uckfield TN22 ....78 C6
Forge Field TN5 .....42 F6
Forge La TN32 ....65 E1
Forge Lane Cotts TN32 65 E1
Forge Rd TN3 ....15 C2
Forge Rise TN22 ....78 C6
Forge Way
Burgess Hill RH15 ...73 A4
Hastings TN37 ......136 C5
Forgefield Cotts TN18 47 A4
Forstal The Cobham TN3 15 F3
Pembury TN2 ....9 E8
Forstall TN3 ....7 A4
Fort Gate BN9 ......179 C5
Fort Haven BN43 ...161 C6
Fort La BN22 ....185 D6
Fort Newhaven BN9 .179 C5
Fort Rd Eastbourne BN22 185 D6
Newhaven BN9 ....179 C5
Forward CI BN9 .....179 D5
Forward Ct BN9 .....168 E2
Foster CI BN25 .....180 E4
Foster Ct BN3 ......163 E6
Foundry La RH15 ...73 B3

Foundry La BN7 .....123 E1
Foundry St BN1 .....189 B3
Fountains Cl Brighton BN1 143 B2
Eastbourne BN22 ....173 E3
Founthill Ave BN2 ..177 B5
Founthill Rd BN2 ...177 B5
Fourteen Acre La TN35 115 D4
Fourth Ave BN3 ....163 B6
Fowey Cl BN43 .....161 A6
Fowey Ct TN39 .....156 E5
Fowly La TN22 ......56 C7
Fox Cl RH15 ....72 F1
Fox Hill RH16 ......50 E1
Fox Hill CI RH16 ...50 F1
Fox Hill Village RH16 50 F1
Fox in the Wood TN5 .29 C6
Fox Way BN41 ......141 B2
Foxcote TN37 ......136 D5
Foxdown Rd BN2 ...165 F7
Foxglove Cl
Broyle Side BN8 ....125 A7
Burgess Hill RH15 ..72 D4
Foxglove Rd BN23 ..174 B3
Foxhill Bexhill TN39 156 E5
Peacehaven BN10 ..167 B1
Foxhill Ct 🖪 RH16 ..50 E3
Foxhole La
Four Throws TN18 ...46 D8
Wadhurst TN5 ......30 B4
Foxhunters Rd BN41 141 B2
Foxwarren RH16 ....50 C5
Framelle Mount TN22 79 B6
Framfield 🖪 BN2 ...164 F5
Framfield CE Prim Sch
TN22 ....79 B6
Framfield CI BN1 ...143 A3
Framfield Rd Buxted TN22 56 B3
Uckfield TN22 ......78 D6
Framfield Way BN21 184 D6
Francis CI RH16 ....50 B8
Francis St BN1, BN2 189 B4
Francislea RH16 ...50 E2
Frankfield Rise TN2 .8 A1
Franklands Cl RH15 .73 B1
Franklands Gdns RH15 98 A8
Franklands Way RH15 98 A8
Franklin Rd Brighton BN2 164 C7
Portslade-by-Sea BN41 162 C7
Shoreham-by-Sea BN43 140 D1
Franklin St BN2 ....164 C8
Fransway TN5 ......40 B3
Frankton Ave RH16 .51 A3
Frant Ave TN39 ....156 C5
Frant CE Prim Sch TN3 .17 B4
Frant CI TN39 .....156 C5
Frant Rd Hove BN3 ..142 A2
Royal Tunbridge
Wells TN2,TN3 ......17 A7
Frant Sta TN3 .....17 F5
Frary Wlk TN21 ....82 A8
Fraser Ave BN23 ...185 E7
Fraser Ct 🖪 BN23 ..161 C8
Freckley Hollow TN33 111 C1
Fred Emery Ct 🖪 BN1 163 E5
Freda Gardham
City Prim Sch TN31 .93 D6
Frederic Ho BN2 ...177 B5
Frederick Cotts RH16 51 B7
Frederick Gdns BN1 189 B3
Frederick Pl BN1 ..189 B3
Frederick Rd TN35 .137 C3
Frederick St BN1 ..189 B3
Frederick Thatcher Place
TN33 ....112 A4
Free Heath Rd TN3,TN5 19 C3
Freehold Terr 🖪 BN2 164 C8
Freek's La RH15 ...73 A5
Freeland Cl BN25 ..180 A6
Freeman Ave BN22 .173 E1
Freemans Rd BN41 .162 A8
Freezeland La TN39 .156 A5
Fremlin Cl TN4 ....7 B4
French Gdns RH16 .51 A6
Frenches Farm Dr TN21 82 A5
Frenchgate Cl BN22 173 F2
Frenchgate Rd BN22 173 F2
Freshfield Bank RH18 11 E2
Freshfield Halt RH17 52 B8
Freshfield La RH17 .33 E2
Freshfield Pl BN2 .164 D6
Freshfield Rd BN2 .164 D6
Freshfield St BN2 .164 D6
Freshfield Way BN2 164 C6
Freshford Cl BN23 ..174 D2
Freshwater Ave TN34 136 E2
Freshwater Sq BN22 173 B3
Freshway BN22 ....173 C3
Frewen Cl TN31 ...67 B7
Frewen Coll TN31 ..67 C5
Frewyn Ct TN38 ...135 F2
Friar Cl BN1 ....143 A4
Friar Cres BN1 ....143 A3
Friar Rd BN1 ......143 A3
Friar Wlk TN34 ...142 F4
Friar's Cres TN35 .138 B7
Friar's Hill Terr TN35 138 C7
Friar's Way TN34 ..136 E4
Friars Bank TN35 .138 B7
Friars Cl BN6 ......97 E4
Friars Hill TN35 ...137 F7
Friars Oak Rd RH16 .97 E5
Friars Rd TN36 ....117 F7
Friars Way TN32 ..80 C6
Friars Wlk BN10 ..178 E6
Friars' Wlk BN23 ..123 C1
Friday St BN23 ....174 C3

Fridays The BN20 ...187 B7
Friezland Rd TN4 ...7 D1
Frimley CI BN2 ....165 F7
Friston Ave BN22 ..173 C1
Friston CI Brighton BN2 143 F4
Friston BN20 ....183 A1
Seaford BN25 ......180 C4
Friston Downs BN20 183 B2
Frith Pk RH19 ......11 E3
Frobisher Cl BN23 .185 E7
Frobisher Ho BN10 .167 D1
Frog Hole La TN20,TN21 58 C5
Frog La TN1 ....8 A2
Front Cotts TN5 ...31 E1
Fruitfields TN5 ....32 C3
Fry Cres RH15 .....72 E5
Fryatts Way TN39 .156 F6
Fryman's La TN21 .58 E6
Fulford CI TN38 ...159 A8
Fulford Ct TN38 ...159 A8
Fuller Cl TN5 ......29 E5
Fuller Rd BN7 .....123 A3
Fuller's Pas 🖪 BN7 123 D1
Fullers La TN31 ...67 B6
Fullwood Ave BN9 .179 B7
Fulmar Cl BN2 ....142 D1
Fulmar Dr RH19 ..2 B3
Fulmer Pl 🖪 TN40 .157 C4
Furlongs The BN26 170 F3
Furnace Ave TN3 ..24 C8
Furnace La TN21 ..82 C2
Furnace Way TN7 ..78 E7
Furness Rd BN20,BN21 184 F2
Furnival Ct TN2 ...16 F8
Furze Croft Hove BN3 163 D6
St Leonards TN38 ..159 B8
Furze Hill BN3 ....163 D6
Furze Hill Ct BN3 .163 E6
Furze Hill Ho BN3 .163 E6
Furze La RH19 .....1 B4
Furzedene BN3 ....163 C6
Furzefield Ave TN2 .7 A8
Furzefield Chase RH19 1 E6
Furzefield Rd RH19 .1 C4
Fyning Pl TN3 .....156 C5
Fyrsway TN35 .....138 E4
Fysie La TN19 .....44 D3

G

Gables Ct 🖪 BN21 ..185 A3
Gables The TN34 ..136 E3
Gableson Ave BN1 .142 B4
Gage Ridge RH13 ..11 E2
Gages The BN27 ..152 D7
Gainsborough Cres
BN23 ....174 D1
Gainsborough Ho 🖪
BN3 ....163 C7
Gainsborough La BN26 172 E6
Gainsborough Rd TN40 157 D4
Galley Hill View TN40 157 E4
Galliers Cl BN1 ...143 B6
Gallipoli Hill TN7 ..13 C3
Gallops The BN7 ..123 A1
Gallows Cl BN24 ..174 A6
Gallows La BN24 ..174 E6
Galveston Cl BN23 185 F7
Gammons Way TN18 .88 E1
Gander Cl RH15 ...73 A5
Gander Ct BN20 ...184 F4
Gander Hill RH16 ..50 F7
Gannet Ho
🖪 Eastbourne BN21 185 A2
Hove BN3 ....142 B1
Ganton CI TN38 ...158 F8
Garden Cl 🖪 Bexhill TN40 157 D7
East Grinstead RH19 10 F7
Portslade-by-Sea BN41 162 C8
Shoreham-by-Sea BN43 140 B1
Garden Cotts 🖪 TN34 160 B4
Garden Cl Bexhill TN40 157 D7
Shoreham-by-Sea BN43 140 B1
Garden Ho The BN1 189 A3
Garden House La RH19 10 F7
Garden Mews BN20 188 D8
Garden Pl BN7 ....123 C1
Garden St Lewes BN7 123 C1
Royal Tunbridge Wells TN1 .8 B4
Garden Wood Rd RH19 10 C8
Gardens The BN2 ..162 B8
Gardner Centre Rd BN1 144 B6
Gardner CI BN23 ..185 E7
Gardner Rd BN41 ..162 A7
Gardner St Brighton BN1 189 B2
Herstmonceux BN27 130 D6
Gardner's Hill TN31 70 B6
Garfield Rd BN27 ..152 C7
Garland Rd 🖪 RH19 .1 D2
Garnet Dr BN20 ...184 C2
Garnet Ho 🖪 BN24 .62 F6
Garth Cl TN39 ....157 A5
Gatehouse Cl TN39 157 A5
Gatehouse La
Burgess Hill BN6,RH15 72 C4
Framfield TN22 ....79 C7
Gatelands Dr TN39 157 B6
Gatesmead RH16 ..50 F8
Gattons Cty Inf Sch The
RH15 ....72 E3

Gattons The RH15 ..72 E3
Gatwick Farm Cotts RH19 3 A4
Gaudick CI BN20 ...184 E1
Gaudick Rd BN20 ..184 E1
Gavin Astor CI TN40 158 A6
Geary Pl TN35 ....114 E3
Geary Rd BN27 ...152 D7
Geering Rd BN24 ..174 B5
Geers Wood TN21 .81 F6
Geerswood Cotts 🖪 TN21 82 A6
Gemma Cl BN27 ...152 A7
Geneva Rd BN9 ...179 D6
Genistos Thee BN6 .97 E4
Gensing Rd TN38 .159 C7
George Hill TN32 ..64 B3
George Rainey Sch TN38 159 C7
George Rd BN9 ....189 B2
Hailsham BN27 ....152 C7
Hastings TN34 .....160 A3
Hove BN3 ....163 B6
Portslade-by-Sea BN41 162 C7
Royal Tunbridge Wells TN2 .8 C3
Southwick BN41 ....162 A7
Sparrow's Green TN5 .29 F5
Georgian CI TN40 .157 E5
Georgian Wlk TN38 158 F8
Gerald CI RH15 ...73 D3
Gerald Rd BN25 ...180 F1
Gerard St BN1 ....189 B5
German St TN36 ..117 E7
Ghyll Rd Crowborough TN6 25 E4
Heathfield TN21 ...82 A6
Ghyll Side Rd TN31 .67 B7
Ghyllside Dr TN34 .136 C4
Ghyllside Ave TN34 136 C4
Ghyllside Way TN34 136 C4
Gibb Cl TN40 ......158 A5
Gibbetts TN1 ......6 F3
Gibbon Rd BN9 ...179 C6
Gibraltar Rise TN21 82 A7
Gibson Ct BN7 ....123 D2
Giffards Cl TN14 ..1 F1
Gilbert Rd
Eastbourne BN22 .185 B4
St Leonards TN37,TN38 159 B8
Gilbert Way BN27 .152 B5
Gilberts Dr BN20 .187 B8
Gilda Cres BN26 ..173 A6
Gildredge Rd
Eastbourne BN21 .184 F2
Seaford BN25 ......180 F3
Gilham La RH18 ...12 B1
Gill The TN2 ......9 E8
Gillham Wood Ave TN39 156 D3
Gillham Wood Rd TN39 156 D3
Gilligans The TN5 .72 F5
Gillridge Gn TN6 ..25 F4
Gillsman's Dr TN35 135 F1
Gillsman's Hill TN34 136 A1
Gillsman's Pk TN38 135 F1
Gilmile Way TN7 ..9 D8
Gingerbread La TN18 ..32 F2
Gipps Cross La TN3 .8 F2
Girton Ho BN3 ....162 F6
Glade Rd TN35 ....160 C6
Glade The Hailsham BN27 151 F6
Mayfield TN20 .....40 A3
Portslade TN42 ....78 D7
Gladepoint RH16 ..50 E5
Glades The Bexhill TN40 157 B6
East Grinstead RH19 ..2 B1
Gladstone Bldgs BN8 160 A3
Gladstone Cl BN22 173 E1
Gladstone Pl BN2 .164 C8
Gladstone Rd
Burgess Hill RH15 ..73 C4
Crowborough TN6 ..25 F1
Hastings TN34 .....160 A3
Portslade-by-Sea BN41 162 B7
Rusthall TN4 ......7 B4
Gladys Ave TN40 ..157 D5
Gladys Rd BN3 ...162 C6
Glanfield Ct TN1 ..8 C5
Glassenbury Dr TN40 157 C5
Glastonbury Rd BN3 162 D6
Gleave Cl RH19 ..2 A2
Glebe Cl Bexhill TN39 156 D3
Hailsham BN27 ....151 E6
Lewes BN7 ....146 A8
Southwick BN42 ..161 F7
Glebe Cotts TN33 .134 A7
Glebe Cty Mid Sch BN42 161 D8
Glebe Dr BN25 ....180 E3
Glebe The
Felbridge RH19 ....1 A4
Hastings TN34 .....160 B5
Hurstpierpoint BN6 97 A6
Lindfield RH16 ....51 A8
Pembury TN2 ......9 D8
Pett TN35 ....115 E5
Glebe Villas BN3 ..163 D7
Glebelands Cl BN43 161 B8
Glebelands The TN6 25 E3
Glen Cl BN26 ......172 F4
Glen Cotts BN26 ..172 F3
Glen Rise BN1 ....142 B5
Glen Rise Cl BN1 .142 B5
Glen The TN22 ....55 D1
Glenburn Ct TN39 157 C7
Glencoe TN6 ......25 F2
Glendale Ave BN21 184 C5
Glendale Ct TN2 ..8 D6

Glendale Rd
Burgess Hill RH15 . . . . 73 B2
Hove BN3 . . . . 163 D7
Glendor Rd BN3 . . . . 162 E6
Glendyne Way RH19 . . . . 11 A8
Gleneagles Cl
Bexhill TN40 . . . . 157 E5
Seaford BN25 . . . . 180 A6
Gleneagles Ct 13 RH16 . . . . 50 E4
Gleneagles Dr
Hailsham BN27 . . . . 152 A8
St Leonards TN38 . . . . 158 F7
Glenfalls Ave BN21 . . . . 143 A7
Glenfergus RH16 . . . . 50 E6
Glengorse TN33 . . . . 112 F3
Glenham Pl RH19 . . . . 21 A5
Glenleigh Ave TN39 . . . . . . 156 F6
Glenleigh Park Rd TN39 . . 157 A6
Glenleigh Wlk TN32 . . . . 64 A4
Glenmore Mews 4 BN21 . 185 A3
Glenmore Pk TN6 . . . . 16 F8
Glenmore Rd TN6 . . . . 25 C3
Glenmore Rd The TN6 . . . . . 25 D3
Glenside 1 RH19 . . . . 1 E1
Glenthorn Rd TN39 . . . . 157 A4
Glenthorne Ho 11 BN21 . . 184 F4
Glenview Ct TN35 . . . . 160 D5
Glessing Rd BN24 . . . . 174 B6
Gleton Ave BN3 . . . . 141 D2
Gloucester Ave TN40 . . . . . 158 A5
Gloucester Cl
East Grinstead RH19 . . . . . . 11 A8
Eastbourne BN22 . . . . 173 C2
Gloucester Cotts 3
TN34 . . . . 160 A4
Gloucester Ct BN23 . . . . . . 174 E1
Gloucester Pas 2 BN1 . . . 189 B3
Gloucester Pl BN1, BN2 . . 189 B3
Gloucester Rd
Brighton BN1 . . . . 189 B3
Burgess Hill RH15 . . . . 72 F3
Sparrow's Green TN5 . . . . . . 29 F6
Gloucester St BN1, BN2 . . 189 B3
Glovers La TN39 . . . . 157 C7
Glynde Ave
Eastbourne BN22 . . . . 173 E1
Saltdean BN2 . . . . 177 D6
Glynde Cl BN9 . . . . 168 D2
Glynde Gdn BN6 . . . . 163 D6
Glynde Rd BN2 . . . . 164 D6
Glynde Sta BN8 . . . . 147 F6
Glyndebourne Ave BN2 . . 177 C6
Glyndebourne Gdns
TN37 . . . . 136 C6
Glyndley Manor
Cottage Est BN24 . . . . 152 F2
Glyne Ascent TN40 . . . . 157 F5
Glyne Barn Cl TN40 . . . . . . 158 A5
Glyne Dr TN40 . . . . 158 A5
Glyne Gap Sch TN40 . . . . . 158 A5
Glynleigh 17 BN2 . . . . 189 C3
Glynleigh Dr BN26 . . . . 173 C6
Glynleigh Rd BN24 . . . . 153 A1
Glynn Rd BN10 . . . . 167 C1
Glynn Rd W BN10 . . . . 167 C1
Glynn Rise BN10 . . . . 167 B1
Goatham La TN21 . . . . 89 E5
Godden Cl TN31 . . . . 67 B7
Godden Rd BN8 . . . . 76 C7
Goddens Gill TN31 . . . . 67 B7
Godfrey Rd Hastings TN35 . 160 C5
Hove BN3 . . . . 141 D1
Goffs The BN21 . . . . 184 B3
Golby Ct BN10 . . . . 178 A7
Gold La BN10 . . . . 167 C2
Goldbridge Rd BN8, TN22 . 76 E7
Golden Cl BN10 . . . . 73 D3
Golden La BN11 . . . . 167 C2
Golden Miller La BN26 . . . 172 F6
Goldhurst Gn TN36 . . . . . . 116 C5
Golding Rd 1 . . . . 174 F2
Goldland Rd BN1, BN3 . . . 163 E7
Goldsmith Cl BN23 . . . . 174 E3
Goldsmiths Ave 25 D3
Goldsmiths L Ctr TN6 . . . . . 25 D3
Goldstone Cl BN3 . . . . 142 A2
Goldstone Cres BN3 . . . . . 142 A3
Goldstone Ct BN3 . . . . 142 A3
Goldstone Cty Jun Sch
BN3 . . . . 141 E1
Goldstone Ho 4 BN3 . . . . 163 B7
Goldstone La BN3 . . . . 163 B8
Goldstone Rd BN3 . . . . 163 B7
Goldstone Ret Pk BN3 . . . . 141 F1
Goldstone St BN3 . . . . 163 B7
Goldstone Villas BN3 . . . . . 163 B7
Goldstone Way BN3 . . . . . . 142 A2
Golf Dr BN1 . . . . 143 B3
Goods Station Rd TN1 . . . . . 8 B4
Goodtrees La TN6 . . . . 4 B2
Goodwin Cl BN27 . . . . 129 A2
Goodwins The TN7 . . . . 7 F1
Goodwood Cl
Bexhill TN40 . . . . 157 D6
Willingdon BN20 . . . . 173 B2
Goodwood Ct 2 BN3 . . . . 163 D7
Goodwood Way BN2 . . . . . 143 F3

Gooseberry La TN31 . . . . . . 67 A3
Gordon Ave BN43 . . . . 161 A7
Gordon Cl RH16 . . . . 50 E6
Gordon Ho RH15 . . . . 73 C4
Gordon Pl TN39 . . . . 157 B6
Gordon Rd Brighton BN1 . . 142 F2
Burgess Hill RH15 . . . . 73 C4
Buxted TN22 . . . . 56 C3
Crowborough TN6 . . . . 25 F3
Hailsham BN27 . . . . 152 B7
Hastings TN34 . . . . 160 A4
Haywards Heath RH16 . . . . . 50 E6
Portslade-by-Sea BN41 . . . 162 C7
Royal Tunbridge Wells TN4 . . 8 C2
Shoreham-by-Sea BN43 . . . 161 A7
Southwick BN41 . . . . 162 A7
Gore Park Ave BN21 . . . . . . 184 D4
Gore Park Rd BN21 . . . . . . 184 D4
Gorham Ave BN2 . . . . 177 A6
Gorham Cl BN2 . . . . 177 A6
Gorham Ct BN10 . . . . 177 E4
Gorham Way BN10 . . . . 177 A6
Goring Ct BN1 . . . . 143 F5
Gorringe Cl
Lower Willingdon BN20 . . . . 173 A3
Shoreham-by-Sea BN43 . . . 161 D7
Gorringe Dr BN20 . . . . 173 A3
Gorringe Rd BN22 . . . . 185 A4
Gorringe Valley Rd BN20 . 173 A3
Gorse Cl Eastbourne BN20 . 184 B5
Portslade-by-Sea BN41 . . . 140 F4
Gorse Dr BN25 . . . . 180 F6
Gorse Hill TN21 . . . . 59 F1
Gorse Rd BN22 . . . . 185 A4
Gorselands TN33 . . . . 88 E1
Gorses The TN39 . . . . 156 C6
Gorsethorn Way TN35 . . . . 138 C4
Gorseway The TN35 . . . . . . 156 C5
Gosford Way BN26 . . . . 172 F6
Gosse Cl 8 TN38 . . . . 159 B6
Goudhurst Cl BN20 . . . . 174 D1
Gower Rd RH16 . . . . 50 E1
Gows Croft BN7 . . . . 145 E5
Grace Ct BN6 . . . . 97 E5
Gradwell End BN6 . . . . 100 D7
Graffham Cl BN2 . . . . 164 E6
Grafton St BN2 . . . . 189 C1
Graham Ave Brighton BN1 . 142 F5
Portslade-by-Sea BN41 . . . 140 F4
Graham Cl BN41 . . . . 140 F4
Graham Cres BN41 . . . . 140 F4
Grammer Ct BN8 . . . . 75 D7
Grampian Cl
Eastbourne BN23 . . . . 174 C3
Royal Tunbridge Wells TN2 . . 8 B5
Granary Cotts TN33 . . . . . . 112 E4
Grand Ave Bexhill TN40 . . . 158 B5
Hassocks BN6 . . . . 97 F4
Hove BN3 . . . . 163 C6
Seaford BN25 . . . . 180 E2
Grand Avenue Mans 4
BN3 . . . . 163 C6
Grand Cres BN2 . . . . 177 A5
Grand Ct Eastbourne BN21 . 185 A1
10 St Leonards TN37 . . . . 159 C6
Grand Hotel Bldgs BN21 . 185 A1
Grand Junction Rd
BN1, BN2 . . . . 189 B1
Grand Par Brighton BN2 . . 189 B2
Polegate BN26 . . . . 173 B5
St Leonards TN37, TN38 . . 159 C6
Grand Parade Mews BN2 . 189 B2
Grange Ave TN34 . . . . 136 A4
Grange Cl Brighton BN1 . . . 142 E1
Burgess Hill RH15 . . . . 73 C5
Crowborough TN6 . . . . 26 D2
Horam TN21 . . . . 116 A2
Grange Court Dr TN39 . . . 157 B6
Grange Ct
Eastbourne BN20 . . . . 184 F2
Lewes BN7 . . . . 146 C8
6 Haywards Heath RH16 . . . 50 D6
Grange End BN20 . . . . 184 F1
Grange Gdns
Eastbourne BN20 . . . . 184 F2
6 Barcombe Cross BN8 . . . 101 D4
Eastbourne BN21 . . . . 184 F1
Hastings TN34 . . . . 136 E5
Hove BN3 . . . . 162 E8
Lewes BN7 . . . . 146 C8
Rusthall TN4 . . . . 7 C5
Uckfield TN22 . . . . 78 C7
Grange The
6 Barcombe Cross BN8 . . . 101 D4
Saltdean BN2 . . . . 177 D4
Uckfield TN22 . . . . 78 C7
Grangeways BN1 . . . . 142 E5
Granoon Cotts BN20 . . . . . 187 A4
Grantham Bank BN8 . . . . . 101 D4
Grantham Cl BN8 . . . . 100 E7
Grantham Rd BN1 . . . . 143 A1
Grants Hill Ho TN22 . . . . . . 78 C7
Granville Cl
6 Eastbourne BN20 . . . . . . 184 F1
6 Hove BN3 . . . . 163 B7
6 Seaford BN25 . . . . 180 E2
Granville Rd
Eastbourne BN20 . . . . 184 F1
Hove BN3 . . . . 163 B7

Granville Rd continued
Royal Tunbridge Wells TN1 . . 8 C5
Grapelies The 3 BN2 . . . . 164 C5
Grasmere Cl BN43 . . . . 174 B4
Grassington Rd BN20 . . . . 184 F1
Grassmere Ave BN10 . . . . . 177 F4
Grassmere Ct BN10 . . . . . . 178 A8
Gratton Ct TN39 . . . . 157 A3
Gravelye Cl RH16 . . . . 51 B5
Gravelye La
Haywards Heath RH16 . . . . . 51 A4
Haywards Heath RH16 . . . . . 51 B6
Gravett Ct RH15 . . . . 72 F2
Graycoats Dr TN6 . . . . 26 A1
Grays Cots TN33 . . . . 112 F3
Grays Cty Inf Sch BN9 . . . 179 C6
Graystone La TN35 . . . . 137 D3
Grazebrook Cl TN39 . . . . . 156 C4
Great Brooms Rd TN4 . . . . . 8 C8
Great Cliffe Rd BN23 . . . . . 174 E1
Great College St BN2 . . . . 164 C4
Great Courtlands 7 . . . . 7 A3
Great Dixter TN31 . . . . 67 F7
Great Footway TN3 . . . . 6 F3
Great Hall Arc 3 TN1 . . . . . 8 B3
Great Heathmead RH16 . . . 51 A4
Great House Ct 4 RH19 . . . 10 F8
Great Knelle Farm
(Childrens Farm) TN31 . . . 66 F6
Great Oak TN19 . . . . 45 A3
Great Rough BN8 . . . . 76 A6
Great Sanders Ho TN33 . . . 88 D4
Great Walstead Sch RH16 . 51 F4
Great Wilkins BN1 . . . . 144 B5
Greater Paddock BN8 . . . . 124 E6
Greatham Ct BN1 . . . . 142 E6
Grecian Rd TN1 . . . . 8 B2
Greeba Ct 8 TN38 . . . . 159 B6
Green Cl Ringmer BN8 . . . . 124 E6
Green Cl BN42 . . . . 161 E7
Green Field Cl BN42 . . . . . . 161 E8
Green Gate BN10 . . . . 167 C1
Green Gr TN27 . . . . 152 B8
Green Hedges TN32 . . . . . . 63 E4
Green Hedges Ave RH19 . . . 1 D2
Green Hedges Cl RH19 . . . . 1 D2
Green La Bexhill TN40 . . . . 156 D5
Broyle Side BN8 . . . . 103 B1
Crowborough TN6 . . . . 26 C6
Eastbourne BN20 . . . . 184 E2
Heathfield TN21 . . . . 82 B6
Jevington BN26 . . . . 172 C1
Lewes BN7 . . . . 146 C8
Seaford BN25 . . . . 180 E2
Green Mdws RH16 . . . . 51 B8
Green Park TN37 . . . . 74 B4
Green Rd RH17 . . . . 34 B4
Green Ridge BN1 . . . . 142 B5
Green Sq TN5 . . . . 29 F5
Green St BN21 . . . . 184 C4
Green The Blackboys TN22 . 80 A6
Bodiam TN32 . . . . 65 F7
Catsfield TN33 . . . . 133 E8
Ewhurst Green TN32 . . . . . . 66 B5
Frant TN3 . . . . 17 B3
Hailsham BN27 . . . . 129 C2
Langton Green TN3 . . . . 6 A3
Ninfield TN33 . . . . 133 B5
Ringmer BN8 . . . . 124 D5
Rottingdean BN2 . . . . 177 F6
Sedlescombe TN33 . . . . 113 E8
Southwick BN42 . . . . 161 E7
St Leonards TN38 . . . . 159 B8
Green View RH15 . . . . 72 E3
Green Way TN2 . . . . 9 D4
Green Wlk Hailsham BN27 . 129 C1
Seaford BN25 . . . . 181 B2
Green Wlk The BN22 . . . . . 173 B3
Greenacres Brighton BN1 . 142 F1
Peacehaven BN10 . . . . 167 D2
Telscombe Cliffs BN10 . . . . 178 A7
Westfield TN35 . . . . 114 E3
Greenacres Dr
Hailsham BN27 . . . . 152 C7
Ringmer BN8 . . . . 124 D4
Greenacres Way BN27 . . . 152 D8
Greenbank Ave BN2 . . . . . 177 D6
Greene Ct BN7 . . . . 146 B8
Greenfield Cl
Brighton BN1 . . . . 143 A5
Rusthall TN4 . . . . 7 C5
Greenfield Cres BN1 . . . . . 143 F5
Greenfield Dr TN22 . . . . . . 78 C7
Greenfield Rd
Burwash TN19 . . . . 62 C7
Eastbourne BN21 . . . . 184 D4
Greenfields BN27 . . . . 152 D7
Greenfields Cl TN37 . . . . . 136 B6
Greenhall Pk RH17 . . . . 35 A2
Greenhill Way
Haywards Heath RH17 . . . . . 51 A2
Peacehaven BN10 . . . . 167 C2
Greenlands RH15 . . . . 98 B8
Greenlands Dr RH15 . . . . . 98 B8
Greenleaf Gdns BN26 . . . . 173 A8
Greenleas Hove BN3 . . . . . 141 D2
Pembury TN2 . . . . 9 C6
Greenstede Ave RH19 . . . . . 1 F2
Greenway BN20 . . . . 184 B6
Greenway Ct TN39 . . . . 177 A5
Greenways Bexhill TN39 . . 156 F7

Greenways continued
Haywards Heath RH16 . . . . . 50 F6
Ovingdean BN2 . . . . 165 D3
Portslade-by-Sea BN42 . . . 161 A8
Southwick BN42 . . . . 140 F1
Greenways Cnr BN2 . . . . . . 165 D4
Greenways Cres BN43 . . . 140 A1
Greenwell Cl BN25 . . . . 181 A4
Greenwich Rd BN27 . . . . . . 152 D7
Greenwich Way BN10 . . . . 178 C7
Greenwoods La TN21 . . . . . 83 D7
Greggs Wood Rd TN2 . . . . . 8 E7
Gregory Ct 2 BN21 . . . . . . 185 B3
Gregory La BN24 . . . . 174 F5
Gregory Wlk TN43 . . . . 113 E8
Grenada 4 TN39 . . . . 157 A2
Grenada Cl TN39 . . . . 156 D4
Grenham Ct TN35 . . . . 137 C3
Grenville Ho TN6 . . . . 167 D1
Grenville Rd BN24 . . . . 175 C4
Grenville St BN1 . . . . 189 A2
Gresham BN24 . . . . 175 B6
Gresham Cl BN21 . . . . 184 C6
Gresham Way TN38 . . . . . . 159 A8
Gresley Rd TN38 . . . . 135 F5
Greville Rd TN35 . . . . 137 C3
Grey Alders RH16 . . . . 51 B6
Grey Tower Bglws
BN24 . . . . 175 C3
Greyfriars BN3 . . . . 163 D8
Greyfriars Ct BN7 . . . . 123 D1
Greyfriars Pl TN36 . . . . 118 B6
Greyhorses TN39 . . . . 156 B4
Greys Rd BN20 . . . . 184 D3
Greystones Ct TN6 . . . . 25 D4
Grimley Ct 5 TN40 . . . . . . 157 C4
Grinstead La 3 RH19 . . . . . 21 C7
Grinstead Mount 4
BN2 . . . . 164 F5
Grommefield TN3 . . . . 15 C7
Groombridge Hill TN3 . . . . 6 D1
Groombridge Rd TN3 . . . . 15 C8
Groombridge Place Gdns
TN3 . . . . 15 C8
Groombridge Rd TN3 . . . . . 6 A1
Groombridge Sta TN3 . . . . 6 A1
Grosvenor Bridge TN1 . . . . 8 A4
Grosvenor Cl BN26 . . . . . . 172 F5
Grosvenor Cres TN38 . . . . 159 A6
Grosvenor Gdns TN38 . . . . 158 F6
Grosvenor Mans 1 BN3 . . 163 B6
Grosvenor Pk TN1 . . . . 8 A4
Grosvenor Rd
East Grinstead RH19 . . . . . . 1 D1
Royal Tunbridge Wells TN1 . . 8 A4
Seaford BN25 . . . . 180 E4
Grosvenor St BN2 . . . . 189 C2
Grosvenor Wlk TN1 . . . . . . 8 A4
Grove Ave TN1 . . . . 8 A2
Grove Bank 3 BN2 . . . . . . 142 E1
Grove Ct 2 BN3 . . . . 163 C6
Grove Hill Brighton BN2 . . 189 C3
Grove Hill Rd TN1 . . . . 8 B2
Grove La TN11 . . . . 70 C4
Grove Park Sch TN6 . . . . . 25 E1
Grove Rd
Burgess Hill RH15 . . . . 73 B3
Eastbourne BN21 . . . . 184 F2
Hastings TN35 . . . . 137 D4
Seaford BN25 . . . . 180 F3
Grove Sch TN38 . . . . 135 F2
Grove St BN2 . . . . 189 C3
Grove The Battle TN33 . . . 112 F3
Bexhill TN39 . . . . 156 F7
Crowborough TN6 . . . . 25 E1
Eastbourne BN20 . . . . 184 B7
Hailsham BN27 . . . . 152 B6
Haywards Heath RH16 . . . . . 51 B3
Mayfield TN20 . . . . 40 D3
Newhaven BN9 . . . . 168 E2
Pembury TN2 . . . . 9 D8
Rye TN31 . . . . 93 C6
Willingdon BN20 . . . . 172 F3
Grove Villa 8 BN1 . . . . 189 A3
Grovebury BN27 . . . . 152 C7
Grovelands Cl RH15 . . . . . . 72 F1
Grovelands Cty Prim Sch
BN27 . . . . 129 A1
Grovelands Rd BN27 . . . . . 129 A1
Growely La TN21 . . . . 84 A6
Grower St 3 TN1 . . . . 8 B4
Growers End BN8 . . . . 76 D7
Guardian Ct BN26 . . . . 172 F7
Guardswell Pl BN25 . . . . . 180 F3
Guestling Rd BN22 . . . . . . 185 D5
Guestling-Bradshaw
Prim Sch TN35 . . . . 138 A8
Guildford Rd 7 BN1 . . . . . . 8 B3
Guildford St BN1 . . . . 189 A3
Guilford Rd BN1 . . . . 189 A3
Guinness Ct BN9 . . . . 168 E2
Guinness Trust Bglws
BN9 . . . . 168 E2
Guldeford La TN29,TN31 . . 71 F3
Guldeford Lane Cnr
TN31 . . . . 71 D2
Guldeford Rd TN31 . . . . 93 E7
Gun Gdn TN31 . . . . 93 C6
Gun Rd TN35 . . . . 160 C5
Gwent Ct 2 BN2 . . . . 185 C4
Gwydir Mans 3 BN1 . . . . 163 D6
Gwyneth Gr TN40 . . . . 157 F7

H

Hackenden Cl RH19 . . . . 2 A4
Hackenden Cotts RH19 . . . . 2 A4
Hackenden La RH19 . . . . . . 2 A4
Hackhurst La BN27 . . . . 128 F8
Hackhurst Lane Ind Est
BN27 . . . . 128 E8
Hackwood TN32 . . . . 64 D6
Haddington Cl BN3 . . . . 163 C6
Haddington St 11 BN3 . . . 163 C7
Hadley Ct Polegate BN26 . . 173 B5
Royal Tunbridge Wells TN4 . . 7 F1
Hadley Ho 4 BN21 . . . . 185 A3
Hadlow Ave BN23 . . . . 174 E3
Hadlow Ct TN39 . . . . 156 C4
Hadlow Down Rd TN6 . . . . . 3 A3
Hadlow La TN21 . . . . 84 B6
Hadrian Gdns TN37 . . . . . . 136 C3
Haig Ave BN1 . . . . 142 F2
Hailsham Ave BN2 . . . . 164 E5
Hailsham Com Coll BN27 . 152 A6
Hailsham Ct 2 TN40 . . . . . 157 C5
Hailsham Rd
Heathfield TN21 . . . . 82 E7
Herstmonceux BN27 . . . . . . 131 A6
Polegate BN26 . . . . 173 E7
Stone Cross BN24,BN26 . . 173 A5
Hairpin Croft BN10 . . . . 167 C5
Half Mile Dro BN8 . . . . 122 A5
Hall La TN22 . . . . 56 A2
Hall's Grove Rd TN2 . . . . . . 4 A8
Hall's Hole Rd TN2 . . . . 9 E7
Halland Cl BN23 . . . . 174 E2
Halland Rd BN2 . . . . 164 D6
Hallands The RH15 . . . . 73 C3
Hallett Rd BN2 . . . . 164 D6
Halley Pk BN27 . . . . 152 D8
Halley Rd Cade Street TN21 . 82 D3
Warbling BN27 . . . . 131 F8
Halls Cotts TN5 . . . . 29 F2
Hallyburton Rd BN3 . . . . . . 162 F8
Halsford Croft RH19 . . . . . . 1 C1
Halsford Gn RH19 . . . . 1 C1
Halsford La RH19 . . . . 1 C1
Halsford Park Cty Prim Sch
RH19 . . . . 1 C1
Halsford Park Rd RH19 . . . 1 D1
Halton Cres TN34 . . . . 160 A5
Halton Pl TN34 . . . . 160 A5
Halton Rd BN22 . . . . 185 C5
Halton Shaws BN6 . . . . 98 F6
Halton Terr TN34 . . . . 160 A5
Ham Bsns Ctr BN43 . . . . . . 161 C4
Ham La Burwash TN19 . . . . . 62 C7
Lewes BN7 . . . . 146 C8
Ringmer BN8 . . . . 124 E6
Scaynes Hill RH17 . . . . 52 A7
Ham Rd BN43 . . . . 161 C4
Hamble Rd BN20 . . . . 174 C2
Hambleton Cl BN23 . . . . . . 174 C3
Hambrook RH15 . . . . 72 D7
Hamelsham Ct BN27 . . . . . 152 C6
Hamilton Cl BN41 . . . . 141 A4
Hamilton Ct Brighton BN2 . 165 F5
Royal Tunbridge Wells TN4 . . 8 A8
Hamilton Gdns TN35 . . . . . 137 C3
Hamilton Ho
6 Eastbourne BN21 . . . . . . 185 A3
Royal Tunbridge Wells TN4 . . 8 A8
Seaford BN27 . . . . 180 E4
Hamilton Lodge Sch
BN2 . . . . 164 F6
Hamilton Mans 8 BN3 . . . 163 A6
Hamilton Rd BN1 . . . . 189 A4
Hamilton Terr TN39 . . . . . . 152 B8
Hamlands La BN22 . . . . 172 F1
Hamlin's Cnr BN6 . . . . 72 A1
Hammer La BN27,TN21 . . . 102 A8
Hammerwood Pk RH19 . . . . 3 C1
Hammerwood Rd RH19 . . . . 3 D2
Hammonds Dr BN23 . . . . . . 185 A8
Hammonds Gardens RH15 . 72 A1
Hammonds Ridge RH15 . . . 72 A1
Hampden Ave BN22 . . . . . . 173 C1
Hampden Ct TN33 . . . . 113 E8
Hampden Gdns BN9 . . . . . . 168 D6
Hampden Park
Cty Inf Sch BN22 . . . . . . 173 C1
Hampden Park Sch BN22 . 173 B1
Hampden Park Sports Ctr
BN22 . . . . 173 C1
Hampden Park Sta BN22 . 173 C1
Hampden Rd BN2 . . . . 164 E6
Hampden Terr 6 BN22 . . . 185 C4
Hampshire Ct
Brighton BN2 . . . . 189 C3
6 Eastbourne BN21 . . . . . . 185 A1
Hampstead Rd BN1 . . . . . . 142 F2
Hampton Pl BN1 . . . . 189 A2
Hampton St 6 BN1 . . . . . . 189 A2
Hampton Terr 7 BN1 . . . . 163 A5
Hampton Way RH19 . . . . . . 1 D1
Hamsey Cl Brighton BN2 . . 164 F5
Eastbourne BN20 . . . . 184 B7
Hamsey Cres BN7 . . . . 123 D1
Hamsey Cty Prim Sch
BN8 . . . . 123 F6
Hamsey La
Cooksbridge BN8 . . . . 123 F3
Seaford BN25 . . . . 181 A2
Hamsey Rd Saltdean BN2 . 177 D6

sey Rd *continued*
pthorne RH19 21 A6
shaw Ct BN22 184 F8
sland RH17 33 C4
oury La RH16 51 A5
oury Park Sports Stad
6 51 A5
ing Birch La TN21 81 D1
leton Cl BN3 141 D2
leton
Inf & Jun Sch BN3 141 E2
leton Gdns BN3 141 D1
leton La
e BN3, BN41 141 C2
slade-by-Sea BN41 141 B2
leton Manor Cl
141 D2
gleton Rd BN3 141 E2
gleton Valley Dr
141 D4
leton Way BN3 141 D3
kham Cty Prim Sch
4 174 B8
kham Hall Rd BN24 174 D7
kham Rd BN24 174 B6
kham St BN24 174 B8
ye La RH17 50 B8
nington Pl BN6 97 A7
over Cl Bexhill TN40 157 C5
ford BN25 180 B6
over Cres BN2 189 C4
over Ct Brighton BN2 189 C4
bourne BN21 184 D5
wards Heath RH16 50 D4
over Mews BN2 189 C4
over Rd
tbourne BN22 185 C4
al Tunbridge Wells TN1 8 A4
over St BN2 189 C4
over Terr BN2 189 C4
son Rd BN9 179 C6
bour Barn TN36 118 B6
bour Ct BN42 161 F7
bour Farm TN36 118 B6
bour Rd TN31 93 D4
bour View Cl BN25 180 B6
bour View Rd BN9 179 B5
bour Way
reham-by-Sea BN43 161 B6
eonards TN38 135 E7
bour's Yd TN33 112 E4
court Cl TN22 78 C6
court Rd TN22 78 D6
ling Ave BN22 185 B6
rada Rise TN34 136 E3
dwick Rd
tbourne BN21 185 A2
e BN3 141 E3
dwick Way BN3 141 E3
dwicke Rd TN34 160 B6
dy Dr BN23 185 F6
e Way TN37 136 C5
ebeating Cl BN27 129 C2
ebeating Cres BN27 129 C2
ebeating Dr BN27 129 C2
ebeating Gdns BN27 129 C2
ebeating La BN27 129 D1
ebell Cl BN23 174 C3
ebell Dr BN41 141 A3
ecombe Rd TN6 37 F8
ecombe Rise TN6 37 F8
emere Hall Gdns TN19 44 E2
emere Hill TN19 44 D2
escroft TN2 16 F7
ewood Cl TN39 157 A3
ewood Ct 8 BN3 163 C6
field Cl BN9 168 F2
gate Cl TN2 16 F8
greaves Rd BN23 174 A1
son Rd BN25 181 A4
kness Dr TN34 137 B5
ands Cl RH16 50 C6
ands Cty Prim Sch
wards Heath RH16 50 D7
field TN22 78 D5
ands Rd RH16 50 D6
equin Gdns TN37 136 A6
equin La TN6 37 E8
equin Pl TN6 37 E8
ey La TN21 82 A6
ey Shute Rd TN38 158 E7
ey Way TN38 158 E6
mans Dr RH19 2 B1
mans Mead RH19 2 B1
mers Hay Rd BN27 129 B1
mers Hill BN8 76 C7
mony St TN4 7 D4
mony Wood TN34 136 F5
msworth Cres BN3 141 E3
old Cl BN24 175 F7
old Dr BN23 185 F8
old Ho TN2 8 C7
old Mews 2 TN38 159 C6
old Pl TN34 159 F7
old Rd TN35 160 C5
old Terr TN33 112 F3
pers Rd BN9 179 C7
rier La TN33 112 F4
riers Ct BN27 152 D7
ries Rd TN2 8 E7
rington Ct BN1 142 E2
rington Mans BN1 142 E2
rington Pl BN1 143 B2
rington Rd BN1 142 E2
rington Villas BN1 142 F2
ris Ct BN21 185 A3
risons La BN8 124 E5
row Cl BN25 181 A4
Harrow La TN37 136 B5
Hart Cl TN22 78 A7
Hartfield Ave BN1 143 A5
Hartfield La BN21 184 F4
Hartfield Mdw TN38 135 D3
Hartfield Rd Bexhill TN39 156 E2
Cowden TN8 4 C6
Eastbourne BN21 184 F3
Forest Row RH18 12 B2
Saltdean BN2 177 D5
Seaford BN25 181 A3
Harting Combe TN38 159 B8
Hartington Mansions
BN21 185 A2
Hartington Pl
Brighton BN2 164 C8
Eastbourne BN21 185 A2
Hartington Rd BN2 164 C8
Hartington Terr BN2 164 C8
Hartington Villas BN3 163 B8
Hartwood Lodge 6
TN40 157 C4
Harvard Cl BN7 123 C3
Harvard Rd BN8 124 D5
Harvest Cl Lindfield RH16 51 B7
Telscombe Cliffs BN10 167 B2
Harvest Hill RH19 10 E8
Harvest Way TN37 136 C5
Harvesters RH16 50 D2
Harvey Cl TN38 135 F4
Harvey's La BN8,TN22 103 D4
Harveys Way BN7 123 E1
Harvington Bsns Pk
BN22 184 F8
Harwood Cl BN23 185 E7
Harwoods Cl 3 RH19 10 F7
Harwoods La RH19 10 F7
Haslam Cres TN40 157 F6
Hasletts Cl TN1 8 B6
Hassock Cl BN23 173 F4
Hassocks Cty Inf Sch BN6 97 F4
Hassocks Lodge BN6 97 F3
Hassocks Rd BN6 97 B5
Hassocks Sta BN6 97 E4
Hastings Ave BN25 181 C5
Hastings Castle TN34 160 A4
Hastings Cl BN26 173 B7
Hastings Coll of Arts
& Tech TN38 159 B6
Hastings Mus & Art Gall
TN34 159 E7
Hastings Mus
of Local History TN34 160 A4
Hastings Rd Battle TN33 113 B2
Bexhill TN40 157 E5
Bexhill TN40 157 F5
Brighton BN2 164 C8
Newenden TN17,TN18 48 C6
Pembury TN2 9 D6
Pembury TN2 9 F5
The Moor TN18 45 F6
Hastings Sea Life Ctr
TN34 160 B3
Hastings Sports Ctr
TN34 159 D8
Hastings Sta TN34 159 E8
Hatch End RH18 11 F2
Hatchgate Cl RH17 50 A6
Hatchgate La RH17 50 A6
Hatfield Ct 13 BN3 163 C6
Hatherley Rd TN37 159 C7
Havana Ct 10 BN23 185 F8
Havelock Rd Bexhill TN40 157 C6
Brighton BN1 142 F1
Eastbourne BN22 185 B4
Hastings TN34 159 F7
Haven Brow BN25 181 A4
Haven Cl Beachlands BN24 175 E6
Lower Willingdon BN22 173 B3
Haven Rd TN38 158 D6
Havering Cl TN2 8 F6
Hawkenbury Cl TN2 8 D2
Hawkenbury Mead TN2 8 D1
Hawkenbury Rd TN2, TN3 8 E1
Hawkenbury Way BN7 123 A1
Hawkes Farm
Cty Prim Sch BN27 129 B3
Hawkhurst CE Prim Sch
TN18 45 F8
Hawkhurst Cl BN23 174 D2
Hawkhurst Pl BN1 143 D6
Hawkhurst Rd
Brighton BN1 143 D6
Flimwell TN5,TN18 32 E2
Hawkhurst Way TN39 156 E3
Hawkins Cl BN43 140 C1
Hawkins Cres BN43 140 D2
Hawkins Rd BN43 140 D1
Hawkins Way BN27 152 B8
Hawks Farm Cl BN27 129 B2
Hawks Rd BN27 129 B2
Hawks Town Cres BN27 129 C2
Hawksbridge Cl BN22 173 C3
Hawkstown Cl BN27 129 B3
Hawkstown Gdns BN27 129 B3
Hawkstown View BN27 129 B3
Hawkswood Dr BN27 129 C3
Hawkswood Rd BN27 129 C3
Hawth Cl BN25 180 C4
Hawth Cres BN25 180 C4
Hawth Gr BN25 180 C4
Hawth Hill BN25 180 C5
Hawth Park Rd BN25 180 C4
Hawth Pl BN25 180 C4
Hawth Rise BN25 180 C5
Hawth Valley Ct 1 BN25 180 C4
Hawth Way BN25 180 D4
Hawthorn Ave TN39 156 D3
Hawthorn Bank BN2 143 F4
Hawthorn Cl
Burgess Hill RH15 73 D5
Saltdean BN2 177 C6
Hawthorn Ct BN26 173 B6
Hawthorn Rd
Eastbourne BN23 185 C7
Hastings TN35 160 D6
Hawthorn Rise BN9 179 B7
Hawthorn Way BN41 141 A3
Hawthorn Wlk TN2 8 E8
Hawthorne Cl TN21 82 B6
Hawthornes The TN31 90 B4
Hawthorns The
Burgess Hill RH15 73 A5
Hailsham BN27 152 A7
Hawthylands Cres BN27 129 B2
Hawthylands Dr BN27 129 B2
Hawthylands Rd BN27 129 B2
Haybourne Cl BN2 164 E7
Haybourne Rd BN2 164 E7
Hayes Cl
Portslade-by-Sea BN41 162 C8
Ringmer BN8 124 D5
Hayes La TN31 91 C5
Hayes Plat TN31 67 C5
Hayland Gn BN27 129 C1
Haylind Rd RH16 51 B5
Haystoun Cl BN22 173 C2
Haystoun Pk BN22 173 C2
Hayward Rd BN7 123 A3
Haywards Heath Coll
RH16 50 D6
Haywards Heath Sta RH16 50 E6
Haywards Rd
Brighton BN1 143 A6
Haywards Heath RH16 50 E3
Haywood Way TN35 137 C4
Hazel Bank 3 BN2 189 C4
Hazel Cl Newhaven BN9 179 B7
Portslade-by-Sea BN41 141 C3
Hazel Court Sch BN23 174 B3
Hazel Court Sec Sch
BN23 174 A3
Hazel Ct TN35 136 F6
Hazel Gr Burgess Hill RH15 73 B1
Lower Willingdon BN20 173 A3
Hazelbank TN3 6 F3
Hazeldene BN25 181 B3
Hazeldene Meads BN1 142 D3
Hazeledene La BN8 75 F7
Hazelgrove Gdns 8 RH16 50 E4
Hazelgrove Rd RH16 50 E4
Hazelholt BN41 140 F3
Hazelwood BN1 142 D3
Hazelwood Ave BN22 173 D4
Hazelwood Cl
Bexhill TN39 156 C3
Royal Tunbridge Wells TN2 8 E8
Hazelwood Cotts TN5 31 D1
Hazelwood Gdns TN37 136 D5
Hazleden Cross RH19 10 B6
Headland Ave BN25 181 A3
Headlands Cl BN10 178 E7
Headway Ct TN4 7 B4
Heansill La TN18 45 E8
Heath Cl 9 RH16 50 E4
Heath Ct RH16 50 E5
Heath Hill Ave BN2 144 A2
Heath Rd RH16 50 E5
Heath Sq RH16 50 D5
Heathcote Dr RH19 1 C2
Heathdown Cl BN10 167 D2
Heather Bank RH16 50 C5
Heather Cl BN23 174 B3
Heather Ct 8 BN1 163 E6
Heather Way TN35 138 F4
Heather Wlk TN6 26 D1
Heatherdune Rd TN39 157 A5
Heathfield Ave BN2 177 D6
Heathfield CE Prim Sch
TN21 82 D6
Heathfield Cl TN34 136 F5
Heathfield Cres BN41 140 F3
Heathfield Dr BN41 140 F4
Heathfield Gdns TN32 64 B3
Heathfield L Ctr TN21 82 D7
Heathfield Rd BN25 180 F3
Heathfield Sch
& Com Coll TN21 82 E7
Heathfields TN2 8 D4
Heathlands TN35 114 E3
Heathy Brow BN10 167 B1
Heavegate Rd TN6 37 C8
Heaven Farm RH17 34 B1
Hectors La RH19 11 C7
Heighton Cl TN39 156 D3
Heighton Cres BN9 168 D2
Heighton Rd BN9 168 E2
Heights The Brighton BN1 142 B5
Hastings TN35 137 E4
6 Haywards Heath RH16 50 E4
Helena Cl BN41 141 C2
Helena Ct TN38 159 B7
Helena Rd BN2 144 C1
Helensdene Wlk TN37 159 D8
Helenswood Sch
(Lower) TN37 136 D6
Helenswood Sch
(Upper) TN34 137 B4
Hellingly Cl BN2 164 F5
Hellingly Cty Prim Sch
BN27 128 F5
Helvellyn Dr BN23 174 C4
Hempstead Gdns TN22 78 D7
Hempstead La
Hailsham BN27 128 F1
Uckfield TN22 78 D7
Hempstead La *continued*
Uckfield TN22 78 E8
Hempstead Rd
Saltdean BN2 166 D3
Uckfield TN22 78 C7
Hempstead Rise TN22 78 C7
Hemsley Ho TN21 81 F8
Henderson Cl TN34 136 F3
Hendon St BN2 164 D5
Henfield Cl BN2 164 F5
Henfield Rd BN22 173 E2
Henfield Way BN3 141 F3
Henge Way BN41 141 B2
Hengist Cl BN23 185 F8
Henleaze BN21 184 E3
Henley Cl
Royal Tunbridge Wells TN2 8 C4
Rye TN31 93 A6
Henley Ct BN2 164 F4
Henley Rd BN2 164 F4
Henley's Hill BN27 131 F7
Henry Burt Way RH15 72 E1
Henry Terr 3 TN34 160 B4
Henwood Green Rd
TN12, TN2 9 E6
Henwoods Cres TN2 9 D6
Henwoods Mount TN2 9 E6
Herbert Rd BN1 142 F2
Herbrand Wlk TN39 156 A1
Hereford Ct
15 Brighton BN2 189 C2
1 Eastbourne BN23 174 E1
15 Hove BN3 163 C7
Hereford St BN2 164 C5
Hereward Rd BN23 185 F8
Hereward Way BN7 123 D3
Hermitage La RH19 10 F8
Hermitage Rd RH19 1 D3
Hermitage The TN34 159 E8
Herne Down TN6 38 A7
Herne Jun Sch TN6 37 F8
Herne Rd TN6 37 F8
Heron Cl Eastbourne BN23 174 C2
St Leonards TN38 158 E8
Uckfield TN22 78 D5
Heron Cotts TN18 48 D3
Heron Ct BN27 152 D7
Heron Pl RH19 10 F8
Heron Ridge BN26 173 B6
Heron's Tye BN6 97 F3
Herons Dale Sch BN43 140 C1
Herons The BN43 161 A8
Herons Way TN2 9 E8
Heronsdale Rd BN2 165 F8
Herontye Dr RH19 11 A8
Herring's Rd TN21,TN33 109 F8
Herstmonceux Castle
Gdns BN27 131 A1
Herstmonceux
CE Prim Sch BN27 130 E6
Hertford Cl TN38 136 A4
Hertford Cty Inf Sch BN1 143 B2
Hertford Cty Jun Sch
BN1 143 C2
Hertford Rd BN1 143 B2
Heskett Pk TN2 9 E6
Hestingas Plat 2 TN34 160 B4
Heston Ave BN1 142 F7
Hever Cl BN23 174 D2
Hever Cres TN39 156 F5
Heyworth Cl BN2 165 F8
Heyworth Cty Prim Sch
RH16 50 F4
Hickling Cl BN23 174 B4
Hickman Way TN34 136 D4
Hickman's Cl RH16 51 B8
Hickman's La RH16 51 A8
Hidden Spring Vineyard
TN21 107 B8
Hide Hollow BN23 174 D3
Hligglers Cl TN22 56 C3
High Bank TN35 137 C3
High Bank Cl TN35 160 C6
High Beach Ho BN25 180 C3
High Beech Cl TN37 135 F6
High Beech Country Club
The TN37 135 F6
High Beech La RH16 50 F8
High Beeches TN2 8 D6
High Branches TN39 156 E4
High Broom Ind Pk TN2 8 C8
High Broom La TN6 37 E7
High Broom Rd TN6 37 F7
High Brooms Rd TN4 8 C7
High Brooms Sta TN4 8 C7
High Cl East Dean BN20 183 C2
Portslade-by-Sea BN41 141 A1
High Cross Fields TN6 25 F3
High Fords TN36 116 E5
High Fords Cl TN36 116 E5
High Heath La BN6 72 B4
High Hurst Cl BN8 76 D7
High Hurstwood
CE Prim Sch TN22 37 A1
High Mdw TN31 67 B7
High Park Ave BN3 141 E3
High Pk TN31 67 A7
High Point RH16 51 A3
High Rocks TN3 7 B1
High Rocks La TN3, TN4 7 C1
High Sh Hall The 15
BN25 180 E2
High St Alfriston BN26 171 A2
Barcombe Cross BN8 101 E4
Battle TN33 112 D4
Bexhill TN40 157 D5
Brighton BN2 189 C2
Burwash TN19 62 A6
High St *continued*
Buxted TN22 56 C3
Cowden TN8 4 B5
Crowborough TN6 25 F3
Ditchling BN6 98 D3
East Grinstead RH19 10 F8
East Hoathly BN8 105 A5
Eastbourne BN21 184 E3
Etchingham TN19 44 C1
Flimwell TN5 32 C3
Frant TN3 17 C4
Hailsham BN27 152 C8
Hartfield TN7 13 D4
Hastings TN34 160 B4
Heathfield TN21 82 A8
Hurstpierpoint BN6 97 A5
Lamberhurst TN3 20 B5
Lewes BN7 123 C1
Lindfield RH16 51 B8
Maresfield TN22 55 B4
Mayfield TN20 40 B2
Newhaven BN9 179 C7
Newick BN8 76 D7
Ninfield TN33 133 A6
Nutley TN22 35 C3
Pembury TN2 9 C6
Pevensey BN24 175 B6
Polegate BN26 173 A6
Portslade-by-Sea BN41 141 A1
Robertsbridge TN32 64 B4
Rotherfield TN6 39 B8
Rottingdean BN2 165 F1
Royal Tunbridge Wells TN1 8 A2
Rye TN31 93 C5
Seaford BN25 180 E2
Ticehurst TN5 31 C1
Uckfield TN22 78 C6
Wadhurst TN5 29 F4
Westham BN24 175 A6
Winchelsea TN36 117 F7
High St (School Hill) TN22 55 B4
High Trees
3 Eastbourne BN21 184 F4
Haywards Heath RH16 50 F5
Uckfield TN22 78 C5
High View TN21 82 B8
High View Rd TN21 59 E1
High Wickham TN35 160 B5
High Woods La TN2 9 B3
Higham Gdns TN35 138 A8
Higham La TN31 67 A7
Highbank BN1 142 C5
Highbridge La BN7 100 B4
Highbrook Cl BN2 143 D3
Highcliff Ct BN2 177 A5
Highcombe BN20 188 D7
Highcroft Cres TN21 82 A7
Highcroft Lodge BN1 163 E8
Highcroft Rd RH19 21 A6
Highcroft Villas BN1, BN3 163 E8
Highden 2 BN2 164 C6
Highdown BN41, BN42 140 F1
Highdown Cl BN42 140 F1
Highdown Cotts TN17 20 F3
Highdown Ct BN1 142 E3
Highdown Rd
Hove BN1, BN3 163 E7
Lewes BN7 123 A2
Highfield RH17 33 C4
Highfield Cl TN2 9 D6
Highfield Cres BN1 143 A5
Highfield Ct 7 RH16 50 E4
Highfield Cty Jun Sch
BN22 174 A1
Highfield Dr
Hurstpierpoint BN6 97 C5
St Leonards TN38 135 D3
Highfield Gdns TN39 157 C7
Highfield Ind Est N BN23 174 A1
Highfield Ind Est S BN23 174 A1
Highfield Rd
East Grinstead RH19 1 D3
Horam TN21 106 F7
Royal Tunbridge Wells TN4 8 C7
Highfields Brighton BN1 143 E5
Burwash TN19 62 A6
Forest Row RH18 11 F2
Rye TN31 93 B7
Highgate Flats TN6 27 B1
Highgate Rd RH18 11 F1
Highgrove Battle TN33 112 B4
Royal Tunbridge Wells TN2 17 A8
Highland Ct RH16 50 E4
Highland Grange TN6 25 E3
Highland Lodge BN21 184 F4
Highland Rd RH16 50 F3
Highlands TN2 8 D7
Highlands Ave TN22 78 D4
Highlands Cl Bexhill TN39 156 F7
Crowborough TN6 25 E3
Keymer BN6 98 A3
Highlands Ct TN6 25 E3
Highlands Dr
Burgess Hill RH15 73 A4
St Leonards TN38 159 B7
Highlands Gdns TN38 159 B7
Highlands Mews 2 TN38 159 B6
Highlands Rd
Portslade-by-Sea BN41 141 B1
Seaford BN25 180 F3
Highlands The
Bexhill TN39 156 F7
Cuckfield RH17 50 A8
Highlea Cl TN37 136 C5
Highleigh 7 BN2 189 C3

Highsted Pl BN10 ....167 D2
Highview Ave N BN1 ......142 E6
Highview Ave S BN1 ......142 E6
Highview Cl
  St Leonards TN37 ....136 D5
  Windmill Hill BN27 ....131 B5
Highview Ct BN20 ....184 F1
Highview La TN22 ....78 D4
Highview Rd Brighton BN1 .142 E6
  Telscombe Cliffs BN10 ....177 F4
Highview Way BN1 ....142 E6
Highwater View TN37 ......135 F7
Highway Cl BN2 ....143 D2
Highway The
  Brighton BN2 ....143 D2
  Brighton BN2 ....143 D3
  Newhaven BN10, BN9 ......179 A6
Highways BN41 ....141 D2
Highwoods Ave TN39 ......156 C6
Highwoods Ct TN39 ....156 E5
Hiham Bglws TN36 ....117 E7
Hiham Gn TN36 ....117 E7
Hilary Cl BN26 ....172 F5
Hilary Lodge 2 BN42 .....164 C5
Hilbert Cl TN2 ....8 C5
Hilders Farm Cl TN6 ....26 B1
Hilgrove Rd BN2 ....166 D3
Hill Brow BN3 ....142 B3
Hill Cl TN6 ....25 E1
Hill Crest Dormans Park RH19 .1 E6
  Royal Tunbridge Wells TN4 ..8 B8
Hill Crest Ct BN9 ....179 C6
Hill Crest Rd BN9 ....179 D6
Hill Dr BN3 ....142 B3
Hill Farm Way
  BN42, BN43 ....140 E2
Hill Mead TN22 ....35 C4
Hill Rd Eastbourne BN20 .184 B5
  Fairlight TN35 ....138 C4
  Lewes BN7 ....123 B2
  Newhaven BN9 ....168 F2
  Saltdean BN2 ....177 B5
Hill Rise Newhaven BN9 ...168 F2
  Seaford BN25 ....180 C5
Hill Side BN9 ....179 D7
Hill St Hastings TN34 .....160 A4
  Royal Tunbridge Wells TN1 ..8 B5
Hill Top BN1 ....140 E2
Hill Top Cl BN41 ....140 F2
Hill View Rd TN4 ....7 C4
Hillary Cl RH19 ....2 C2
Hillbank Cl BN41 ....140 F3
Hillbert Rd TN2 ....8 C5
Hillborough Cl TN39 ....156 C6
Hillbrow (Brighton Univ)
  BN20 ....184 E1
Hillbrow Rd BN1 ....142 D4
Hillbury Gdns TN5 ....31 D1
Hillcrest Brighton BN1 .....142 C5
  Rye TN31 ....93 B7
Hillcrest Ave TN39 ....157 A6
Hillcrest Cl RH17 ....51 F3
Hillcrest Ct BN1 ....142 C5
Hillcrest Dr TN2 ....8 D7
Hillcrest La RH17 ....51 F3
Hillcrest Sch TN35 ....137 C5
Hillcroft BN41 ....140 F2
Hillgarth TN4 ....8 A8
Hillman Cl BN7 ....123 E1
Hillrise TN6 ....26 B2
Hillside Brighton BN2 .....143 E2
  Forest Row RH18 ....11 E3
  Friston BN20 ....183 D1
  Mayfield TN20 ....40 B2
  Portslade-by-Sea BN41 ...141 C1
  Southwick BN42 ....140 F1
Hillside Ave BN25 ....181 C5
Hillside Cl RH19 ....1 E3
Hillside Cotts TN5 ....30 B8
Hillside Dr TN21 ....149 B6
Hillside Rd Bexhill TN40 ..157 C5
  Hastings, Silverhill
  Park TN34 ....136 C5
  Hastings, St Helen's
  Wood TN34 ....136 E3
Hillside Sch BN41 ....141 B2
Hillside Way Brighton,
  Moulsecoomb BN2 ....143 C2
  Brighton, Westdene BN1 ..142 C4
Hillside Wlk RH17 ....50 C6
Hilltop Dr TN31 ....93 B7
Hillview Rd BN2 ....165 B8
Hillyfield BN7 ....146 B8
Hillyglen Ct TN34 ....159 E8
Hindleap Warren
  Activity Ctr RH18 ....22 D5
Hindover Cres BN25 ......181 A4
Hindover Rd BN25 ....181 A4
Hinton Cl BN1 ....143 C2
Hither Chantlers TN3 ....7 A2
Hoad Rd BN22 ....185 B4
Hoad's Wood Rd TN34 ...137 A3
Hoadleys La TN6 ....25 D5
Hoadswood Cross TN21 ...84 B2
Hoath Hill TN22 ....87 C5
Hoathdown Ave BN9 ......179 A7
Hobbs La TN31 ....68 D6
Hoblands RH16 ....51 B4
Hobney Rise BN24 ....174 F5
Hockington La BN27 ......173 B4
Hodcombe Cl BN23 ....174 F4
Hoddern Ave BN10 ....178 B8
Hoddern Cty Jun Sch
  BN10 ....178 B8
Hodshrove La BN2 ....143 E3

Hodshrove Pl BN2 ....143 E3
Hodshrove Rd BN2 ....143 E3
Hoe The TN37 ....136 B6
Hogarth Ho TN38 ....159 A8
Hogarth Rd
  Eastbourne BN23 ....174 D1
  Hove BN3 ....162 F7
Hoghole La TN3 ....19 F2
Hogs Edge BN2 ....144 A2
Hogtrough La TN36 ......117 E7
Holbrook Cl BN20 ....188 E8
Holden Park Rd TN4 ....7 A6
Holdings The
  Kingston near Lewes BN7 .145 F5
  Upper Wellingham BN8 ..124 B7
Hole Farm Cl TN34 ......136 E2
Hollamby Pk BN27 ....152 D7
Holland Ave TN39 ....156 C4
Holland Mews BN3 ......163 D5
Holland Rd BN3 ....163 D6
Holland St BN2 ....189 C3
Hollands Way RH19 ....2 A4
Hollier's Hill TN40 ....157 C6
Hollies The 40 A2
Hollin Cl TN4 ....7 C4
Hollingbourne Ct 2 BN2 .164 E4
Hollingbury Copse BN1 ..143 A4
Hollingbury Cres BN1 ....143 A2
Hollingbury Ind Est BN1 .143 C7
Hollingbury Park Ave
  BN1 ....143 A2
Hollingbury Rd BN1 ......143 B3
Hollingbury Rise BN1 ...143 B2
Hollingbury Rise W BN1 .143 A3
Hollingbury Terr BN1 ....143 B2
Hollingdean La BN1 ......164 B8
Hollingdean Rd BN2 ......164 B8
Hollingdean St BN1 ....143 B1
Hollingdean Terr BN1 ....143 B2
Hollinghurst Cl TN37 .....136 B5
Hollinghurst Rd TN37 ....136 B4
Hollington Cl TN38 ....159 B8
Hollington Cty Inf Sch
  TN38 ....136 A4
Hollington Cty Jun Sch
  TN38 ....136 A4
Hollington Old La TN38 ..136 A4
Hollington Park Cl TN38 .136 A1
Hollington Park Rd TN38 .136 A1
Hollow La Blackboys TN22 .80 B4
  Dormansland RH19, RH7 ...2 D6
Hollow The RH16 ....51 B5
Holly Bank 3 BN2 ....189 C5
Holly Bank Ct TN6 ....26 B2
Holly Cl Bexhill TN39 .....156 C6
  Brighton BN1 ....142 E3
  Hailsham BN27 ....152 B6
  Heathfield TN21 ....82 A6
Holly Ct TN6 ....25 E2
Holly Dr TN21 ....82 A6
Holly Rd RH16 ....51 A3
Hollybank Gdns TN38 ...136 B1
Hollycroft BN27 ....100 A3
Hollydene Rd TN5 ....29 D6
Hollyshaw Cl TN2 ....8 C2
Hollywood Cl TN16 ....50 E5
Holm Oak Cl TN33 ....156 E3
Holmbush Cl
  Haywards Heath RH16 ....50 E2
  Shoreham-by-Sea BN43 ..140 D2
Holmbush Ct 3 BN41 ...161 C8
Holmbush Cty Fst Sch
  BN43 ....140 D1
Holmbush Way
  BN42, BN43 ....140 D1
Holmdale Rd BN9 ....169 A1
Holmbury Ho 1 BN3 ....159 E7
Holmes Ave BN3 ....141 F1
Holmes Cl BN25 ....180 A6
Holmes Farm Cotts TN39 .156 A8
Holmes Hill Cotts BN8 ..127 C6
Holmesdale Cl TN5 ....29 E5
Holmesdale Ct TN34 ....159 E8
Holmesdale Gdns TN34 .159 E7
Holmesdale Rd
  Bexhill TN39 ....157 A4
  Burgess Hill RH15 ....73 A1
Holmewood Ho TN3 ......7 A2
Holmewood Rd TN4 ......8 C7
Holmewood Ridge TN6 ...6 A3
Holmhurst Cl TN4 ....7 F4
Holmhurst La TN37 ......136 B5
Holmstead BN2 ....189 C4
Holmwood Cl BN6 ....97 F4
Holt Lodge 1 BN2 ....189 C4
Holtt The Burgess Hill RH15 .73 C2
  Hailsham BN27 ....152 A6
  Seaford BN25 ....180 F5
Holters Way BN25 ....180 F5
Holton Hill BN2 ....165 E7
Holtview Rd BN2 ....165 B8
Holtye Ave RH19 ....2 A3
Holtye Golf Club TN8 ......3 F3
Holtye Rd RH19 ....1 E3
Holy Cross CE Prim Sch
  TN22 ....87 C6
Holyhead Cl BN27 ....129 A1
Holyrood RH19 ....11 A8
Holywell Cl BN20 ....188 E7
Holywell Rd BN20 ....188 E7
Holywell Wlk BN27 ......152 B7
Home Farm Bsns Ctr
  BN1 ....143 D2
Home Farm Cl Frant TN3 .17 C4
  Horsted Keynes RH17 ....33 C5
Home Farm La BN2 ......143 D3

Home Farm Rd BN1 BN2 .143 D3
Home Platt RH19 ....21 A6
Home Rd BN1 ....142 E1
Homebush Ave
  Saltdean BN2 ....177 D5
  Telscombe BN7 ....166 F3
Homecoast Ho BN10 ....178 B7
Homedrive Ho 8 TN34 .159 F7
Homedrive Rd BN3 ......163 C8
Homefield Cl BN25 ....180 F4
Homefield Rd BN25 ......180 F4
Homegate Ho 3 BN21 ..184 F3
Homeglade Ho BN20 ....188 E8
Homehill Ho 7 TN40 ....157 C7
Homelands Cl TN31 ......157 A6
Homelatch Ho 4 BN21 ..185 A3
Homelawn Rd 3 TN40 ..157 A7
Homeleigh BN1 ....142 E5
Homeridge Ho BN2 .....177 D5
Homestall Rd RH19 ....11 E8
Homestead La RH15 .....73 C6
Homestead The TN5 .....15 C7
Hometye Ho BN25 ....180 D3
Homewarr Rd 4 TN40 ..157 A7
Homewood Cl TN31 .....157 A6
Homewood Rd TN3 ....6 F3
Homoeopathic Hospl TN1 .8 A3
Honey Croft BN3 ....141 D4
Honey La BN8 ....149 D7
Honeycrag Cl BN26 .....173 A7
Honeypot La BN7, BN8 ..100 B7
Honeysuckle Cl
  Eastbourne BN23 ....174 B3
  Hailsham BN27 ....152 B5
  St Leonards TN37 ....136 C5
Honeyway Cl BN26 ......172 F3
Honies Ct TN39 ....157 C6
Hoo Gdns BN20 ....173 B1
Hoo The BN20 ....173 B1
Hood Cl BN23 ....185 E7
Hooe Rd TN33 ....133 A3
Hook Hill TN5 ....31 A6
Hookswood Cl TN6 ....26 A3
Hoopers Cl BN7 ....123 C3
Hoover Cl TN37 ....135 F7
Hop Gdn TN22 ....36 C2
Hope Cotts BN42 ....161 E8
Hopehouse La TN17,TN18 ..47 F7
Hopfield Gdns TN22 ....78 E8
Hopgarden Cl TN34 .....159 E8
Hoppers Croft La TN19 ..62 B6
Hopwood Gdns TN4 ....8 A6
Horam Park Cl TN21 .....106 F7
Horebeech La TN21 .....107 A6
Horizon Cl TN4 ....8 A8
Horleigh Green Rd TN20 .39 C1
Horley Pl BN2 ....164 E6
Hornbeam TN19 ....62 A2
Hornbeams The RH15 ...72 D4
Hornblower Cotts TN19 ..44 C1
Hornbuckles Cl BN8 .....100 E7
Hornby Pl BN2 ....144 A1
Hornby Rd BN2 ....144 A1
Horning Cl BN23 ....174 B4
Horns Rd TN18 ....45 D8
Horntye Pk TN37,TN38 .159 D6
Horntye Rd TN37 ....136 C1
Horsa Cl BN23 ....185 E8
Horsegrove Ave TN5 .....31 F1
Horsegrove La TN6 ....39 B8
Horseshoe Cl TN38 .....136 B2
Horseshoe La TN31 .....157 A6
Horsewalk BN27,TN33 ..154 E7
Horsfield Rd BN7 ....123 B3
Horsgate Ho RH17 ....50 A8
Horsgate La RH17 ....50 A6
Horsham Ave BN10 ......178 D8
Horsham Ave N BN10 ...178 C8
Horsham Cl BN2 ....164 F6
Horsham Rd TN6 ....11 A6
Horsted Ho 1 RH16 ......50 D7
Horsted Keynes Ind Est
  RH17 ....33 B7
Horsted Keynes Sta RH17 .33 A7
Horsted La Danehill RH17 ..34 A4
  Isfield TN22 ....102 F7
Horsted Pond La TN22 ...78 A3
Horsted Sq TN22 ....78 A6
Horsye Rd BN27 ....185 B7
Horton Rd BN1 ....143 B1
Hoskins Pl RH17 ....2 A1
Hosmers Field TN6 ....39 D8
Hospital Villas RH16 .....50 F3
Houghton Green La TN31 .70 C2
Houghton La TN31 ....70 C3
Houndean Ct BN7 ....146 A8
Houndean Rise BN7 .....145 F8
Hova Villas BN3 ....163 B6
Hove Bsns Ctr BN3 .....163 B8
Hove Ent Ctr BN41 ......162 C6
Hove General Hospl BN3 .163 A7
Hove Manor 8 BN3 ......163 A6
Hove Mus & Art Gall
  BN3 ....163 A6
Hove Park Gdns
  Hove BN3 ....142 B1
  Hove BN3 ....162 B8
Hove Park Rd BN3 ......142 C1
Hove Park Villas
  (Lower) BN3 ....163 D2
Hove Park Villas
  (Upper) BN3 ....142 A1
Hove Park Way BN3 .....142 B1
Hove Pk BN3 ....163 B5
Hove St BN3 ....163 A6
Hove Sta BN3 ....163 B8
Hovedene BN3 ....163 C7

How's Cl TN31 ....90 B5
Howard Ave RH15 ....72 E4
Howard Cl BN27 ....152 D6
Howard Ct Hove BN3 ...142 D2
  Peacehaven BN10 ....178 B7
Howard Gdns TN2 ....8 C5
Howard Ho Bexhill TN39 .156 E4
  Peacehaven BN10 ....167 D1
Howard Pl BN1 ....189 A4
Howard Rd BN2 ....164 C7
Howard Sq BN21 ....185 A2
Howards Cres TN39 .....156 C4
Howbourne La TN22 ......56 E5
Howes Cotts TN18 ....45 F8
Howey Cl BN9 ....168 F1
Howlett Cl TN38 ....135 F4
Howlett Dr BN27 ....129 B2
Howletts Cl BN21 ....173 F1
Hoyle Rd BN10 ....178 A8
Hudson Cl BN23 ....185 G7
Hudson Rd BN2 ....185 G6
Huggett's La BN22 ......173 B3
Hughenden Cl 2 TN34 ..136 F2
Hughenden Pl 1 TN34 ..136 F2
Hughenden Rd TN34 ....160 A6
Hughes Rd BN2 ....164 B8
Hughes Way TN22 ....78 C8
Hugletts La TN21 ....83 A7
Humboldt Ct TN2 ....8 D5
Humphrey Lodge RH15 ..73 D3
Humphrey's Gap BN41,BN3 .161 A7
Hundred Acre La
  BN6, RH17 ....74 B2
Hundredhouse La TN31 ..90 F2
Hungershall Park Cl TN4 ..7 E1
Hungershall Pk TN4 ....7 E2
Hunloke Ave BN22 ......185 B6
Hunston Cl BN22 ....165 F7
Hunt's Gate RH17 ....52 E3
Hunters Way
  Royal Tunbridge Wells TN4 ..7 F1
  Uckfield TN22 ....78 B8
Hunting Cl TN40 ....157 C5
Huntingdon Rd TN4 ....8 C7
Huntingdon Way RH15 ..73 D5
Huntington Cl 1 BN27 ..123 E1
Huntley Mill Rd TN5 ......31 E3
Huntleys Pk TN4 ....7 F5
Hurdis Rd BN25 ....180 A6
Hurrell Rd TN34 ....160 B6
Hurst Cres BN41 ....162 B8
Hurst Farm Rd RH19 ....10 D7
Hurst Green CE Sch TN19 .45 A2
Hurst Hill BN1 ....143 C5
Hurst La Eastbourne BN21 .184 D5
  Sedlescombe TN33 ....88 F3
  Windmill Hill BN27 ....131 B5
Hurst Rd Eastbourne BN21 .184 D5
  Hassocks BN6 ....97 D4
Hurst Shaw TN21 ....107 C8
Hurst The TN2 ....8 D4
Hurst Way TN5 ....31 A6
Hurst Wickham La BN6 ..97 C5
Hurstfield Cl RH17 ....51 A2
Hurstpierpoint Coll BN6 ..97 B8
Hurstwood BN2 ....164 F5
Hurstwood Cl TN40 .....158 B5
Hurstwood La
  Haywards Heath RH17 ....51 A2
  Royal Tunbridge Wells TN4 ..7 F3
  Sharpthorne RH17, RH19 .21 D1
Hurstwood Pk TN4 ....7 F3
Hurstwood Rd TN22 .....56 A6
Hurtis Hill TN6 ....37 E7
Hutton Rd BN1 ....143 B3
Hyde Cl BN7 ....145 C5
Hyde Gdns BN21 ....185 A2
Hyde Rd BN21 ....184 F2
Hyde The BN24 ....164 F8
Hyde Tynings Cl BN20 ...188 D8
Hydehurst Cl TN6 ....25 C5
Hydney St BN22 ....185 C5
Hydneye The BN22 ......173 F1
Hylden Cl BN2 ....165 B8
Hyperion Ave BN26 .....172 E6
Hythe Ave TN38 ....158 B5
Hythe Cl Polegate BN26 ..173 C7
  Seaford BN25 ....181 D5
Hythe Cres BN25 ....181 C4
Hythe Rd BN1 ....143 A2
Hythe View BN25 ....181 C4

I

Ian Cl TN40 ....157 F7
Icklesham CE Prim Sch
  TN36 ....116 E6
Icklesham Dr TN38 ......135 D3
Iden Cl BN2 ....164 E5
Iden Ct TN34 ....136 D3
Iden Hurst BN6 ....97 A7
Iden Rd TN31 ....69 B3
Iden St BN22 ....174 A2
Iden's La RH17 ....182 D8
Ifield Cl BN2 ....177 E6
Ifield Mill Cl BN24 ......174 B5
Ifford & Kingston
  CE Prim Sch BN7 ....145 F5
Ifford Cl BN9 ....168 D1
Ilex Ct BN42 ....161 F8
Ilex Gn 8 BN27 ....129 B1
Image Cross Flats RH19 ..21 A5
Imberhorne Bsns Ctr RH19 .1 B3
Imberhorne La RH19 .....1 B2
Imberhorne Lower Sch
  RH19 ....1 D3

Imberhorne Sch RH19 .....
Imberhorne Way RH19 ...
Impala Gdns TN4 ....
Imperial Arc BN1 18
Independent Bsns Pk The
  RH19 ....
Ingham Dr BN1 14
Inglesea Sch TN38 13
Ingleside TN38 13
Ingleside Dr TN6 ....
Inglewood Gdns TN38 ...13
Ingram Cres E BN2 ......
Ingram Cres W BN3 ......
Ingram Ct BN3 ....
Ingrams Ave TN39 15
Ingrams Way BN27 15
Inholmes Cl RH15 ....
Inholmes Park Rd RH15 ...7
Inkerman Terr TN31 ......
Innham's Wood TN6 .....
Innings Dr BN24 17
Innovation Dr RH15 .....
Insley Ct TN39 15
Inverness Rd 4 BN2 16
Inwood Cres BN1 14
Iona Cl BN27 12
Iona Way 12 RH16 5
Irelands La BN7 ....
Ironlatch Ave TN38 13
Ironlatch Cl TN38 13
Ironstone Way TN22 7
Ironstones TN1 ....
Irving Ho TN1 ....
Isaac's La RH16, RH15 5
Isabel Cl BN25 18
Isabel Cres BN41 16
Isfield BN7 14
Isfield Rd Brighton BN1 .14
Isfield TN8,TN22 10
Isherwood TN33 11
Isle of Thorns
  (Univ of Sussex) RH17 ..2
Islingword Pl BN2 16
Islingword Rd BN2 16
Islingword St BN2 16
Ismay Lodge TN39 15
Ive Grange TN33 13
Iveagh Cres BN9 16
Ivor Rd BN2 14
Ivors La BN8 12
Ivory Pl BN2 18
Ivy Cotts BN8 10
Ivy Dene La RH19 ....
Ivy Mews 8 BN3 16
Ivy Pl BN1 18
Ivy Terr BN21 ....
ivyhouse
  Employment Area TN35 .13
Ivyhouse La TN35 13
Ivylands Yd TN31 9

J

Jack O'Dandy Cl BN21 ...18
Jackdaws The TN22 7
Jackies La BN8 7
Jacks Hill TN7 ....
Jackson Mews BN9 17
Jackson St BN2 18
Jacobs Acre TN40 15
Jacqueline Du Pré Ct
  BN2 ....
Jamaica Way BN23 18
James Ave BN27 13
Jameson Cres TN40 13
Jameson Rd TN40 15
Jane Murray Way
  BN6,RH15 ....
Janes Cl RH15 7
Janes La RH15 7
Janeston Ct 4 BN3 .....
Japonica Cl BN43 14
Jardine Ct TN6 ....
Jarretts CI TN31 9
Jarvis Brook Ctry Pk TN6 .3
Jarvis Brook Sch TN6 3
Jarvisbrook Cl TN39 15
Jasmine Cotts TN31 .....
Jasmine Ct Brighton BN1 .14
  Hove BN3 16
Jasmine Gn 2 BN27 12
Jasmine Cl BN10 17
Jay Cl BN23 17
Jay Rd BN10 17
Jays The Burgess Hill RH15 .7
  Uckfield TN22 7
Jefferies RH17 3
Jefferies Way TN6 2
Jefferson Way TN37 13
Jeffreys Way TN22 5
Jellicoe Cl BN23 ....
Jenner's La TN35 13
Jephson Cl BN20 18
Jerome Cl BN23 ....
Jersey St BN2 18
Jervis Ave BN23 ....
Jesmond Cl BN3 16
Jesmond Rd BN3 16
Jesters RH16 7
Jevington Ct TN39 15
Jevington Ct BN43 16
Jevington Dr
  Brighton BN2 14
  Polegate BN26 18
Jevington Gdns BN21 ...18
Jevington Ho 7 BN21 ...18
Jevington Rd BN26 17
Jew St BN1 18

Jireh Ct RH16 ....50 E5
Joan Hughes Ct BN26 ....173 A6
Joan Nightingale Ho
RH16 ....50 C4
Job's La BN6 ....72 A6
Joe's La BN7 ....131 B5
John Dann Cl TN22 ....80 A6
John Macadam Way
TN37 ....136 A6
John Spare Ct TN4 ....8 A6
John St Brighton BN2 ....189 C3
  Royal Tunbridge Wells TN4 ..8 A5
John Whittle Lodge BN2 .143 C1
John's Cross Rd TN32 .....87 C8
Johns Cl BN10 ....167 C2
Johnson Bank 4 BN2 ....164 C7
Johnson Cl TN37 ....135 F6
Johnson Dr RH15 ....73 D3
Jonas Dr TN5 ....29 E5
Jonas La TN5 ....29 E5
Jordan Cl BN3 ....162 E8
Jordans La BN23 ....173 D3
Jordans La E BN22 ....173 D3
Jordans La W BN22 ....173 C3
Jordans The RH19 ....10 E8
Joyce Villas TN21 ....106 E5
Jubilee Cl RH16 ....51 A4
Jubilee Ct BN2 ....143 E2
Jubilee Gdns BN25 ....181 A5
Jubilee Ho BN9 ....179 C7
Jubilee Rd Bexhill TN39 ..157 A7
  Burgess Hill RH15 ....72 E2
  Portslade-by-Sea BN41 ....162 A8
Jubilee St BN1 ....189 B3
Judge's Terr RH19 ....10 E8
Jugg's Rd BN7 ....146 B7
Juggs Cl BN7 ....146 B8
Juggs Rd BN7 ....146 A7
Julian Cl 3 BN43 ....161 C8
Julian Rd BN3 ....163 E7
Junction Cl RH15 ....73 C4
Junction Rd
  Bodiam TN18, TN32 ....46 A3
  Brighton BN1 ....189 A3
  Burgess Hill RH15 ....73 B3
  Cripp's Corner TN32 ....65 C5
  Cripp's Corner TN32,TN33 ..108 B5
  Eastbourne BN21 ....185 A3
  St Leonards TN37 ....136 B7
Junction St BN26 ....173 B6
Juniper Cl
  Portslade-by-Sea BN41 .....141 B3
  Seaford BN25 ....181 C3
  St Leonards TN38 ....135 E3
Juniper Wlk BN43 ....140 C1
Jury's Gap
  Coastguard Cotts TN31 ......95 E1
Jury's Gap Rd TN29 ....96 F5

K

Kammond Ave BN25 ......181 B5
Kane Hythe Rd TN33 .....111 C6
Karenza Ct BN1 ....164 A8
Katherine Way BN25 ......180 D5
Keaton Ho RH16 ....50 E6
Keats Cl TN38 ....158 F6
Keats Pl RH13 ....1 D1
Kebbell Lodge 6 BN22 ..189 C2
Kedale Rd BN25 ....180 E4
Keel Gdns TN4 ....7 E8
Keere St BN7 ....146 C8
Keith Wlk BN23 ....185 F6
Keld Ave TN22 ....78 D6
Keld Dr TN22 ....78 D6
Keld Rd BN3 ....142 D1
Keld Way BN23 ....185 F6
Kelley Cotts BN8 ....124 E6
Kelsey Ct RH15 ....73 D3
Kemble Cl TN2 ....12 A2
Kemp Ct BN2 ....164 E4
Kemp St BN1 ....189 B3
Kemp Town 11 8 BN2 ...164 D4
Kemps Farm Rd TN6 ....26 B1
Kemps Way TN2 ....64 C5
Kemptown Mews 11 BN2 .164 E4
Kendal Ct BN9 ....179 E7
Kendal Pk TN4 ....7 E5
Kendal Rd BN3 ....162 F8
Kenilworth Cl BN22 ....144 A2
Kenilworth Rd TN38 ....159 B7
Kenmure Ave BN1 ....143 A7
Kennard Ct RH18 ....11 E3
Kennedy Ave RH19 ....13 C6
Kennedy Cl TN21 ....82 B6
Kennedy Ct TN38 ....136 B3
Kennedy Rd TN40 ....157 E4
Kennedy Way BN23 ....179 B8
Kennel Cnr BN8 ....124 F6
Kennel La TN39 ....156 C4
Kennett Cl TN34 ....154 C4
Kennett Ct TN34 ....173 F5
Kenrith Ct TN34 ....136 E2
Kensington Cl TN38 ....135 D3
Kensington Gdns BN1 ....189 B3
Kensington Pl BN1 ....189 B3
Kensington St BN1 ....189 B3
Kent & East Sussex
  Rly TN17 ....49 C5
Kent Ho BN3 ....163 B5
Kent Sussex Hospl TN4 .....8 A4
Kent Cl Bexhill TN40 ......158 A5
  Eastham-by-Sea BN43 ....161 C7
  Chelsea TN36 ....117 E7
Kent BN20 ....184 B6
Kent Fields BN7 ....145 E5
Kent Ho TN1 ....8 C6
Kent La TN32 ....85 F6

Kent Rd
  Royal Tunbridge Wells TN4 ..8 A6
  St Leonards TN38 ....135 F4
Kent St TN3 ....114 A3
Kent's La TN6 ....99 C7
Kenton Cl BN3 ....157 A5
Kenton Cl TN39 ....185 A1
Kenton Rd BN3 ....162 D7
Kents Rd RH15 ....50 F3
Kenwards BN1 ....143 D7
Kenwood Cl TN34 ....137 B4
Kenya Ct 2 BN2 ....163 E6
Kenwood Cl TN34 ....137 B4
Kenya Ct 2 BN2 ....163 E6
Keppel Rd TN34 ....136 A5
Kepplestone BN20 ....188 E8
Kerrara Terr BN22 ....185 B5
Kerrison Mews 7 BN3 ....163 D5
Kestrel Ct Bexhill TN40 ..157 E4
  Hove BN3 ....163 D6
Kestrel Ct BN27 ....152 D7

Kestrels The
  Shoreham-by-Sea BN43 ....161 A8
  St Leonards TN38 ....135 F5
Ketcham Cnr BN24 ....174 E6
Ketche's La RH17,TN22 ..52 E7
Kevin Gdns BN2 ....165 E8
Kew St BN1 ....189 A3
Kewhurst Ave TN39 ....156 D3
Key West BN23 ....185 G8
Keymer Ave BN10 ....178 D7
Keymer Cl
  Eastbourne BN23 ....174 E1
  St Leonards TN38 ....158 E6
Keymer Gdns RH15 ....73 B2
Keymer Par RH15 ....73 B2
Keymer Pk BN6 ....98 B3
Keymer Rd Brighton BN1 .143 B6
  Burgess Hill RH15 ....97 F3
  Hassocks BN6 ....97 F3
Kibbles La TN4 ....7 E8
Kidbrook RH16 ....51 B6
Kidbrooke Park
  (Michael Hall Sch) RH18 ..11 D1
Kidbrooke Rise RH18 ......11 E2
Kidd's Hill TN7 ....24 A4
Kilburn Terr 6 BN2 ....185 A3
Kilda St 1 BN22 ....185 B4
Kildare Ct TN34 ....137 B4
Kildare Ct BN20 ....184 C3
Kiln Cl TN22 ....78 D4
Kiln Dr TN22 ....78 D6
Kiln La
  Haywards Heath RH16 ....51 B5
  Hove TN33 ....155 B7
  Isfield TN22 ....102 E5
Kiln Rd BN8 ....125 A8
Kiln The RH15 ....73 C3
Kilnbank TN2 ....8 C7
Kilnbank Ho RH16 ....50 D2
Kilnbarn Way RH16 ....50 D2
Kilnwood La BN8 ....100 E7
Kilpatrick Cl BN23 ....174 D3
Kimberley Ct TN39 ....157 C6
Kimberley Rd
  Brighton BN2 ....143 D1
  Seaford BN25 ....180 C4
Kindersley Cl RH19 ....13 A2
Kinfauns Ave BN22 ....185 B6
King Alfred (Swimming
  Pool & Sports Ctr) BN3 ..163 A6
King Charles Pl 3 BN43 .161 A6
King Edward Ave TN34 ..136 C3
King Edward Cl TN34 .....136 C3
King Edward's Par BN20 .188 E8
King George Ave RH19 .....1 C3
King George Rd BN43 ......161 D8
King George V Hill TN1 .....8 C5
King George VI Ave
  BN1, BN3 ....142 A3
King George VI Dr BN3 ..142 A4
King George VI Mans
  BN3 ....141 F2
King Henry's Rd TN2 .....123 B2
King Offa Prim Sch
  TN39 ....157 B5
King Offa Way TN40 ......157 C5
King Pl BN1 ....189 A2
King St Brighton BN1 .....189 B2
  East Grinstead RH19 ....1 E1
King Wood Hill TN1 ....90 A3
King's Ave
  Eastbourne BN20 ....184 E5
  Newhaven BN9 ....168 E1
  Rye TN31 ....93 D6
King's Bank La TN31 ......108 A4
King's Cl BN21 ....184 E5
King's Gdns BN3 ....163 A5
King's Hill Rd TN19 ....62 B3
King's Manor Sch BN43 ..161 D8
King's Mead La BN25 .....180 D4
King's Rd
  Brighton BN1 ....163 E5
  Haywards Heath RH16 ......50 F3
  St Leonards TN37 ....159 C7
Kingfisher Cl TN22 ....78 E5
Kingfisher Ct BN27 ....152 D7
Kingfisher Dr BN23 ....174 C2
Kingfisher Rise RH19 ....10 F4
Kings Chase TN6 ....25 D3
Kings Cl Bexhill TN40 ......157 C4
  Eastbourne BN21 ....184 F5
  Telscombe Cliffs BN10 ....167 B1
Kings Copse 9 RH19 ....10 F8

Kings Ct TN6 ....25 E2
Kings Ct E BN23 ....185 F8
Kings Ct 5 6 BN2 ....185 F8
Kings Ct W 5 BN2 ....185 F8
Kings Dr BN6 ....63 C8
Kings Gate BN3 ....163 C6
Kings Mead St BN20 ......188 D7
Kings Mews BN3 ....163 B6
Kings Par TN1 ....143 A2
Kings Par TN2 ....8 D3
Kings Rd BN42 ....160 E8
Kings Ride Alfriston BN26 .170 F3
  Burgess Hill RH15 ....73 D1
  Seaford BN25 ....180 D4
Kings Toll Rd TN2 ....9 F6
Kings Way RH15 ....73 D2
Kings Wlk 6 TN34 ....159 F8
Kingsbury Rd BN1 ....189 B4
Kingsbury St BN1, BN2 ..189 B4
Kingscote Lodge BN1 ....143 F5
Kingscott Cl TN39 ....157 B6
Kingsdale Cl TN38 ....112 F3
  St Leonards TN37 ....136 C6
Kingsfield BN42 ....161 E8
Kingsfield Cotts BN26 ....149 E8
Kingsfold 2 BN2 ....164 A8
Kingsfold Cl 3 BN25 ......180 F2
Kingsland Cl BN43 ....185 D7
Kingsland Ct BN1 ....142 F6
Kingsley Cl TN37 ....136 A5
Kingsley Rd
  2 Brighton BN1 ....163 E5
  Wadhurst TN5 ....30 A4
Kingsley Rd Brighton BN1 .142 F6
Lewes BN7 ....123 B2
Kingsmarsh Cotts TN20 ..58 B6
Kingsmead BN25 ....180 D4
Kingsmead St BN20 ......184 D6
Kingsmead Way BN25 ....180 E4
Kingsmead Wlk BN25 .....180 E4
Kingsmere 2 BN1 ....142 E2
Kingsmere Cl 2 BN1 ....164 A8
Kingsmere Way BN23 .....185 F8
Kingsthorpe Rd BN3 ......162 F8
Kingston Ave BN25 ....184 A2
Kingston Bay Rd BN43 ...161 C6
Kingston Broadway
  BN42,BN43 ....140 D1
Kingston Buci Cty Fst Sch
  BN43 ....161 B8
Kingston Cl Brighton BN1 .143 E6
  Hove BN3 ....161 B8
  Seaford BN25 ....181 B3
  Shoreham-by-Sea BN43 ....161 C8
Kingston Gn 7 BN2 ....161 C8
Kingston Ho BN42,BN43 .161 D7
Kingston La BN42,BN43 ..161 D7
Kingston Rd
  Eastbourne BN22 ....173 F2
  Lewes BN7 ....146 B7
Kingston Ridge BN7 ....145 D6
Kingston Villas TN1 ....8 D3
Kingston Way
  Seaford BN25 ....181 B3
  Shoreham-by-Sea
  BN42,BN43 ....140 D1
Kingsway Hove BN3, BN41 .163 A5
Kingsway Ct 11 BN3 ....163 C5
Kingswood Ave TN34 .....136 F6
Kingswood Cl TN2 ....8 C3
Kingswood Flats BN1 .....189 C2
Kingswood Rd TN2 ....8 C3
Kinnoss Cl 5 BN21 ....185 A4
Kinsale Cl 4 BN13 ....163 E7
Kinver La TN40 ....158 A6
Kipling Ave BN2 ....165 E7
Kipling Ct Bexhill TN40 ..157 F5
  5 Haywards Heath RH16 .50 D5
Kipling Way RH19 ....1 C1
Kipling Wlk 1 BN23 ....174 E2
Kirby Dr BN10 ....167 A1
Kirdford Ct RH15 ....73 C1
Kirk Way BN20 ....184 B5
Kirkdale Rd TN1 ....8 C5
Kirkstall Cl BN22 ....173 E3
Kitchenour La TN31 ....68 E5
Kite Cl TN38 ....158 E8
Kites Nest Wlk TN39 ......156 B4
Kitilear Ct BN3 ....162 A8
Knebworth Rd TN39 ......156 F5
Knelle Rd TN32 ....84 B6
Knelle View 2 TN31 ....67 B7
Knepp Cl BN2 ....143 F2
Knight's Ridge TN2 ....9 D7
Knights Cl TN2 ....9 D7
Knights Gate Rd BN1 .....144 C7
Knights La TN39 ....156 B6
Knightsbridge Cl TN4 ....7 F5
Knole Cl 4 TN40 ....157 F4
Knole Gr RH19 ....1 C3
Knole Rd Bexhill TN40 ....157 D3
  Rottingdean BN2 ....177 A5
Knoll Bsns Ctr The BN3 ..162 D8
Knoll Cl BN3 ....162 D8
Knoll Cres BN22 ....174 A1
Knoll Inf Sch TN37 ....141 D1
Knoll Rd BN22 ....174 A2
Knoll Rise TN38 ....159 A7
Knowle Cl
  Crowborough TN6 ....38 C8
  Langton Green TN3 ....6 F3
Knowle Cotts TN3 ....17 E1

Knowle Ct TN38 ....136 B1
Knowle Hill Bodiam TN32 .65 D8
  Mayfield TN20 ....40 A1
Knowle La BN6 ....104 A6
Knowle Pk
  Crowborough TN6 ....25 D2
  Mayfield TN20 ....40 A1
Knowle Rd TN35 ....138 E5
Knoyle Rd BN1 ....142 E2
Knyveton Ct RH15 ....73 B3
Kylemore BN24 ....175 B6
Kymer Gdns BN6 ....98 A3

L

La Marne Ct TN34 ....136 E2
Laburnam Wlk BN22 .....173 D3
Laburnham Gn 6 BN27 ..129 B1
Laburnum Ave BN23 ......141 E1
Laburnum Ct TN2 ....9 A2
Laburnum Gdns TN40 ....157 F6
Laburnum Gr BN1 ....143 B3
Laburnum Way RH16 ....51 B4
Lacys Hill BN8 ....147 F8
Ladies Mile Brighton BN1 .143 B7
  Hailsham BN27 ....129 D1
Ladies Mile Cl BN1 ....143 A7
Ladies' Mile CE BN1 ....142 F6
Ladies' Mile Cl BN1 ....142 E6
Ladies' Mile Rd BN1 ......143 A7
Lady Bee Ind Est BN9 ....161 E6
Lady Oak La TN5,TN17 ....32 C7
Lady's Gift Rd TN4 ....7 F8
Ladycross Cl BN25 ....181 C3
Ladyfern Ct TN2 ....8 C4
Ladymead RH15 ....73 C5
Ladysmith Rd BN2 ....164 D8
Lagwood Cl BN6 ....97 F3
Laine Cl BN1 ....142 F3
Laines The BN26 ....170 F3
Lake Dr BN10 ....178 C7
Lake House Cl TN39 ......156 D4
Lake Rd TN4 ....7 E4
Lake St TN20,TN6 ....40 C7
Lake View BN2 ....164 C5
Lake View Rd RH19 ....1 F1
Lakehurst La TN33 ....110 B8
Lakelands Cl BN22 ....174 A1
Lakelands Dr TN39 ....156 A4
Lakeman Way TN4 ....8 B7
Lakeside Ave BN26 ....149 C8
Lakeside Ct BN22 ....174 A1
Laleham Cl
  Eastbourne BN22 ....184 E4
  St Leonards TN37 ....136 C5
Lamb Cl TN2 ....9 D8
Lamberhurst CE Prim Sch
  TN3 ....20 B6
Lamberhurst Rd TN4 .... 8 A8
Lamberhurst Vineyard
  TN3 ....20 A4
Lambert Pl BN7 ....123 D3
Lambert Rd BN7 ....174 E3
Lamberts Cotts TN3 ....112 E3
Lamberts Rd TN2 ....8 D8
Lambourn Ave BN24 ......174 A5
Lambourn Cl RH19 ....1 C2
Lambourn Way 8 D1
Lambourne Cl BN1 ....143 C2
Lambourne Rd BN1 ....143 C2
Lampington Row TN3 ....6 E3
Lampool Cnr TN22 ....55 A7
Lanark Ct BN20 ....184 B6
Lancaster Ct
  Eastbourne BN22 ....189 C5
  11 Hove BN3 ....163 A6
Lancaster Dr RH19 ....1 C2
Lancaster House Rd BN1 .144 B7
Lancaster Rd
  Brighton BN1 ....189 A4
  St Leonards TN38 ....135 F5
Lancaster St BN7 ....123 D1
Lancing Cl TN34 ....136 D3
Lancing Cl 5 BN2 ....164 F5
Lancing Way BN24 ....172 F4
Landgate TN31 ....93 D6
Landport Farm Rd BN7 ..123 A3
Landport Rd Lewes BN7 ..123 B3
  Lewes BN7 ....123 C2
Landsdown Rd BN25 ......181 C5
Landsdown Way TN37 ....157 E5
Landseer Rd BN3 ....162 F8
Lane The TN3 ....6 C5
Langdale Cl BN23 ....174 C4
Langdale Gdns BN3 ....162 F6
Langdale Rd BN3 ....162 F6
Langham Cl Hastings TN34 .136 F4
  Ringmer BN8 ....124 D5
Langham Rd
  Hastings TN34 ....136 F4
  Robertsbridge TN32 ....63 F4
Langholm Rd RH19 ....1 C3
Langhurst 9 BN2 ....164 E4
Langley Cl TN39 ....157 B8
Langley Cres BN2 ....144 E1
Langney Cty Prim Sch
  BN23 ....174 E1
Langney Gn BN23 ....185 E8
Langney La BN23,BN27 ..185 B3
Langney Rise BN23 ....174 D2
Langney Sh Ctr BN23 .....174 C2
Langridge Dr
  East Grinstead RH19 ....10 E8
  Portslade-by-Sea BN41 ....141 B3
Langridge La RH16 ....51 A5
Langridge Way RH15 ....72 E5
Langridges Cl BN8 ....52 E6
Langton Cl TN33 ....112 E4

Langton Green
Cty Prim Sch TN3 ....6 E4
Langton Rd Rusthall TN3, TN4 ..7 C3
  Speldhurst TN3 ....7 A7
Langton Ridge TN3 ....7 B3
Langtye La BN26,BN8 .....149 E6
Lansdown Pl BN7 ....146 D8
Lansdown Pl W BN7 ....82 B6
Lansdowne Cres BN27 ...129 B2
Lansdowne Dr BN27 ......129 A2
Lansdowne Mews 7
  BN3 ....163 D6
Lansdowne Pl BN3 ....163 D6
Lansdowne Rd
  Hailsham BN27 ....129 B2
  Hove BN1, BN3 ....163 D6
  Royal Tunbridge Wells TN1 ..8 B4
Lansdowne Sq
  1 Hove BN3 ....163 D5
  6 Royal Tunbridge Wells TN1 ..8 B4
Lansdowne St BN3 ....163 D6
Lansdowne Way BN27 ...129 B3
Lapierre Rd BN9 ....179 B7
Lapwing Cl BN23 ....174 C2
Lapwing Ct BN27 ....152 E7
Larch Cl Heathfield TN21 ..82 B5
  St Leonards TN38 ....136 A3
  Woodingdean BN2 ....165 F7
Larch Gdns BN22 ....173 D3
Larch Way BN41 ....51 B4
Lark Hill BN3 ....141 E3
Larke Cl BN43 ....161 C7
Larkfield Cl TN38 ....136 A3
Larkfield Way BN1 ....143 A4
Larkhill TN40 ....157 C4
Larkspur Dr BN23 ....174 B3
Larnach Cl TN22 ....78 B7
Lascelles Terr BN21 ....185 A1
Lashbrooks Rd TN22 ....78 B7
Latimer Rd BN22 ....185 C8
Laton Rd TN34 ....136 D2
Laughton Cl BN23 ....174 A4
Laughton Cty Prim Sch
  BN8 ....126 C6
Laughton Lodge BN8 .....126 A8
Laughton Rd
  Broyle Side BN8 ....125 D6
  Woodingdean BN2 ....165 F8
Laundry La RH17 ....22 D1
Laurel 2 RH16 ....50 D6
Laurel Bank Bexhill TN40 .157 F5
  Royal Tunbridge Wells TN4 ..8 B8
  Wadhurst TN5 ....30 A4
Laurel Cl RH15 ....73 D5
Laurel Dene RH19 ....1 F1
Laurel La TN36 ....116 F5
Laurel Rd TN2 ....8 D7
Laurel Way TN38 ....135 E3
Laurels The
  8 Brighton BN2 ....189 C5
  Uckfield TN22 ....78 E8
Lauren Ct TN38 ....158 F7
Lauriston Rd BN1 ....142 E2
Lavant Cl TN39 ....156 C6
Lavender Cl BN24 ....174 B5
Lavender Ct BN23 ....174 B3
Lavender Gdns BN1 ....31 E1
Lavender Hill BN43 ....140 B1
Lavender Ho BN2 ....189 C1
Lavender Line TN22 ....102 E8
Lavender St BN2 ....189 C1
Lawes Ave BN9 ....179 C7
Lawn The TN3 ....159 C2
Lawns Ave BN21 ....184 D4
Lawns The
  Eastbourne BN22 ....185 C5
  Hailsham BN27 ....152 C6
  Willingdon BN20 ....173 B1
  Willingdon BN22 ....173 B2
Lawrence Cl BN23 ....174 D1
Lawrence La TN33 ....78 C7
Lawrence Rd BN3 ....162 F8
Lawrie La RH16 ....51 B5
Laylands Cl BN41 ....162 A7
Laylands Rd BN41 ....162 A7
Layne The TN3 ....93 A6
Lea Ave TN31 ....93 A6
Lea Ct BN9 ....179 C8
Lea Rd BN10 ....178 B8
Leach Ct BN2 ....164 C5
Leaf Hall Rd 10 BN22 ....185 B3
Leaf Hospl
  (Univ of Brighton) BN21 .184 F4
Leaf Rd BN21 ....185 A3
Leahurst Court Rd BN1 ..142 E1
Leahurst Ct 1 BN1 ....142 E1
Lealands Cl TN3 ....15 C6
Lealands Dr TN22 ....55 C1
Leamland Wlk BN27 ......152 B7
Leap Cross
  Small Bsns Ctr BN27 ......129 A1
Leas The Burgess Hill RH15 .72 F4
  Peacehaven Heights BN10 .178 F6
  St Leonards TN38 ....159 A6
  Turner's Green TN5 ....30 A6
Leasam La TN31 ....93 B8
Leasingham Gdns TN39 ..157 A5
Ledsham Ave TN37 ....136 B5
Ledsham Cl TN37 ....136 B5
Ledsham Pk TN37 ....136 B5
Ledsham Way TN37 ....136 B5
Lee Rd BN7 ....123 B2

ee Ave BN9 ....179 C8
eeds Ave BN23 ....185 D7
eeds La TN35 ....137 D4
eeds La TN20 ....58 D6
eeford Cotts TN33 ....88 A1
eeves Cl TN21 ....82 A6
eeves Way TN21 ....185 F8
eepward Quay BN21 ....185 F8
.eggs' La TN3 ....6 E5
.egsheath La RH18, RH19 ...21 F8
.eicester Cl BN22 ....185 B4
.eicester Dr TN2 ....16 F8
.eicester Rd BN7 ....123 B1
.eicester St BN1 ....189 C4
.eicester Villas BN3 .....162 D7
.eighton Cl TN4 ....8 A7
Leighton Rd
  Horsted Keynes RH17 .....33 C5
  Hove BN3 ....163 A8
.Leighton Villas RH17 ....33 C5
.eigh La TN2 ....16 E8
.enham Ave BN2 ....177 B5
.enham Rd E BN2 ....177 B5
.enham Rd W BN2 ....177 B5
.ennox Cl BN26 ....184 B5
.ennox Ct TN21 ....82 B8
.ennox Rd Hove BN3 ....162 F8
  Shoreham-by-Sea BN43 ...161 B8
.Lennox St TN31 ....189 C2
.eopold Rd BN11 ....157 B4
.epeland BN27 ....129 A1
.eslie Cl TN40 ....157 F7
.eslie St BN2 ....185 B4
.etheren Pl BN1 ....184 D3
.eveller End BN8 ....76 D7
.eveller Rd BN8 ....76 D7
.evett Cl BN26 ....173 C6
.evett Ct BN26 ....173 C6
.evett Rd BN26 ....173 C6
.evetts La TN32 ....46 D1
.ewes Bsns Ctr BN7 ....123 C2
.ewes Cl Bexhill TN39 ..157 A6
  Saltdean BN2 ....177 E5
.Lewes Cres BN2 ....144 A8
.ewes Ct BN1 ....148 A8
.ewes High St BN7 ....123 B1
.ewes Ho 5 BN21 ....184 F4
.ewes Mews 12 BN21 ...164 E4

Lincoln Ave BN10 ....178 A7
Lincoln Ave S BN10 ......178 A7
Lincoln Cl
  Eastbourne BN20 ....188 C8
  2 St Leonards TN38 ......136 A4
Lincoln Cotts BN2 ....189 C3
Lincoln Ct
  Eastbourne BN20 ....184 B7
  Hove BN3 ....163 C8
  Peacehaven BN10 ....1 C4
Lincoln Rd BN41 ....163 A7
Lincoln St BN2 ....189 C4
Lincoln Way TN6 ....38 A8
Lincoln Wood RH16 ....50 C5
Linden Ave RH19 ....1 C2
Linden Chase TN22 ....79 B1
Linden Ct Eastbourne BN22 ...173 E2
  Royal Tunbridge Wells TN4 ....8 A2
Linden Ct TN22 ....78 C7
Linden Gdns 7 F1
Linden Gr Hailsham BN27 ...129 C3
  Lindfield RH16 ....51 B7
Linden Park Rd TN2 ....8 A2
Linden Rd TN40 ....157 C3
Lindens The 4 BN2 ......189 C4
Lindfield RH16 ....51 B7
Lindfield Ave BN25 ....181 C2
Lindfield Cl BN2 ....177 B6
Lindfield Ct BN1 ....143 C2
Lindfield Cty Inf Sch
  RH16 ....51 A7
Lindfield Cty Jun Sch
  RH16 ....51 B7
Lindfield Dr BN27 ....152 B7
Lindfield Ent Pk RH16 ...51 C6
Lindfield Rd BN22 ....173 D1
Lindfield Sch The BN22 ...173 D2
Lindon Cl BN20 ....184 C2
Lindsay Cl BN20 ....184 C2
Lindfield Rd RH19 ....1 D3
Link Rd BN20 ....184 D1
Link The Friston BN20 ...183 C2
  Rye TN31 ....9 E8
Link Way TN2 ....8 B8
Linden Cotts TN18 ....47 E5
Links Ave BN10 ....179 A7
Links Cl Crowborough TN6 ...25 D2
  Portslade-by-Sea BN41 ...162 C8
Links Dr TN45 ....157 A4
Links Rd
  Portslade-by-Sea BN41 ...162 C8
  Seaford BN25 ....181 A2
Links St TN57 ....157 A4
Links The 6 Bexhill TN40 ...158 F8
  St Leonards TN38 ....158 F8
Links Way TN31 ....94 E2
Linkswood BN21 ....184 E2
Linkway Eastbourne BN20 ...184 B7
  Westham BN24 ....174 E6
Linkway The BN1 ....143 B1
Linley Ct TN34 ....137 A3
Linnet Ct BN23 ....63 A4
Linnet Ct TN22 ....78 D5
Linosa Ct 10 BN22 ....185 B3
Linthouse Cl RH16 ....167 D2
Linton Cres TN34 ....159 E8
Linton Ct TN34 ....159 E8
Linton Rd Hastings TN34 ...159 E8
  Hove BN3 ....162 F8
Lion Hill BN23 ....174 B5
Lion Hill Cotts BN24 .....174 B5
Lion La BN21 ....162 F7
Lion Mews 8 BN3 ....162 F7
Lion St TN31 ....93 C5
Lionel Rd TN40 ....157 E3
Lions Ct BN26 ....164 E5
Lions Dene BN1 ....142 D4
Lions Gdns BN1 ....142 D4
Lions Pl BN25 ....180 F2
Liphook Cl BN1 ....143 C1
Lipscombe Rd TN2 ....78 C5
Liptraps La TN2 ....8 D7
Lismore Rd BN21 ....185 A2
Lister Ave RH19 ....10 F6
Lister Rd BN23 ....174 A1
Litlington Ct 4 BN25 ....180 C4
Little Bapham Cotts TN3 ...18 F4
Little Bentswood RH16 ....50 F5
Little Bentswood TN6 .....50 F5
Little Black Hill RH16 ....51 F5
Little Common
  Cty Prim Sch TN39 ......156 D4
Little Common Rd TN39 ...156 C5
Little Copse Rd BN6 ......97 E4
Little Cranfield Ct RH19 ...1 D1
Little Cres TN21 ....177 B5
Little East St Brighton BN2 ...189 B2
  Lewes BN7 ....123 D1
Little Footway TN3 ....6 F3
Little George St BN2 ......189 C2
Little Horsted
  CE Prim Sch TN22 ....78 D8
Little Iridge Farm Cotts
  TN35 ....45 C1
Little King St RH19 ....1 E2
Little London Rd RH17 ...106 F8
Little Mallett TN3 ....6 F3
Little Mead BN8 ....58 A8
Little Mount Sion TN1 ....8 A2
Little Paddock
  Crowborough TN6 ....25 E1
  Heathfield TN21 ....82 A7
  Ringmer BN8 ....124 E6
Little Parks Cotts TN33 ..112 E5
Little Pk TN5 ....29 E5
Little Preston St BN1 .....163 B5
Little Ridge Ave TN37 ....136 C5

Little Ridge Cty Prim Sch
  TN37 ....136 C5
Little Sherwood Ind Pk
  TN36 ....116 C5
Little Sunnyside TN6 ......25 F1
Little Trogers La TN6 ......25 F1
Little Twitten TN35 ....156 C3
Little Western St 1 BN1 ...163 E5
Littlemead TN22 ....54 C4
Littlewood La TN22 ....56 C4
Littleworth Cl BN2 ....165 F7
Living World The BN25 ..181 F4
Livingstone Ho 5 BN1 ....163 B7
Livingstone Rd
  Burgess Hill RH15 ....72 F3
  Hove BN3 ....163 C8
Livingstone St BN2 ....164 D5
Lloyd Cl BN3 ....163 C8
Lloyd Rd BN3 ....163 C8
Lockhart Ch RH16 ....50 F2
Lockitt Way BN7 ....145 E5
Locks Cres BN41 ....141 B1
Locks Ct 10 BN41 ....141 B1
Locks Hill BN41 ....141 B1
Lockwood Cl BN22 ....165 F7
Lockwood Cres BN22 ....165 F7
Loder Pl BN1 ....142 F2
Loder Rd BN1 ....142 F2
Lodge Ave BN22 ....173 C1
Lodge Ct East Grinstead RH19 ...146 A8
  Lewes BN7 ....140 F2
Lodge Hill La BN6 ....98 C4
Lodge La BN8 ....98 A2
Lodge La TN35 ....160 C6
Lodge Rd BN26 ....189 C5
Lodge The Brighton BN2 ...185 A2
  6 Eastbourne BN21 ......185 A2
Lodsworth BN2 ....164 F7
Lodsworth Cl BN22 ....164 F7
Loewy Cl Bexhill TN39 ...157 B3
Lomaria Cl BN22 ....173 C1
Lomas La TN18 ....47 F5
Lomond Ave BN1 ....143 B7
London Meed
  Cty Prim Sch RH15 ....73 A1
London Rd Bexhill TN39 ...157 B5
  Brighton BN1 ....189 B4
  Brighton, Withdene BN1 ...142 D4
  Burgess Hill RH15 ....72 F5
  Crowborough TN6 ....25 E4
  Danehill RH17 ....34 A4
  East Grinstead RH19 ....1 C3
  East Hoathly BN8 ....105 A5
  Flimwell TN5 ....32 D3
  Forest Row RH18 ....11 E4
  Hailsham BN27 ....129 A2
  Hassocks BN6, BN9 ....45 A3
  John's Cross TN32,TN33 ...87 D3
  Mansfield TN22 ....55 B4
  Pyecombe BN1,BN45 .....119 C4
  Royal Tunbridge Wells TN4 ...8 A8
  Royal Tunbridge Wells,
    MountSion TN1 ....8 A3
  St Leonards TN37,TN38 ...159 C8
  Uckfield TN22 ....55 D2
London Road Sta BN1 ...164 A8
London Terr BN1 ....189 B4
Londrina Ave BN21 ....185 C2
Londrina Terr BN21 ....185 C2
Long Ave TN40 ....158 A6
Long Barn Motor Mus
  TN21 ....80 F8
Long Beach Mews BN23 ...175 B1
Long Beach View BN23 ..175 B1
Long Hos TN32 ....85 D5
Long La TN33 ....88 E1
Long Man The BN26 ......171 F1
Long Meads TN3,TN4 ......7 B4
Long Park Crw BN6 ....98 D2
Long Slip TN3 ....7 A3
Long Wlk RH16 ....51 B4
Longacre Ct TN40 ....158 C7
Longbury TN22 ....78 C5
Longfield Rd TN2 ....8 D8
Longhill Cl BN2 ....165 E4
Longhill Rd BN2 ....165 E4
Longhill Sch BN2 ....165 E4
Longhurst RH15 ....73 D2
Longhurst Cotts BN6 ......75 D7
Longland Rd BN20 ....184 C4
Longridge Ave BN2 ....177 D5
Longstone Rd BN21 ......185 A3
Longview TN21 ....82 A7
Longwood Cl BN27 ....129 A2
Lonsdale Gdns TN1 ....7 F4
Lookout The BN10 ....167 D3
Loose Farm Barns TN33 ...113 A2
Loose Farm Cotts TN33 ...113 A2
Lordine La TN32 ....137 D3
Lords La TN35 ....137 D3
Lords The BN25 ....180 E6
Lordslaine Cl BN20 ....188 D8
Lordswell La TN6 ....167 E8
Lorinors Ct BN3 ....162 D8
Lorna Rd BN3 ....163 D7
Lorne Rd BN1 ....189 B5
Lorraine Ct 2 Hove BN3 ...163 B6
  11 Hove BN3 ....163 B6
Lorraine Rd BN10 ....167 F4
Losssenham La TN18 ......48 D3
Lottbridge Dr BN22 ....173 F1
Lottbridge Dro
  Eastbourne BN23 ....185 B7
  Eastbourne BN22 ....185 B7
Lottbridge Rdbt BN23 ...185 A8
Lorat Mead TN38 ....158 D6
Love La Eastbourne BN23 ...184 D3
  Mayfield TN20 ....39 F2

Love La continued
  Rye TN31 ....93 B6
Lovegrove Ct BN3 ....162 E8
Lovell Ct BN21 ....184 D5
Lover's Wlk BN1 ....163 F8
Lover's Wlk Cotts BN1 ...163 F8
Lowdells Cl RH19 ....1 C4
Lowdells Dr RH19 ....1 C4
Lowdells La RH19 ....1 C4
Lower Bevendean Ave
  BN2 ....143 E1
Lower Chalvington Pl
  BN2 ....164 E5
Lower Church Rd RH15 ...72 F3
Lower Cross TN31 ....91 E2
Lower Dene RH19 ....1 A4
Lower Dicker BN27 ....128 C3
Lower Dr Seaford BN25 ...180 F5
  Southwick BN42 ....140 E1
Lower Glen Rd TN37 .....136 B4
Lower Green Rd
  Pembury TN2 ....9 D7
  Rusthall TN3, TN4 ....7 C6
Lower Hazelhurst TN5 .....31 A4
Lower High St TN5 ....30 A4
Lower Lake TN33 ....112 E4
Lower Market St 6 BN3 ...163 D5
Lower Mere TN35 ....10 F8
Lower Mere BN2 ....162 F8
Lower Platt TN34 ....179 C7
Lower Platt BN9 ....31 F1
Lower Rd
  Eastbourne BN21 ....184 D4
  Forest Row RH18 ....11 E4
  Golden Cross BN27 ....130 E3
Lower Rock Gdns BN2 ...189 C1
Lordale (The Swedish
  Folk High Sch) BN41 ...141 B1
Loxfield Cl BN20 ....184 D2
Loxfield Gdns TN6 ....26 B1
Loxwood Cl Bexhill TN39 ...156 D5
  Eastbourne BN22 ....173 C1
Loyal Par BN1 ....142 C5
Lucas Cl BN9 ....33 D5
Lucas Cl RH19 ....2 A1
Lucas Grange RH16 ....50 D6
Lucas Shadwell Way TN31 ...93 F2
Lucas Way RH16 ....50 C5
Lucastes Ave RH16 ....50 C6
Lucastes La RH16 ....50 C6
Lucastes Rd RH16 ....50 D6
Lucerne Cl BN41 ....141 B1
Lucerne Rd BN1 ....143 A1
Lucinda Way BN25 ....180 F6
Lucraft Rd BN1,BN2 ......144 A5
Ludley Hill TN31 ....91 A6
Ludlow Rise BN2 ....144 A1
Ludwig La TN32 ....63 C6
Luke Lade Ct BN27 ....152 C7
Lulham Cl BN10 ....167 B2
Lullington Ave BN3 ....162 F8
Lullington Cl
  Bexhill TN40 ....158 A6
  Eastbourne BN21 ....184 C7
  Seaford BN25 ....181 B2
Lullington Gdns TN37 ...136 C5
Lullington Ho 5 BN21 ...184 E4
Lunce's Hill RH16,RH17 ...73 F8
Lundy Wlk
  7 Eastbourne BN23 ....185 F8
  Hailsham BN23 ....129 A2
Lureland Ct BN10 ....178 C6
Lurgashall RH15 ....73 C4
Lushington La BN21 ......185 A2
Lushington Rd BN21 .....185 A2
Lustrells Cl BN2 ....177 B6
Lustrells Cres BN2 ....177 C6
Lustrells Rd BN2 ....177 B6
Lustrells Vale BN2 ....177 C6
Luther St BN2 ....164 C7
Luton Cl BN21 ....184 C6
Luxford Cl TN22 ....78 C7
Luxford Gdns TN6 ....38 A8
Luxford Dr TN6 ....38 A8
Luxford La TN6 ....38 A8
Luxford Rd
  Crowborough TN6 ....38 A8
  Lindfield RH16 ....51 B6
Luxford's La RH17 ....107 D5
Lychgates Cl TN40 ....157 D5
Lydd Cl BN23 ....174 D2
Lydd Rd TN31 ....94 F2
Lymden La TN5 ....43 A7
Lyminster Ave BN1 ....143 A5
Lynchet Cl BN1 ....143 C3
Lynchet Down BN1 ....143 C3
Lynchet Wlk BN1 ....143 C3
Lynchets Cres BN3 ....143 A3
Lynchets The BN7 ....123 D2
Lynchets The TN6 ....38 A8
Lynden Ct 11 BN1 ....142 E2
Lyndhurst Ave TN34 ......137 A4
Lyndhurst Cl BN23 ....173 C6
Lyndhurst Rd BN26 ....173 C6
Lynholm Rd BN26 ....173 C6

Lynton Cl
  East Grinstead RH19 ....2 A2
  Hurstpierpoint BN6 ....97 B5
Lynton Park Ave RH19 .....2 A2
Lynton St BN2 ....164 C7
Lynwood TN3 ....136 C5
Lynwood Cl TN37 ....136 D5
Lynwood Rd BN2 ....177 C4
Lyon Cl BN3 ....163 D7
Lyoth La RH16 ....51 C4
Lyoth Villas RH16 ....51 C4
Lytham Cl TN38 ....158 F8

M

Mabb's Hill TN5 ....42 F7
Maberley Rd TN40 ....157 C6
Mackenzie Ho RH19 ....1 A4
Mackerel Hill TN31 ....68 F4
Mackerel's Rocks BN8 ....76 F3
Mackie Ave Brighton BN1 ...143 A7
  Keymer BN6 ....98 A5
Macmillan Dr BN21 ....184 C5
Madehurst Cl BN2 ....164 D5
Madeira Dr BN2 ....164 C4
Madeira Pk TN1 ....8 B2
Madeira Pl BN2 ....189 C1
Madeira Way BN23 ....185 F8
Madeira Dr TN34 ....136 C3
Mafeking Rd BN2 ....143 D1
Magdalen Ct 5 TN40 ....174 C3
Magdalen Ct TN40 ....157 D4
Magdalen Rd Bexhill TN40 ...157 D4
  St Leonards TN37 ....159 D7
Magellan Way TN40 .....185 D7
Magna Ct TN40 ....157 B4
Magnolia Cl BN21 ....184 D5
Magnolia Dr BN22 ....173 D2
Magnolia Wlk BN22 ....173 D2
Magpie Cl Bexhill TN39 ...156 C6
  St Leonards TN38 ....158 E8
Magreed La TN21 ....59 C2
Maidstone Rd TN1 ....9 E8
Main Rd
  Icklesham TN35,TN36 ...116 D
  Westfield TN35 ....11 B6
Main St TN36 ....70 B6
  Northiam TN31 ....67 B
  Peasmarsh TN31 ....69 B
Mainstone Rd 1 BN23 ...162 F
Maitland Cl TN34 ....136 A
Major Cl BN1 ....143 B
Major York's Rd TN4 ....7 F
Malcolm Gdns BN2 ....173 A
Maldon Rd BN1 ....142 D
Malines Ave BN10 ....178 B
Malines Ave S BN10 ......178 B
Mallard Cl BN27 ....184 F
Mallard Dr TN22 78
Mallard Pl RH19 10
Mallett Cl 5 BN23 180
Malling Cl BN7 123
Malling Down BN7,BN8 ...123
Malling Hill BN7 123
Malling House
  (Sussex Pol HQ) BN7 ...123
Malling Ind 2 Lewes BN7 ...123
Malling St 1 Lewes BN7 ...123
  Lewes BN7 123
Mallory Rd BN3 142
Malt House Trad Est
  BN43 161
Malthouse Bsns Pk The
  TN31 69
Malthouse Ct 14 BN2 ...189
Malthouse La
  Brighton BN2 189
  Burgess Hill RH15 71
  Peasmarsh TN31 69
  Peasmarsh TN31 69
  St John's Common RH15 ...72
Malthouse Trad Est
  BN43 161
Maltings Barn The 7
  BN7 123
Maltings The
  Burgess Hill RH15 65
  Peasmarsh TN31 69
Malton Way TN2 17
Malvern Cl BN23 17
Malvern Ho 1 TN39 157
Malvern St 12 BN3 16
Malvern Way TN34 13
Manaton Cl RH16 5
Manchester Rd TN33 13
Manchester St BN2 18
Mandalay Ct BN1 14
Manhattan Ct BN1 14
Manhattan Gdns TN35 ...13
Manifold Rd BN22 18
Mann St TN34 5
Manner Ct BN8 7
Manning Cl RH19 ....
Manor Ave BN6 9
Manor Cl Brighton BN2 ...16
  Broyle Side BN8 1
  Burgess Hill RH15 ....
  Horam TN21 1
  Uckfield TN22 ....
  Royal Tunbridge Wells TN4 ...
  Seaford BN25 1
  Southwick BN42 1
  Uckfield TN22 ....
  Willingdon BN20 1
Manor Cotts TN3 ....

or Cres BN2 ...... 164 E5
or Ct Seaford BN25 ...... 181 B3
hwick BN42 ...... 162 A7
or Cty Prim Sch TN22 ...... 78 D8
or Dr BN10 ...... 167 B1
or End TN22 ...... 78 C8
or Field Cty Prim Sch
...... 73 C4
or Gdns BN2 ...... 164 E5
or Gn BN2 ...... 164 E5
or Hall Cty Fst Sch
...... 161 F7
or Hall Cty Mid Sch
...... 161 F8
or Hill BN2 ...... 164 E6
or House Ct TN22 ...... 78 C8
or Paddock BN2 ...... 164 E6
or Park Cl BN27 ...... 129 A3
or Park Ct BN26 ...... 173 A6
or Park Rd BN27 ...... 129 A3
or Pk TN4 ...... 7 E3
or Rd BN2 ...... 164 E4
or Rd Bexhill TN40 ...... 157 D4
ton BN2 ...... 164 E5
ess Hill RH15 ...... 73 D3
Grinstead RH19 ...... 1 C2
bourne BN22 ...... 174 A2
bourne BN26 ...... 173 A6
nn TN21 ...... 160 A5
slade-by-Sea BN41 ...... 141 B1
hall TN4 ...... 7 C4
or Rd BN25 ...... 181 B3
ters La BN27 ...... 128 C3
field Rd BN3 ...... 162 E7
ion Cl RH15 ...... 73 D3
ryton Way TN34 ...... 136 C7
 ll Cl BN7 ...... 123 C4
ell Ho Rd BN2 ...... 189 C2
on Ct BN23 ...... 185 D8
on Rd BN2 ...... 143 E1
ters Rd BN20 ...... 184 B3
le Ave TN39 ...... 156 C3
s Cl Bexhill TN39 ...... 156 C3
less Hill RH15 ...... 73 B5
vards Heath RH16 ...... 51 B3
esfield TN22 ...... 55 A4
Tunbridge Wells TN2 ...... 8 B3
ngedean BN2 ...... 165 E7
or Ct Chailsham BN27 ...... 152 A8
hn's Common RH15 ...... 73 A5
or Dr Burgess Hill RH15 ...... 73 D3
Grinstead RH19 ...... 2 A1
e Gdns BN3 ...... 141 F1
e Hts TN37 ...... 136 B7
e Leaf Cl BN9 ...... 179 B7
e Rd
bourne BN25 ...... 185 D7
shaven Heights BN10 ...... 178 F6
e Wlk TN36 ...... 156 C3
hurst Cl TN37 ...... 136 B7
hurst Ct TN37 ...... 136 C8
hurst Rd
hurst Rd 173 D2
slade-by-Sea BN41 ...... 141 A1
ments TN37 ...... 136 B7
hurst Rise TN37 ...... 136 B7
eleaf Gdns BN26 ...... 173 A8
es Cotts TN22 ...... 80 A6
ewood **4** BN1 ...... 142 E3
Rd BN8 ...... 76 D7
ants Cl BN6 ...... 97 A6
ants Dr TN31 ...... 94 E2
ants La BN6 ...... 97 A6
ants Way RH15 ...... 72 F5
s Cl BN20 ...... 184 A8
s Gdns TN37 ...... 136 A5
an Ct TN38 ...... 159 B7
an Ct BN8 ...... 124 C4
an Ct TN37 ...... 157 A3
an's Hill TN6 ...... 25 B6
Bay Cl TN38 ...... 135 E7
sfield Bonners
an Ct TN21 ...... 55 B4
sfield Dr BN24 ...... 174 C3
sfield Rd BN27 ...... 152 B8
aret Ct BN10 ...... 178 B7
aret St BN2 ...... 189 C1
ery Rd BN3 ...... 162 D8
e Ct BN2 ...... 164 E4
se Bexhill TN40 ...... 157 C3
nards TN38 ...... 159 B6
a Court Ave **4**
...... 157 C3
ole Dr TN39 ...... 157 D6
a Heights TN38 ...... 159 A6
a Way BN2 ...... 164 F3
a Wlk BN23 ...... 185 E8
e Ave
alands BN24 ...... 175 F6
e BN3 ...... 162 E6
e Cl
nlands BN24 ...... 175 F6
an BN2 ...... 177 B5
e Cotts TN31 ...... 94 E2
e Cres BN25 ...... 180 F2

Marine Ct
Rottingdean BN2 ...... 177 A5
Seaford BN25 ...... 180 C3
4 St Leonards TN38 ...... 159 C6
Telscombe Cliffs BN10 ...... 177 F3
Marine Dr
Rottingdean BN2 ...... 165 C2
Seaford BN25 ...... 180 B5
Marine Gdns BN2 ...... 189 C1
Marine Par Brighton BN2 ...... 165 C4
Eastbourne BN21,BN22 ...... 185 B3
Hastings TN34 ...... 160 A3
Seaford BN25 ...... 180 C3
Marine Parade Rd **15**
BN2 ...... 164 C4
Marine Rd
Pevensey Bay BN24 ...... 175 D5
Eastbourne BN22 ...... 185 B3
Tre Sq BN2 ...... 164 C4
Marine Terr BN24 ...... 175 D5
Marine Terrace Mews
BN2 ...... 164 C4
Marine View **3** BN2 ...... 189 C2
Mariners Quay BN2 ...... 164 C4
Mariteau Ho TN36 ...... 117 E7
Marjoram Pl BN43 ...... 140 B1
Mark Cl BN25 ...... 181 C2
Mark Cross BN8 ...... 126 B2
Mark Cross CE Prim Sch
TN6 ...... 28 A3
Mark La BN1 ...... 185 A2
Market La **7** BN7 ...... 123 D1
Market Pas
6 Hailsham TN34 ...... 160 A3
St Leonards TN38 ...... 159 C6
Market Pl Burgess Hill RH15 ...... 73 B2
Hailsham BN27 ...... 152 C7
Haywards Heath RH16 ...... 50 D6
14 Royal Tunbridge Wells TN2 ...... 8 B3
Rye TN31 ...... 93 C5
Market Sq Battle TN33 ...... 112 C5
1 Hailsham BN27 ...... 152 C7
Royal Tunbridge Wells TN1 ...... 8 B4
Market St Brighton BN1 ...... 189 B2
Hailsham BN27 ...... 152 C7
Lewes BN7 ...... 123 D1
Rye TN31 ...... 93 C5
St Leonards TN38 ...... 159 C6
Market Terr **1** TN38 ...... 159 C6
Markland Way TN22 ...... 78 A7
Marklye La Heathfield TN21 ...... 59 B2
Rushlake Green TN21 ...... 83 C3
Markstakes Cnr BN8 ...... 101 A6
Markstakes La BN8 ...... 76 C2
Markwick Terr TN38 ...... 159 B8
Marlborough Cl
Eastbourne BN23 ...... 174 D3
Royal Tunbridge Wells TN4 ...... 7 A4
Marlborough Ct
Burgess Hill RH15 ...... 72 E3
Eastbourne BN21 ...... 184 F3
1 Hove BN3 ...... 162 E5
Marlborough Dr RH15 ...... 73 C2
Marlborough Mews BN1 ...... 189 A2
Marlborough Pl BN1,BN2 ...... 189 B3
Marlborough St BN1 ...... 189 A2
Marle Ave RH15 ...... 73 A4
Marle Green Cotts TN21 ...... 84 B3
Marley La TN33 ...... 112 F4
Marley Gdns TN33 ...... 112 F4
Marley La TN33 ...... 113 B6
Marley Lodge BN9 ...... 189 C4
Marley Rise TN33 ...... 112 F4
Marline Ave TN38 ...... 136 A4
Marline Rd TN38 ...... 136 A4
Marlinspike The BN43 ...... 161 A6
Marlow Ave BN22 ...... 185 B6
Marlow Dr
Haywards Heath RH16 ...... 51 C4
St Leonards TN37 ...... 136 C5
Marlow Rd BN22 ...... 185 B6
Marlowes The TN40 ...... 157 F3
Marlpit Cl RH19 ...... 1 E4
Marlpit Gdns TN6 ...... 31 E1
Marlpit Rd RH19 ...... 21 A6
Marlpit The TN6 ...... 29 E5
Marlpits La TN33 ...... 133 F7
Marmion Rd BN3 ...... 162 F7
Marsden Rd BN23 ...... 174 E1
Marsh Ho **3** BN2 ...... 161 D7
Marsh Quarter La TN18 ...... 47 C3
Marshall Ct BN22 ...... 173 D1
Marshall La BN9 ...... 179 C7
Marshall Rd BN23 ...... 185 A8
Marshall Rdbt BN23 ...... 174 A1
Marshall Way RH15 ...... 141 F1
Marshalls Row BN1 ...... 189 B4
Marshfoot La BN27 ...... 152 D8
Marshlands Cty Prim Sch
BN27 ...... 152 D8
Marshlands La TN21 ...... 82 A7
Marston Ct **10** BN3 ...... 163 E7
Marston Rd TN31 ...... 93 B4
Martello Ct
Pevensey Bay BN24 ...... 175 C3
South Heighton BN9 ...... 168 D2
Martello Mews **1** BN24 ...... 175 E8
Martello Rd
Eastbourne BN22 ...... 185 D6
Seaford BN25 ...... 180 E2
Martello Tower Mus
BN25 ...... 180 E1
Martens Field BN7 ...... 146 E1

Martha Gunn Rd BN2 ...... 143 E1
Martin Cl BN22 ...... 173 D1
Martin Ct BN22 ...... 173 D1
Martineau La TN35 ...... 137 F5
Martingale Cl TN37 ...... 136 C5
Martins The BN10 ...... 167 B1
Martlet Ho Brighton BN1 ...... 164 A8
Martlet Rd Brighton BN1 ...... 164 A8
Martlet The BN3 ...... 142 D1
Martletts Bexhill TN40 ...... 157 E5
Lower Willingdon BN22 ...... 173 B3
Martletts The
Broad Oak TN31 ...... 90 C4
Burgess Hill RH15 ...... 73 A3
Crowborough TN6 ...... 25 F1
Hailsham BN27 ...... 152 A7
Hastings TN34 ...... 136 E2
Lewes BN7 ...... 123 D3
South Chailey BN8 ...... 100 D7
Martletts The
Burwash Common TN19 ...... 60 F3
Ringmer BN8 ...... 124 E6
Martyn's Cl BN2 ...... 165 E4
Martyns Pl RH19 ...... 11 A8
Martyns Way TN40 ...... 158 A5
Marwick Ct TN38 ...... 159 B8
Mary Burfield Ct **3** TN21 ...... 82 A7
Mary Stamford Gn TN31 ...... 94 A3
Maryan Ct BN27 ...... 152 C7
Maryland Rd TN4 ...... 8 D1
Marylands RH16 ...... 50 F5
Maskelyne Rd BN27 ...... 131 A1
Mason Cl RH19 ...... 2 A2
Mason Rd Rye TN31 ...... 93 A5
Seaford BN25 ...... 180 F4
Matlock Rd Brighton BN1 ...... 142 D2
Eastbourne BN20 ...... 188 E8
Maudlin Ct TN37 ...... 159 C8
Maunsell Cl RH16 ...... 50 F3
Maunsell Rd TN38 ...... 135 F5
Maurice Rd BN25 ...... 180 F1
May Ave RH25 ...... 180 A8
May Cotts BN7 ...... 123 C4
May Rd BN2 ...... 164 D7
May Tree Gdns TN40 ...... 157 F6
Mayfair Cl BN26 ...... 172 F4
Mayfair Rd BN20 ...... 173 B1
Mayfield Ave BN10 ...... 178 D6
Mayfield CE Prim Sch
TN20 ...... 40 B3
Mayfield Cl Brighton BN1 ...... 143 A5
Hastings TN35 ...... 39 F2
Royal Tunbridge Wells TN4 ...... 7 F4
Mayfield Cres BN1 ...... 142 F5
Mayfield Ct Broad Oak TN21 ...... 59 E1
Burgess Hill RH15 ...... 73 B3
Saltdean BN27 ...... 177 C6
Mayfield Flat TN21,TN22 ...... 81 A8
Mayfield La Durgates TN5 ...... 29 D4
St Leonards TN38 ...... 135 D2
Mayfield Pl TN5 ...... 29 E5
Mayfield Pl BN27 ...... 185 A4
Mayfield Rd
East Grinstead RH19 ...... 10 D6
Forest Row RH18 ...... 12 A2
Royal Tunbridge Wells TN4 ...... 7 F4
Mayflower Rd
Haywards Heath RH16 ...... 50 F4
3 Shoreham-by-Sea BN43 ...... 161 A6
Mayflower Rd BN43 ...... 50 F4
Mayflower Sq BN1 ...... 189 B4
Mayhew Way BN7 ...... 123 D2
Mayhouse Rd RH15 ...... 72 F1
Maynard's Green
Cty Prim Sch TN21 ...... 82 A2
Mayne Way TN34 ...... 137 B4
Mayo Ct **5** BN2 ...... 164 B8
Mayo La BN2 ...... 164 B8
Mayo Rd BN2 ...... 164 B8
Mayo Rise BN2 ...... 164 B8
Maypole Cotts TN22 ...... 56 B8
Maypole Rd
Ashurst Wood RH19 ...... 11 E6
East Grinstead RH19 ...... 1 D6
Maytree Rd TN17 ...... 9 C7
Maytree Cotts BN9 ...... 100 C7
Maytree Wlk BN3 ...... 141 E1
Mayvern Ct TN6 ...... 25 E1
Mayview Ct TN21 ...... 59 E1
Maywood Ave BN22 ...... 173 E2
Maze Hill TN38 ...... 159 B7
Maze Hill Terr TN38 ...... 159 B7
Mcbechie Ho RH19 ...... 1 D3
McIndoe Rd RH19 ...... 1 D3
McMichael Way TN19 ...... 45 A3
McWilliam Rd BN2 ...... 144 C1
Meachants Cl BN20 ...... 173 B2
Meachants La BN20 ...... 173 B2
Mead The TN39 ...... 156 D4
Meadow Bank TN21 ...... 82 A8
Meadow Cl
Hailsham BN27 ...... 129 B1
Hove BN3 ...... 142 B3
Portslade-by-Sea BN41 ...... 141 B2
Rottingdean BN2 ...... 177 B6
Southwick BN42 ...... 162 A8
St Leonards TN38 ...... 136 A4
Meadow Cres TN37 ...... 157 C7
Meadow Ct RH16 ...... 51 B6
Meadow Ho BN10 ...... 178 C6
Meadow Hill Rd **8** TN6 ...... 26 C1
Meadow La
Burgess Hill RH15 ...... 72 F1
Lindfield RH16 ...... 51 B6
Meadow Par BN27 ...... 165 F3
Meadow Pl TN22 ...... 78 C6

Meadow Rd
Groombridge TN3 ...... 15 C7
Hove BN3 ...... 142 A6
Royal Tunbridge Wells TN1 ...... 8 A4
Rusthall TN4 ...... 7 C4
Meadow Rise TN21 ...... 106 F7
Meadow The TN2 ...... 9 E8
Meadow Vale BN20 ...... 165 E5
Meadow View
Rotherfield TN6 ...... 39 B7
Westfield TN35 ...... 114 C4
Meadow View Cotts TN19 ...... 45 A3
Meadow Way
Fairlight Cove TN35 ...... 138 C4
Heathfield TN21 ...... 82 A6
Seaford BN25 ...... 181 B3
Meadowcroft Cl RH19 ...... 1 C2
Meadowlands Ave BN22 ...... 173 D1
Meadows Ave BN26 ...... 97 F5
Meadows Rd BN22 ...... 173 B2
Meadows The
Crowborough TN6 ...... 25 F2
Hove BN3 ...... 141 C3
Lewes BN7 ...... 123 C6
Meadowside TN33 ...... 88 E1
Meadowside Cotts TN5 ...... 31 F1
Meadowview
Eastbourne BN20 ...... 143 E1
Lower Street TN33 ...... 133 B5
Rye Harbour TN31 ...... 95 A3
Meadow View Bexhill TN39 ...... 156 C4
Hove BN3 ...... 141 C3
Meads Brow BN20 ...... 188 D8
Meads CE Prim Sch
BN20 ...... 188 D7
Meads Cl BN3 ...... 141 C3
Meads St BN20 ...... 184 E1
Meads St BN20 ...... 188 E8
Meads The Brighton BN1 ...... 143 D5
East Grinstead RH19 ...... 10 E7
Royal Tunbridge Wells TN2 ...... 8 C2
Meadway BN26 ...... 188 E8
Meadway Cres BN3 ...... 141 F2
Meadway Ct BN42 ...... 141 F2
Meadway The
Brighton BN2 ...... 164 F5
Shoreham-by-Sea BN43 ...... 161 A6
Mealla Cl BN2 ...... 123 C3
Medina Dr BN24 ...... 163 B6
Medina Pl BN3 ...... 163 B5
Medina Terr Hove BN3 ...... 163 B5
St Leonards TN38 ...... 159 A6
Medina Villas BN3 ...... 163 B5
Medmerry Hill BN2 ...... 143 E2
Medway Crowborough TN6 ...... 26 C1
Hailsham BN27 ...... 129 A1
Medway Dr
East Grinstead RH19 ...... 10 D6
Forest Row RH18 ...... 12 A2
Medway La BN24 ...... 174 C4
Medway Rd TN1 ...... 8 B5
Medway View TN40 ...... 12 A2
Meeching Cl BN9 ...... 179 C7
Meeching Pl BN9 ...... 179 C7
Meeching Rd BN9 ...... 179 C7
Meeching Valley
Cty Prim Sch BN9 ...... 179 B7
Meeds Rd RH15 ...... 73 A2
Meeting House La BN1 ...... 189 B2
Megrims Hill TN18 ...... 47 A6
Melbourne Rd BN22 ...... 185 A4
Melbourne St BN2 ...... 164 C8
Melfort Rd TN6 ...... 25 D1
Melrose Ave BN1 ...... 141 A1
Melrose Cl Brighton BN1 ...... 143 C1
Hailsham BN27 ...... 152 A8
Melvill La BN1 ...... 173 B1
Melville Rd BN3 ...... 163 E7
Mendip Ave BN23 ...... 174 D3
Mendip Gdns TN34 ...... 137 B3
Mendip Wlk TN2 ...... 9 B3
Menzies Rd TN38 ...... 136 B3
Meon Cl BN20 ...... 184 A5
Mercatoria TN38 ...... 159 C6
Mercer St TN1 ...... 8 A5
Mercers TN5 ...... 42 F3
Mercerad Rd BN25 ...... 180 F3
Merchland Rd BN2 ...... 144 B2
Merevale BN1 ...... 143 A2
Merewood CI BN23 ...... 184 E4
Mereworth Rd TN4 ...... 8 A6
Meridian Ct BN10 ...... 178 C8
Meridian Cty Prim Sch
BN10 ...... 167 C1
Meridian Ind Est The
BN10 ...... 178 C7
Meridian L Ctr BN10 ...... 178 C7
Meridian Rd BN7 ...... 123 B2
Meridian Way
East Grinstead RH19 ...... 1 F3
Peacehaven BN10 ...... 178 C7
Merivale TN35 ...... 137 A6
Merlin CI BN3 ...... 163 D8
Merlin Ct BN27 ...... 152 E7
Merlin Way RH19 ...... 2 A3
Mermaid Pas TN31 ...... 93 B5
Mermaid St TN31 ...... 93 B5
Merrimac Ho **1** TN40 ...... 157 E4
Merrimede Cl TN38 ...... 159 A7

Merriments La TN18,TN19 ...... 45 D5
Merrion Cl TN4 ...... 8 B7
Merrion Way TN4 ...... 8 B7
Merston Ct BN2 ...... 165 E6
Merton Ct **7** TN40 ...... 157 E4
Meryon Ct TN31 ...... 93 C5
Metcalfe Ave BN9 ...... 179 B8
Metropole Ct
12 Brighton BN1 ...... 163 E5
11 Eastbourne BN21 ...... 185 B3
Mewetts Ct BN20 ...... 173 B3
Mews Cl RH19 ...... 10 F6
Mews Rd TN38 ...... 159 C6
Mews The Brighton BN1 ...... 142 E2
East Hoathly BN8 ...... 105 A5
Pembury TN2 ...... 9 C5
3 Royal Tunbridge Wells TN1 ...... 8 B3
Seaford BN25 ...... 181 B4
Meyners Cl BN3 ...... 141 C1
Michael Fields RH18 ...... 11 C3
Michael Tetley Hall
(Nursery Trng Coll, Dr
Barnardo's Home) TN2 ...... 8 D6
Michel Cl BN20 ...... 183 C3
Michel Dene Cl BN20 ...... 183 C1
Michel Dene Rd BN20 ...... 183 C1
Michelbourne Ct RH15 ...... 72 E1
Michele Cl **1** TN38 ...... 136 B1
Michelham Cl BN23 ...... 174 A4
Michelham Priory BN27 ...... 151 B7
Michelham Rd BN22 ...... 173 C1
Michelson Cl TN33 ...... 135 F4
Micklefield Sch BN25 ...... 181 B3
Middle Dr TN22 ...... 55 A6
Middle Field 9 E8
Middle Furlong BN25 ...... 180 F3
Middle La TN21 ...... 83 E3
Middle Rd
Bells Yew Green TN3 ...... 18 A5
Brighton BN1 ...... 142 B5
Hastings TN35 ...... 137 C4
Shoreham-by-Sea BN43 ...... 161 B7
Middle Row **R** RH19 ...... 10 F8
Middle St Brighton BN1 ...... 189 A2
Falmer BN1 ...... 144 C6
Hastings TN34 ...... 159 F8
Portslade-by-Sea BN41 ...... 162 B6
Middle Street
Cty Prim Sch BN1 ...... 189 A2
Middle Way
Burgess Hill RH15 ...... 73 B3
Lewes BN7 ...... 123 A1
Middle Wlk TN2 ...... 8 E8
Middleham Ct BN23 ...... 174 C4
Middleham Way BN23 ...... 174 C4
Middlesex Ct **4** BN22 ...... 185 B4
Middleton Rd BN40 ...... 157 F3
Middleton Dr BN20 ...... 162 D6
Middleton Rise BN1 ...... 143 C5
Middleway RH27 ...... 131 B5
Midfields Cl RH15 ...... 73 B3
Midfields Wlk RH15 ...... 73 B4
Midhurst Rd BN23 ...... 173 F4
Midhurst Rise BN1 ...... 143 B6
Midhurst Wlk BN3 ...... 141 D3
Midway Rd BN2 ...... 165 C8
Midway The TN4 ...... 7 D2
Mighell St BN2 ...... 189 C2
Milchester Ho BN10 ...... 188 E8
Mildenhall Dr TN37 ...... 136 B8
Mildmay Cl BN8 ...... 124 B8
Mildmay Rd BN7 ...... 123 A1
Mile End Cotts BN1 ...... 142 E6
Mile Oak Cres BN42 ...... 140 F1
Mile Oak Cty Prim Sch
BN41 ...... 140 F3
Mile Oak Gdns BN41 ...... 141 A1
Mile Oak Rd
Portslade-by-Sea BN41 ...... 140 F3
Southwick BN42 ...... 141 B1
Milestones TN21 ...... 82 B8
Milfoil Dr BN23 ...... 174 B3
Military Rd TN30,TN31 ...... 70 F3
Mill Brooks BN8 ...... 100 D7
Mill Cl East Grinstead RH19 ...... 10 E7
Friston BN20 ...... 183 A1
Hastings TN35 ...... 137 E4
Heathfield TN21 ...... 82 A4
Portslade-by-Sea BN41 ...... 141 C1
Ringmer BN8 ...... 124 C5
South Chailey BN8 ...... 100 D7
Staplecross TN32 ...... 65 E2
Wannock BN26 ...... 172 F4
Westfield TN35 ...... 114 E5
Mill Cnr TN31 ...... 67 E7
Mill Cotts RH19 ...... 10 E7
Mill Cres TN6 ...... 25 F3
Mill Dr Crowborough TN6 ...... 25 F3
Hove BN3 ...... 142 A3
Seaford BN25 ...... 181 A3
Mill Gap Rd BN21 ...... 184 F4
Mill Gdns Heathfield TN21 ...... 82 A5
Ringmer BN8 ...... 124 D5
Mill Green Rd RH16 ...... 50 E7
Mill Hill Ho 23 E2
Mill Hill La Barcombe BN8 ...... 101 D2
Clayton BN6,BN45 ...... 119 E2
Crowborough TN6 ...... 25 E2

Mill La continued
Dormansland RH7 . . . . .1 F8
East Hoathly BN8 . . . . .105 A5
Flackley Ash TN31 . . . . .68 F3
Goddards' Green BN6 . . . . .72 A3
Hastings TN35 . . . . .137 C5
Hellingly BN27 . . . . .129 A6
Hooe Common TN33 . . . . . . .132 F2
Mark Cross TN6 . . . . .28 A3
Portslade-by-Sea BN41 . . . . .141 B1
Punnett's Town TN21 . . . . .83 D6
Rodmell BN7 . . . . .167 D8
Uckfield TN22 . . . . .78 C6
Westfield TN35 . . . . .114 E5
Mill Mead BN8 . . . . .124 E5
Mill Path BN8 . . . . .124 E5
Mill Pk RH15 . . . . .73 B3
Mill Race BN6 . . . . .97 E8
Mill Rd Brighton BN1 . . . . . .142 C6
Burgess Hill RH15 . . . . .73 B3
Eastbourne BN21 . . . . .184 D3
Hailsham BN27 . . . . .152 D6
Heathfield TN21 . . . . .81 F7
Lewes BN7 . . . . .123 E3
Ringmer BN8 . . . . .124 D5
Rye TN31 . . . . .93 C2
Southwick BN41 . . . . .162 B7
Winchelsea TN36 . . . . .117 E8
Mill Rd Ind Est BN41 . . . . . .162 B7
Mill Rise Brighton BN1 . . . . .142 C5
Heathfield TN21 . . . . .82 A2
Robertsbridge TN22 . . . . .64 A3
Mill St BN1 . . . . .144 C7
Mill Stream Mdw RH16 . . . . .50 D7
Mill View BN8 . . . . .124 C4
Mill View Cl BN24 . . . . .174 D6
Mill View Hospl BN3 . . . . . .141 E1
Mill View Rd TN39 . . . . .157 B7
Mill Way
East Grinstead RH19 . . . . .10 E7
Wannock BN26 . . . . .172 E4
Mill Wood RH15 . . . . .73 B3
Milland Cl TN40 . . . . .157 E6
Milland Rd BN27 . . . . .129 B1
Millbank RH15 . . . . .73 B3
Millberg Rd BN25 . . . . .181 C4
Millbrook Bsns Pk TN6 . . . . .38 D8
Millbrook Cl TN21 . . . . .107 A7
Millbrook Gdns BN20 . . . . .184 B6
Millbrook Ind Est TN6 . . . . .38 D8
Millbrook Rd TN6 . . . . .26 A3
Millcroft BN1 . . . . .142 C5
Millcroft Ave BN42 . . . . .140 E1
Millcroft Gdns BN42 . . . . . .140 E1
Millcross Rd BN41 . . . . .141 B1
Milldown Rd BN25 . . . . .180 F3
Miller's Hill TN35 . . . . .114 E6
Miller's Rd BN1 . . . . .142 E1
Millers Rise BN27 . . . . .152 A6
Millers Way RH15 . . . . .73 B4
Millfield Bexhill TN40 . . . . . .157 C4
Ninfield TN33 . . . . .133 A6
Millfield Cl Newick BN8 . . . . .76 C7
Seaford BN25 . . . . .181 B4
Millfield Cotts BN8 . . . . .76 C7
Millfield Ct TN40 . . . . .157 C4
Millfield Rise TN40 . . . . . . .157 C4
Millfields BN26 . . . . .173 A7
Millfields Ct BN26 . . . . .173 A7
Millham Cl TN39 . . . . .156 F7
Millington Ct TN22 . . . . .78 C6
Millrace The BN26 . . . . .172 F4
Millstream Cl TN3 . . . . .6 D1
Millstream Gdns BN26 . . . .172 F4
Millward Rd BN24 . . . . .175 C3
Millwood Cl TN22 . . . . .55 D4
Millwood La TN22 . . . . .55 C4
Millwood Rd TN39 . . . . .157 A8
Milnard Cres BN42 . . . . .157 C4
Milner Flats BN2 . . . . .189 C2
Milner Rd BN2 . . . . .143 D1
Milnthorpe Rd
Eastbourne BN20 . . . . .188 E8
Hove BN3 . . . . .162 F8
Milton Cres
East Grinstead RH19 . . . . .10 C8
Eastbourne BN21 . . . . .184 C4
Milton Ct RH16 . . . . .50 D5
Milton Dr
Royal Tunbridge Wells TN2 . . . . .9 E7
Southwick BN42 . . . . .161 F8
Milton Rd Brighton BN2 . . . .189 C4
Eastbourne BN21 . . . . .184 C4
Hayward Heath RH16 . . . . .50 D6
Milton St BN2 . . . . .174 B7
Milward Cres TN34 . . . . . . .160 A4
Milward Ct TN34 . . . . .161 C8
Milward Rd TN34 . . . . .160 A5
Mimosa Cl BN26 . . . . .173 A7
Mimosa Ct BN1 . . . . .143 B3
Mimram Rd BN24 . . . . .174 A5
Mindleheim Ave RH19 . . . . . .2 B2
Minnels The BN6 . . . . .98 A3
Minsted Sq TN19 . . . . .156 C2
Minster Cl BN26 . . . . .173 A7
Mint The TN31 . . . . .93 B5
Mistley Cl TN40 . . . . .158 A6
Mitchelldean BN10 . . . . . . .167 C1
Mitre Ho BN1 . . . . .163 E5
Mitten Rd TN40 . . . . .157 C4
Moat Croft BN21 . . . . .184 E4
Moat Croft Rd BN21 . . . . . .184 E4
Moat Farm TN7 . . . . .17 A2
Moat La Cowden TN8 . . . . . . .4 E7

Moat La continued
Waldron TN21 . . . . .80 D2
Westfield TN33 . . . . .114 B3
Moat Rd RH19 . . . . .1 E2
Mocatta Way TN21 . . . . .72 D5
Modena Rd BN3 . . . . .163 C6
Moira House Sch BN20 . . . .188 D8
Molesey Ct TN22 . . . . .78 C7
Molesworth St BN3 . . . . . . .162 F8
Molyneux Almshouses TN4 . .7 B4
Molyneux Ct TN4 . . . . .7 F4
Molyneux Park Gdns TN4 . . . .7 F4
Molyneux Park Rd TN4 . . . . . .7 F4
Mona Rd BN22 . . . . .185 B5
Monarch Gdns
Eastbourne BN23 . . . . .174 F1
Seaford BN25 . . . . .181 A5
Monarch St TN34 . . . . .136 A5
Monarch Ho BN22 . . . . .185 E5
Monastery Gdns TN6 . . . . . . .39 F8
Monceux Rd
Eastbourne BN21 . . . . .184 C4
Herstmonceux BN27 . . . . .130 C6
Monckton Way BN7 . . . . . . .145 E5
Monger's Mead BN8 . . . . . . .101 E4
Monk Cl BN1 . . . . .143 E6
Monk's House TN4 . . . . .146 E1
Monks La Lewes BN7 . . . . . .146 C8
Newbury's TN5 . . . . .30 B8
Monks Way Lewes BN7 . . . . .123 C3
Northiam TN31 . . . . .67 D4
Monk's Wlk TN36 . . . . .117 C7
Monmouth St BN3 . . . . .163 B7
Monson Rd TN1 . . . . .8 B4
Monson Way BN1 . . . . .8 B4
Montacute Gdns TN2 . . . . . . .7 F2
Montacute Rd Lewes BN7 . .146 A8
Royal Tunbridge Wells TN2 . . . .7 F2
Montacute Way TN22 . . . . . .78 D8
Montague Cl BN43 . . . . .161 D7
Montague Ct
6 Brighton BN2 . . . . .164 C4
2 Peacehaven-by-Sea BN43 .161 D7
Montague Pl BN2 . . . . .164 C4
Montague St *4* BN2 . . . . . .164 C4
Montague Way BN24 . . . . . .174 F5
Montana Ct TN38 . . . . .135 E6
Montargis Way TN6 . . . . .26 A1
Montefiore Rd BN3 . . . . .163 E7
Monteith Cl TN3 . . . . .7 A3
Monterey Cl TN39 . . . . .156 E3
Monterey Gdns TN39 . . . . .156 E3
Montes Hill RH16 . . . . .51 F8
Monteswood La
RH16,RH17 . . . . .52 B8
Montfort Cl BN43 . . . . .161 C6
Montfort Ct BN24 . . . . .174 F6
Montfort Rd BN24 . . . . .174 F6
Montgomery Rd
Hastings TN35 . . . . .137 D5
Montgomery St BN3 . . . . . .163 A7
Montgomery Way TN4 . . . . . .8 B7
Montpelier Cres BN1 . . . . . .163 E6
Montpelier Lodge *9*
BN1 . . . . .163 E6
Montpelier Rd BN1 . . . . . . .163 E5
Montpelier St BN1 . . . . .163 E6
Montpelier Villas BN1 . . . . .163 E6
Montreal Rd BN2 . . . . .143 D1
Montserrat *2* TN39 . . . . . .157 A2
Monument View BN2 . . . . . .164 D6
Moons Hill La RH19, RH7, TN8 . .2 E8
Moons Hill TN33 . . . . .133 B6
Moor Hall Dr TN33 . . . . .132 F6
Moor Hill TN18 . . . . .45 F8
Moor La Ashton Green BN8 .125 B3
Westfield TN35 . . . . .114 E3
Moor Pl RH19 . . . . .1 D2
Moor Rd TN35 . . . . .114 E3
Moor The TN18 . . . . .45 F8
Moore Pk BN27 . . . . .152 D7
Moore's La TN31 . . . . .90 E8
Moorhen Cl TN38 . . . . .158 E8
Moorhurst Rd TN38 . . . . . . .135 F5
Moorings The
East Grinstead RH19 . . . . .1 A3
Eastbourne BN20 . . . . .188 E8
Lewes BN7 . . . . .123 E1
Shoreham-by-Sea BN43 . . . . .161 C6
Moray Wlk BN27 . . . . .129 A2
Morecambe Rd BN1 . . . . . . .143 A6
Morestead BN10 . . . . .167 D1
Morgan Cl TN39 . . . . .156 F7
Morgay Wood La TN35 . . . . .115 E2
Morlais Pl TN36 . . . . .118 B6
Morlais Ridge TN36 . . . . . . .118 B6
Morland Dr TN3 . . . . .20 B5
Morlands Cl TN33 . . . . .133 B5
Morley Cl BN7 . . . . .146 A7
Morley St BN2 . . . . .189 C3
Morningside Cl BN25 . . . . . .180 F4
Mornington Cres BN3 . . . . .162 D7
Mornington Mansions
BN3 . . . . .162 D7
Morris Rd BN7 . . . . .123 E1
Morten Rd BN7 . . . . .162 D7
Mortain Rd BN24 . . . . .174 F6
Mortimer Gdns BN26 . . . . .172 F4
Mortimer Rd
Eastbourne BN22 . . . . .185 A6
Hove BN3 . . . . .163 A8
Morton Rd RH19 . . . . .10 E7
Moscow Rd TN35 . . . . .137 C3
Motcombe Cl *8* BN2 . . . . .157 D3
Motcombe Cty Inf Sch
BN21 .184 C5
Motcombe La BN21 . . . . . . .184 D4

Motcombe Rd BN21 . . . . . .184 D4
Motte Field TN7 . . . . .13 E4
Mottins Hill TN6 . . . . .38 D8
Moulsecoomb Cty Inf Sch
BN2 . . . . .143 E3
Moulsecoomb
Cty Jun Sch BN2 . . . . .143 E3
Moulsecoomb Sta BN2 . . . .143 D2
Moulsecoomb Way BN2 . . .143 F4
Mount Caburn Cres
BN10 .167 C2
Mount Cl BN9 . . . . .179 F8
Mount Dr BN2 . . . . .177 D6
Mount Edgcumbe Rd TN4 . . .8 A3
Mount Ephraim TN4 . . . . .8 A4
Mount Ephraim Rd TN1 . . . . .8 A4
Mount Harry Rd BN7 . . . . . .123 A2
Mount Idol View TN39 . . . . .157 A8
Mount Joy TN33 . . . . .112 D5
Mount Pl *9* BN2 . . . . .123 C1
Mount Pleasant
Blackboys TN22 . . . . .80 A6
Brighton BN2 . . . . .189 C2
Crowborough TN6 . . . . .38 B7
Hook Green TN3 . . . . .19 E6
Mount Pleasant BN8 . . . . .101 E6
Sparrow's Green TN5 . . . . .29 E5
6 St Leonards TN38 . . . . . .159 C4
The Moor TN18 . . . . .45 F8
Uckfield TN22 . . . . .78 C6
Mount Pleasant Ave *2* TN1 . .8 B3
Mount Pleasant Cres *2*
TN34 .136 F1
Mount Pleasant La TN34 . .160 A6
Mount Pleasant La TN20 . . . .20 A6
Mount Pleasant Rd
Hastings TN34 . . . . .160 A6
Royal Tunbridge Wells TN1 . . . .8 A3
Mount Rd
Eastbourne BN20 . . . . .188 F8
Hastings TN35 . . . . .160 C6
Newhaven BN9 . . . . .179 F8
Mount Sion TN1 . . . . .8 A2
Mount St Battle TN33 . . . . . .112 D5
Lewes BN7 . . . . .146 C8
Mount The Hailsham BN27 . .152 C6
St Leonards TN38 . . . . .159 B7
Uckfield TN22 . . . . .78 C8
Mount View Terr BN27 . . . . .152 C6
Mount Zion Pl BN1 . . . . .189 A3
Mountain Ash BN27 . . . . . . .152 A8
Mountbatten Cl TN35 . . . . .137 D5
Mountbatten Dr BN3 . . . . . .162 E8
Mountbatten Dr BN23 . . . . .185 F7
Mountfield & Whatlington
CE Prim Sch
TN32 . . . . .87 D7
Mountfield Ct *4* TN1 . . . . . .8 B3
Mountfield Gdns TN1 . . . . . . .8 B3
Mountfield La TN32 . . . . .86 C8
Mountfield Rd
Eastbourne BN22 . . . . .173 F1
Lewes BN7 . . . . .146 D8
Royal Tunbridge Wells TN1 . . . .8 B3
Mountfield Villas TN32 . . . . .87 C5
Mountfields BN1 . . . . .143 C2
Mountney Bridge Bsns Pk
BN24 .174 F4
Mountney Dr BN24 . . . . .175 F7
Mountney Rd BN21 . . . . . . .184 C4
Mountreed TN20 . . . . .52 B7
Mowden Sch BN1 . . . . .142 D1
Moy Ave BN22 . . . . .185 B5
Moyne Cl BN1 . . . . .141 E1
Muirfield Ct *4* RH16 . . . . . .50 E7
Muirfield Rise TN38 . . . . . . .158 E8
Mulberry Cl Bexhill TN39 . . .156 C4
Brighton BN1 . . . . .142 F3
Eastbourne BN22 . . . . .173 E3
Shoreham-by-Sea BN43 . . . . .140 D1
Mulberry Ct BN26 . . . . .173 A6
Mulberry La RH16 . . . . .50 D4
Mulberry Way TN21 . . . . .81 F7
Mulberry Wlk TN37 . . . . . . .136 D5
Munns Dr RH15 . . . . .73 B4
Munster Cotts BN8 . . . . . . .101 E4
Munster Gn BN8 . . . . .101 E4
Murray Ave BN9 . . . . .179 C7
Museum of Natural Life
TN32 . . . . .64 B4
Museum of Shops BN21 . . . .185 A2
Musgrave Ave RH19 . . . . .10 E8
Mushroom Field BN7 . . . . . .145 E5
Muster Cl N RH16 . . . . .50 D4
Muster Gn N RH16 . . . . .50 D4
Muster Gn S RH16 . . . . .50 D4
Mutton Hall Hill TN21 . . . . . .82 B8
Mutton Hall La TN21 . . . . . . .82 B8
Mutton Hill RH7 . . . . .2 B7
Myrtle Cotts TN35 . . . . .25 F3
Myrtle Rd Crowborough TN6 . .25 F1
Eastbourne BN22 . . . . .185 D6

N

Namrik Mews BN3 . . . . .163 A6
Nan Kemp's Grave BN7 . . . .145 E6
Nan Tucks La TN22 . . . . .56 C2
Nanson Rd BN1 . . . . .143 D6
Naomi Cl BN20 . . . . .184 E1
Napier Ho *6* BN2 . . . . .164 C7
Napier Rd
Royal Tunbridge Wells TN2 . . . .8 D2
St Leonards TN38 . . . . .135 E4
Nash La RH17 . . . . .52 A4
Natal Rd BN2 . . . . .143 D1

Neale Cl RH19 . . . . .1 B3
Neath Rd TN29 . . . . .96 A2
Neaves La BN8 . . . . .125 A5
Neill's Cl BN9 . . . . .179 C7
Neills Rd TN32 . . . . .19 D2
Neilson Ct TN34 . . . . .136 D1
Nellington Ct TN4 . . . . .7 B4
Nellington Rd TN3, TN4 . . . . . .7 B4
Nelson Dr BN23 . . . . .185 E6
Nelson Ho TN3 . . . . .156 E4
Nelson Row BN2 . . . . .189 C3
Nelson Rd Hastings TN34 . . .160 A5
Royal Tunbridge Wells TN2 . . . .8 D2
Nelson Row BN2 . . . . .189 C2
Neptune Ct BN2 . . . . .164 F3
Nesbitt Rd BN2 . . . . .143 D1
Nestor Ct BN1 . . . . .163 E8
Nether La TN22 . . . . .57 A4
Netherfield Ave BN23 . . . . .174 F2
Netherfield CE Prim Sch
TN33 . . . . .86 C2
Netherfield Gn BN2 . . . . . . .165 F8
Netherfield Hill TN33 . . . . . .112 B7
Netherfield Hill Cotts
TN33 .112 B7
Netherfield Rd TN33 . . . . . . .111 B6
Netherfield Way TN33 . . . . . .86 D2
Netherwood Cl TN34 . . . . . .136 F5
Nettleton Cl BN1 . . . . .143 B1
Nevill Ave
Eastbourne BN22 . . . . .173 E1
Hove BN3 . . . . .141 F1
Nevill Cl
Crowborough Warren TN6 . . . . .37 C8
Hove BN3 . . . . .142 A2
Nevill Cres BN7 . . . . .123 A1
Nevill Ct
Crowborough Warren TN6 . . . . .37 C8
Hove BN3 . . . . .142 A1
Nevill Gate TN2 . . . . .8 B3
Nevill Gdns BN3 . . . . .142 A2
Nevill Gn TN22 . . . . .55 D1
Nevill Lodge TN22 . . . . .8 C4
Nevill Pk TN4 . . . . .7 E3
Nevill Pl BN3 . . . . .142 A2
Nevill Rd Crowborough TN6 . .25 F3
Hove BN3 . . . . .142 A2
Lewes BN7 . . . . .123 A2
Rottingdean BN2 . . . . .165 F1
Uckfield TN22 . . . . .55 D1
Nevill Ridge TN4 . . . . .7 D3
Nevill St TN2 . . . . .8 A2
Nevill Terr
Crowborough TN6 . . . . .25 F3
Royal Tunbridge Wells TN2 . . . .7 F2
Nevill Way BN3 . . . . .142 A2
Neville
8 Eastbourne BN22 . . . . . .185 B4
Peacehaven BN10 . . . . .178 D6
New Barn Cl
Hailsham BN27 . . . . .152 C6
Portslade-by-Sea BN41 . . . . . .140 A3
Shoreham-by-Sea BN43 . . . . .140 B1
New Barn Rd
Rottingdean BN2 . . . . .165 F3
Shoreham-by-Sea BN43 . . . . .140 B1
New Church Rd BN3 . . . . . . .162 E2
New Coastguards Cotts
BN25 .180 C4
New College Ct BN23 . . . . . .174 C4
New Cotts
Crowborough TN6 . . . . .38 C8
Eastbourne BN20 . . . . .188 D8
Five Ashes TN20 . . . . .58 B6
Scaynes Hill RH17 . . . . .51 F1
New Cut Westfield TN32 . . . . .87 C1
Westfield TN35 . . . . .114 E4
New Dorset St BN1 . . . . . . .189 A3
New England Ho BN1 . . . . . .189 B4
New England La
Rye TN31 . . . . .93 C8
Sedlescombe TN33 . . . . .113 F6
New England Rd
Brighton BN1 . . . . .189 A4
Haywards Heath RH16 . . . . . . .50 F4
Royal Tunbridge Wells TN4 . . . .7 B4
New England Rise BN41 . . . .141 A4
New England St BN1 . . . . . .189 A4
New Farthingdale RH7 . . . . . .2 B8
New Forest Lodge TN6 . . . . .37 C8
New Langney Ct BN23 . . . . .174 E1
New Lydd Rd TN31 . . . . .94 E2
New Moorsite TN35 . . . . . . .114 E6
New Park Ave TN40 . . . . . . .157 C4
New Pl Eastbourne BN21 . . .184 D3
Uckfield TN22 . . . . .78 C5
New Pond Hill TN21 . . . . . . .81 D6
New Rd Brighton BN1 . . . . . .189 A3
Crowborough TN6 . . . . .25 F3
Eastbourne BN22 . . . . .185 B4
Fairlight TN35 . . . . .138 D4
Hailsham BN27 . . . . .129 C4
Hastings TN35 . . . . .160 D6
Keymer BN6 . . . . .98 B2
Lewes BN7 . . . . .123 C1
Mill Corner TN32 . . . . .67 B3
Polegate BN26 . . . . .173 B6
Ringmer BN8 . . . . .124 D3
Rotherfield TN6 . . . . .39 C8
Rye TN31 . . . . .93 D6
South Heighton BN9 . . . . .168 D1
Uckfield TN22 . . . . .78 C5
New Steine BN2 . . . . .189 C1
New Steine Mews BN2 . . . . .189 C1
New Sussex Hospl BN3 . . . .163 E6

New Upperton Rd *7*
BN21 1
New Way La BN6 1
New Winchelsea Rd
TN31, TN36 1
Newark Pl BN2 1
Newbury Cotts TN5 1
Newbury La TN5 1
Newcomen Rd TN4 1
Newdigate Ho *2* TN40 1
Newells Cl BN2 1
Newfield La BN9 1
Newgate Rd TN37 1
Newgate Rd TN37 1
Newhaven Harbour Sta
BN9 1
Newhaven Hts BN9 1
Newhaven Local
& Maritime Mus BN9 1
Newhaven Marine Sta
BN9 1
Newhaven Rd BN25 1
Newhaven Sq BN9 1
Newhaven St BN2 1
Newhaven Town Sta
BN9 1
Newhaven Wlk TN38 1
Newhaven Wlk TN38 1
Newick CE Prim Sch BN8 . . .1
Newick Cl BN25 1
Newick Dr BN8 1
Newick House Sch RH15 1
Newick La TN20,TN21 1
Newick Rd Brighton BN1 1
Eastbourne BN20 1
Newington Ct TN5 1
Newlands
Hastings TN34 1
Keymer BN6 1
Newlands Cres RH19 1
Newlands Manor Sch
(Senior) BN25 1
Newlands Park Way BN8 1
Newlands Pl RH18 1
Newlands Rd
Rottingdean BN2 1
Newlands Rise TN4 1
Newlands Sch BN25 1
Newmans Way TN35 1
Newmarket Rd BN2 1
Newmarket Terr *8* BN2 1
Newnham Way TN21 1
Newnham Way TN21 1
Newport Rd RH15 1
Newport St BN2 1
Newstead BN1 1
Newtimber Dr BN41 1
Newton Ave RH19 1
Newton Cl RH16 1
Newton Pk BN27 1
Newton Rd Lewes BN7 1
Lindfield RH16 1
Peacehaven BN10 1
Royal Tunbridge Wells TN1 1
Newton Willows TN3 1
Newton's Hill TN7 1
Newtown Rd BN3 1
Nicholson Ct BN23 1
Nicolson Dr BN43 1
Nightingale Cl
East Grinstead RH19 1
Eastbourne BN23 1
Nightingale La RH15 1
Nightingale Rise TN22 1
Nightingales The
Royal Tunbridge Wells TN4 1
Uckfield TN22 1
Nile St BN1 1
Ninfield CE Prim Sch
TN33 1
Ninfield Pl BN2 1
Ninfield Rd TN39 1
Nizells Ave BN3 1
Noahs Ark La RH16 1
Noble Ct BN3 1
Nodes La BN27 1
Noel Gn RH15 1
Noel Rise RH15 1
Nolan Rd BN2 1
Nook Cl TN35 1
Nook The TN22 1
Norbury Cl TN6 1
Nore Rd BN9 1
Norfolk Bldgs *5* BN1 1
Norfolk Cl BN8 1
Norfolk Ct *2* Brighton BN1 .1
4 Eastbourne BN22 1
Norfolk Ho *2* BN1 1
Norfolk Pl *5* BN1 1
Norfolk Rd Hove BN1 1
Royal Tunbridge Wells TN1 1
Norfolk Sq BN1 1
Norfolk St BN1 1
Norfolk Terr BN1 1
Norfolk Way TN22 1
Norlington Cl BN8 1
Norlington Fields BN8 1
Norlington La BN8 1
Norman Cl Battle TN33 1

Palmers Row BN27 ....152 B7
Palmerston Rd BN9 ....168 F1
Pangdean La BN6 ....72 C4
Pangdene Cl RH15 ....72 E1
Pankhurst Ave BN2 ....164 D6
Pankhurst Cl TN39 ....157 A8
Pankhurst Rise TN39 ....157 A8
Pannel La TN35,TN36 ....116 E2
Pannell Cl RH19 ....1 D1
Pannett RH15 ....72 E4
Pantiles The
  Royal Tunbridge Wells TN2 ..8 A2
  Royal Tunbridge Wells TN4 ....7 F2
Parade The
  Beachlands BN24 ....175 F6
  Brighton BN1 ....142 B4
  East Grinstead RH19 ....1 B3
  Hove BN3 ....141 E2
  Pevensey Bay BN24 ....175 E5
Paradise Dr BN20 ....184 D2
Paradise Family L Pk
  BN9 ....168 D1
Paragon The BN20 ....172 F3
Parham Cl BN2 ....164 D5
Parham Ho 15 BN3 ....163 D7
Park Ave Bexhill TN39 ....157 A8
  Eastbourne BN21,BN22 ....184 D7
  Hastings TN34 ....136 D3
  Hove BN3 ....162 E7
  Keymer BN6 ....98 A2
  Shoreham-by-Sea BN43 ....161 C8
  Telscombe Cliffs BN10 ....178 A8
Park Cl Brighton BN1 ....143 E5
  Burgess Hill RH15 ....72 F4
  Eastbourne BN20 ....184 D3
  Hailsham BN27 ....152 B6
  Hastings TN34 ....136 D3
  Hove BN3 ....141 E3
  Hurstpierpoint BN6 ....98 F8
  Portslade-by-Sea BN41 ....141 B1
Park Cnr BN8 ....104 F2
Park Cres Brighton BN2 ....189 C4
  Crowborough TN6 ....25 F3
  Forest Row RH18 ....12 A2
  Hastings TN34 ....136 D2
  Portslade-by-Sea BN41 ....141 B1
  Rottingdean BN2 ....177 A5
Park Crescent Pl BN2 ....189 C4
Park Crescent Rd BN2 ....189 C4
Park Crescent Terr BN2 ....189 C4
Park Croft BN26 ....173 D5
Park Ct
  Brighton, Patcham BN1 ....142 E6
  Brighton, Preston BN1 ....142 F1
  Burgess Hill RH15 ....73 A3
  4 Haywards Heath RH16 ....50 F7
  Hove BN3 ....163 D7
Park Dr TN34 ....136 D2
Park Drive Cl RH9 ....168 F2
Park Farm Cl TN19 ....63 B8
Park Gate Brighton BN1 ....163 F8
  Hailsham BN27 ....129 D3
  Hove BN3 ....163 D6
Park Gates 16 Eastbourne BN21 ....185 A2
  Hove BN3 ....163 D8
Park Hill BN2 ....189 C2
Park La Ashurst Wood RH19 ..11 D6
  Battle TN33 ....112 D4
  Bexhill TN39 ....157 A8
  Crowborough TN6 ....25 F3
  Eastbourne BN21 ....184 C8
  Laughton BN8 ....126 E7
  Southwick BN42 ....161 D7
  Whatlington TN32 ....88 A5
Park Lodge
  10 Eastbourne BN21 ....185 A2
  Hove BN3 ....163 D8
Park Lodge Ct TN38 ....159 B7
Park Manor BN1 ....142 C4
Park Mead Cty Prim Sch
  BN27 ....151 A7
Park Par RH16 ....50 E4
Park Rd Bexhill TN39 ....157 B3
  Brighton BN1 ....143 E5
  Burgess Hill RH15 ....73 A3
  Crowborough TN6 ....25 F3
  Dormans Park RH19 ....1 F6
  East Grinstead RH19 ....1 D1
  Forest Row RH18 ....12 A2
  Hailsham BN27 ....129 B8
  Haywards Heath RH16 ....50 E4
  Heathfield TN21 ....82 B7
  Heathfield TN21 ....82 C6
  Lewes BN7 ....123 C1
  Peacehaven Heights BN10 ....178 F6
  Rottingdean BN2 ....165 F1
  Royal Tunbridge Wells TN4 ....8 B3
  Seaford BN25 ....180 D3
  Shoreham-by-Sea BN43 ....161 C8
Park Rise BN3 ....141 E3
Park Road Toter 4 BN2 ....189 C2
Park Royal BN1 ....163 E6
Park Shaw TN33 ....88 E1
Park St Brighton BN2 ....189 C2
  Falmer BN1 ....144 C6
  Royal Tunbridge Wells TN4 ....8 C3
Park Terr BN21 ....185 A1
Park The Crowborough TN6 ....25 F2
  Rottingdean BN2 ....177 A5
Park View Brighton BN1 ....163 E8
  Brighton BN2 ....164 B2
  Buxted TN22 ....56 C4
  Hastings TN34 ....136 D2
  Haywards Heath RH16 ....50 E6
  Northiam TN31 ....69 A1

Park View continued
  Peasmarsh TN31 ....69 B2
Park View Cl BN10 ....167 A1
Park View Rd BN3 ....142 B1
Park View Rise BN10 ....178 A8
Park View Terr
  Brighton BN1 ....163 E8
  Westfield TN35 ....114 E4
Park Village Rd BN1 ....144 B8
Park Village The BN1 ....144 A8
Park Villas TN21 ....82 B6
Park Way Hastings TN34 ....136 D3
  Southwick BN42 ....161 F8
Park Way Cl BN42 ....161 F8
Park Wood Rd TN34 ....136 F6
Parker Cl BN21 ....184 E5
Parker Ct BN41 ....141 B2
Parker Rd TN34 ....137 A3
Parkfield Ave BN22 ....173 E1
Parkhurst Rd TN40 ....178 C8
Parkland Cty Inf Sch
  BN22 ....173 E1
Parkland Cty Jun Sch
  BN22 ....173 D1
Parklands Maresfield TN22 ....55 A5
  Royal Tunbridge Wells TN4 ....7 C8
  Shoreham-by-Sea BN43 ....161 C8
Parklands Rd BN6 ....97 F3
Parkmead BN2 ....189 C4
Parkmore Terr BN1 ....189 C4
Parks The BN41 ....141 B3
Parks Yd TN33 ....112 D4
Parkside Burgess Hill RH15 ....72 F3
  East Grinstead RH19 ....1 C1
  Heathfield TN21 ....82 B8
  Keymer BN6 ....98 A4
  Portslade-by-Sea BN43 ....140 A1
Parkside Cty Prim Sch
  TN21 ....82 C5
Parkside Rd BN25 ....180 F4
Parkstone Par TN34 ....136 D4
Parkstone Rd TN34 ....136 D4
Parkstone Terr TN34 ....136 D4
Parkview
  Hurstpierpoint BN6 ....97 A5
  Royal Tunbridge Wells TN2 ....8 A2
Parkview Rd TN22 ....55 D1
Parkway BN20 ....184 B8
Parkwood TN31 ....70 B4
Parkwood Cl TN6 ....8 C6
Parnell Ct 2 BN2 ....189 C2
Parochial Terr BN2 ....189 C2
Parrock La TN7 ....12 E2
Parry Cl BN23 ....174 E3
Parsonage Cl TN4 ....7 B5
Parsonage La
  Icklesham TN36 ....116 F6
  Lamberhurst TN3 ....20 B6
  Westfield TN35,TN36 ....114 C4
Parsonage Rd
  Eastbourne BN21 ....184 D4
  Hastings TN35 ....7 B5
Parsons Cl TN38 ....135 F4
Partridges La TN5 ....28 E6
Pashley Down Cty Inf Sch
  BN20 ....184 D2
Pashley Manor Gdns TN5 ..44 B7
Pashley Rd BN20 ....184 D2
Paston Ho TN1 ....163 F8
Paston Pl BN2 ....164 D4
Pasture Hill Rd RH16 ....50 D6
Patagonia Ho TN2 ....8 C3
Patcham By-Pass BN1 ....142 E6
Patcham Cty Inf Sch BN1 ..142 E6
Patcham Cty Jun Sch
  BN1 ....142 E6
Patcham Grange BN1 ....142 E6
Patcham High Sch BN1 ....142 E6
Patcham House Sch BN1 ....142 E6
Patcham Mill Rd BN24 ....174 B5
Patchdean BN1 ....142 F5
Patching Lodge 5 BN2 ....164 C5
Paton Rd TN39 ....157 A8
Paul Cl BN27 ....129 A3
Pavilion Bldgs BN1 ....189 B2
Pavilion Cl 15 BN6 ....97 E5
Pavilion Ct 16 BN1 ....163 E7
Pavilion Par BN2 ....189 B2
Pavilion Rd BN1 ....144 C7
Pavilion Ret Pk BN2 ....143 C1
Pavilion St 21 BN2 ....189 B2
Pavilion Way RH10 ....10 E8
Paxhill Cl TN38 ....135 E6
Paygate Rd TN33 ....113 E7
Payne Ave BN3 ....162 F8
Payne Terr BN1 ....143 B1
Paynsbridge Way TN21 ....107 A7
Paynters Way BN6 ....76 C7
Paynton Rd TN37 ....136 B3
Pathorne Cl BN42 ....140 D1
Payton Dr RH15 ....72 F2
Payton Rd RH15 ....72 F2
Peace Cl BN1 ....143 C1
Peacehaven Cty Inf Sch
  BN10 ....178 B7
Peacock Ind Est BN8 ....163 D7
Peacock La BN1 ....142 E4
Peakdean Cl BN20 ....183 B2
Peakdean La BN20 ....183 B2
Pearl Cl 3 BN21 ....185 A2
Pearse Pl TN2 ....20 B5
Peartree Cl RH15 ....72 E3
Peartree Field TN36 ....116 F6
Peartree Hill TN5 ....44 E2
Peartree La TN39 ....156 D6
Peasmarsh CE Prim Sch
  TN31 ....69 B1
Pebble Rd BN24 ....175 E5

Pebsham Cty Prim Sch
  TN40 ....158 A5
Pebsham Dr TN40 ....158 A6
Pebsham La TN38,TN40 ....158 A6
Peckham Cl BN7 ....123 C3
Peel Rd BN2 ....164 F4
Peelings La BN24 ....174 D6
Peeps La TN6 ....39 A6
Pegasus Way RH19 ....2 B3
Pegler Ave BN9 ....179 B6
Pegwell Cl TN34 ....136 E2
Pelham Arc 1 TN34 ....160 A3
Pelham Cl
  Peacehaven BN10 ....167 D1
  Westham BN24 ....174 F5
Pelham Cres
  Hailsham BN27 ....152 C6
  Hastings TN34 ....160 A3
Pelham Ct 15 BN25 ....180 E2
Pelham Pl TN34 ....160 A3
Pelham Place Cotts RH16 ..51 A7
Pelham Rd Lindfield RH16 ....51 A6
  Seaford BN25 ....180 E2
Pelham Rise BN10 ....167 D1
Pelham Sq BN1 ....189 B3
Pelham St Brighton BN1 ....189 B3
  Hastings TN34 ....159 F7
Pelham Terr Brighton BN2 ..143 C1
  Lewes BN7 ....123 C2
Pelham Yd 4 BN25 ....180 E2
Pell Cl TN5 ....30 A6
Pellbrook Rd BN7 ....123 B3
Pellings Farm Cl TN6 ....26 B2
Pellings Rise TN6 ....26 B3
Pells CE Prim Sch
  Lewes BN7 ....123 C1
  Lewes BN7 ....123 C2
Pelwood Rd TN31 ....95 A2
Pembroke Ave BN3 ....163 A7
Pembroke Cl BN27 ....129 C3
Pembroke Cres BN3 ....163 A7
Pembroke Ct 2 BN3 ....163 A6
Pembroke Gdns BN3 ....163 A6
Pembury
  Haywards Heath RH16 ....51 B3
  Pembury TN2 ....9 D7
Pembury Cty Prim Sch TN2 ..9 D8
Pembury Gr TN39 ....157 A7
Pembury Grange TN2 ....9 E8
Pembury Hospl TN2 ....9 C8
Pembury Rd
  Eastbourne BN23 ....174 D1
  Royal Tunbridge Wells TN2 ....8 E4
Pendean RH15 ....73 C1
Pendragon Ct BN3 ....163 A8
Pendrill Pl TN5 ....29 F5
Penhale Rd BN2 ....185 D5
Penhurst Cl
  Eastbourne BN22 ....174 A1
  St Leonards TN37 ....136 D5
Penhurst Dr TN40 ....158 A6
Penhurst La TN33 ....110 E6
Penhurst Pl BN2 ....164 F6
Penland Cl RH16 ....50 D7
Penland Ct 9 TN40 ....157 F4
Penland Rd Bexhill TN40 ....157 F5
  Haywards Heath RH16 ....50 D7
Penn Cres
  Haywards Heath RH16 ....51 A5
  Ringmer BN8 ....124 D5
Penn Yd TN2 ....9 C6
Pennine Rise TN34 ....137 B4
Pennine Way BN13 ....174 D3
Pennine Wlk TN2 ....8 D5
Pennington Ho RH16 ....51 A3
Penny La TN40 ....158 A5
Pennybridge La TN40 ....40 D5
Penrith Way BN23 ....174 C4
Pensford Dr BN23 ....174 D3
Penshurst Rd TN11,TN3 ....6 B8
Penstock Terr TN31 ....93 F3
Penstone Ct 4 BN43 ....161 C8
Pentland Cl
  Eastbourne BN23 ....174 D3
  St Leonards TN37 ....136 C5
Pentlands BN26 ....183 C7
Pepper Dr RH15 ....72 F1
Pepper Hall Cotts RH17 ....74 B5
Peppercombe Rd BN20 ....184 B4
Pepys Wlk BN23 ....174 C3
Percival Cres BN22 ....173 F1
Percival Rd BN22 ....173 F1
Percival Terr 14 BN2 ....164 D4
Percy Rd TN35 ....137 C3
Percy Terr TN4 ....8 A2
Perry Ave RH19 ....1 E1
Perry Hill BN2 ....166 C3
Perryfields RH15 ....72 E2
Perryhill Cotts TN7 ....13 E8
Perryhill La TN7 ....13 E8
Perryman's La RH17 ....34 D3
Perrymans La TN22 ....36 F1
Perrymount Rd RH16 ....50 F6
Perth Cl BN25 ....181 C3
Perth Ct 8 BN21 ....185 A4
Perth Rd TN37 ....136 B3
Peter Gladwin
  Cty Prim Sch BN41 ....141 B2
Peter James Cl TN31 ....94 E2
Peter James La TN35 ....138 C6
Petersfield TN2 ....8 F1
Petland Gdns RH16 ....50 F3
Petlands Rd RH16 ....50 F3
Pett Cl BN2 ....164 F6
Pett La TN36 ....117 A4
Pett Level Rd TN35 ....139 B7
Pett Rd TN35 ....138 C8
Petworth Dr RH15 ....73 A4

Petworth Ho 18 BN3 ....163 D7
Petworth Pl BN22 ....173 E2
Petworth Rd BN1 ....143 B6
Pevensey & Westham
  CE Prim Sch BN24 ....175 A6
Pevensey & Westham Sta
  BN24 ....174 F5
Pevensey Bay Rd BN23 ....175 A2
Pevensey Bay Sta BN24 ....175 C6
Pevensey Castle BN24 ....175 A6
Pevensey Cl BN25 ....181 B4
Pevensey Ct
  3 Bexhill TN39 ....157 B3
  Pevensey Bay BN24 ....175 D4
  Pevensey Park Rd BN24 ....174 F6
Pevensey Rd
  7 Brighton BN2 ....164 C8
  Eastbourne BN21,BN22 ....185 B3
  Newhaven BN9 ....179 B6
  Polegate BN26 ....173 C6
  St Leonards TN38 ....159 B7
Peverells The BN25 ....181 A5
Peyton Cl BN23 ....185 F7
Philip Cole Cl 18 TN34 ....160 B4
Philip Cl 8 BN3 ....163 C7
Phoenix Brewery Halls
  BN2 ....189 C4
Phoenix Cl
  Eastbourne BN23 ....185 C8
  Hailsham BN27 ....152 E7
Phoenix Cres BN42 ....161 D8
Phoenix Cswy BN7 ....123 D1
Phoenix Ct 9 BN2 ....185 B3
Phoenix Pl Brighton BN2 ....189 C3
  Lewes BN7 ....123 D1
Phoenix Rise BN2 ....189 C3
Phoenix Way BN42 ....161 D8
Phyllis Ave BN10 ....178 B8
Piazza The BN23 ....185 D7
Picardy Cl TN13 ....112 C4
Piccadilly La TN20 ....40 C1
Pickers Gn RH16 ....51 A8
Picketts La TN22 ....54 D8
Pickforde La TN5 ....31 D1
Picton St BN2 ....164 C5
Piddinghoe Ave BN10 ....178 D6
Piddinghoe Cl BN10 ....178 D7
Piddinghoe Mead BN9 ....168 B1
Pilgrim Ct RH16 ....51 A5
Pilgrims Old Sch BN7 ....146 A7
Pilgrims Way TN24 ....136 F4
Pilmer Rd TN6 ....25 F4
Pilot Ho 1 BN2 ....189 C2
Pilot Rd TN34 ....137 B4
Piltdown Ct Bexhill TN39 ....157 B4
  Hastings TN34 ....136 E1
Piltdown Rd BN2 ....164 F6
Piltdown Rise TN22 ....78 D8
Piltdown Way BN22 ....174 A4
Pinders Rd TN35 ....164 D6
Pinders Wlk TN35 ....137 D3
Pine Ave TN34 ....137 B4
Pine Gr Crowborough TN6 ....25 E3
  East Grinstead RH19 ....1 A3
Pine Tree Cl
  Hurstpierpoint BN6 ....97 B5
  Newhaven BN9 ....179 C7
Pine Tree Rd TN21 ....82 A6
Pine Trees BN6 ....97 D4
Pine Trees Cl BN6 ....97 D4
Pine Way BN27 ....152 A7
Pine Way Cl RH19 ....10 E7
Pine Wlk TN2 ....78 D8
Pineham Copse RH16 ....50 F4
Pinehurst RH15 ....73 A1
Pinehurst Cl TN40 ....157 E6
Pines The 2 Brighton BN2 ..189 C4
  Hastings TN34 ....137 B3
  Haywards Heath RH16 ....51 B4
  Hove BN3 ....163 E6
Pinewood 4 BN1 ....142 E3
Pinewood Chase TN6 ....25 D3
Pinewood Cl
  Eastbourne BN22 ....173 D2
  Hove BN3 ....142 D2
Pinewood Cl RH16 ....50 D2
Pinewood Rd TN2 ....8 D5
Pinewood Way
  Haywards Heath RH16 ....50 D2
  St Leonards TN38 ....135 E3
Pinewoods TN39 ....156 E4
Pinewoods Cl TN39 ....156 E4
Pinfold 4 RH16 ....50 D6
Pinfold Cl BN2 ....165 E6
Pinton Hill TN5 ....31 B3
Pinwell Rd BN7 ....146 D8
Pipe Pas 5 BN7 ....123 C1
Piper's Gate TN22 ....78 D4
Pipers Cl Bexhill TN40 ....157 C5
  Hove BN3 ....141 C3
  Wadhurst TN5 ....30 A4
Pipers Field RH16 ....78 D4
Pipers La TN22 ....64 B3
Pipit Mdw TN22 ....78 D5
Pit La BN6 ....97 A5
Pitcairn Ave BN23 ....175 E3
Pitreavie Dr BN27 ....152 A8
Pitt Dr BN25 ....181 A5
Pitt Gdns BN2 ....165 D7
Place La BN25 ....180 E3
Plainfields Ave BN1 ....143 A7
Plaistow Cl BN2 ....164 F6
Plashett Park Gates
  TN22 ....102 F5
Plat The TN31 ....67 B6
Platt The Dormansland RH7 ....2 A8

Platt The continued
  Frant TN3 1
  Haywards Heath RH16 1
Plaw Hatch La RH18, RH19 ..2
Playden Cl 3 BN2 1
Playden Gdns TN34 13
Playden La TN31 7
Playden St Michael's
  CE Prim Sch TN31 7
Pleasant View Cotts TN6 2
Pleasant View Rd TN6 2
Pleasure Island TN34 16
Plemont Gdns TN38 15
Pleyden Rise TN39 15
Plough La TN37 1
Plover Cl BN23 17
Plover Cr Hailsham BN27 15
  St Leonards TN38 13
Plum Tree Cotts TN38 4
Plumey Feather Cotts TN3 3
Plumpton Agricultural Coll
  BN6 12
Plumpton Bostall BN7 12
Plumpton Cl Bexhill TN40 15
  Eastbourne BN23 17
Plumpton Cross BN7 9
Plumpton Crossways
  BN7, BN8 9
Plumpton Cty Prim Sch
  BN7 9
Plumpton La BN7 9
Plumpton Race Course
  BN7 9
Plumpton Rd BN2 16
Plumpton Sq BN2 5
Plymouth Ave BN2 17
Plymouth Cl BN23 17
Plynlimmon Rd TN34 16
Pocock's Rd BN21 18
Polegate By-Pass BN26 17
Polegate Cty Prim Sch
  BN26 17
Polegate Sta BN26 17
Polesden Rd TN
Polley Cl TN2 9
Pollington Pl TN6 2
Pomper La BN6 9
Pond Cl TN31 9
Pond Way RH19
Pondcroft Rd RH16 5
Pondsyde Ct BN25 18
Ponswood Rd TN38 13
Pont Cl TN21 8
Pook Reed Cl TN21 8
Pook Reed La TN21 8
Pool Valley BN2 18
Poona Rd TN1
Popes Cott TN17 2
Poplar Ave BN3 14
Poplar Cl Brighton BN1 14
  Hove BN3 14
Poplar Wlk BN22 17
Poplars The BN6 9
Poppinghole La TN32 8
Popps La TN39 15
Poppyfield TN31 7
Port Hall Ave BN1 16
Port Hall Mews BN1 16
Port Hall Pl BN1 16
Port Hall Rd BN1 16
Port Hall St BN1 16
Port Rd BN22
Port View BN9
Porters Way BN26
Portfield Ave BN1 14
Portfield Cl TN40 15
Portland Ave BN3 16
Portland Ave BN3 16
Portland Cotts 11 TN34 15
Portland Gate BN3 16
Portland Ho 6 RH19 1
Portland Mews 1 BN2 16
Portland Pl
  18 Brighton BN2 16
  12 Hastings TN34 15
Portland Rd
  Burgess Hill RH15 7
  East Grinstead RH19 1
  Hove BN3 16
Portland Road Trad Est
  BN3 16
Portland Sq TN21 8
Portland St BN1 18
Portland Terr
  15 Hastings TN34 15
  South Heighton BN9 16
Portland Villas
  Hove BN3 16
Portlands BN23 18
Portsdown Way BN20
Portside Com Coll
  (Lower) BN41 14
Portside Com Coll
  (Sixth Form)
  Portslade-by-Sea BN41 14
  Portslade-by-Sea BN41 14
Portside Cty Inf Sch
  BN41 14
Portslade Sta BN41 16
Portsmouth La RH16 1
Portsmouth Wood Cl RH16 ..1
Portsmouth Wood Cl
  RH16 1
Portsmouth Wood Dr
  RH16 1
Posey Cotts BN27 13

ıgworth Cl TN21 .....80 F8
lorn Cl RH18 ....12 B1
lorn La RH18 ....12 B2
ffice Pas 10 TN34 ...160 A4
ı La BN8 ....124 F5
n's La TN33, TN39 ...133 F4
s Mill La TN21 ....59 F4
's La BN7 ....146 C8
ies Cotts BN27 ......128 D3
ies The TN22 ....78 D4
s Field BN8 ....124 D6
s La RH15 ....72 F1
Cl TN31 ....90 A2
Cotts BN6 ....74 A1
y La TN31 ....90 A2
gfield Rd TN31 ....93 A6
Marsh Ind Est
...................174 F4
lands Dr BN8 ....100 C7
Cl BN23 ....185 F6
Cnr BN8 ....101 D4
Gate BN6 ....97 D3
La Framefield TN22 ...79 E7
ton BN8 ....126 C7
The RH15 ....72 F4
field Farm TN6 ......26 B2
field Rd
orough TN6 ....26 B2
urst TN18 ....47 B5
sbridge Hill
TN3 ....6 D7
Cl RH15 ....72 D3
r Mill La TN4 ....8 B8
rmill Cl TN4 ....8 C8
rmill La
TN33 ....112 C1
m Green TN31, TN33 ...89 D3
Gdns BN9 ....168 D1
Rd BN8 ....76 D7
Gr BN1 ....189 A3
Rd BN1 ....163 E6
Sq BN1 ....163 E6
Villas BN1 ....189 A3
gs Cl BN25 ....181 C2
gs Dr BN3 ....141 F3
r Rd BN3 ....163 A8
Folly La TN6 ....25 E1
tt Gdns RH15 ....73 A3
n Cir BN1 ....189 B4
n Dro BN1 ....142 F2
n Gr TN22 ....79 B6
n Grange BN1 ....142 E1
n Manor (Mus)
...................142 E1
n Park Ave BN1 .....142 F1
n Park Sta BN1 .....142 D2
n Rd Bexhill TN39 ....157 B7
n BN1 ....163 F8
n St BN1 ....163 E5
n Village Mews
...................142 E1
nville Ct
hton BN1 ....163 E7
hton BN1 ....189 A4
nville Rd BN1, BN3 ..189 A4
ux Rd BN21 ....184 E5
se Cl
s Hill RH15 ....72 D4
urne BN23 ....174 B3
se Hill Bexhill TN39 ..156 F6
t Cove TN35 ....138 F5
se La RH18 ....12 A1
Albert St BN1 ....189 B2
Charles Cl
BN42 ....141 A1
Charles Rd BN7 .....123 E3
Edward's Rd BN7 ....123 B1
Of Wales Ct BN41 ...162 F6
Regent's Cl BN2 ....164 E4
Regent's Ct 2
...................164 E4
William Par BN23 ...185 F6
s Cres BN2 ....189 C5
's Pl BN1 ....189 B2
s Rd Brighton BN2 ...164 B8
ards TN37 ....159 D7
s St Brighton BN2 ...189 B2
unbridge Wells TN2 ......8 C3
s Terr BN2 ....164 E4
s Ave BN3 ....163 A6
s Cl Seaford BN25 ...180 E5
d TN22 ....78 A7
s Cres BN3 ....163 A6
s Ct 6 BN3 ....163 A6
s Field BN26 ....150 B3
s Rd BN23 ....185 E7
s Sq BN3 ....163 A6
s Dr BN25 ....180 D5
s La BN27 ....109 C1
s Rd BN3 ....163 A8
Way TN8 ....4 A6
Ave TN34 ....136 E1
Cl Hastings TN34 .....136 E1
ey Bay BN24 ....175 D5
Cres BN7 ....146 C8
Ct Brighton BN1 .....163 F8
tbourne BN20 ....184 F1
BN7 ....146 D8
Ct CT TN40 ....157 E5
Flats 7 BN7 ....146 C8
Ho BN7 ....146 D8
Hts BN20 ....184 A5
La BN23 ....174 E3
Meadow Sh Ctr
...................159 F8
Orch 8 BN23 ....174 E1
Rd Burgess Hill RH15 ...73 A1
urne BN23 ....174 E2

Priory Rd *continued*
Forest Row RH18 ....11 D2
Hassocks BN6 ....97 E5
Hastings TN34 ....160 B5
Priory Sch BN7 ....146 E8
Priory St Hastings TN34 ...159 F7
Lewes BN7 ....146 C8
Priory The Brighton BN1 ...142 D5
5 Hove BN3 ....163 B5
Priory Way RH16 ....50 F4
Promenade BN10 ....178 C6
Promenade The BN24 .....175 D4
Prospect Cotts
Crowborough TN6 ....25 E3
Lamberhurst TN3 ....20 A3
Prospect Gdns 10 BN21 ...184 D4
Prospect Pl TN34 ....159 E7
Prospect Rd
Heathfield TN21 ....82 B6
Royal Tunbridge Wells TN2 ...8 C3
Royal Tunbridge Wells TN4 ....7 F8
Prospect Terr TN21 ....82 A7
Providence Cotts
Crowborough TN6 ....25 D4
Groombridge TN3 ....15 C7
Providence Pl BN1 ....189 B4
Prowting Mead TN39 .....156 C4
Pudding Cake La TN22 .....78 C7
Pulborough Ave BN22 .....173 E2
Pulborough Cl BN2 ....164 F7
Pump Ho The BN3 ....162 D8
Pump La TN22 ....79 D4
Punnetts Town
Cty Prim Sch TN21 ....83 B6
Purbeck Cl BN23 ....174 C4
Putlands Cres TN39 ......157 A8
Pyecombe St BN45 ....119 A6

Q

Quadrangle The BN8 ......105 C5
Quadrant BN1 ....189 A2
Quadrant The
Eastbourne BN21 ....184 E4
Keymer BN6 ....98 A4
Quail Ct BN27 ....152 D7
Quakers La RH16 ....51 A5
Quantock Cl
Eastbourne BN23 ....174 D3
Royal Tunbridge Wells TN2 ....8 D5
Quantock Gdns TN34 .....137 B3
Quarry Bank Rd BN1 .....143 B2
Quarry Cl RH15 ....73 D3
Quarry Cotts TN5 ....29 D7
Quarry Cres TN34 ....160 A5
Quarry Hill
Haywards Heath RH17 .....50 C6
St Leonards TN38 ....159 B7
Quarry Ho TN38 ....159 B6
Quarry La BN25 ....181 A5
Quarry Rd Hastings TN34 ...160 A5
Newhaven BN9 ....179 D5
Royal Tunbridge Wells TN1 ....8 B5
Quarry Rise RH19 ....2 A3
Quarry Terr TN34 ....136 F1
Quay Ct BN43 ....161 B6
Quay The 5 BN43 ....161 A6
Quebec Cl Bexhill TN39 ...157 A5
Eastbourne BN23 ....185 F7
Quebec Mans TN38 ....159 A8
Quebec Rd TN38 ....136 A4
Quebec St BN2 ....189 C3
Queen Alexandra Ave
BN3 ....142 A3
Queen Anne's Cl BN7 .....123 C1
Queen Caroline Cl BN3 ...142 A3
Queen Elizabeth Ave
RH15 ....73 A2
Queen Mary Ave BN3 .....142 A3
Queen Sq BN1 ....189 A2
Queen St TN18 ....47 B5
Queen Victoria Ave BN3 ...142 A3
Queen Victoria Hospl The
RH19 ....1 F3
Queen's Ave 4 TN34 .....159 F7
Queen's Cres BN23 ....185 E7
Queen's Ct RH16 ....50 F6
Queen's Gdns
Brighton BN1 ....189 B3
Eastbourne BN21 ....185 B3
Hove BN3 ....163 C5
Royal Tunbridge Wells TN4 ....8 B6
Queen's Par
Eastbourne BN22 ....173 F1
Hove BN3 ....141 E2
Queen's Park
Cty Prim Sch BN2 ......164 C5
Queen's Park Rd BN2 .....164 C6
Queen's Park Rise BN2 ...164 C6
Queen's Park Terr BN2 ...164 C6
Queen's Pl Brighton BN1 ...189 B4
Hove BN3 ....163 C6
Queen's Rd
Brighton BN1 ....189 A3
East Grinstead RH19 ....1 E1
Eastbourne BN23 ....185 D7
Hastings TN34 ....159 F8
Lewes BN7 ....123 D3
Royal Tunbridge Wells TN4 ....8 B6
Queen's Wlk RH19 ....1 E1
Queens App TN22 ....55 D1
Queens Cotts TN5 ....29 E6
Queens Cres RH15 ....73 A2
Queens Ct 8 TN39 ....157 B3
Queens Dr Hassocks BN6 ....97 F4
Maresfield TN22 ....54 F4
Queens Park Gdns BN25 ...180 C4

Queens Rd
Crowborough TN6 ....25 F1
Haywards Heath RH16 ......50 E6
Herstmonceux BN27 ....130 E5
Southwick BN42 ....140 E1
Queens Sq TN34 ....159 F8
Queensbury Mews BN1 ....163 E5
Queensdown Sch BN1 .....143 C3
Queensdown School Rd
BN1, BN2 ....143 D2
Queensmount TN20 ....58 B7
Queensway Brighton BN2 ..164 D6
East Grinstead RH19 ....1 E1
Seaford BN25 ....181 A6
St Leonards TN37, TN38 ....135 E5
Querneby Cl BN43 ....161 D7
Quickbourne La TN31 ......67 C7
Quinnell Dr BN27 ....129 B2
Quintin Cl BN27 ....152 A5
Quintins The BN27 ....152 C8

R

Radcliffe Cl TN37 ....136 C3
Radinden Dr BN3 ....142 D1
Radinden Manor Rd BN3 ...163 D8
Radnor Mews TN38 ....135 E2
Ragged Dog La TN21 ....81 B3
Raglan Ct Brighton BN1 ...189 A2
Pevensey Bay BN24 ......175 C3
Railway App
East Grinstead RH19 ....1 E1
Newhaven BN9 ....179 D7
Railway Cotts Cowden TN8 ....4 D8
Horsted Keynes RH17 ......33 A8
Ripe BN8 ....149 A6
St Leonards TN38 ....158 F6
Railway La BN7 ....123 D1
Railway Rd BN9 ....179 D7
Railway St BN1 ....189 A3
Railway View TN6 ....38 C8
Raleigh Cl BN23 ....185 F7
Ramsay Way BN23 ....185 F7
Ramslye Cotts TN3 ....16 D8
Ramslye Rd TN4 ....16 E8
Ranalah Est BN9 ....179 D8
Randiddles Cl BN6 ....97 B4
Randolph La TN31 ....70 B3
Ranelagh Ct BN23 ....185 E6
Ranelagh Villas BN3 .....163 B8
Rangemore Dr BN21 ......184 D6
Rankine Rd TN2 ....8 D7
Ranmore Cl TN34 ....136 E6
Rannoch Rd TN6 ....25 D2
Rannoch Rd W TN6 ....25 D2
Ranscombe Hill BN8 .....147 A6
Ranscombe La BN8 ....147 D6
Ranworth Cl BN23 ....174 B4
Raphael Rd BN3 ....162 F7
Rapson's Rd BN20 ....173 A3
Rastrick Cl RH15 ....72 F1
Rattle Rd BN24 ....174 D6
Ratton Dr BN20 ....184 B7
Ratton Gdn BN20 ....184 B7
Ratton Rd BN21 ....184 E4
Ratton Sch BN21 ....184 C7
Ratton Village BN20 .....184 B8
Raven Ct Battle TN33 .....112 F4
St Leonards TN38 ....135 E3
Ravens Cl TN39 ....156 C3
Ravens Croft BN20 ......188 F8
Ravens Ct BN20 ....188 F8
Ravenside Ret & L Pk
TN40 ....158 A4
Ravenswood BN6 ....97 E4
Ravenswood Ave TN2 ....8 D6
Ravenswood Dr BN2 ......165 F6
Ravenswood Rd RH15 ......73 B3
Ravine Cl TN34 ....137 A3
Rayford Cl BN10 ....178 C7
Rayford Ct
2 Bexhill TN40 ....157 D4
8 Seaford BN25 ....180 E2
Raymond Cl BN25 ....181 A5
Rayner Cl TN6 ....25 F3
Raystede Ctr
for Animal Welfare BN8 .103 D1
Readers La TN31 ....69 F5
Reading Rd BN2 ....164 F4
Reba Ct BN2 ....177 D4
Rectory Cl Burwash TN19 ....62 B6
East Hoathly BN8 ....105 A5
Eastbourne BN20 ....184 D3
Hove BN3 ....162 D7
Newhaven BN9 ....179 C6
Shoreham-by-Sea BN43 ...161 D7
St Leonards TN38 ....136 B2
Rectory Ct 16 BN43 .....161 C8
Rectory Field TN7 ....13 E4
Rectory La Beckley TN31 ....67 F4
Iden TN31 ....70 B4
Rye TN31 ....93 C8
Winchelsea TN36 ....117 E7
Rectory Rd Newhaven BN9 ..168 E2
Shoreham-by-Sea BN43 ...161 D7
Rectory Way TN40 ....157 D5
Red Dyke Cotts BN24 ....173 F6
Red Lake Cty Prim Sch
TN35 ....137 D4
Red Lake Terr TN35 .....137 D4
Red Oak TN18 ....45 E8
Red Oast Cotts TN5 ....32 C3
Redbridge La TN6 ....37 D5
Redbrook La TN22 ....56 D4
Redford Cl BN23 ....174 E1
Redgarth Ct RH19 ....1 B3
Redgeland Rise TN38 ....135 F2

Redgill La BN8 ....53 B1
Redhill Cl BN1 ....142 C5
Redhill Dr BN1 ....142 C5
Redleaf Cl TN2 ....8 D6
Redman King Ho BN20 ....184 F2
Redmayne Dr TN34 ....159 E7
Redoubt Fortress & Mus
BN22 ....185 C4
Redoubt Rd BN22 ....185 C4
Redshank Ct BN27 ....152 D7
Redvers Rd BN2 ....143 D1
Redwell Ave TN39 ....157 B8
Redwood Dr RH16 ....50 D3
Reed Ct BN7 ....123 D3
Reed Ho BN8 ....100 E7
Reed Pond Wlk RH16 ....51 A4
Reedham Rd BN23 ....174 B4
Reedswood Rd
Broad Oak TN31 ....90 B4
St Leonards TN38 ....158 E8
Reeves Ct TN3 ....6 B5
Reeves Hill BN1 ....143 D5
Reeves Terr TN5 ....31 E1
Refectory Rd BN1 ....144 B7
Regal Dr 10 RH19 ....10 F8
Regency Cl TN22 ....78 C8
Regency Ct BN1 ....142 D3
Regency Gdns TN38 .....159 A8
Regency Hall 19 TN2 ....8 A2
Regency Ho TN2 ....8 B2
Regency Mews
15 Brighton BN1 ....163 E5
Eastbourne BN20 ....185 A1
Regency Rd BN1 ....189 A2
Regency Sq BN1 ....163 E5
Regent Arc BN1 ....189 B2
Regent Bsns Pk RH15 ......72 E2
Regent Hill BN1 ....189 A2
Regent Pl
Royal Tunbridge Wells TN2 ....8 D3
St Leonards TN37 ....135 F7
Regent Row BN1 ....189 A2
Regent Sq TN31 ....93 C6
Regent St BN1 ....189 B2
Regents Cl BN25 ....180 E5
Regina Ct TN4 ....7 F4
Reginald Rd TN39 ......157 B4
Regnum Cl BN22 ....173 E4
Reigate Rd BN1 ....142 D1
Renascent Ho 18 BN21 ...185 B3
Renfrew Ct BN22 ....185 A1
Resting Oak Hill BN8 ....100 F3
Reynolds Dr TN40 ......157 E5
Reynolds La TN4 ....7 F6
Reynolds Rd
Eastbourne BN23 ....174 E1
Hove BN3 ....162 F7
Reynoldstown La BN26 ...172 F6
Ribbetts Cotts BN6 ....97 A5
Ribbetts Ho BN6 ....97 A5
Riccards La TN33 ....88 A2
Rices Hill RH19 ....1 E1
Richard Allen Ct BN2 ....143 C1
Richardson Ct 5 BN3 ....162 F7
Richardson Rd Hove BN3 ..162 F7
Royal Tunbridge Wells TN4 ....8 A5
Richborough Cl TN34 ....136 D4
Richington Way BN25 ....181 B5
Richland Cl TN35 ....137 E4
Richmead Gdns TN20 ......40 B2
Richmond Ave TN39 .....156 F3
Richmond Cl TN39 ......157 A3
Richmond Ct 9 BN3 .....163 E7
Richmond Gr TN39 ......157 A2
Richmond Hts 11 BN2 ....189 C3
Richmond Par BN2 ......189 C3
Richmond Pl
Brighton BN2 ....189 B3
Eastbourne BN21 ....184 F4
Royal Tunbridge Wells TN2 ....8 B1
Richmond Rd
Bexhill TN39 ....157 A3
Brighton BN2 ....164 B8
Pevensey Bay BN24 .....175 D5
Seaford BN25 ....180 E3
Richmond Sq RH19 ....1 D2
Richmond St
Brighton BN2 ....189 C3
Hastings TN35 ....160 C6
Richmond Terr
Brighton BN2 ....189 C4
1 Seaford BN25 ....180 E3
Richmond Way RH19 ....10 F8
Riddens Cl BN7 ....99 E5
Riddens La BN7 ....99 E6
Riddens The BN7 ....99 E5
Riddlesdale Ave TN4 ....8 A6
Ride The BN1 ....142 F1
Riders Bolt TN39 ....156 E5
Ridge Cl Nutley TN22 ......35 C5
Portslade-by-Sea BN41 ...141 A4
Ridge Rd BN1 ....144 C7
Ridge The Groombridge TN3 ..15 A6
Hastings TN34, TN37 ....136 D6
Winchelsea Beach TN36 ...118 C6
Ridge View BN1 ....143 E5
Ridge W The TN37 ......136 A7
Ridge Way RH17 ....51 B2
Ridgelands Cl BN20 .....184 C3
Ridgeside Ave BN1 .....142 E5
Ridgeway
East Grinstead RH19 ......10 E7
Hurst Green TN19 ....45 A3
Pembury TN2 ....9 D7
Southwick BN41, BN42 ....140 F1
The Moor TN18 ....45 E8
Ridgeway Cl
Heathfield TN21 ....82 A8

Ridgeway Cl *continued*
Southwick BN42 ....140 F1
Ridgeway Gdns BN2 ......165 E7
Ridgeway The
Burgess Hill RH15 ....73 B4
Friston BN20 ....183 B1
Herstmonceux BN27 .....130 E6
Seaford BN25 ....180 F4
Ridgewood Ave BN2 .....166 C3
Ridgewood Cl TN22 ....78 D4
Ridgewood Gdns
Bexhill TN40 ....157 F4
Hastings TN34 ....136 E5
Ridgewood Ind Pk TN22 ....78 E4
Ridgway Cl BN2 ....165 D8
Ridgway Paddock BN7 ....145 E6
Ridgway The BN2 ....165 D8
Ridings The Bexhill TN39 ...156 F8
Burgess Hill RH15 ....73 C2
Newick BN8 ....76 C7
Ovingdean BN2 ....165 C4
Royal Tunbridge Wells TN2 ....8 F6
Seaford BN25 ....180 F5
St Leonards TN37 ....136 C5
Telscombe Cliffs BN10 ...167 B2
Rigden Rd BN3 ....142 C1
Riley Rd BN2 ....143 C1
Rill Wlk RH19 ....2 B1
Ringle Gn TN18 ....47 C5
Ringmer Bsns Pk BN8 ....124 F6
Ringmer Cl BN1 ....143 E4
Ringmer Com Coll BN8 ...124 E6
Ringmer Cty Prim Sch
BN8 ....124 E5
Ringmer Rd Brighton BN1 ..143 E4
Brighton BN1 ....143 F4
Newhaven BN9 ....179 B6
Seaford BN25 ....180 E2
Ringmer Way BN23 ......174 A4
Ringwood Cl BN22 ......185 B5
Ringwood Ct 5 BN22 ....185 C5
Ringwood Rd
Bexhill TN39 ....157 C7
Eastbourne BN22 ....185 B5
Ripe La BN8 ....126 E2
Ripley Chase BN21 .....184 E3
Ripsley Cl BN23 ....174 E2
Risden La TN18 ....46 D7
Rise Park Gdns BN23 ....174 E2
Rise The
East Grinstead RH19 ......10 F8
Haywards Heath RH16 .....51 B5
Horam TN21 ....106 F7
Portslade-by-Sea BN41 ...140 F2
Riseden Rd TN5 ....29 C1
Rising The BN23 ....174 E2
Rissom Ct BN1 ....142 E2
River La BN26 ....171 A3
River Way TN22 ....78 C6
Riverbourne Ho 10 BN22 ..185 B4
Riverbridge Cotts TN33 ...113 E8
Riverdale BN7 ....123 C2
Riverhall Hill TN5 ....28 F8
Riverside Forest Row RH18 ..11 E3
Hadlow Down TN22 ....57 D1
Newhaven BN9 ....179 D6
Southwick BN42 ....161 E7
Riverside Bsns Ctr BN43 ..161 A7
Riverside Gdns TN6 ....38 C8
Riverside Ind Est BN7 ...123 D2
Riverside Rd BN43 ......161 A6
Rixons Cl RH17 ....33 C5
Rixons Orch RH17 ....33 C5
Roadean Cl BN25 ......181 A4
Robert Lodge BN2 ......164 F4
Robert Mitchell Sch
TN39 ....157 B7
Robert St BN1 ....189 B3
Robert Tressell Cl TN34 ...136 E1
Robert Tressell
Workshops 7 TN34 ......159 F8
Robert's Hill TN36 ......117 E8
Roberts Row TN31 ....68 C5
Robertsbridge Com Coll
TN32 ....63 F4
Robertson Pas TN34 .....159 F7
Robertson Rd BN1 ......142 D1
Robertson St TN34 .....159 F7
Robertson Terr 1 TN34 ...159 F7
Robertsons Hill TN34 ...160 B6
Robian Cl TN22 ....55 A4
Robin Cl East Grinstead RH19 ..1 F2
Eastbourne BN23 ....174 C2
Robin Ct TN39 ....157 A3
Robin Davis Cl BN2 ....143 E1
Robin Dene BN2 ....164 E4
Robin Hill TN39 ....156 D4
Robin Post La BN26 ....151 B1
Robin Rd RH15 ....72 D2
Robinia Lodge BN1 .....142 E2
Robins Row BN41 ....141 A1
Robinson Rd BN9 ....179 C8
Robinsons Ct BN22 .....185 C6
Roborough Ct BN21 .....185 A4
Robsack Ave TN38 ......135 E2
Robsack Wood
Cty Prim Sch TN38 ....135 E2
Rochdale Ho TN1 ....8 C5
Rochdale Rd TN1 ....8 C6
Rochester Cl
Eastbourne BN20 ....188 C8
5 Hove BN3 ....163 D6
Rochester Ct 4 BN3 ....163 D6
Rochester Gdns BN3 ....163 D6
Rochester Ho TN6 ....26 C1

Rochester Rd **4** TN37 .....136 B2
Rochester St BN2 ....164 D5
Rochester Way TN6 ....26 B1
Rochford Way BN25 ......180 B6
Rochmans Way TN6 ....38 A8
Rock Channel TN31 ....93 C5
Rock Channel Quay TN31 .93 C5
Rock Cl Hastings TN35 ...137 D4
Rock **2** Southwick BN42 ....161 E7
Rock Cotts TN3 ....17 B1
Rock Gr BN2 ....164 E4
Rock Hall Cotts TN22 ......78 D8
Rock La TN35 ....137 D7
Rock Lodge Vineyard
RH17 ....52 A2
Rock Pl BN2 ....189 C1
Rock St BN2 ....164 E4
Rock Villa Rd TN1 ....8 A4
Rock's Hill TN35 ....114 E7
Rock-a-Nore Par TN34 ...160 B4
Rock-a-Nore Rd TN34 ....160 B3
Rockall Ave BN23 ....185 F8
Rockall Dr BN27 ....122 D2
Rockhurst Dr BN20 ......184 B6
Rockington Way TN6 ....38 B8
Rocklands Cotts BN27 ....131 B5
Rocklands La TN35 ....160 C5
Rockmead Rd TN35 ......138 F4
Rocks Hill TN22 ....64 E7
Rocks La TN22 ....55 F7
Rocks Park Cty Prim Sch
TN22 ....78 B8
Rocks Park Rd TN22 ......78 B7
Roderick Ave
Peacehaven BN10 ....178 B7
Peacehaven BN10 ....178 C8
Roderick Ave N BN10 ....167 C2
Rodmell Ave BN2 ....177 D5
Rodmell CE Prim Sch
BN7 ....146 E1
Rodmell Ct **5** BN25 .....180 C4
Rodmell Ho BN9 ....168 D3
Rodmell Pl BN1 ....143 A6
Rodmell Rd
Royal Tunbridge Wells TN2 ..8 A2
Seaford BN25 ....181 B2
Rodmill Dr BN21 ....184 D6
Rodmill Rd BN21 ....184 D5
Rodwell TN6 ....26 C1
Roebuck St **10** TN34 ....160 B4
Roedale Rd BN1 ....143 B1
Roedean Cl TN39 ....157 A5
Roedean Cres BN2 ....165 A4
Roedean Hts BN2 ....165 A4
Roedean Path BN2 ....165 A3
Roedean Rd Brighton BN2 .164 F4
Royal Tunbridge Wells TN2 ..8 A2
Roedean Sch BN2 ....165 C3
Roedean Terr BN2 ....165 B3
Roedean Vale BN2 ....165 B3
Roedean Way BN2 ....165 B3
Roeheath BN8 ....75 F4
Roffrey Ave BN22 ....173 D1
Rolfe Dr RH15 ....73 D3
Romaine Cl RH15 ....73 D5
Roman Cl BN25 ....180 B6
Roman Cres BN42 ....161 E8
Roman Croft BN21 ....184 E4
Roman Rd Hove BN3 .....162 D6
Southwick BN42 ....161 E8
Roman Way
Southwick BN42 ....161 E8
Uckfield TN22 ....78 E7
Romans Way BN24 ....174 E6
Romney Cl BN41 ....162 B8
Romford Rd TN1,TN12 .....9 F7
Romney Cl BN25 ....181 C4
Romney Rd Polegate BN26 .173 E7
Rottingdean BN2 ....177 A5
Romney St BN22 ....185 C5
Romsey Cl BN1 ....143 C2
Rookery Cl Hove BN1 ....142 E1
South Heighton BN9 .....168 E2
Rookery La
Rushlake Green TN21 .....83 E2
Winchelsea TN36 ....117 F7
Rookery The BN23 ....174 C4
Rookery Way
Haywards Heath RH16 ....50 E1
Newhaven BN9 ....168 F2
Seaford BN25 ....180 B5
Rookhurst Rd TN40 ......157 F5
Rookley Cl TN2 ....8 D2
Rookwood Cl TN22 ....78 E8
Roopers TN3 ....7 A7
Roosevelt Ct TN38 ....136 B3
Rope Wlk Hailsham BN27 .152 B8
Rye TN31 ....93 C6
Rope Wlk The TN18 ......47 B5
Roper's Gate TN2 ....7 C2
Rosary Ct RH15 ....73 B2
Rose Cotts RH17 ....34 A4
Rose Ct BN6 ....97 E4
Rose Hill Cl BN1 ....189 A4
Rose Hill Cl BN1 ....189 B4
Rose Hill Ct BN1 ....189 B4
Rose Hill Ho TN1 ....8 A3
Rose Hill Terr BN1 ......189 B4
Rose Wlk Cl BN9 ....179 C7
Rose Wlk BN25 ....180 F4
Rose Wlk The BN9 ......179 C7

Rosebarn Cl RH15 ....73 C1
Rosebery Ave
Eastbourne BN22 ....173 E1
Woodingdean BN2 ....165 C8
Rosedale Pl BN22 ....173 D3
Rosedene Cl BN2 ....165 E6
Rosefield Cotts TN32 .....65 F1
Rosehill Gdns TN6 ....26 C1
Rosehill Wlk TN1 ....8 A3
Roselands Bexhill TN39 ..156 F6
Sedlescombe TN33 ....88 E1
Roselands Ave
Eastbourne BN22 ....185 C5
Wellbrook TN20 ....39 F1
Roselands Cty Inf Sch
BN22 ....185 B5
Roseleigh Gdns RH17 ....51 F3
Rosemary Cl
Haywards Heath RH17 .....50 B6
Peacehaven BN10 ....167 C1
Rosemary Dr BN43 ....140 C1
Rosemary La
Shellies Green TN35 .....138 D6
Stonecrouch TN5 ....32 A5
Rosemount Cl BN25 ....180 A6
Rosetti Rd BN24 ....175 D4
Roseveare Rd BN22 .....185 C6
Rossdale TN2 ....8 D5
Rosslyn Ave BN43 ....161 A7
Rosslyn Rd BN43 ....161 A7
Rotary Lodge BN1 ....143 E6
Rotary Point BN41 ....141 B1
Rothbury Rd BN3 ....162 D7
Rother Ave BN24 ....173 F5
Rother Cl Burwash TN19 ..62 A6
Crowborough TN6 ....38 A7
Rother Ct TN29 ....157 B6
Rother Rd BN25 ....181 A2
Rother Valley Railway Mus
TN32 ....64 A4
Rother View TN19 ....62 B7
Rotherfield Ave
Bexhill TN40 ....157 D4
Eastbourne BN23 ....174 A4
Hastings TN34 ....160 B5
Rotherfield Cl BN1 ....143 B6
Rotherfield Cres BN1 ....143 B5
Rotherfield Cty Prim Sch
TN6 ....39 B8
Rotherfield La TN20 ......39 F4
Rotherfield Rd TN6 .....159 B8
Rotherfield Rd TN6 ....38 A7
Rotherhurst La TN6 ......39 B6
Rothermead TN20 ....39 F1
Rotherview TN32 ....64 C5
Rothley Chase RH16 ......50 F4
Rothsay Rd TN38 ....159 B7
Rothwell Ct BN9 ....179 A7
Rotten Row BN7 ....146 B8
Rottingdean CE Prim Sch
BN2 ....177 A6
Rottingdean Pl BN2 .....165 F4
Rotunda Rd BN23 ....185 D8
Rotyngs The BN2 ....165 F2
Rough Brow BN25 ....181 A4
Rough Field RH19 ....1 D4
Rough The BN6 ....97 F2
Round Hill Rd **2** BN2 ..164 B8
Round Hill St **3** BN2 ..164 B8
Roundacres Way TN40 ..157 E6
Roundel The TN17 ....136 D5
Roundhay Ave BN10 ....178 E6
Roundhill Cres BN2 .....164 B8
Roundhill Rd TN2 ....8 D1
Roundhouse Cotts TN21 ..82 D7
Roundway BN1 ....143 E5
Roundwood La RH16 .....50 F8
Roundwood Rd TN37 ...136 B5
Rowan Ave
Eastbourne BN22 ....173 D3
Hove BN3 ....141 E1
Rowan Cl
Haywards Heath RH16 ....51 B4
Heathfield TN21 ....82 A5
Portslade-by-Sea BN41 ..141 A1
Seaford BN25 ....181 C3
St Leonards TN37 ....136 D6
Rowan Ct Hove BN1 ....142 E1
Polegate BN26 ....173 A6
Rowan Gdns TN40 ......157 F6
Rowan Tree Rd TN2 ......7 E1
Rowan Way BN1 ....165 E4
Rowan's Cl **1** BN2 ....164 C3
Rowanden Cl BN2 ....177 C4
Rowans The RH15 ....72 D4
Rowbarns TN33 ....112 C6
Rowe Ave BN10 ....178 B7
Rowe Ave N BN10 ....178 B8
Rowsley Rd BN20 ....188 D7
Royal Alexandra Hospl
for Sick Children The
BN1 ....189 A3
Royal Chase TN4,TN1 .....7 F4
Royal Cres BN2 ....164 C4
Royal Crescent Mans
BN2 ....164 C4
Royal Crescent Mews
BN2 ....164 C4
Royal Dr BN25 ....180 E6
Royal George Par BN43 .140 C1
Royal George Rd RH15 ..72 E3
Royal Mews TN34 ....159 A6
Royal Military Rd TN36 .118 A8
Royal Oak La TN22 ....56 B8
Royal Par
Eastbourne BN22 ....185 C4
Eastbourne BN22 ....185 D5

Royal Pavilion BN1 ......189 B2
Royal Sovereign View
BN23 ....185 F6
Royal Sussex Cres BN20 .184 E5
Royal Sussex Ct BN7 ....146 D8
Royal Sussex Cty Hospl
(General) BN2 ....164 D4
Royal Terr **4** TN37 .....159 C7
Royal Victoria Place Sh Ctr
TN1 ....8 B4
Royles Cl BN2 ....177 A6
Royston Cl BN20 ....183 A1
Royston Gdns BN20 .....157 F6
Rudyard Cl BN2 ....165 E8
Rudyard Kipling
Cty Prim Sch BN2 ......165 E7
Rudyard Rd BN2 ....165 E8
Rue De Bayeux TN33 ...112 D5
Ruffet Ct TN2 ....7 E1
Rufus Cl BN7 ....123 C1
Rugby Cl BN25 ....181 B4
Rugby Ct **3** BN2 ......164 E4
Rugby Pl BN2 ....164 E4
Rugby Rd BN1 ....143 A1
Rumbolds La RH14 ....50 D2
Rumsey Ct TN6 ....25 F1
Rusbridge La **4** BN7 ..123 E1
Rush Ct **4** BN22 ......185 B3
Rushers Cross TN20 ......40 E5
Rushes The RH16 ....51 C4
Rushetts TN3 ....6 F4
Rushey Cl BN8 ....124 E5
Rushlake Cl BN1 ....143 E5
Rushlake Cres BN21 ....184 D6
Rushlake Rd BN1 ....143 E5
Rushlye Cl TN7 ....12 E7
Rushmere Rise TN38 ....135 E1
Rushwood Cl RH16 ....51 B4
Ruskin Rd Hove BN3 ....162 F8
Willingdon BN20 ....173 B1
Rusper Rd Brighton BN1 .143 D6
Brighton BN1 ....184 B6
Ruspers RH15 ....73 D2
Russell Cotts **5** BN21 .184 E4
Russell Cres **2** BN1,BN3 .189 A4
Russell Mews **8** BN1 ..163 E5
Russell Pl BN1 ....189 A2
Russell Rd BN1 ....189 A2
Russell Row BN7 ....123 C3
Russell Sq BN1 ....189 A2
Russell St **10** TN34 ....159 A8
Russell Cl BN20 ....173 C6
Rusthall Grange TN4 ......7 D4
Rusthall High St TN4 .....7 C4
Rusthall Pk TN4 ....7 D4
Rusthall Rd TN4 ....7 D4
Rustic Cl BN10 ....167 B1
Rustic Rd BN10 ....167 B2
Rustington Cl BN20 ....188 F8
Rustington Rd BN1 .....143 A5
Rustlings Cl RH16 ....51 B5
Rustwick TN4 ....7 D4
Rutherfords Bsns Pk
TN33 ....113 B7
Rutland Cl BN21 ....184 D6
Rutland Ct
3 Eastbourne BN23 ..174 E1
Hove BN3 ....162 F6
Rutland Gdns BN3 ......162 F7
Rutland Rd BN3 ....163 A7
Rutley Cl TN2 ....64 C5
Ruxley Ct BN23 ....174 D2
Rydal Cl TN4 ....7 E5
Rydal Dr TN4 ....7 E5
Rydal Way BN23 ....174 C4
Ryde Cl BN3 ....141 D1
Ryde Rd BN2 ....164 E7
Ryders TN3 ....7 A3
Rye Cl Polegate BN26 ...173 C7
Saltdean BN2 ....177 F6
Seaford BN25 ....181 C4
Rye Harbour
Nature Reserve TN31 ....94 B1
Rye Ind Est TN31 ....93 D4
Rye Rd Four Throws TN18 .46 D8
Hastings TN35 ....137 D5
Iden TN30,TN31 ....70 A8
Rye Foreign TN31 ....69 E2
Rye St BN22 ....185 D6
Rye Sta TN31 ....93 B6
Ryecroft **12** Brighton BN2 .164 F5
Haywards Heath RH16 ....50 E3
Ryefield Cl BN21 ....184 C7
Ryelands Dr BN2 ....143 D3
Rylstone Rd BN22 ......185 C4
Rymers Cl TN2 ....8 D7
Rymill Rd TN38 ....136 A3
Ryst Wood Rd RH18 .....12 B1

S

Sackville Cl
East Grinstead RH19 ......1 C3
Lewes BN7 ....123 C1
Sackville Coll RH19 ....1 F1
Sackville Ct Bexhill TN40 .157 D5
3 East Grinstead RH19 ..10 F8
Sackville Gdns
East Grinstead RH19 ......1 C3
Hove BN3 ....162 F6
Sackville La RH19 ....1 C3
Sackville Rd Bexhill TN39 .157 B3
Eastbourne BN22 ....173 E2
Hailsham BN27 ....152 C6
Hove BN3 ....163 A7
Sackville Sch RH19 ....2 A1

Sackville Trad Est BN3 ..163 B8
Sacred Heart RC Prim Sch
TN35 ....160 B5
Sacred Heart Sch TN5 ...29 D6
Saddler's Cl **4** TN38 ...159 B6
Saddlers Cl RH15 ....73 D1
Sadler Way BN2 ....164 F6
Sadlers Way BN8 ....124 D4
Saffrays Ct TN38 ....159 B7
Saffron Cl BN43 ....140 C1
Saffron Gate BN3 ....163 C7
Saffron Gdns BN26 .....170 F3
Saffrons Ct BN21 ....184 E2
Saffrons Mead BN20 ...184 F2
Saffrons Pk BN20 ....184 E1
Saffrons Rd BN21 ....184 F2
Saffrons The RH15 ....72 F5
St Agnes Rd RH19 ....1 E2
St Andrew's CE Inf Sch
BN22 ....185 D6
St Andrew's CE Prim Sch
BN1 ....163 B6
St Andrew's Dr BN9 ....179 B7
St Andrew's Dr BN25 ...180 B6
St Andrew's La **1** BN7 .123 D1
St Andrew's Rd
Bexhill TN40 ....157 C5
Brighton BN1 ....143 A1
Portslade-by-Sea BN41 ..162 C7
St Andrew's Sq **8** TN34 .159 F8
St Andrews Cl BN27 ....129 A1
St Andrews Rd BN41 ....73 C4
St Ann's Cl BN3 ....163 D7
St Anne's Cl TN40 ....157 D5
St Anne's Cres BN7 ....123 B1
St Anne's Ct
5 Brighton BN1 ......189 A4
2 Brighton BN1 ......164 C4
St Anne's Gdns BN6 .....98 A3
St Anne's Ho **7** BN1 ..189 A4
St Anne's Rd BN21 .....184 F4
St Anne's Sch BN42 ....184 F4
St Annes Gn TN19 ....62 A6
St Annes Rd BN20 ......173 B3
St Anns Well Ho **6**
BN3 ....163 D6
St Ans Mans BN3 ....163 E7
St Anthony's Ave BN23 .185 E8
St Anthonys Ave BN23 .128 E6
St Aubyn's Cres BN41 ..162 B7
St Aubyn's Gdns **13** BN3 .163 A6
St Aubyn's Mead BN2 ..177 A5
St Aubyn's Rd
Eastbourne BN22 ....185 B3
Portslade-by-Sea BN41 ..162 C7
Southwick BN41 ....162 A7
St Aubyns BN3 ....163 A6
St Aubyns Rd BN3 ......163 A5
St Aubyns S BN43 ......163 A5
St Aubyns Cl RH17 ......165 F1
St Augustine Cl RH17 ....51 F3
St Augustine's Ct TN39 .156 F3
St Augustine's
RC Prim Sch TN4 ....8 A7
St Barnabas CE Prim Sch
BN3 ....163 B5
St Barnabas' Cl TN1 ......8 B5
St Bartholomew's
CE Prim Sch BN1 ....189 B4
St Bede's Prep Sch BN20 .188 E7
St Bernadette's
RC Prim Sch BN1 ....142 E2
St Boswells Cl BN27 ....152 A8
St Bretades BN21 ....185 B2
St Catherine's Cl TN37 .159 D8
St Catherine's Terr **6**
BN3 ....163 B5
St Christopher's (Trng Coll,
Dr Barnardo's Home)
TN2 ....8 D4
St Christopher's Rd BN6 .97 A6
St Christopher's Sch
BN3 ....163 A6
St Clement's Caves TN34 .160 A4
St Clement's Ct BN21 ..184 D6
St Clements Pl **5** TN38 .159 C6
St Crispians BN25 ....180 D3
St Crispians Ct BN25 ...180 D3
St Cuthmans Cl BN2 ...164 F6
St David's Ave TN40 ....157 C5
St David's Cl BN10 .....178 B8
St David's Rd TN4 ....8 A6
St Davids Cl BN22 ......173 D4
St Dominic Cl TN38 ....159 A8
St Edmund's Rd RH16 ...50 F3
St Edward's Cl RH19 .....1 C1
St Elizabeth's BN25 ....180 F4
St Francis Chase TN39 ..157 A5
St Francis Cl RH16 ....50 F2
St George's La BN6 ......97 B5
St George's Mews BN1 ..189 B3
St George's Pk TN2 ......16 F8
St George's Pl
Brighton BN1 ....189 B3
Hurstpierpoint BN6 ......97 B5
St George's Rd
Bexhill TN40 ....157 C5
Brighton BN2 ....164 D4
Eastbourne BN21 ....185 A2
Hastings TN34 ....160 A5
St George's Sch TN2 .....9 A5
St George's Terr **5** BN2 .164 C4
St Georges Cl BN43 ....181 C3
St Giles CE Prim Sch
RH17 ....33 C6
St Giles Cl
Shoreham-by-Sea BN43 ..161 B8
Winchelsea TN36 ....117 E7

St Gregory Cl BN20 ......
St Gregory's
Catholic Comp Sch TN4 .
St Helen's Ave TN34 ....
St Helen's Cres
Hastings TN34 ....
Hove BN3 ....
St Helen's Ct TN34 .....
St Helen's Down TN34 ..
St Helen's Rd **2**
St Helen's Rspl TN35 ...
St Helen's Park Rd TN34 .
St Helen's Rd
Brighton BN2 ....
Hastings TN34 ....
St Helena's Ct **1** BN21 .
St Helens Wood Rd
TN34 ....
St Heliers Ave BN3 ......
St James BN24 ....
St James La TN22 ......
St James Rd BN22 .....
St James St BN7 ....
St James' Ave TN40 ....
St James' Cl TN40 .....
St James' CE Inf Sch TN2 .
St James' Cl TN40 .....
St James' Cres TN40 ....
St James' Ho **8** BN2 ..
St James' Pk TN1 ......
St James' Rd Bexhill TN40 .
Royal Tunbridge Wells TN1 .
St James's Ave TN40 ...
St James's Ct TN1 ......
St James's Rd
East Grinstead RH19 .....
Hastings TN34 ....
St James's St BN2 .....
St James's Street Mews
BN2 ....
St John Bank BN3 ......
St John St **6** BN7 .....
St John the Baptist
RC Prim Sch BN2 ......
St John's Ave RH15 .....
St John's CE Prim Sch
Crowborough TN6 ....
Royal Tunbridge Wells TN4 .
St John's Cl
Crowborough TN6 ....
East Grinstead RH19 .....
South Chailey BN8 ......
St John's Dr BN24 ......
St John's Hill **2** BN7 ..
St John's Ho BN20 .....
St John's Mount **6** BN2 .
St John's Pk TN4 ....
St John's Pl Brighton BN2 .
2 Hove BN3 ....
St John's Rd Bexhill TN40 .
Crowborough TN6 ....
East Grinstead RH19 .....
Eastbourne BN20 ....
Haywards Heath RH16 ..
Hove BN3 ....
Polegate BN26 ....
Royal Tunbridge Wells TN4 .
Seaford BN25 ....
St Leonards TN37 ......
St John's Sch BN7 .....
Brighton BN2 ....
Seaford BN25 ....
St John's Terr **3** BN7 ..
St Johns CE Prim Sch TN2 .
St Johns Ct RH15 ......
St Joseph's Cl BN3 .....
St Joseph's
RC Cty Prim Sch BN2 ..
St Joseph's RC Prim Sch
RH16 ....
St Joseph's Trad Est BN3 .
St Josephs Way RH16 ..
St Julian's La BN43 ....
St Julians Cl BN43 .....
St Keyna Ave BN3 ......
St Kitts **3** TN39 ......
St Laurence Cl BN10 ...
St Lawrence
CE Prim Sch BN6 ......
St Lawrence Mews BN23 .
St Lawrence Pl BN23 ...
St Lawrence Rd TN39 ..
St Lawrence Way
Hurstpierpoint BN6 ......
Pevensey Bay BN23 .....
St Leonard's Ave BN3 ..
St Leonard's Gdns BN3 .
St Leonard's Pl BN20 ..
St Leonard's Rd
8 Brighton BN2 ......
Eastbourne BN21 ....
Hove BN3 ....
Newhaven BN9 ....
St Leonards CE Prim Sch
TN38 ....
St Leonards Cl BN9 ....
St Leonards Ct TN38 ...
St Leonards Pk RH19 ...
St Leonards Rd TN39 ..
St Leonards Terr BN26 ..
St Leonards
Warrior Square Sta TN37 .
St Louie Cl BN9 ....
St Lucia **1** TN39 .....
St Lucia Wlk BN23 .....

's CE Inf Sch TN4 ....8 C7
's Cty Inf Sch
........................164 C6
's La BN9 ....179 C7
's Rd
...............164 C6
nbridge Wells TN4 ....8 B6
's Terr TN27 ....164 C6
s CE RH15 ....73 A3
garet CE Prim Sch
........................98 D3
garet's Ave RH19 .....1 F6
garet's Pl BN1 ....189 A2
garet's Rd
rinstead RH19 ....1 F3
nards TN37 ....159 D7
garet's Rise BN25 ....180 A6
garet's Terr TN37 ....159 D7
garets Cres TN39 ....156 B8
garets Terr TN31 ......93 C5
k's CE Prim Sch
n BN2 ....164 E5
y Down TN22 ....57 C5
nbridge Wells TN4 .....7 D1
k's Rd TN4 ....16 F7
k's St BN2 ....164 E4
ks Cl TN39 ....156 D5
ks Field TN22 ....57 B5
tin's Flats 6 BN2 ....164 C7
tin's La 4 BN7 ....146 C8
tin's Pl BN2 ....89 A3
tin's St BN2 ....189 C5
tins TN33 ....112 D5
tins CE Prim Sch
........................164 C8
tins Cres BN11 ....184 C4
tins Ho BN8 ....124 E6
tins Rd BN22 ....173 D3
y Magdalen
im Sch BN1 ....163 E5
y Magdalen's
m Sch TN40 ....157 F6
y Magdalene St
........................189 C5
y Star of the Sea
im Sch TN37 ....159 D8
y the Virgin
im Sch TN7 ....13 D4
's CE Sch RH19 ....1 D2
's Cl
Street TN31 ....90 A2
rst TN5 ....31 D1
on BN22 ....173 B2
's Cnr 3 BN21 ......184 D3
's Cotts
........................112 E3
TN33 ....156 F8
tbourne BN20 ....184 D3
's Ct
tbourne BN21 ....184 D3
eonards TN37 ....159 C7
's Farmhouse
........................112 E3
's Gdns TN13 ....112 E3
's La Bexhill TN39 ...156 F8
urst TN3 ....7 A8
's Pl
st TN5 ....31 D1
on BN22 ....189 C2
's RC Prim Sch
borough TN6 ....8 A6
by-Sea BN41 ....162 B7
's Rd
Hill RH15 ....72 F4
borne BN21 ....184 D4
's La TN34 ....160 A5
's Rd W RH15 ....72 E4
's Sch
TN40 ....157 E6
y's Green TN21 ....82 A1
y's Sq 12 BN2 ......164 D4
's Terr
........................112 F3
s TN30 ....160 A5
's Villas TN33 ....112 E3
s Wlk BN27 ....152 C7
-in-the-Fields
........................40 B2
rs TN21 ....80 E7
ry Ave BN27 ....152 C7
ry Garth TN22 ....93 C3
ry Pl 3 BN43 ....161 A6
hew's Dr TN38 ......136 C1
hew's Gdns TN38 ...136 B1
hew's High Brooms
m Sch TN4 ....8 B8
hew's Rd TN38 ......136 B5
hews CE Sch BN27 ...164 C8
ion Cl BN27 ....151 F8
hael's Cty Prim Sch
........................14 B5
hael's Pl
n BN1 ....163 E6
tings TN34 ....159 E7
hael's Rd
by-Sea BN41 ....162 B7
nbridge Wells TN4 .....8 B7
hael's Terr BN7 .....123 D3
naels Cl
........................38 B8
naels Rd BN2 ....174 A6
naels Rd RH19 ....1 E2
olas Cl TN36 ....51 A6
olas La 13 BN7 .....123 D1
olas Lodge BN1 ....189 A2
olas Rd BN43 ......161 A6

St Nicholas Rd
Brighton BN1 ....189 A3
Portslade-by-Sea BN41 .162 B8
St Nicholas' CE Jun Sch
BN41 ....162 B8
St Nicolas & St Mary
CE Sch BN43 ....161 A8
St Nicolas Cl BN24 ....175 B6
St Olive's Cl TN21 ......81 C7
St Pancras Gdns TN6 ...146 B8
St Pancras Rd BN7 ....146 C8
St Pancras RC Prim Sch
BN7 ....123 B1
St Pancras Rd BN7 ....146 C8
St Patrick's Cres TN40 .157 C5
St Patrick's Rd BN3 ...163 A7
St Paul's CE Prim Sch
BN1 ....189 A3
St Paul's CE Prim Sch
TN37 ....136 D1
St Paul's Cl TN16 ......50 F5
St Paul's Cl Rushall TN4 .7 C4
St Leonards TN37 ....159 D8
St Paul's Pl TN37 ....159 D8
St Paul's RC Sec Sch
RH16 ....72 C3
St Paul's Rd TN37 ....136 C1
St Paul's St Brighton BN2 .189 C5
Rusthall TN4 ....7 C4
St Pauls CE Inf Sch TN4 .7 B4
St Pauls Cl Jun Sch TN4 .7 B4
St Pauls Cl BN22 .....173 D3
St Peter & St Paul
CE Prim Sch TN40 ....157 C4
St Peter's Ave BN10 ...178 A8
St Peter's CE Prim Sch TN2 .8 C3
Seaford BN25 ....180 E5
St Peter's Cl Hove BN3 .141 F2
St Peter's Terr TN40 ...157 E4
St Peter's Cty Inf Sch
BN41 ....162 B7
St Peter's Mews TN40 .157 E4
St Peter's Pl BN1, BN2 .189 B3
St Peters RC Prim Sch
BN43 ....161 A8
St Peter's RC Sch RH19 .1 C1
St Peter's Rd
Portslade-by-Sea BN41 .162 B7
Seaford BN25 ....180 E5
St Leonards TN37 ....159 C8
St Peters St Brighton BN1 .189 B4
Royal Tunbridge Wells TN2 .8 C3
St Peters Mdw TN6 ....39 A7
St Peters Pl TN27 ....123 C1
St Peters Row TN5 ....73 A4
St Peters Row TN6 ....1 F1
St Philip's Ave BN22 ..185 B5
St Philip's RC Prim Sch
TN22 ....78 C5
St Philips Ct TN2 ......8 D6
St Philips Mews 8 TN2 .8 D6
St Richard's Cl BN3 ...141 D1
St Richard's Flats BN41 .162 B7
St Richard's RC Sch
TN40 ....157 E4
St Richard's Rd BN41 .162 B7
St Richards Ho 3 TN38 .159 C7
St Richards Rd TN6 ....38 A4
St Saviour's Rd TN38 ..158 F6
St Saviours Cl 8 BN41 .146 C8
St Stephens Ct TN1 ....8 B5
St Swithun's Cl RH19 ...1 F1
St Swithun's La 1 BN7 .146 C8
St Swithun's Terr BN7 .146 C8
St Thomas 5 TN39 ....157 A4
St Thomas a' Becket
RC Inf Sch BN21 .....184 D5
St Thomas a' Becket
RC Jun Sch BN21 .....184 D5
St Thomas CE Prim Sch
TN36 ....117 F7
St Thomas's Cl TN34 ..160 A5
St Thomas's St TN36 ..117 F7
St Vincent's Dr TN2 ....65 A3
St Thomas of Canterbury
Ct TN20 ....40 A2
St Thomas' CE Prim Sch
TN3 ....15 C6
St Thomas's Rd TN34 .160 A5
St Thomas's St TN36 ..117 F7
St Vincent's Flats TN37 .82 A5
St Vincents Pl BN20 ...184 E1
St Vincents Rd TN38 ..158 F7
St Wilfred's Ct 5 RH16 .50 E4
St Wilfred's Pl BN25 ..181 B3
St Wilfreds Rd RH15 ...73 A4
St Wilfrid's CE Prim Sch
RH16 ....72 F2
St Wilfrid's Gn BN27 ...152 C6
St Wilfrid's Way RH16 ..50 E4
St Wilfrids RC Prim Sch
RH15 ....72 F2
Saint Hill Manor RH19 ..10 C4
Saint Hill Rd RH19 .....10 C5
Saints Hill TN11 ....11 C6
Salcey Cl TN18 ....74 A8
Salehurst CE Prim Sch
TN32 ....64 B4
Salehurst Gdns TN38 ..135 D7
Salehurst Rd BN21 ....184 C4
Salisbury Cl BN27 ....173 C2
Salisbury Dr Bexhill TN40 .157 B5
Eastbourne BN20 .....188 C8
Hove BN3 ....163 C6
Langton Green TN3 .....6 F3
Royal Tunbridge Wells TN4 .8 C3

Salisbury Rd continued
Seaford BN25 ....180 E3
St Leonards TN37 .....136 C1
Salisbury Terr TN31 ....81 B8
Salisbury Yd TN37 ....136 C1
Salix Cl 3 BN27 ......185 B3
Salmons Rd TN4 ....7 C4
Saltcote La TN31 ......93 C7
Saltcote Mews TN31 ...93 C7
Saltdean Cl TN39 .....156 E3
Saltdean Cty Prim Sch
BN2 ....177 C6
Saltdean Dr BN2 ......177 B5
Saltdean Park Rd BN2 .177 C5
Saltdean Vale BN2 ....177 D6
Saltdean Way TN39 ...156 D3
Salters La TN34 ......160 B4
Salvador Cl BN20 ....181 C4
Salvington Cres TN39 .156 F4
Samoa Way BN23 .....175 B2
San Feliu Ct RH19 .....2 B2
San Jose Cl TN35 ....160 C6
Sancroft Rd BN20 ....184 B3
Sanctuary The BN20 ..184 B4
Sand Hill La BN8,TN22 .104 B8
Sand Rd TN4 ....20 A4
Sandbanks Cl BN27 ...152 A5
Sandbanks Gdns BN27 .152 A5
Sandbanks Rd BN27 ..152 B6
Sandbanks Rd BN27 ..152 B6
Sandbrook BN6 ....97 F3
Sanders Ho BN3 ......162 E8
Sanderstead 8 BN2 ..164 F5
Sandfield Rd TN11 .....6 A2
Sandgate Cl BN25 ....181 C5
Sandgate Rd BN1 .....143 A2
Sandhawes Hill RH19 ..2 A2
Sandhill La Boarshead TN6 .26 E7
Churches Green BN27 .109 B6
Sandhurst Ave Pembury TN2 .17 B5
Woodingdean BN2 .....144 D1
Sandhurst Cl
Royal Tunbridge Wells TN2 .8 C6
Sandhurst Cross TN18 .47 A4
Sandhurst Cty Prim Sch
TN18 ....47 C5
Sandhurst Gdns TN34 .136 F5
Sandhurst Ho TN2 .....8 D5
Sandhurst La TN39 ....156 B6
Sandhurst Pk TN2 .....8 C6
Sandhurst Rd TN2 .....8 C6
Sandhurst Vineyards TN18 .47 E5
Sandore Cl BN25 .....181 A4
Sandore Rd BN25 ....181 A4
Sandown Cl
Eastbourne BN23 .....174 B4
Royal Tunbridge Wells TN2 .8 B6
Sandown Court Com Coll
TN2 ....8 B6
Sandown Cl BN23 ....174 B4
Sandown Gr TN2 ......8 B6
Sandown Pk TN2 ......8 B6
Sandown Rd Brighton BN2 .164 D7
Hastings TN35 ....137 C3
Southwick BN42 ......161 E8
Sandown Way TN40 ...157 B6
Sandpiper Wlk BN23 ..174 C2
Sandridge TN6 ....26 B1
Sandringham Cl
East Grinstead RH19 ...11 A8
Hove BN3 ....142 A3
Seaford BN25 ....180 A6
Sandringham Dr BN3 ..142 A3
Sandringham Hts TN38 .135 E7
Sandringham Lodge 17
BN3 ....163 C6
Sandrock Hall TN34 ..160 A5
Sandrock Hill TN33,TN38 .135 A4
Sandrock Pk TN37 .....8 D4
Sandrock Pk TN34 ....136 F5
Sandrocks Way RH16 .50 E2
Sandwich Dr TN38 ....158 F8
Sandwich St BN25 ....185 C6
Sandy Cl TN37 ....136 B5
Sandy Cross Cotts TN21 .82 A5
Sandy Cross La TN21 .82 B5
Sandy La
Chelwood Gate RH17 .34 C8
Coleman's Hatch TN7 ..23 D6
East Grinstead RH19 ...1 F1
Framefield TN22 ......79 A7
Lions Green TN21 .....81 C2
Sandy Vale RH16 ....50 E2
Sanshaw Cl BN27 ....184 E3
Santa Cruz Dr BN23 ..185 F7
Santer Ho TN18 ....45 E8
Sanphils Ave BN1 ....142 F7

Saxon Cl BN2 ....177 C6
Saxon Ct Hove BN3 ...162 D6
St Leonards TN37 ....159 C8
Saxon Ground BN21 ..184 C4
Saxon Mews BN27 ...152 C4
Saxon Mount Sch TN38 .158 F7
Saxon Rd Hastings TN35 .137 D3
Hove BN3 ....162 D6
Newhaven BN9 ....179 C7
Saxon Rise TN40 .....157 E4
Saxon St TN37 ....159 C6
Saxonbury 8 BN2 ....189 C3
Saxonbury Cl TN6 .....39 A4
Saxonhurst Ct TN37 ..136 B4
Saxons TN39 ....156 A3
Saxonwood Rd TN33 ..112 C5
Sayerland La BN26 ...173 A8
Sayerland Rd BN26 ..173 A8
Sayers The 8 RH19 ....1 C1
Scamps Hill RH16 .....51 C6
Scanlon Cl BN20 .....173 A3
Scarborough Rd BN1 .142 D1
Scarletts Cl TN2 ......8 C6
Scaynes Hill CE Prim Sch
RH17 ....51 F3
Sceptre BN1 ....142 E2
Schofield Way BN21 ..185 F7
School Cl Burgess Hill RH15 .72 F2
8 Southwick BN42 ...161 E8
School Cotts
East Chiltington BN7 ..100 B3
Maresfield TN22 ....55 C5
School Field BN8 ....101 E5
School Hill
Barcombe Cross BN8 .101 E4
Lamberhurst TN3 ......20 B6
Old Heathfield TN21 ..82 D5
Ticehurst TN36 ....117 E8
School La
Ashurst Wood RH19 ...11 F4
Blackboys TN22 ......80 A6
Crowborough, Blackness TN6 .25 C7
Crowborough, St John's TN6 .25 D4
Danehill RH17 ....34 B5
Forest Row RH18 .....11 F2
Hadlow Down TN22 ...35 C5
Nutley TN22 ....35 C5
Peasmarsh TN31 .....69 B2
Polegate BN26 ....173 A7
Pembe BN45 ....119 C6
Saltdean BN2 ....177 C6
School Path BN2 ......164 B3
School Rd Hastings TN35 .137 C3
Hove BN3 ....162 F8
School Rise Brighton BN2 .164 E6
Royal Tunbridge Wells TN2 .7 F3
School Terr TN32 ......64 C5
Schwerte Way TN38 ..159 E7
Science Park Rd BN1 .144 B2
Science Park Sq BN1 .144 B6
Scotland St BN2 .....189 C3
Scotlands Dr TN20 ....20 D3
Scotney Castle TN3 ...20 D3
Scotney Castle Gdns TN3 .20 D3
Scotsford Cl TN21 ....59 F1
Scotsford Rd TN21 ...59 F2
Scott Rd BN3 ....162 F7
Scotts Acre TN31 .....94 D2
Scotts Way TN2 ......16 E8
Scrace Hill Terr RH16 ..73 D8
Scraper's Hill BN8 ...128 A8
Scrase Lodge RH15 ..73 D3
Scutes Cl TN34 ......137 A3
Sea Cotts 5 BN25 ...180 F7
Sea Ho 8 BN42 ......161 E7
Sea Rd Bexhill TN40 ..157 D3
Camber TN31 ....94 F2
Fairlight Cove TN35 ..139 A5
Hastings TN38 ....158 F5
Pevensey Bay BN24 ..175 D5
Winchelsea Beach TN36 .118 B7
Seabeach La BN2 ....185 C3
Seabourne Rd
Bexhill TN40 ....158 A6
Bexhill TN40 ....158 B5
Seacliffe BN10 ....177 F3
Seafield Cl BN25 .....181 B5
Seafield Rd BN3 .....163 B6
Seaford Cty Prim Sch
BN25 ....180 E4
Seaford Head Com Coll
(Lower) BN25 ....180 F2
Seaford Head Com Coll
(Upper) BN25 ....181 A2
Seaford Rd
Eastbourne BN22 .....185 C5
Hove BN3 ....162 C6
Newhaven BN9 ....179 F8
Seaford Sta BN25 ....180 E3
Seagrave Cl BN25 ...180 A6
Seagrove Way BN25 .180 F5
Searle Ave BN10 .....178 E6
Seasaw Way BN2 ....164 F7
Seaside
Eastbourne BN22 .....185 C5
St Leonards TN38 ....158 F6
Seaside Rd TN38 ....158 F6
Seaside Rdbt BN23 ..185 C4
Seaside Way TN38 ...158 F6
Seaview Ave BN10 ...178 E6
Seaview Rd
Newhaven BN9 ....168 F1

Seaview Rd continued
Peacehaven BN10 ....178 E6
Woodingdean BN2 ....165 B8
Seaview Terr
Icklesham TN36 ......116 E5
Rye TN31 ....93 C5
Seaville Dr
Eastbourne BN23 ....185 D8
Pevensey Bay BN24 .175 D5
Second Ave Bexhill TN40 .157 F5
Camber TN31 ....94 F2
Hove BN3 ....163 C6
Newhaven BN9 ....179 C6
Second Rd BN10 .....178 A7
Sedgebrook Gdns TN34 .136 E2
Sedges The TN38 ....135 E1
Sedgewick Rd TN40 ..157 C6
Sedlescombe
CE Prim Sch TN33 ...88 E1
Sedlescombe Gdns TN38 .136 B2
Sedlescombe Rd N TN37 .136 B4
Sedlescombe Rd S TN38 .136 B1
Sedlescombe Vineyard
TN32 ....88 D5
Sefton Chase TN6 ....26 A3
Sefton Rd BN41 ......140 F3
Sefton Way TN6 ......26 A3
Segrave Cl BN27 .....123 B2
Selba Dr BN1 ....143 B3
Selborne Pl BN3 .....163 C7
Selborne Rd BN3 ....163 C6
Selby Cl TN22 ....78 D5
Selby Ct RH16 ....50 E3
Selby Gdns TN38 .....78 D5
Selby Rd Eastbourne BN21 .184 D5
Uckfield TN22 ....78 D6
Selby Rise TN22 .....78 D5
Selham Cl BN1 ......143 D6
Selham Dr BN1 ......143 D6
Selham Pl BN1 ......143 D6
Selhurst Rd BN2 .....165 E6
Selbourne Pk TN3 ....17 C4
Selmeston Cl TN34 ..136 D1
Selmeston Ct 2 BN25 .180 C4
Selmeston Ho 6 BN21 .184 D4
Selmeston Pl BN2 ...164 F6
Selmeston Rd BN21 .184 C7
Selmestone Rd BN2 ..164 F5
Selsey Cl BN1 ....143 A6
Selsfield Cl BN1 .....143 D3
Selsfield Dr BN2 .....143 D3
Selwyn Dr BN21 .....184 E4
Selwyn Ho TN13 .....117 C4
Selwyn Park Ct 9 BN21 .184 E4
Selwyn Rd BN21 .....184 E4
Semley Lodge BN6 ...97 E4
Semley Rd Brighton BN1 .143 A1
Hassocks BN6 ....97 E4
Sempstead La TN31,TN32 .66 C4
Senlac Gdns TN33 ...112 C5
Senlac Green TN22 ...78 E8
Senlac Pk TN3 ....15 C7
Senlac Rd BN9 ....179 D7
Senlac Way TN37 ....136 C5
Sergison Cl RH16 ....50 C5
Sergison Rd RH16 ...50 D5
Setfords Field BN8 ....75 E1
Sevelands Cl TN13 ...164 F7
Seven Acre Ct TN37 ..136 A5
Seven Dials BN1 .....189 A4
Seven Sisters Ctry Pk
BN25 ....182 A2
Seven Sisters Rd BN22 .173 C3
Sevenfields RH15 .....72 D4
Sevenoaks Rd TN37 .174 D2
Seville St BN2 ....164 C7
Sewell Ave TN40 .....157 C5
Seymour Ho 3 BN2 ..164 D4
Seymour Sq 7 BN2 ..164 D4
Seymour St 4 BN2 ...164 D4
Seymour Villas TN34 .137 A3
Shaftesbury Ct TN22 .78 C8
Shaftesbury Pl BN1 ..164 A8
Shaftesbury Rd
Brighton BN1 ....189 B5
Royal Tunbridge Wells TN4 .8 A5
Shakespeare St BN3 ..163 A8
Shakespeare Wlk BN23 .174 F4
Shalesbrook La RH18 ..12 A1
Shalfleet Cl BN23 ....174 B3
Shandon Cl TN2 ....8 C4
Shands BN6 ....97 F3
Shanklin Cl BN23 ....174 F4
Shanklin Ct
11 Brighton BN2 .....164 C8
Hove BN3 ....141 D1
Shanklin Rd BN2 .....164 C8
Shannon Cl BN10 ....167 B1
Shannon Way BN23 ..185 F8
Sharp's Cnr TN21 ....106 E3
Sharpthorne Cres BN41 .141 C1
Sharrow Ct RH16 .....50 E5
Shaw The TN2 ....8 C2
Shawcross Ho BN1 ..142 E2
Shawfield TN6 ....26 B2
Shaws Cnr 5 TN31 ...67 B7
Shearwater Terr TN34 .136 D4
Shedden Ct TN21 ....82 A8
Sheddingdean Bsns Ctr
RH15 ....72 F5
Sheddingdean Cl RH15 .73 A4
Sheddingdean Cty Inf Sch
RH15 ....73 A5

Saxon Cl BN2 ....177 C6

Sheddingdean
Neighbourhood Ctr
RH15 . . . . .73 A5
Sheep End BN22 . . . . .185 B4
Sheep Pen La **3** BN25 . . . . .181 A3
Sheep Plain TN6 . . . . .37 D8
Sheep Wlk BN2 . . . . .165 F1
Sheepbell Cl BN41 . . . . .141 B3
Sheepfair BN7 . . . . .123 A2
Sheepfold The BN10 . . . . .167 C1
Sheepsetting La TN21 . . . . .81 E7
Sheepstreet La TN19,TN5 . . . . .43 E5
Sheepwash La TN22 . . . . .80 C8
Sheerwater Cres TN4 . . . . . . .136 D4
Sheffield Mill La TN22 . . . . . . .53 C8
Sheffield Park Gdns TN22 . . .53 D5
Sheffield Park Sta TN22 . . . . .53 A4
Sheffield Park Way BN23 . . .174 A4
Sheiling Rd TN6 . . . . .25 E3
Shell La **9** TN34 . . . . .160 A3
Shelldale Ave BN41 . . . . .162 B7
Shelldale Cres BN41 . . . . .162 B7
Shelldale Rd BN41 . . . . .162 B8
Shelley Cl BN7 . . . . .123 B1
Shelley Cl **4** RH16 . . . . .50 D5
Shelley Pk **4** TN21 . . . . .82 A7
Shelley Rd
East Grinstead RH19 . . . . .1 D1
Hove BN3 . . . . .162 F7
Ringmer BN8 . . . . .124 E5
Shelley Wood RH15 . . . . .72 D4
Shelly Wlk **3** BN23 . . . . .174 E2
Shenfield Way BN1 . . . . .143 B3
Shenstone RH16 . . . . .51 B8
Shepham Ave BN2 . . . . .177 D6
Shepham La BN26 . . . . .173 C8
Shepherd St **3** TN38 . . . . . . .159 C6
Shepherd's Cl TN39 . . . . .156 D4
Shepherd's Hill TN7 . . . . .23 D8
Shepherd's Way TN35 . . . . . .138 E4
Shepherds Cl
Eastbourne BN22 . . . . .173 F3
Piddinghoe BN9 . . . . .168 B2
Ringmer BN8 . . . . .124 E5
Shepherds Cot BN10 . . . . . . .167 D2
Shepherds Croft BN1 . . . . . . .142 C4
Shepherds Ct TN35 . . . . .138 E4
Shepherds Mead RH15 . . . . . . .72 F4
Shepherds Way
Ringmer BN8 . . . . .124 E5
South Chailey BN8 . . . . .100 C7
Uckfield TN22 . . . . .78 C5
Shepherds Wlk
Crowborough TN6 . . . . .26 C1
Hassocks BN6 . . . . .97 F5
Royal Tunbridge Wells TN2 . . . . .8 D4
Shepherdsgrove La RH19 . . . . .3 A4
Sheppard Way BN41 . . . . .141 A3
Sheppey Wlk BN27 . . . . .129 A3
Sheppeys RH16 . . . . .50 D2
Shepway The BN25 . . . . .181 B4
Sheraton Cl BN21 . . . . .184 F2
Sherborne Ct **3** BN21 . . . . .184 D4
Sherborne Cl Hove BN3 . . . . .141 D3
Royal Tunbridge Wells TN2 . . . . .8 D3
Sherbourne Rd BN3 . . . . .141 D3
Sherbourne Way BN3 . . . . . . .141 D3
Sheridan Cl RH19 . . . . .1 C1
Sheridan Mans BN3 . . . . .163 A8
Sheridan Terr BN3 . . . . .163 A8
Sheriff's La TN6 . . . . .39 D7
Sheringham Cl TN32 . . . . .165 E2
Sherrington Rd BN2 . . . . .165 F8
Sherwood Cl TN34 . . . . .136 F1
Sherwood Dr RH16 . . . . .50 C5
Sherwood Gn BN27 . . . . .152 B6
Sherwood Park
Cty Prim Sch TN2 . . . . .8 D6
Sherwood Pl TN2 . . . . .6 E3
Sherwood Rd
Royal Tunbridge Wells TN2 . . . . .8 E5
Seaford BN25 . . . . .180 F4
Sherwood Rise BN25 . . . . . . .180 F4
Sherwood Way TN2 . . . . .8 D6
Shinewater Ct BN23 . . . . .174 B3
Shinewater Cty Prim Sch
BN23 . . . . .174 B4
Shinewater La BN23 . . . . .174 B4
Shinewater Rdbt BN23 . . . . . .174 B1
Shingle Cl TN38 . . . . .135 E7
Shingle Rd BN43 . . . . .161 A6
Ship St Brighton BN1 . . . . . .189 A2
East Grinstead RH19 . . . . .10 E8
Newhaven BN9 . . . . .179 C8
Ship Street Gdns BN1 . . . . . .189 A2
Shipley La TN39 . . . . .156 D3
Shipley Mill Cl BN24 . . . . .174 B5
Shipley Rd BN2 . . . . .165 E7
Shipwreck Heritage Ctr
(Mus) TN34 . . . . .160 B3
Shipyard La TN31 . . . . .93 C5
Shirlea View TN33 . . . . .112 E4
Shirley Ave BN3 . . . . .142 B2
Shirley Cl BN43 . . . . .161 D8
Shirley Dr Hove BN3 . . . . .142 C2
St Leonards TN37 . . . . .136 B4
Shirley Gdns TN4 . . . . .7 C5
Shirley Rd BN3 . . . . .163 C8
Shirley St BN3 . . . . .163 B7
Shirleys BN6 . . . . .98 E2
Shoreham Beach
Cty Fst Sch BN43 . . . . .161 A6
Shoreham By–Pass
BN41,BN43 . . . . .140 D2

Shoreham Coll BN43 . . . . .161 D7
Short Brow BN25 . . . . .181 A4
Short Brow Cl BN22 . . . . .173 B3
Shortbridge Rd BN21 . . . . . . .184 D4
Shortgate La
Laughton BN8 . . . . .126 B8
Shortgate BN8 . . . . .104 B2
Shortgate Rd BN2 . . . . .143 F4
Shortlands Cl BN22 . . . . .173 C1
Shorts Cl RH16 . . . . .50 E3
Shotters RH15 . . . . .72 E1
Shovelstrode La RH19 . . . . . . .11 D8
Showfields Rd TN2 . . . . .7 F1
Shropshire Ct BN20 . . . . .184 B7
Shrub La TN19 . . . . .62 C7
Shrublands Ct TN2 . . . . .8 C4
Shrublands The TN39 . . . . . . .156 E3
Sicklehatch La TN21 . . . . .82 B2
Sidcup Cl BN23 . . . . .174 D2
Sidehill Dr BN41 . . . . .140 F2
Sidley Cty Prim Sch
TN39 . . . . .157 C7
Sidley Gn TN39 . . . . .157 C7
Sidley Rd BN22 . . . . .185 C5
Sidley St TN39 . . . . .157 C7
Sidney Cl TN22 . . . . .16 F8
Silchester Rd TN38 . . . . .159 C7
Sillwood Cl **10** BN1 . . . . .163 E5
Sillwood Hall **2** BN1 . . . . . .163 E5
Sillwood Pl **17** BN1 . . . . .163 E5
Sillwood Rd BN1 . . . . .163 E5
Sillwood St BN1 . . . . .163 E5
Sillwood Terr **22** BN1 . . . . . .163 E5
Silva Cl TN40 . . . . .158 A6
Silvan Rd TN38 . . . . .135 E4
Silver Bank Cotts TN19 . . . . . .64 B8
Silver Birches
Haywards Heath RH16 . . . . .51 A4
Hove BN1 . . . . .142 E1
Silver Hill TN19 . . . . .45 B1
Silverdale Ave BN3 . . . . .163 D7
Silverdale Rd BN3 . . . . .98 B3
Silverdale Ave BN3 . . . . .163 D7
Silverdale Rd BN27 . . . . .152 B8
Silverdale Cty Prim Sch
TN38 . . . . .136 B3
Silverdale La
Royal Tunbridge Wells TN4 . . . . .8 B6
Sandhurst Cross TN18 . . . . .46 F5
Silverdale Rd
Burgess Hill RH15 . . . . .73 B2
Eastbourne BN20 . . . . .184 F1
Hove BN3 . . . . .163 D7
Silverden Cotts TN18 . . . . .46 F4
Silverhill Ave TN37 . . . . .136 C4
Silverlands Rd **1** TN37 . . . . .136 B2
Silvester Rd TN40 . . . . .157 C5
Silwood Cl TN2 . . . . .8 E7
Simmonds Ct TN4 . . . . .7 B4
Simons Cl TN6 . . . . .26 A1
Singleton Mill Rd BN24 . . . . .174 C5
Singleton Rd BN1 . . . . .143 A6
Singleton Way RH15 . . . . .73 C1
Sinnock Sq **11** TN34 . . . . . . .160 B4
Sir Henry Fermor
CE Prim Sch TN6 . . . . .26 A2
Six Bells Mews TN31 . . . . .67 C5
Skinner's La TN33 . . . . .133 D8
Skinners' Sch The TN4 . . . . .8 A6
Skippers Hill Manor
Prep Sch TN20 . . . . .58 B7
Skyline View BN10 . . . . .167 D1
Slade The TN3 . . . . .20 A3
Sleeches Cross TN3 . . . . .17 B2
Sleepers Stile Rd TN5 . . . . .19 B1
Slider's La TN22 . . . . .53 A7
Slides The TN38 . . . . .135 F3
Slimbridge Rd RH15 . . . . .72 F3
Slindon Ave BN10 . . . . .178 D6
Slindon Cres BN23 . . . . .174 E1
Slinford Cl BN2 . . . . .164 D5
Sliverick's La TN33 . . . . .109 F7
Sloane Ct **4** BN2 . . . . .164 C5
Sloe La BN26 . . . . .171 A3
Slonk Hill Rd BN43 . . . . .140 A1
Sloop La BN17 . . . . .52 D5
Slugwash La RH17 . . . . .74 B7
Smeatons La TN36 . . . . .118 B5
Smith Cl TN33 . . . . .133 B5
Smithy The Durgates TN5 . . . . .29 A3
Uckfield TN22 . . . . .78 B6
Smith's Cl TN37 . . . . .136 C5
Smolletts RH19 . . . . .10 C8
Smugglers Cl BN26 . . . . .170 F3
Smugglers La TN6 . . . . .25 D5
Smugglers Way TN35 . . . . . . .138 F4
Snape La TN5 . . . . .29 D1
Snape View TN5 . . . . .29 F4
Snatt's Rd TN22 . . . . .55 C1
Snednore BN7 . . . . .145 F5
Snipe Cl TN2 . . . . .9 E8
Snowdon Cl BN23 . . . . .174 D3
Snowdon Rd RH16 . . . . .51 C4
Snowflakes La RH16 . . . . .51 D6
Soames Ct RH15 . . . . .72 F4
Solomon's La TN32 . . . . .67 C4
Solomons Cl BN23 . . . . .175 B2
Solway BN27 . . . . .129 A2
Solway Ave BN3 . . . . .142 F7
Somerhill Ave BN3 . . . . .163 D7
Somerhill Ct **10** BN3 . . . . . . .163 D7
Somerhill Cty Jun Sch
BN3 . . . . .163 D6
Somerhill Lodge BN3 . . . . . . .163 D6
Somerhill Rd BN3 . . . . .163 D6
Somerset Ct
Eastbourne BN23 . . . . .174 E1
3 Hove BN3 . . . . .163 C7

Somerset Point **1** BN2 . . . . .164 C4
Somerset Rd TN4 . . . . .8 A6
Somerset St BN2 . . . . .164 C5
Somerset Villas TN3 . . . . .15 C7
Somerville Cl BN23 . . . . .185 E7
Somerville Gdns TN4 . . . . .7 F4
Sompting Cl BN2 . . . . .164 F7
Sompting Ct **3** BN43 . . . . . .161 B8
Sorrel Cl BN23 . . . . .174 C3
Sorrel Dr BN23 . . . . .174 C3
South Ave Brighton BN2 . . . .164 C5
Eastbourne BN20 . . . . .184 B5
Hurstpierpoint BN6 . . . . .97 A5
South Bank BN6 . . . . .97 E3
South Brooks Rd TN29 . . . . . . .96 F2
South Cl Beachlands BN24 . . .175 F6
Burgess Hill RH15 . . . . .72 E3
Hailsham BN27 . . . . .152 B6
South Cliff Bexhill TN39 . . . .156 F2
Eastbourne BN20 . . . . .188 F8
South Cliff Ave
Bexhill TN39 . . . . .156 E2
Eastbourne BN20 . . . . .184 F1
South Cliff Tower BN20 . . . .188 F8
South Cliffe 3 BN7 . . . . .123 E1
South Coast Rd
Peacehaven BN10 . . . . .178 D6
Telscombe Cliffs BN2,BN10 . .177 E4
South Cliffe **5** Lewes BN7 . .123 E1
Royal Tunbridge Wells TN4 . . . . .8 A6
South Downs BN7 . . . . .99 E5
South Downs Bsns Pk
BN7 . . . . .123 E2
South Downs Rd BN7 . . . . . . .123 D2
South Dr RH15 . . . . .72 E3
South Gr TN1 . . . . .8 A2
South La Newhaven BN9 . . . .179 C7
Wood's Corner TN21 . . . . .84 E2
South Lodge **3** BN2 . . . . . . .164 F5
South Lodge Cl RH15 . . . . .72 F4
South Lynn Dr BN21 . . . . .184 F4
South Malling
CE Prim Sch BN7 . . . . .123 E3
South Pl 3 BN2 . . . . .123 D1
South Point 7 BN43 . . . . . . .161 A6
South Rd Brighton BN1 . . . . .142 E1
Hailsham BN27 . . . . .152 B6
Haywards Heath RH16 . . . . .51 C4
Newhaven BN9 . . . . .179 D7
Wivelsfield Green RH17 . . . . . . .74 D4
South Rough BN8 . . . . .76 C7
South Side TN21 . . . . .59 E1
South St Brighton BN1 . . . . . .189 A2
Crowborough TN6 . . . . .26 C5
Ditchling BN6 . . . . .98 D3
East Hoathly BN8 . . . . .104 F4
Eastbourne BN21 . . . . .185 A2
Falmer BN1 . . . . .144 C6
Lewes BN7 . . . . .123 E1
Mayfield TN20 . . . . .40 B2
Portslade-by-Sea BN41 . . . . . .141 A1
Rotherfield TN6 . . . . .39 B8
Seaford BN25 . . . . .180 E2
St Leonards TN37 . . . . .159 C7
South Terr Broad Oak TN21 . .59 E1
Hastings TN34 . . . . .159 F8
Westfield TN35 . . . . .114 E3
South Undercliff TN31 . . . . . .93 C5
South View Ditchling BN6 . . . .98 E3
Eastbourne BN21 . . . . .184 E4
Hastings TN34 . . . . .160 B4
1 South Heighton BN9 . . . . .168 E2
South View Rd
Crowborough TN6 . . . . .25 E1
Royal Tunbridge Wells TN4 . . . . .8 B8
Turner's Green TN5 . . . . .29 F6
South Way Lewes BN7 . . . . . .123 A1
Newhaven BN9 . . . . .179 D7
Seaford BN25 . . . . .181 C1
South Woodlands BN1 . . . . .142 E5
Southall Ave BN2 . . . . .143 D2
Southampton Cl BN23 . . . . . .185 E8
Southampton St BN2 . . . . . . .189 C3
Southborough
CE Prim Schs TN4 . . . . .7 E8
Southbourne Rd BN22 . . . . . .185 C6
Southcourt Ave TN39 . . . . . . .156 F2
Southdown Ave
Brighton BN1 . . . . .143 A1
Hastings TN34 . . . . .137 B3
Lewes BN7 . . . . .146 A8
Lower Willingdon BN20 . . . . . . .173 A3
Peacehaven BN10 . . . . .178 C6
Portslade-by-Sea BN41 . . . . . .162 C8
Southdown Cl
Haywards Heath RH16 . . . . .50 D2
Newhaven BN9 . . . . .179 B6
Portslade-by-Sea BN41 . . . . . .141 A2
Seaford BN25 . . . . .181 A2
Southwick BN42 . . . . .161 E7
Southease Sta BN9 . . . . .168 A7
Southenden Cl BN27 . . . . .152 C7
Southern Ave BN26 . . . . .173 B6

Southern Rd BN22 . . . . .173 F2
Southern Ring Rd BN1 . . . . . .144 B6
Southfield BN26 . . . . .172 F5
Southfield Rd TN4 . . . . .8 A6
Southfields
Sparrow's Green TN5 . . . . .29 F6
Speldhurst TN3 . . . . .7 A7
Southfields Cl **5** BN21 . . . . .184 F3
Southfields Rd BN21 . . . . .184 F3
Southfields Way TN4 . . . . .8 B8
Southgate TN4 . . . . .7 D7
Southlands Ave RH19 . . . . .1 E7
Southlands Ave TN39 . . . . . . .157 A7
Southlands Ct **1** BN41 . . . . .161 B8
Southlands General Hospl
BN43 . . . . .161 B8
Southlands Rd TN39 . . . . .157 A7
Southmead Cl TN20 . . . . .40 D3
Southmount BN1 . . . . .143 B1
Southon Cl BN41 . . . . .140 F3
Southover CE Prim Sch
BN7 . . . . .146 C8
Southover High St BN7 . . . . . .146 C8
Southover Manor Ho 10
BN7 . . . . .146 C8
Southover Pl BN2 . . . . .189 C4
Southover Rd BN7 . . . . .146 C8
Southover St BN2 . . . . .189 C3
Southridge Rd TN6 . . . . .37 E8
Southridge Rise TN6 . . . . .37 E8
Southview RH17 . . . . .51 F3
Southview Cl
Crowborough TN6 . . . . .25 E1
Peacehaven BN10 . . . . .140 E1
Southview Dr TN22 . . . . .78 D8
Southview Rd
Peacehaven BN10 . . . . .178 C8
Southwick BN42 . . . . .161 E8
Southwater Cl BN2 . . . . .164 D6
Southwater Rd TN37 . . . . .159 C8
Southway RH15 . . . . .72 D3
Southwater Cty Jun Sch
RH15 . . . . .72 D3
Southwick Cl RH19 . . . . .1 D2
Southwick Ho **6** RH19 . . . . . .1 D2
Southwick Sq BN42 . . . . .161 E7
Southwick St BN42 . . . . .161 E8
Southwick Sta BN42 . . . . .161 E7
Southwood Ave TN4 . . . . .8 A6
Southwood Cl TN38 . . . . .136 A1
Southwood Rd TN4 . . . . .7 B5
Sovereign Cl
Hastings TN34 . . . . .137 A4
Seaford BN25 . . . . .181 A5
Sovereign Ct
Brighton BN2 . . . . .165 C3
Eastbourne BN22 . . . . .185 C5
Sovereign Ctr
Burgess Hill RH15 . . . . .72 E2
Eastbourne BN22 . . . . .185 E6
Spa Cl BN3 . . . . .163 B5
Spa Ind Est TN2 . . . . .8 E8
Spa Valley Rly TN4 . . . . .7 E1
Spaldings The TN38 . . . . .135 E1
Spanish Cl RH15 . . . . .73 B4
Sparks Gdns TN33 . . . . .133 A6
Sparrow Way RH15 . . . . .72 D3
Sparrows Green Rd TN5 . . . . . .29 F5
Sparrows The BN10 . . . . .167 D1
Spatham La BN6 . . . . .98 F4
Speldhurst CE Prim Sch
TN3 . . . . .7 A7
Speldhurst Hill TN3 . . . . .7 B8
Speldhurst Rd
Langton Green TN3 . . . . .6 F4
Royal Tunbridge Wells . . . .
Spencer Ave BN3 . . . . .141 D3
Spencer Mews **8** TN1 . . . . . . .8 A2
Spencer's Mews **4** TN1 . . . . . .8 B4
Spences Field BN7 . . . . .123 E2
Spences La BN7 . . . . .123 E2
Spicers Cl RH15 . . . . .72 F5
Spindlewood Dr TN39 . . . . . . .156 C4
Spinnals Gr BN42 . . . . .161 D7
Spinney Cl RH15 . . . . .97 C5
Spinney The Battle TN33 . . . .112 F3
Brighton BN1 . . . . .156 D3
Burgess Hill RH15 . . . . .73 A4
Hastings TN34 . . . . .136 E1
Haywards Heath RH16 . . . . .50 D8
Hove BN3 . . . . .142 C3
Robertsbridge TN32 . . . . .63 F3
Spinneys The
Heathfield TN21 . . . . .82 B6
Lewes BN7 . . . . .123 C1
Spital Rd BN7 . . . . .123 B8
Spithurst Rd BN8 . . . . .101 E6
Spode La TN8 . . . . .4 A7
Sponden La TN18 . . . . .47 A7
Sportcentre Rd BN1 . . . . .144 A6
Spotted Cow La TN22 . . . . .56 E5
Spout Hill TN6 . . . . .27 D1
Spray Hill TN3 . . . . .20 B4
Spray's La TN33,TN35 . . . . . . .114 B4
Spring Cl BN20 . . . . .173 B1
Spring Copse RH19 . . . . .1 D3
Spring Gdns
Brighton BN1 . . . . .189 B2
Glynde BN8 . . . . .147 F5
Lewes BN7 . . . . .123 C1
Rushlall TN4 . . . . .8 B3
6 Southwick BN42 . . . . .161 E7
Spring Hill Northiam TN31 . . . .67 B7
Saint's Hill TN11, TN3 . . . . .6 A7

Spring Hill Wildfowl Pk
RH18 . . . .
Spring La Bexhill TN39 . . . .
Burwash TN19 . . . .
Clayton BN6 . . . .
Five Ashes TN20 . . . .
Spring Lodge Cl BN23 . . . .
Spring Mdw RH18 . . . .
Spring Park TN21 . . . .
Spring St Brighton BN1 . . . .
St Leonards TN37 . . . .
Spring Steps TN36 . . . .
Spring Way RH19 . . . .
Springate Rd BN43 . . . .
Springett Almshouses
TN18 . . . .
Springett Ave BN8 . . . .
Springett Cotts BN8 . . . .
Springfield RH14 . . . .
Springfield Ave BN10 . . . .
Springfield Cl
Crowborough TN6 . . . .
Westham BN24 . . . .
Springfield Cotts
Cackle Street TN31 . . . .
Rotherfield TN6 . . . .
Springfield Rd
Bexhill TN40 . . . .
Brighton BN1 . . . .
Eastbourne BN22 . . . .
Groombridge TN3 . . . .
St Leonards TN38 . . . .
Springfield Valley Rd
TN38 . . . .
Springfields BN3 . . . .
Springfields Farm Ind Est
RH17 . . . .
Springhead TN2 . . . .
Springhead Way TN6 . . . .
Springside Wlk TN38 . . . .
Springview Apartments
TN2 . . . .
Springwood Rd TN21 . . . .
Spur Rd BN26 . . . .
Spurway Pk BN41 . . . .
Squab La BN27 . . . .
Square The
Beachlands BN24 . . . .
Brighton BN1 . . . .
Cowden TN8 . . . .
Hailsham BN27 . . . .
Wadhurst TN5 . . . .
Squirrel Cl Bexhill TN39 . . . .
St Leonards TN38 . . . .
Squirrel Way TN2 . . . .
Stable Ctyd TN22 . . . .
Stable Mews TN37 . . . .
Stabledene Way TN2 . . . .
Stablefield TN35 . . . .
Stables La **3** BN21 . . . .
Stacey's Cnr TN21 . . . .
Stafford Ct **2** BN23 . . . .
Stafford Cty Jun Sch
BN22 . . . .
Stafford Rd Brighton BN1 . . . .
Royal Tunbridge Wells TN2 . . . .
Seaford BN25 . . . .
Stafford House F Ed Ctr
BN6 . . . .
Stafford Rd Brighton BN1 . . . .
Royal Tunbridge Wells . . . .
Seaford BN25 . . . .
Stafford St BN6 . . . .
Stag Rd TN2 . . . .
Stainsby St **1** TN37 . . . .
Stalkers La BN8 . . . .
Stamford **8** RH16 . . . .
Stamford Ct TN35 . . . .
Stamford Lodge **2** BN1 . . . .
Stanam Rd TN2 . . . .
Standard Hill Cl TN33 . . . .
Standean Cl BN1 . . . .
Standen (NT) RH19 . . . .
Standen Cl RH19 . . . .
Standen St
Royal Tunbridge Wells TN4 . . . .
Standen Street TN17,TN18 . . . .
Stanford Ave
Brighton BN1 . . . .
Hassocks BN6 . . . .
Stanford Cl Hassocks BN6 . . . .
Hove BN3 . . . .
Stanford Ct BN1 . . . .
Stanford Cty Inf Sch BN1 . . . . . .
Stanford Cty Jun Sch
BN1 . . . .
Stanford Rd BN1 . . . .
Stanford Terr BN1 . . . .
Stanhope Pl **1** TN38 . . . .
Stanhope Rd TN1 . . . .
Stanier Rd TN34 . . . .
Stanley Ave BN41 . . . .
Stanley Ave S BN41 . . . .
Stanley Cl **3** BN2 . . . .
Stanley Deason L Ctr
BN2 . . . .
Stanley Rd Brighton BN1 . . . .
1 Eastbourne BN22 . . . .
Hastings TN34 . . . .
Peacehaven BN10 . . . .
Portslade-by-Sea BN41 . . . .
Royal Tunbridge Wells TN1 . . . .
Stanley St BN2 . . . .
Stanmer BN1 . . . .
Stanmer Ave BN2 . . . .
Stanmer Ct BN1 . . . .
Stanmer Dr BN2 . . . .
Stanmer Ho BN1 . . . .
Stanmer Park Rd BN1 . . . .

nmer St BN1 143 B2
nmer Villas BN1 143 B2
nsfield Rd BN7 123 B2
nstead Cres BN2 165 F6
nsted Rd BN22 185 A4
plecross
ethodist Prim Sch TN32 65 E2
plefield Dr BN2 143 F3
pley Ct BN3 162 D8
pley Rd BN3 141 D1
r La Alfriston BN26 171 A3
ackboys TN22 80 B6
ayfield TN20 40 B2
r Mews TN20 40 B2
r Rd 6 BN21 184 E4
rboard Ct BN2 164 F3
rborough Cotts RH7 1 F7
rfield TN6 25 E1
rling Cl RH15 72 C3
rr's Cotts 10 TN34 160 B4
rr's Green La TN33 113 A3
rrs Mead TN33 113 A3
rvecrow La TN31 91 D6
rwell Cl TN34 136 D3
tion App Battle TN33 112 E3
stbourne BN22 173 F1
chingham TN19 44 C1
'mer BN1 144 B6
ssocks BN6 97 F4
stings TN34 159 E8
athfield TN21 82 A7
rsted Keynes RH17 33 A7
ve BN3 163 B8
yfield TN20 39 F2
aford BN25 180 E3
Leonards TN37 159 C7
tion Cl
mpton Green BN7 99 E5
wn Row TN6 27 D1
tion Cotts
owhurst TN33 135 A6
ssocks BN6 97 E4
nchelsea TN36 92 D1
tion Par 7 BN21 184 F3
tion Rd Bexhill TN40 157 C4
ghton BN1 142 D3
rgess Hill RH15 73 B2
owhurst TN33 134 F5
st Grinstead RH19 1 D1
est Row RH18 11 F3
oombridge TN3 15 C7
ilsham BN27 152 C6
stings TN34 159 F8
athfield TN21 82 A7
lingly BN27 129 A5
rsted Keynes RH17 33 C5
rst Green TN19 45 A3
ield TN22 102 D8
wes BN7 146 D8
yfield TN20 40 A2
whaven BN9 168 F1
rth Chailey BN8 75 F7
rthiam TN31 67 B8
mpton Green BN7 99 E6
egate BN26 173 A6
rtslade-by-Sea
3, BN41 162 C7
bertsbridge TN32 64 B4
ckrobin TN5 29 C6
aford BN25 180 B5
arpthorne RH19 21 A6
Southwick BN42 161 E7
negate TN5 42 E5
wn Row TN6 27 C1
nchelsea TN36 92 E1
khyham TN7 14 B5
tion Road Ind Est
27 152 C6
ion St Brighton BN1 189 B3
Eastbourne BN21 185 A3
wes BN7 123 D1
veley Rd BN20 188 E8
ellands Rise TN5 31 F1
ep Hill Brede La TN31 89 E2
ep Rd TN20, TN6 38 D3
ne Gdns BN2 189 B2
ne La BN1, BN2 189 B2
ne St BN2 189 B1
nings The RH19 1 C3
phen's Rd TN4 8 B6
phens Cl BN8 124 D5
phens Rd BN1 143 B2
phenson Dr RH19 10 F7
vens Cl TN39 157 C7
vens Ct BN3 162 E7
venson Cl BN23 174 E3
venson Rd
ghton BN2 164 C5
St Leonards TN37 136 B3
wards Inn La 3 BN7 146 C8
wart Rd TN4 8 C7
yne Cl 4 BN25 180 F2
yne Ct 11 BN25 180 E2
yne Rd BN25 180 F2
yne The BN25 180 E2
yning Ave Hove BN3 141 F3
acehaven BN10 178 C7
yning Cl BN25 181 C2
yning Ct 7 BN3 163 B7
ning Rd
tingdean BN2 177 A5
ford BN25 181 C2
s The BN27 152 C7
ing Ave BN25 181 C4
ing Cl
gess Hill RH15 73 C4
ford BN25 181 C3
ing Court Rd RH15 73 C4

Stirling Ct 5 BN3 163 C7
Stirling Pl BN3 163 A6
Stirling Rd TN38 135 F5
Stirling Way RH19 2 B3
Stock Dale TN35 138 F4
Stockland Green Rd TN3 7 B8
Stockland La TN22 57 B6
Stockleigh Rd TN38 159 C7
Stocks Mdw TN33 133 B5
Stockwell Ct
Burgess Hill RH15 72 F3
1 Haywards Heath RH16 50 E3
Stockwell Rd RH19 10 E6
Stoddards La TN31 67 F6
Stoke Brunswick Sch
RH19 11 E7
Stoke Cl BN25 181 B3
Stoke Manor Cl BN25 181 B4
Stokes Cotts TN19 60 F3
Stokes Ho 4 TN39 157 A4
Stone Cotts TN3 19 F4
Stone Court La TN2 9 E8
Stone Cross
Eastbourne BN24 174 B5
Mayfield TN20 39 F2
Stone Cross Cty Prim Sch
BN24 174 A5
Stone Cross Rd
Crowborough TN6 38 A7
Wadhurst TN5 30 A4
Stone Pit La TN18 47 E5
Stone Quarry Rd RH17 34 D7
Stone Row TN3 6 B5
Stone Row Cotts TN3 6 D1
Stone St Brighton BN1 163 E5
12 Hastings TN34 159 F8
Royal Tunbridge Wells TN1 8 B4
Stone Works Cotts TN31 93 F3
Stonebeach Rise TN38 135 E7
Stonebridge La TN22 79 F5
Stonecott Cl TN6 37 F8
Stonecroft Cl BN3 141 E4
Stonecross Rd BN2 143 F4
Stonedene Cl RH18 12 B2
Stonefield Pl 2 TN34 159 F8
Stonefield Rd TN34 159 F8
Stonefield Way RH15 72 F5
Stonegate CE Prim Sch
TN5 42 F5
Stonegate Cl BN23 174 A4
Stonegate Ct TN5 42 F5
Stonegate Rd TN5 30 C1
Stonegate Sta TN5 42 D3
Stonegate Way TN21 82 B8
Stoneham Cl BN7 123 C3
Stoneham Rd BN3 162 F7
Stonehaven Ct 5 TN40 157 D3
Stonehouse Dr Hastings,
Beauport Park TN33, TN38 113 F1
St Leonards TN38 136 A2
Stonehurst Ct 10 BN2 164 C6
Stonehurst La TN20, TN22 57 D7
Stoneleigh Ave BN1 142 F6
Stoneleigh Cl
Brighton BN1 142 F6
East Grinstead RH19 1 F1
Stonelink Cl TN37 135 F7
Stonepark Dr RH18 12 A2
Stonepound
Crossroads BN6 97 D4
Stonepound Rd BN6 97 E4
Stonery Cl BN41 141 A2
Stonery Rd BN41 141 A2
Stonestile La TN35 136 F8
Stonewall Park Rd TN3 6 F3
Stonewood Cl
Royal Tunbridge Wells TN4 8 A8
Seaford BN25 181 C4
Stoney La Hailsham BN27 152 C7
Shoreham-by-Sea BN43 161 C8
Stoneywish Ctry Pk BN6 98 E3
Storrington Cl BN3 141 E2
Straight Half Mile TN22 55 B5
Strand TN31 93 B5
Strand Ct TN31 93 B5
Strand Hill TN36 117 F7
Strand Mdw TN19 62 B7
Strand The BN2 165 A3
Stratford St TN1 8 C5
Strathenden Ct 9 BN25 180 E2
Strathfield Cl RH16 50 F4
Stratton Ct 6 BN3 162 F7
Strawberry Cl TN2 16 E7
Strawberry Fields TN31 67 A7
Strawlands BN7 99 E6
Stream La
Fairlight Cove TN35 139 A5
Sedlescombe TN33 88 C2
The Moor TN18 46 F4
Stream Lane Cotts TN18 46 A7
Stream Pit La TN18 47 B5
Stream Pk RH19 1 A3
Streamside Cl TN34 136 E3
Streat Bostall BN6 121 C6
Streat La BN6 99 C4
Streatfield Gdns TN21 81 F8
Streatfield Ho TN22 78 C8
Streatfield Rd
Heathfield TN21 81 F8
Uckfield TN22 78 B7
Streele La TN22 56 D1
Streele View TN22 78 E8
Street End La
Broad Oak TN21 59 E1
Broad Oak TN21 59 E5
Street The Framefield TN22 79 B6
Kingston near Lewes BN7 145 E5
Sedlescombe TN33 88 E1

Street The *continued*
West Firle BN8 148 B3
Westmeston BN6 120 F8
Streetlands TN33 88 E1
Stringer Way BN1 142 F3
Stringwalk The BN27 152 C7
Stroma Gdns BN27 128 F2
Strome Ho TN39 157 C7
Strongs Pas 5 TN34 160 B4
Strood Gate RH17 74 C5
Strood Rd TN37 136 C2
Stuart Ave BN21 184 C6
Stuart Cl TN2 16 F8
Stuart Way RH19 10 F7
Stubb La TN31 90 D2
Stubbygrove Cotts TN3 17 E4
Stud Cotts BN27 151 A8
Studdens La BN27 108 D1
Sturdee Cl BN23 185 F7
Sturdee Pl TN34 160 A3
Sturton Pl BN27 152 B7
Sudeley Pl BN2 164 D4
Sudeley St BN2 164 D4
Sudeley Terr 6 BN2 164 D4
Suffolk Ct 5 BN22 185 C4
Suffolk Rd TN39 157 C7
Suffolk St BN3 162 F8
Sugar La RH17 33 C4
Sugworth Cl RH16 50 D7
Sullington Cl BN2 143 F4
Sullington Way BN43 161 A8
Sumach Cl BN22 173 E2
Summer Cl BN41 162 A7
Summer Ct BN20 188 D7
Summer Hill TN38 159 A8
Summer Hill Rd TN39 156 F6
Summercourt BN27 152 B8
Summerdale Rd BN3 141 D2
Summerdown Cl BN20 184 D3
Summerdown La BN20 183 C1
Summerdown Rd BN20 184 D3
Summerfields Ave BN27 152 A8
Summerheath Rd BN27 152 B8
Summerhill Cl RH16 50 F7
Summerhill Dr RH16 51 A7
Summerhill Grange RH16 50 F7
Summerhill La RH16 50 F7
Summerlands Rd BN22 173 C2
Summersdeane BN42 140 F1
Summervale Rd TN2, TN4 7 E1
Sun La 8 TN34 160 A3
Sun St BN7 123 C1
Sunhill Ct TN2 9 C6
Sunningdale Cl
10 Bexhill TN40 157 E4
Hailsham BN27 129 A1
Seaford BN25 181 A2
Sunningdale Dr TN38 158 F7
Sunninghill Ave BN3 141 F2
Sunninghill Cl BN3 141 E2
Sunnybank TN5 32 E3
Sunnybank Cl TN20 40 B2
Sunnybrooke Cl TN22 78 D7
Sunnycroft Cl RH17 51 E2
Sunnydale Ave BN1 143 A6
Sunnydale Cl BN1 143 A6
Sunnyside Rd TN4 7 C4
Sunnywood Dr RH16 50 D3
Sunset Cl Beachlands BN24 175 F6
Telscombe Cliffs BN10 167 B1
Sunstar La BN26 172 E6
Sunte Ave RH16 50 F7
Sunte Cl RH16 50 E7
Sunview Ave BN10 178 D6
Surrenden Cl BN1 142 F4
Surrenden Cres BN1 142 E4
Surrenden Holt BN1 142 F3
Surrenden Lodge BN1 142 F2
Surrenden Pk BN1 143 A4
Surrenden Rd BN1 142 F3
Surrey Cl
Royal Tunbridge Wells TN2 16 F8
Seaford BN25 180 D4
Surrey Ho 12 BN2 164 D4
Surrey Rd BN25 180 C4
Surrey St BN1 189 A3
Susan's Rd BN21 185 A3
Susans Cl BN8 105 A5
Sussex Ave BN27 152 B8
Sussex Chambers 8
TN34 159 F8
Sussex Cl Bexhill TN39 156 F5
Hailsham BN27 152 B8
Royal Tunbridge Wells TN2 8 C1
Sussex Ct
Eastbourne BN22 185 B5
2 Haywards Heath RH16 50 E3
15 Hove BN3 163 C6
Shoreham-by-Sea BN43 161 A6
Sussex Cty Cricket Gd
BN3 163 C7
Sussex Eye Hospl BN2 164 D4
Sussex Gdns
East Dean BN20 183 C1
Haywards Heath RH17 51 B3
Sussex Ho
6 Eastbourne BN21 185 A2
Telscombe Cliffs BN10 177 F3
Sussex House Bsns Pk
BN3 162 F8
Sussex Hts 13 BN1 163 E5
Sussex Mews
4 Brighton BN2 164 E4
16 Royal Tunbridge Wells TN2 8 A2
Sussex Nuffield Hospl
Hove BN3 162 F7
Woodingdean BN2 165 C8
Sussex Pl BN2 189 C3

Sussex Rd
Haywards Heath RH16 50 E3
Hove BN3 163 B5
St Leonards TN38 159 A6
Sussex Sq Brighton BN2 164 E4
17 Haywards Heath RH16 50 E4
Sussex St BN2 189 C2
Sussex Terr BN2 189 C3
Sussex Toy & Model Mus
BN1 189 B3
Sussex Way
Burgess Hill RH15 72 E5
Telscombe Cliffs BN10 177 F3
Sutherland Ave TN39 157 A4
Sutherland Cl 1 TN39 157 A4
Sutherland Rd
Brighton BN2 164 C5
Royal Tunbridge Wells TN1 8 B3
Sutton Ave
Peacehaven BN10 178 B7
Seaford BN25 181 A3
Sutton Ave N BN10 178 B8
Sutton Cl BN2 144 E1
Sutton Cotts BN7 146 B3
Sutton Croft La 4 BN25 180 E3
Sutton Dro BN25 180 F4
Sutton Park Rd BN25 180 E3
Sutton Pl TN40 157 E4
Sutton Rd
Eastbourne BN21 185 A3
Seaford BN25 181 A3
Sutton Wall BN7 146 D4
Suttons Ind Pk TN36 118 A7
Suttons The Camber TN31 95 A1
St Leonards TN38 135 F2
Swaine's Pas 6 TN34 160 B4
Swaines Way TN21 82 A6
Swainham La TN38 135 B4
Swainsthorpe Cl RH16 50 F3
Swale Cl BN24 174 A5
Swallow Bank TN38 135 F2
Swallow Cl BN23 174 C2
Swallow Ct TN22 78 D5
Swallow Dr Battle TN33 112 F4
Royal Tunbridge Wells TN2 8 F6
Swallow Rest RH15 72 C3
Swallows The BN10 167 B1
Swan Ave 9 TN34 160 A4
Swan Bsns Ctr BN27 152 D6
Swan Cl BN8 100 E7
Swan Rd BN27 152 D6
Swan Terr TN34 160 A4
Swanborough Dr BN2 164 F7
Swanborough Dro BN7 145 F4
Swanborough Hollow
BN7 146 A4
Swanborough Pl BN2 164 F7
Swanley Cl BN23 174 D2
Swann Cl RH15 73 D3
Swannee Cl BN10 167 D1
Swans Ghyll RH18 11 E3
Swansbrook La TN21 106 E2
Swaylands Ave TN6 37 F7
Sweda Ct 18 BN2 164 D4
Sweeps Hill Cl TN2 9 D7
Sweethaws La TN6 37 C6
Sweetings La TN3, TN5 19 D1
Sweetlands BN6 98 B5
Swife La TN21 60 D5
Swift Cl Burgess Hill RH15 72 D3
Crowborough TN6 25 D1
Uckfield TN22 78 D5
Swiftsden Cotts TN19 44 F6
Swinburne Ave BN22 173 C3
Swingate Cross BN27 129 C5
Swissland Hill RH19, RH7 1 E7
Swynford Dr 1 TN38 136 A5
Sybron Way TN6 38 D8
Sycamore Cl Bexhill TN39 156 C4
Eastbourne BN22 173 D3
Heathfield TN21 82 B6
Portslade-by-Sea BN41 141 C3
Seaford BN25 181 C3
St Leonards TN38 136 A1
Woodingdean BN2 165 E8
Sycamore Cotts TN2 9 C6
Sycamore Ct TN22 78 D8
Sycamore Dr
East Grinstead RH19 2 A1
Hailsham BN27 152 B5
Sycamores The BN10 167 D1
Sydenham Ct TN40 157 D3
Sydney Cl TN38 136 B3
Sydney Little Rd TN38 135 D4
Sydney Rd
Eastbourne BN22 185 B4
Haywards Heath RH16 50 E6
Sydney St BN1 189 B3
Sydney Tidy Ho 5 BN2 164 C6
Sylvan Cl RH16 51 B4
Sylvester Way BN3 141 C3
Symbister Rd BN41 162 C7
Syresham Gdns RH16 50 F4

T

Tackleway TN34 160 B4
Taddington Ho 2 BN22 185 C4
Taddington Rd 1 BN22 185 C4
Tainter's Brook TN22 78 E8
Talbot Cres BN1 143 D6
Talbot Pk TN2 8 D5
Talbot Rd TN18 45 F8
Talbot Terr BN7 123 C1
Tall Ash Dr TN37 136 C4
Talland Par 17 BN25 180 E2
Tamar Cl BN24 174 A5
Tamarack Cl BN22 173 D2
Tamerisk Stps 24 TN34 160 B4
Tamplin Terr BN2 189 C3
Tamworth Rd BN3 162 F7
Tan Yard Cotts TN36 117 F8
Tanbridge Rd BN23 174 F2
Tandridge Rd BN3 162 E6
Tangier La TN3 17 B6
Tanglewood Coppice
TN39 156 E3
Tangmere Cl TN39 156 E3
Tangmere Rd BN1 143 A6
Tanhouse La TN31 68 F2
Tanners Field RH17 74 A5
Tanners Way TN6 26 A1
Tanners' Brook BN7 146 D8
Tanyard TN18 47 B5
Tanyard Ave RH19 11 A8
Tanyard Cotts Battle TN33 112 E3
Buxted TN22 56 C1
Tanyard La Chelwood
Common RH17, TN22 34 C4
Winchelsea TN36 117 F8
Tapsell's La TN5 29 D5
Tarland Ho TN2 8 D3
Tarner Rd BN2 189 C3
Tarragon Way BN43 140 C1
Tarring Cl BN9 168 D2
Tas Combe Way BN20 173 B2
Tate Cres RH15 72 F5
Taunton Gr BN2 144 A1
Taunton Pl BN2 144 A1
Taunton Rd BN2 143 F1
Taunton Way BN2 144 A1
Tavistock 8 BN21 185 A2
Tavistock & Summerhill
Sch RH16 50 F7
Tavistock Down BN1 143 C2
Taylor Cl TN38 135 F4
Taylor Ct TN2 8 C7
Taylor St TN4 8 A8
Tea Garden La TN3, TN4 7 C2
Teal Ct Hailsham BN27 152 D7
St Leonards TN38 135 E3
Teasley Mead TN3 5 C4
Tedder Rd TN4 8 B7
Tedder Terr TN35 137 D5
Teg Cl BN41 141 C2
Teise Cl TN2 8 D2
Teknol Ho RH15 72 E2
Telegraph St 12 BN2 164 C4
Telford Rd TN38 136 A5
Telham Cl TN34 137 A5
Telham La TN33 112 E1
Telscombe Cliffs
Cty Prim Sch BN10 178 A8
Telscombe Cliffs Way
BN10 178 A8
Telscombe Pk BN10 167 C2
Telscombe Rd
Eastbourne BN23 174 F2
Peacehaven BN10 167 D2
Temple Gdns BN1, BN3 163 E6
Temple Gr RH15 72 D4
Temple Grove Sch TN22 36 E3
Temple St BN1 163 E6
Tenantry Down Rd BN2 164 E8
Tenantry Rd BN2 164 D8
Tennis Cl BN27 152 B7
Tennis Rd BN3 162 E6
Tennyson Ct 5 RH16 50 D5
Tennyson Rise RH19 10 C8
Tennyson Wlk BN23 174 E3
Tenterden Cl BN23 174 D2
Tenterden Rise TN34 136 E2
Terminus Ave TN39 157 A3
Terminus Pl
9 Brighton BN1 189 A4
6 Hailsham BN27 152 C7
Terminus Rd Bexhill TN39 157 B3
Brighton BN1 189 A4
Eastbourne BN21 185 A3
Terminus St BN1 189 A3
Terrace Rd TN37 159 C7
Tescombe Grange BN10 177 F3
Teynham Ho BN2 177 C4
Thackeray Cl BN23 174 E3
Thakeham Cl TN40 158 A6
Thalia Ho TN40 157 B4
Thames Cl BN2 189 C2
Thanet Way TN34 136 E2
Thatchers Cl RH15 73 D1
Thatchings The BN26 173 A5
Theaklen Dr TN38 136 B2
Theobalds Gn TN21 82 A5
Theobalds Rd RH15 73 D6
Theobold Ho 1 BN1 189 B3
Theodore Cl TN2 8 E7
Third Ave Bexhill TN40 157 F6
Hove BN3 163 B6
Newhaven BN9 179 C6
Third Rd BN10 178 A7
Third St TN3 6 F3
Thirlmere Rd TN4 7 E5
Thomas Brassey Cl TN37 136 B5
Thomas Peacocke
Com Coll TN31 93 B6
Thomas Peacocke Sch
TN31 93 B6
Thomas St Lewes BN7 123 E2
Royal Tunbridge Wells TN4 8 A5
Thomas Turner Dr BN8 105 A5
Thompson Rd
Brighton BN1 143 C1
Newhaven BN9 168 F2

Thorn Cotts TN35 ....116 A4
Thornbank Cres TN39 .....156 F3
Thornbush Cres BN41 .....141 B3
Thorndean Rd BN2 ....143 D3
Thornden Ct TN17 ....49 A8
Thornden La TN17 ....49 A8
Thorne Cres TN39 ....133 E1
Thornfield Gdns TN2 ....8 F5
Thornhill Ave BN1 ....143 A7
Thornhill Cl BN3 ....141 E2
Thornhill Rise BN41 ......141 A4
Thornhill Way BN41 ......141 A3
Thorns The TN35 ....138 A8
Thornsdale 4 BN2 ....189 C3
Thornton Cl 5 BN22 ......185 B3
Thornton Rd BN26 ....171 F7
Thornwood Cl BN22 ....173 E2
Thorny Cl TN21 ....82 A7
Thorpe Works TN4 ....7 F8
Three Gables TN22 ....35 C4
Three Oaks La TN5 ....29 D7
Three Oaks Sta TN35 ......115 D2
Thurrock Cl BN2 ....173 B4
Thyme Cl BN43 ....140 C1
Thyssel La TN31 ....67 B6
Tibbs Mill La TN22,TN6 ....37 E2
Ticehurst Ave TN39 ......155 F4
Ticehurst CE Prim Sch
TN5 ....43 B8
Ticehurst Cl Bexhill TN39 .155 F4
  Hastings TN35 ....137 C3
Ticehurst Rd BN2 ....159 B7
Ticehurst Rd BN2 ....164 F5
Tichborne Cotts RH16 .....51 C6
Tichborne St BN1 ....189 B2
Tickerage La TN22 ....79 F6
Tidebrook TN5,TN20 ......40 F7
Tidebrook Gdns BN23 .....174 F2
Tideswell Rd BN21 ....185 A3
Tideway Sch
  & Sixth Form Ctr BN9 ...179 B6
Tidy St BN1 ....189 B3
Tilbury Pl BN2 ....189 C2
Tilbury Way BN2 ....189 C3
Tile Barn Cl TN22 ....102 D8
Tile Barn Rd TN38 ....135 F4
Tilebarn Ct RH16 ....50 E2
Tilehurst Dr BN27 ....152 A8
Tilekiln La TN35 ....137 E4
Tilers Cl RH15 ....73 D3
Tilford Rd TN40 ....157 F4
  Eastbourne BN21 ......184 D7
Tilgate Dr BN20 ....156 D3
Tilley La BN27 ....131 E6
Tilling Green Cty Inf Sch
TN31 ....93 A5
Tillingham Ave TN31 ......93 B6
Tillingham Ct BN24 ....174 A5
Tillingham La TN31 ....92 A6
Tillingham View TN31 .....90 B5
Tillington BN2 ....166 F7
Tillington Terr TN35 .....160 C6
Tillstone Cl BN2 ....143 D2
Tillstone St BN2 ....189 C2
Tilsmore Cres TN21 ....81 F7
Tilsmore Rd TN21 ....81 E6
Timber Yard Cotts BN1 ...123 E1
Timberlaine Rd BN24 .....175 C4
Timberley La BN22 ....173 D1
Timbers Ct BN27 ....152 C8
Tinclal Cl RH15 ....73 D3
Tinker's La TN22 ....57 E3
Tinkers La TN5 ....31 E3
Tintagel Cl BN3 ....163 A8
Tintern Cl Brighton BN1 ..143 B1
  Eastbourne BN22 ......173 E3
Tisbury Rd BN3 ....163 C6
Titchfield Cl RH15 ....73 D3
Tithe Barn Field TN36 ...116 F5
Titian Rd BN3 ....162 F7
Tiverton Dr TN40 ....157 F7
Tivoli BN1 ....142 E2
Tivoli Cres BN1 ....142 D1
Tivoli Cres N BN1 ....142 D2
Tivoli Pl BN1 ....142 D2
Tivoli Rd BN1 ....142 D2
Tobago 6 TN39 ....157 A2
Tobias Sch of Art RH19 ...10 E6
Tolkien Rd BN23 ....174 F2
Toll La Fairwarp TN22 ....36 A1
  Nutley TN22 ....35 F1
Toll Wood Rd TN21 ......106 F7
Tollgate Lindfield RH16 ...51 B8
  Peacehaven BN10 ......167 B1
Tollgate Cty Jun Sch
BN23 ....185 D7
Tollgate Ct BN23 ....185 D7
Tollgate Lock TN31 ....93 B4
Tollgates TN31 ....112 B4
Tollwood Pk TN6 ....26 B1
Tollwood Rd TN6 ....38 B8
Tomsett's Bank RH18 .....11 F1
Tomtits La RH18 ....2 C6
Tonbridge Rd TN2,TN11 ....9 A7
Tonbridge Way TN31 ......94 E2
Tongdean Ave BN3 ....142 C2
Tongdean Ct BN3 ....142 D4
Tongdean La
  Brighton BN1 ....142 C4
  Brighton BN3 ....142 D4
Tongdean Rd BN3 ....142 C3
Tongdean Rise BN1 ......142 C4
Top Cross TN40 ....158 A7

Top Dr TN22 ....55 A6
Top Rd RH19 ....21 B5
Top Rd BN10 ....167 C1
Tor Rd W BN10 ....167 C2
Torcross Cl BN2 ....143 E1
Torfield Cl TN34 ....160 B4
Torfield Ct BN21 ....184 E4
Torfield Ho TN34 ....160 B4
Torfield Rd BN21 ....160 B4
Torfield Sch TN34 ....160 B5
Toronto Terr
  Brighton BN2 ....164 C6
  Lewes BN7 ....123 C1
Terrance Cl BN1 ....141 F1
Totland Rd BN2 ....164 D7
Tott Hill BN6 ....97 B5
Tott Yew Rd BN20 ....173 A4
Tottington Way BN43 ....140 B1
Tottingworth La TN21 ...184 D6
Tovey Cl BN1
  Beachlands BN24 ......175 F7
  East Grinstead RH19 ....1 E2
Tower Cl RH11 ....1 E2
Tower Ho Brighton BN1 ..142 E2
  Burgess Hill RH15 .....73 B2
Tower Mill Rd BN26 ......173 A5
Tower Rd Brighton BN2 ..164 C6
  St Leonards TN37 ....136 C1
Tower Rd W TN37,TN38 ..159 B8
Tower Ride Uckfield TN22 .55 D1
  Uckfield TN22 ....55 E1
Tower St Heathfield TN21 ..82 B8
  Rye TN31 ....93 C6
Tower View TN22 ....78 D8
Towergate BN1 ....142 E2
Towerscroft Ave TN37 ...136 C5
Town Hill TN3 ....20 A4
Town Place Farm Cotts
  RH17 ....52 C7
Towner Art Gall & Mus
  BN21 ....184 D3
Townlands Rd TN5 ....29 F4
Tozer Ct BN1 ....162 B7
Traders Pas TN31 ....93 B5
Trafalgar Cl
  Peacehaven BN10 ......167 C1
  St Leonards TN37 ....135 F7
Trafalgar Cotts 8 TN34 ..160 B4
Trafalgar Ct BN1 ....189 B3
Trafalgar Gate BN2 .....164 F3
Trafalgar La BN1 ....189 B3
Trafalgar Mews 9 BN2 ...185 C4
Trafalgar Pl BN1 ....189 B3
Trafalgar Rd BN41 ......162 B8
Trafalgar St BN1 ....189 B3
Trafalgar Terr BN1 ......189 B3
Tram Rd TN31 ....94 A2
Transit Rd BN9 ....179 D7
Travellers La TN35 ......137 C4
Trebilco Cl TN4 ....7 B3
Treblers Rd TN20,TN6 ....38 E6
Tredcroft Rd BN1 ....142 C2
Tree Tops Cl BN2 ....165 E8
Treemaines Rd BN23 .....174 F2
Treemans Rd RH17 ....33 B2
Tremola Ave BN2 ....177 C6
Trenches Rd TN5 ....25 F1
Trevor Gdns BN8 ....147 F6
Treyford Ct BN1 ....144 E1
Triangle Ho 4 RH16 ......50 F3
Triangle L Ctr The RH15 ..72 D4
Triangle Rd RH16 ....50 E3
Triangle The BN20 ......173 B3
Triangle Way RH15 ....72 D5
Trickland Cotts TN22 ....53 C5
Trinity Cl TN2 ....8 A4
Trinity Field BN8 ....124 E6
Trinity Mews 3 TN34 ....159 E7
Trinity Pl BN2 ....185 B2
Trinity Rd BN6 ....97 A6
Trinity St Brighton BN2 ..189 C4
  Hastings TN34 ....159 E7
Trinity Trees BN21 ......185 A2
Trinity Villas 2 TN34 ....159 E7
Tristan Gdns TN4 ....7 D4
Trojans Plat TN36 ......117 E7
Troon Cl BN25 ....180 A6
Troon Cl RH16 ....50 E4
Trossachs Cl BN23 ......174 D3
Troy Cl TN6 ....26 A1
Truleigh Cl BN2 ....177 B8
Truleigh Dr BN41 ....141 A4
Truleigh Way BN43 ......140 A1
Truman Dr TN37 ....135 F6
Trumpet La BN27 ....109 C2
Tubwell La
  Crowborough TN6 ......38 D7
  Maynard's Green TN21 ..81 F2
Tudor Ave TN38 ....159 A7
Tudor Cl
  East Grinstead RH19 ....1 D6
  Hove BN3 ....141 F2
  Rottingdean BN2 .....177 A6
  Seaford BN25 ....180 D4
Tudor Ct TN2 ....7 E1
Tudor Gdns RH15 ....72 F4
Tudor Rose Pk Cvn Site
  BN10 ....167 B1
Tudor Wlk TN22 ....79 B5
Tugwell Rd BN20 ....173 F2
Tumulus Rd BN2 ....166 C3
Tunbridge Wells
  Gram Sch for Boys TN4 ..8 A7
Tunbridge Wells
  Gram Sch for Girls TN4 ..8 A6
Tunbridge Wells Ind Hospl
  The TN3 ....6 B3
Tunbridge Wells Mus TN1 ..3 B4

Tunbridge Wells Rd
  Argos Hill TN20,TN6 ...39 E5
  Mark Cross TN6,TN5 ...40 E5
Tunbridge Wells Trade Pk
  TN2 ....8 D8
Tunnel Rd TN1 ....8 B4
Tuppen Ho BN7 ....145 E5
Tuppenney Cl TN35 .....137 C3
Turkey Cock La TN31 ....75 C6
Turkey La RH15 ....73 B3
Turkey Rd TN39 ....156 E7
Turley Cotts TN3 ....7 A8
Turley Rd TN3 ....7 A8
Turnberry Cl TN38 ......158 F7
Turnberry Cl RH16 ......50 E8
Turnberry Dr BN27 ......152 A8
Turner Cl Bexhill TN40 ..157 E5
  Eastbourne BN23 .....174 D1
Turner's Hill Rd RH19 ...10 B6
Turners Green La TN5 ...29 F6
Turners Green Rd TN5 ...29 F6
Turners Mill Cl RH16 ....50 D7
Turners Mill Rd RH16 ....50 D6
Turners Way RH15 ....72 F4
Turnpike Cl
  Broyle Side BN8 ......125 A8
  Peacehaven BN10 .....167 C1
Turnpike Piece BN1 .....144 A6
Turret Ct RH19 ....1 C3
Turton Cl BN2 ....164 D5
Tuscan Ct BN10 ....177 F3
Tutts Barn La BN22 .....185 A5
Tuxford Rd TN4 ....7 B5
Tweedsmuir Cl BN23 ....174 C3
Twineham Cl BN2 ....164 F7
Twineham Rd BN21 .....184 D7
Twitten 7 BN41 ....162 B8
Twitten The Bexhill TN39 .156 D4
  Burgess Hill RH15 .....73 B4
  Crowborough TN6 .....25 E1
  Ditchling BN6 ....98 D3
  Southwick BN42 ......161 E7
Twyford Cres TN37 .....136 C4
Twyford Rd BN1 ....144 A6
Twyfords TN6 ....25 E1
Twyhurst Ct RH19 ....1 D3
Twysden Cotts TN18 .....47 A4
Tye Cl BN2 ....165 F7
Tye Hill Rd BN26 ....151 A4
Tye View BN10 ....167 A1
Tyedean Rd BN10 ......177 F4
Tyler's Gn RH16,RH17 ...50 B4
Tylers La TN22 ....35 E1
Tyndale Ave TN39 ......156 C3
Tyson Pl 2 BN2 ....189 C2

U

Uckfield Cl BN2 ....164 F6
Uckfield Com Coll TN22 ..78 D8
Uckfield Com Hospl TN22 .78 D6
Uckfield Rd Poundgate TN6 .37 B7
  Upper Wellington BN2 ..124 B7
Uckfield Sta TN22 ......78 C6
Uckham La TN33 ....112 E6
Udiam Cotts TN32 ....65 C5
Udimore Rd TN31 ....91 C3
Under Rd BN27 ....130 B3
Undercliff
  St Leonards TN38 ....159 B6
  St Leonards TN38 ....159 B6
Undercliff Terr 7 TN38 ..159 C6
Underdown Rd BN42 ....161 E8
Underhill TN21 ....55 B5
Underhill La Clayton BN6 .119 E8
  Westmeston BN6 .....120 C8
Unicorn Ho 1 TN34 .....160 A4
Union Cl BN27 ....129 B3
Union Rd BN2 ....189 C4
Union Sq 11 TN2 ....8 A2
Union St Brighton BN1 ..189 B2
  St Leonards TN38 ....159 C7
  Union Street TN5 .....32 B3
Univ of Brighton
  Brighton BN1 ....189 B2
  Eastbourne BN20 .....188 D8
  Falmer BN1 ....144 B6
Univ of Brighton
  (Belgrave Street Annexe)
  BN2 ....189 C3
Univ of Brighton
  (Cockcroft/Watts
  Annexes) BN2 ....143 D2
Univ of Brighton
  (Finsbury Road Annexe)
  BN2 ....189 C3
Univ of Brighton
  (St Peter's Ho) BN2 ..189 B3
Univ of Sussex BN1 ....144 C3
Uplands Cl Bexhill TN39 .156 F6
  Uckfield TN22 ....55 C1
Uplands Com Coll TN5 ..30 A4
Uplands Pk TN5 ....59 E1
Uplands Rd BN1 ....143 A6
Uplands Sch BN1 ....143 C2
Uplands The BN1 ....159 F7
Upper Abbey Rd BN2 ...164 D4
Upper Ave BN21 ....185 A4
Upper Bedford St BN2 ..164 C4
Upper Belgrave Rd BN25 .180 F5
Upper Berendean Ave
  BN2 ....143 D1
Upper Broomgrove Rd
  TN34 ....137 B3
Upper Carlisle Rd BN20 .188 D8

Upper Chalvington Pl
  BN2 ....164 E5
Upper Church Rd TN37 ..136 B4
Upper Chyngton Gdns
  BN25 ....181 B4
Upper Cl RH18 ....11 F2
Upper Clarence Rd TN37 .136 C1
Upper Cotts BN2 ....165 D7
Upper Cumberland Wlk
  TN1 ....8 B1
Upper Dr The BN3 .....163 D8
Upper Duke's Dr BN20 ..188 C7
Upper Dunstan Rd TN4 ...8 B6
Upper Gardner St BN1 ..189 B3
Upper Glen Rd TN37 ...136 A5
Upper Gloucester Rd
  BN1 ....189 A3
Upper Greenwoods La
  TN21 ....83 C6
Upper Grosvenor Rd
  TN1,TN4 ....8 B6
Upper Hamilton Rd BN1 .189 A5
Upper Hollingdean Rd
  BN1 ....143 B1
Upper Horsebridge Rd
  BN27 ....129 A3
Upper King's Rd BN20 ..173 B1
Upper Kingston La
  BN42,BN43 ....140 D1
Upper Lake TN33 ......112 E4
Upper Lewes Rd BN2 ...189 C4
Upper Lodges BN1 .....143 D8
Upper Market St BN3 ..163 D5
Upper Maze Hill TN38 ..159 B7
Upper Nellington TN3 ...7 B4
Upper North St BN1 ...189 A2
Upper Park Pl 7 BN2 ...189 C2
Upper Park Rd TN37 ...136 C1
Upper Platts TN5 ....31 F1
Upper Profit TN3 ....7 A3
Upper Ratton Dr BN20 ..184 B8
Upper Rock Gdns BN2 ..189 C2
Upper Roedale Cotts
  BN1 ....143 B4
Upper Sea Rd TN40 ....157 D4
Upper Sherwood Rd
  BN25 ....181 A4
Upper Shoreham Rd
  Shoreham-by-Sea
  BN42,BN43 ....140 D1
  Shoreham-by-Sea BN43 .140 B1
Upper South Rd TN37 ..136 C1
Upper Sq RH18 ....11 E3
Upper St East Dean BN20 .187 B8
  Rushlall TN4 ....7 B4
Upper St James's St BN2 .189 C1
Upper St Johns Rd RH15 .73 A4
Upper Station Rd TN21 ..82 A7
Upper Stephens TN3 .....7 A3
Upper Sudeley St 7
  BN2 ....164 D4
Upper Valley Rd BN9 ...179 B6
Upper Wellington Rd
  BN2 ....164 D4
Upper Winfield Ave BN1 .142 F6
Upper Wish Hill BN20 ..184 B8
Upperton Gdns BN21 ...184 F3
Upperton La BN21 .....184 F3
Upperton Rd BN21 ....184 E4
Upton Ave BN42 ....140 E1
Upton Quarry TN3 ......6 F3
Upwick Rd BN20 ......184 C3

V

Val Mascal TN38 ....136 A1
Val Prinseps Rd BN24 ..175 C4
Vale Ave Brighton BN1 ..142 E7
  Royal Tunbridge Wells TN1 .8 A3
Vale Cl BN25 ....181 B4
Vale Ct BN41 ....162 B7
Vale Gdns BN41 ....162 B7
Vale Rd Battle TN33 ...112 B5
  Haywards Heath RH16 ..50 E2
  Mayfield TN20 ....80 A6
  Portslade-by-Sea BN41 .162 C7
  Royal Tunbridge Wells TN1 .8 A3
  Saltdean BN2 ....166 D3
  Seaford BN25 ....181 A4
  St Leonards TN37 ....136 C2
Vale The BN2 ....165 E5
Vale View Rd TN21 .....82 B6
Valebridge Cl RH15 ....73 C6
Valebridge Dr RH15 ....73 C5
Valebridge Rd RH15 ....73 C6
Valence Rd BN7 ....123 B1
Valentine Ct
  2 Eastbourne BN21 ..185 A2
  14 Hove BN3 ....163 C7
Valentine Dr RH15 ....72 F2
Vallance Cl RH15 ......141 C2
Vallance Ct BN3 ......163 A4
Vallance Gdns BN3 ....163 A5
Vallance Rd BN3 ......163 A6
Vallensdean Cotts BN41 .142 A2
Valley Cl Brighton BN1 ..142 C4
  Newhaven BN9 ....179 B8
Valley Dene BN9 ......179 B7
Valley Dr Brighton BN1 ..142 C4
Valley Rd Crowborough TN6 .25 F1
  Lewes BN7 ....146 A8
  Newhaven BN9 ....179 A7
  Newhaven BN9 ....179 B7
  Peacehaven BN10 ....167 C2
  Portslade-by-Sea BN41 .141 A2

Valley Rd continued
  Rushall TN4 7
Valley Rise BN25 180
Valley Side Rd TN35 ...137
Valley View TN22 53
Valley View Cl TN6 25
Valverde Ho BN43 163
Vanbrugh Ct 7 BN3 ...163
Vancouver Rd BN23 ...175
Vantage Wlk TN38 136
Varndean Cl BN1 142
Varndean Coll BN1 142
Varndean Dr BN1 142
Varndean Gdns BN1 ...142
Varndean Holt BN1 142
Varndean Rd BN1 142
Varndean Sch BN1 142
Vega Cl BN27 152
Ventnor Cl BN23 174
Ventnor Villas BN3 ...163
Venture Cl TN40 157
Verbania Way RH19 2
Verdant Cl TN34 159
Vere Rd BN1,BN2 189
Veric 12 BN2 163
Vermont Rd TN4 7
Vermont Way TN37 ...135
Vernon Ave
  Peacehaven BN10 178
  Woodingdean BN2 ...165
Vernon Cl BN23 185
Vernon Ct 3 BN1 163
Vernon Gdns BN1 163
Vernon Lodge 13 BN21 .185
Vernon Rd
  Royal Tunbridge Wells TN1 .8
  Uckfield TN22 78
Veronica Terr BN2 163
Verrall's Wlk 15 BN7 ..146
Verulam Pl TN37 159
Viaduct Rd BN1,BN2 ..189
Vian Ave BN23 185
Vicarage Cl
  Newhaven BN9 168
  Ringmer BN8 124
  Seaford BN25 180
Vicarage Dr BN20 184
Vicarage Field BN27 ..152
Vicarage La
  Burwash Common TN19 .61
  Eastbourne BN20 184
  Hailsham BN27 152
  Hellingly BN27 152
  Rottingdean BN2 165
  Scaynes Hill RH17 35
  Westfield TN35 114
Vicarage Rd
  Burwash Common TN19 .61
  Eastbourne BN20 184
  Hailsham BN27 152
  Hastings TN34 160
Vicarage Terr BN2 165
Vicarage Way
  Hurst Green TN19 45
  Ringmer BN8 124
Viceroy Lodge 10 BN3 ..163
Victor Cl BN25 181
Victoria Ave
  Burgess Hill RH15 73
  Hastings TN35 137
  Peacehaven BN10 178
Victoria Cl
  Burgess Hill RH15 73
  Burgess Hill RH15 73
  Polegate BN26 173
Victoria Cotts
  High Cross TN6 39
  2 Hove BN3 163
  St Leonards TN37 ...136
  Stone Cross BN24 ...173
Victoria Ct 6 Hove BN3 .163
  Portslade-by-Sea BN41 .162
  St Leonards TN38 ...159
Victoria Dr BN20,BN21 .184
Victoria Gdns
  Burgess Hill RH15 73
  Eastbourne BN20 184
Victoria Gr 7 BN3 163
Victoria Ind Est RH15 ..73
Victoria Mews BN2 165
Victoria Pl 6 BN1 6
Victoria Rd Bexhill TN39 .15
  Brighton BN1 16
  Burgess Hill RH15 73
  Crowborough TN6 3
  Eastbourne BN20 18
  Hailsham BN27 152
  Haywards Heath RH16 ..5
  Mayfield TN20 4
  Polegate BN26 173
  Portslade-by-Sea BN41 .162
  Royal Tunbridge Wells TN1 .3
  Southwick BN42 161
  St Leonards TN37 ...159
Victoria St BN1 189
Victoria Terr Burwash TN19 .62
  1 Hove BN3 163
Victoria Way
  Burgess Hill RH15 73
  East Grinstead RH19 ...1
  Winchelsea Beach TN36 .118
Victory Mews BN2 164
View Bank TN35 137
View Rd BN10 167
View Terr RH7 1

rs Path RH16 . . . . .51 B4
rs Wood Path TN22 . . . .55 D1
ng Cl BN25 . . . . .180 B6
ng Way BN23 . . . . .185 F8
ge Rd TN37 . . . . .159 D7
ge Barn The BN1 . . . . .142 E7
ge Mews TN36 . . . .
ge The BN20 . . . . .188 D8
ge Way BN1 . . . . .144 C6
ge Wks BN8 . . . . .105 A5
ers Cl BN2 . . . . .165 E8
ers Ct BN1 . . . . .189 B3
en Cl BN23 . . . . .185 F7
Cotts TN6 . . . . .38 C7
Farm Cotts BN8 . . . . .104 A5
PI BN1 . . . . .189 A3
Sq BN22 . . . . .185 D6
St BN1 . . . . .189 B3
hall (Prep Sch
  Boys) 87 E6
hall Rd TN34 . . . . . . .137 A5
hall Rd TN32 . . . . .87 E5
ries The
  pess Hill RH15 . . . . . .73 D3
bourne BN23 . . . . . . .174 D2
s BN3 . . . . .163 E6
s Cross Rd
ghton BN2 . . . . .164 F7
an TN21 . . . . .107 B7
yard La TN5 . . . . .31 C2
y The
tbourne BN21 . . . . . . .184 C7
nor TN22 . . . . .35 C4
n's Croft TN13 . . . . . .112 D6
n's La TN33 . . . . .112 D6
Electric Rly
, BN2 . . . . .164 C4
Gris Nez TN36 . . . . . .118 B5

e Cl BN23 . . . . .185 F7
hurst Bsns Pk TN5 . . . .29 B7
hurst CE Prim Sch
  . . . . .29 F5
hurst Cl
tbourne BN22 . . . . . . .173 F2
eonards TN37 . . . . . . .136 B5
hurst La TN33 . . . . . .111 E6
hurst La TN5 . . . . .29 F4
hurst Rd TN6 . . . . .28 C3
hurst Rise BN2 . . . . . .164 F5
hurst Sta TN5 . . . . . . .29 C6
lands Brook Rd RH19 . .1 C5
gy Cl RH19 . . . . .2 A1
horns La TN22 . . . . . .57 C6
wright Cl TN38 . . . . . .135 D3
wright Rd TN39 . . . . . .157 B4
ter Cl BN27 . . . . .123 D2
es La TN35 . . . . .138 E5
efield Rd BN2 . . . . . . .189 C5
degrave Rd BN1 . . . . .143 A1
degrave St 4 TN34 . . .159 F8
en Terr TN33 . . . . .112 E4
ene Cl TN34 . . . . .136 F2
dergrave Ct BN22 . . . .166 D3
dron Ave BN1 . . . . . . .143 D6
dron Cl BN20 . . . . . . .184 D8
dron Ct TN21 . . . . . . .82 D8
dron PI BN1 . . . . .143 D6
dron Rd BN20 . . . . . . .105 A5
dron Thorns TN21 . . . .82 A7
shut Rd BN7 . . . . .123 A3
es Farm Cotts BN7 . . .121 C7
sbeech Rd BN2 . . . . . .177 D4
er Cl BN23 . . . . .185 F7
ks The TN3 . . . . .15 C8
Hill Rd RH18, RH19 . . .11 E5
ace Cl TN17 . . . . .123 D1
ands Cres BN7 . . . .
ands Cty Prim Sch
  . . . . .123 A2
ed Garden The TN22 . .55 D4
ers TN3 . . . . .7 A8
ington Towers 4 TN40 .157 C4
s Ave BN23 . . . . .185 E7
s Cl TN6 . . . . .26 A1
s Field TN3 . . . . .15 B6
s Ho RH19 . . . . .1 E1
s PI BN23 . . . . .185 E8
s Way RH15 . . . . .72 E4
send Rd BN24 . . . . . . .175 C6
mer Cres BN2 . . . . . . .144 B1
mer Rd BN25 . . . . . . .181 C4
nut Cl Brighton BN1 . .142 E3
ghfield TN21 . . . . .82 B6
nut Ct BN26 . . . . .173 A6
nut Pk RH16 . . . . .51 B4
aut Tree Wlk BN20 . . .184 B8
nut Wlk BN26 . . . . . . .173 A6
ole Rd BN2 . . . . .164 D5
ole Terr BN2 . . . . .164 D5
ole Wlk BN23 . . . . . . .174 E3
shes Rd TN6 . . . . .38 B7
ingham Cl BN22 . . . . .173 D3
ingham Rd BN3 . . . . . .164 F7
er May Ho 4 BN2 . . . .164 F5
ers Green Rd TN11 . . . . .5 F6
on Cl
tbourne BN23 . . . . . . .174 E3
eonards TN37 . . . . . . .136 C5
on Pk TN39 . . . . .156 F4
wers La TN4 . . . . .123 D1
derdown Cl BN2 . . . . .165 E4
derdown Dr BN2 . . . . .165 E4
derdown Rd BN2 . . . . .165 E4

Wanderdown Way BN2 . .165 E4
Wannock Ave BN20 . . . .172 F3
Wannock Cl BN20 . . . . .158 A6
Wannock Dr BN26 . . . . .172 F5
Wannock Gdns BN26 . . .172 F3
Wannock La BN20, BN26 . .172 F3
Wannock Rd
  Eastbourne BN22 . . . . .185 D5
  Polegate BN26 . . . . . . .172 F5
War Meml Hospl TN6 . . . .25 E1
Warbleton Cl BN2 . . . . .164 E5
Warburton Cl
  East Grinstead RH19 . . . .11 A8
  Eastbourne BN21 . . . . .184 C8
  Uckfield TN22 . . . . .78 D8
Ward Cl TN5 . . . . .29 E5
Ward Way TN39 . . . . . . .157 A6
Wardrobes Rd
  Friston BN20 . . . . .183 A1
  Hastings TN34 . . . . . . .159 FB
Ward's La TN6 . . . . .30 C4
Warden Ct RH17 . . . . . . .50 A6
Warden Park Sch TN7 . . .50 A5
Wardsbrook Rd TN5 . . . . .43 D7
Ware Ct RH15 . . . . .73 D3
Warelands RH15 . . . . . . .73 F1
Warenne Rd BN3 . . . . . .141 C4
Wares Field TN22 . . . . . .78 D4
Wares Rd TN22 . . . . .78 D4
Warleigh Rd BN1, BN2 . .189 B5
Warmdene Ave BN1 . . . .142 E6
Warmdene Cl BN1 . . . . .142 F5
Warmdene Rd BN1 . . . . .142 F6
Warmdene Way BN1 . . . .142 F6
Warminster Rd BN24 . . .175 D5
Warner Ct RH15 . . . . . . .73 A3
Warnham Ct BN3 . . . . . .142 A4
Warnham Gdns TN39 . . .156 E2
Warnham Rise BN1 . . . . .143 A5
Warren Ave BN2 . . . . . . .165 C8
Warren Cl Crowborough TN6 .25 C7
  Eastbourne BN20 . . . . .188 C8
  Friston BN20 . . . . .183 B1
  Lewes BN7 . . . . .146 B8
  Roser's Cross TN21 . . . . .81 A6
  St Leonards TN38 . . . . .158 E8
  Woodingdean BN2 . . . . .165 B8
Warren Crn TN21 . . . . . . .81 A8

Warren Cotts
  Mayfield TN20 . . . . .40 C3
  North Chailey BN8 . . . . .75 F7
Warren Ct Crowborough TN6 .25 C7
  Southwick BN42 . . . . . .140 E1
Warren Dr BN7 . . . . .146 A8
Warren Farm La TN6 . . . .16 B4
Warren Gdn TN6 . . . . . . .25 E2
Warren Hill BN20 . . . . . .184 A1
Warren La
  Beacon Down TN21 . . . . .81 A7
  Friston BN20 . . . . .183 B1
  North Chailey BN8 . . . . .75 E8
Warren Lodge BN10 . . . .167 A1
Warren Rd
  Crowborough TN6 . . . . .25 C1
  Fairlight TN35 . . . . .138 C4
  Woodingdean BN2 . . . . .165 B8
Warren Ridge
  Crowborough TN6 . . . . .25 D2
  Frant TN3 . . . . .17 C3
Warren Rise BN2 . . . . . .165 B8
Warren The
  Burgess Hill RH15 . . . . .73 C1
  Mayfield TN20 . . . . .40 C2
  Ticehurst TN5 . . . . .31 E1
Warren Way
  North Chailey TN8 . . . . .75 F8
  Telscombe Cliffs BN10 . .167 A1
Warren Wood The 25 D1
Warrenwood Rd 53 A1
Warrior Ct BN41 . . . . . . .141 B2
Warrior Gdns TN37 . . . .159 C7
Warrior Ho BN20 . . . . . .188 E8
Warrior Sq
  6 Eastbourne BN22 . . . .185 C4
  St Leonards TN37 . . . . .159 D7
Warrs Hill La BN8 . . . . . .75 E8
Wartling Cl TN38 . . . . . .135 F3
Wartling Dr TN39 . . . . . .156 D2
Wartling Rd
  Eastbourne BN22 . . . . .185 D6
  Wartling BN27 . . . . . . .131 C2
Warwick Cl BN27 . . . . . .129 C3
Warwick Ct
  4 Eastbourne BN21 . . . .174 E1
  8 Hove BN3 . . . . .163 E7
Warwick Mount 2 BN2 . .164 C4
Warwick Pk TN2 . . . . . . .9 E1
Warwick Rd Bexhill TN39 .156 F5
  4 Royal Tunbridge Wells TN1 . .8 A2
  Seaford BN25 . . . . .180 E3

Waterloo Pl
  1 Brighton BN1 . . . . . . .189 C3
  10 Eastbourne BN21 . . .185 D4
  2 Lewes BN7 . . . . .123 D1
Waterloo Sq BN26 . . . . .171 A3
Waterloo St 163 D5
Watermen's Ct TN34 . . . .136 F3
Watermill Cl Bexhill TN39 .157 B7
  Lower Willingdon BN20 . .173 A5
Watermill Dr TN38 . . . . .135 D3
Watermill La Clayhill TN31 .67 D2
  Icklesham TN35,TN36 . . .116 C3
  Watermill TN39 . . . . . . .134 E2
Waters Cotts TN5 . . . . . .30 A4
Waterside RH19 . . . . .2 B1
Waterside Cl TN35 . . . . .137 C3
Waterworks Cotts
  Hastings TN34 . . . . . . .159 FB
  1 Hastings TN34 . . . . .136 F1
Waterworks Rd
  Eastbourne BN22 . . . . .185 A4
  1 Hastings TN34 . . . . .136 F1
Watling Cl 8 BN42 . . . . .161 E7
Watling Ct 5 BN42 . . . . .161 E7
Watling Rd BN42 . . . . . .161 E7
Wattle's Wish TN33 . . . .112 C6
Watts Cl TN35 . . . . .29 F4
Watts La BN21 . . . . .184 E4
Watts Lodge RH15 . . . . .73 D3
Watt's Palace La TN31 . . .89 D7
Waverley Cl BN1 . . . . . . .143 C1
Waverley Ct
  4 Hastings TN34 . . . . . .159 E7
  7 Seaford BN25 . . . . . .180 F2
Waverley Dr TN2 . . . . . . .8 F6
Waverley Gdns BN43 . . . .162 A3
Wayfaring Down BN26 . .172 D3
Wayfield Ave BN3 . . . . . .141 F1
Wayfield Cl BN3 . . . . . . .141 F1
Wayford Cl BN23 . . . . . .174 D2
Wayland Ave BN1 . . . . . .142 C3
Wayland Hts BN1 . . . . . .142 C4
Wayside Brighton BN1 . . .142 D6
Wayside Wlk TN31 . . . . .81 F6
Weald Ave BN3 . . . . .162 FB
Weald Cl
  Barcombe Cross BN8 . . .101 E4
  Lewes BN7 . . . . .123 C2
Weald Rd RH15 . . . . .72 E3
Weald Rise RH16 . . . . . .50 E1
Weald The RH19 . . . . . . .1 F4
Weald View
  Barcombe Cross BN8 . . .101 E4
  Staplecross TN32 . . . . . .65 E2
  Turner's Green TN5 . . . . .29 F6
Wealden Cl TN35 . . . . . .25 F3
Wealden Cotts TN19 . . . . .61 C3
Wealden Ind Est TN6 . . . .38 C8
Wealden Pk BN22 . . . . . .173 C1
Wealden View TN19 . . . . .62 B7
Wealden Way
  Bexhill TN39 . . . . .156 C6
  Haywards Heath RH16 . .50 F1
Weald Rd TN1 . . . . .81 F7
  8 Hastings TN34 . . . . . .8 C8
Weatherby Cl BN21 . . . . .184 C8
Weavers Cl RH15 . . . . . .73 D1
Weavers La BN20 . . . . . .170 F3
Weavers Rock La TN21 . . .82 C5
Wedderburn Rd BN20 . . .173 B1
Week La BN8 . . . . .124 D2
Weir Wood Resr
  (Nature Reserve) RH19 . .10 D1
Welbeck Ave Hove BN3 . .162 E6
  Royal Tunbridge Wells TN4 .8 C8
  St Leonards TN38 . . . . .159 A7
Welbeck Cl
  Burgess Hill RH15 . . . . .73 D4
  Eastbourne BN23 . . . . .185 E5
Welbeck Ct 8 BN25 . . . .180 E3
Welbeck Dr RH15 . . . . . .73 D4
Welesmere Rd BN41 . . . .166 A3
Welkin (Brighton Univ)
  BN20 . . . . .184 E1
Welland Cl TN34 . . . . . . .36 A8
Wellcombe Cres BN20 . .188 D7
Weller Rd TN4 . . . . .7 F8
Wellesley Cl Bexhill TN39 .156 D3
  Crowborough TN6 . . . . .25 D1
Wellesley Ct 19 TN34 . . .160 B4
Wellesley Rd 7 BN21 . . .185 A3
Wellfield RH19 . . . . .11 C7
Wellgreen La BN7 . . . . . .145 F5
Wellhouse La BN1 . . . . . .98 C7
Wellingham La BN8 . . . .124 A7
Wellington Ct
  Brighton BN2 . . . . .165 A3
  8 Eastbourne BN21 . . . .185 A4
Wellington Gdns TN33 . .112 C5
Wellington Ho 7 TN34 . .159 FB
Wellington Lodge BN1 . .160 A4
Wellington Mews TN34 . .159 FB
Wellington Pk 1 BN25 . .181 A3
Wellington Rd
  Brighton BN2 . . . . .189 C4
  Hastings TN34 . . . . . . .160 A4
  Newhaven BN9 . . . . . . .168 F2
  Peacehaven BN10 . . . . .178 A6
  Portslade-by-Sea BN41 . .162 B6
Wellington Sq TN34 . . . .159 FB
Wellington St
  Brighton BN2 . . . . .164 C7

Wellington St continued
  1 Lewes BN7 . . . . .123 D1
Wellington Terr 14 TN34 .159 FB
Wellington Town Rd RH19 .1 D2
Wellingtonia Cl 8 BN1 . .142 E3
Wellis Ct TN38 . . . . .159 A8
Wellis Gdns TN38 . . . . . .159 A8
Wellplace Cotts TN36 . . .116 F5
Wells Chase BN7 . . . . . . .99 E6
Wells Cl Eastbourne BN20 .188 C8
  Plumpton Green BN7 . . .99 E6
  Royal Tunbridge Wells TN1 .8 A3
Wells Ho TN4 . . . . .7 F4
Wells Lea RH19 . . . . .1 D3
Wells Mdw RH19 . . . . . . .1 D4
Wellsbourne Rd BN24 . . .174 A5
Welsley Mews TN6 . . . . . .25 F2
Wendale Dr BN10 . . . . . .167 D2
Wendover Grange 3
  BN3 . . . . .163 A6
Went Hill Gdns BN22 . . .173 B3
Went Hill Pk BN25 . . . . .181 A3
Went La BN20 . . . . .183 C1
Went Way BN20 . . . . . . .187 B8
Wenthill Cl BN20 . . . . . .187 B8
Wentworth Cl
  Bexhill TN40 . . . . .157 F5
  Hailsham BN27 . . . . . . .129 A1
Wentworth Ct BN23 . . . .185 E6
Wentworth St BN2 . . . . .189 C1
Wentworth Way TN38 . . .158 FB
West Ascent TN38 . . . . . .158 D4
West Beeches Rd TN6 . . .26 B2
West Blatchington Inf Sch
  BN3 . . . . .141 E4
West Blatchington
  Jun Sch BN3 . . . . .141 E4
West Cl Alfriston BN26 . . .170 F3
  Polegate BN26 . . . . . . .173 B7
West Common RH16 . . . .50 F6
West Common Dr RH16 . .51 A7
West Dean Rise BN25 . . .181 A4
West Down Rd TN39 . . . .157 A5
West Dr BN2 . . . . .164 C6
West Dr BN27 . . . . .130 E6
West End Cotts TN19 . . . .60 F3
West End La BN6 . . . . . . .97 A5
West Furlong Cl BN6 . . . .97 A5
West Furlong La BN6 . . . .97 A5
West Gate BN7 . . . . .99 E6
West Hill Arc 3 TN34 . . .160 A3
West Hill Cliff Rly TN34 . .160 A4
West Hill Cl BN27 . . . . . .129 B1
West Hill La TN38 . . . . . .159 B6
West Hill Mews TN38 . . .158 F6
West Hill Rd
  Brighton BN1 . . . . .189 A3
  St Leonards TN38 . . . . .158 F6
West Hill St BN1 . . . . . . .189 A4
West Ho BN3 . . . . .185 A2
West Hoathly Rd RH19 . .10 C4
West Hove Cty Inf Sch
  BN3 . . . . .162 F7
West Kent Coll of F Ed TN4 .8 A7
West La RH19 . . . . .10 D8
West Leigh RH19 . . . . . .10 E7
West Mallion RH16 . . . . .51 A8
West Par TN39 . . . . .157 B2
West Park Rd RH15 . . . . .72 D4
West Point BN43 . . . . . . .161 A6
West Rd Kilndown NT17 . .20 F3
  Portslade-by-Sea BN41 . .162 A7
West Rise Cty Inf Sch
  BN23 . . . . .174 C2
West Rise Cty Jun Sch
  BN23 . . . . .174 C2
West St Alfriston BN26 . . .170 F3
  Brighton BN1 . . . . .189 A2
  Burgess Hill RH15 . . . . .72 E4
  Ditchling BN6 . . . . .98 D3
  Dormansland RH7 . . . . . .2 A8
  East Grinstead RH19 . . . .10 E8
  Hailsham BN27 . . . . . . .129 C4
  Hastings TN34 . . . . . . .160 A3
  Lewes BN7 . . . . .123 D1
  Mayfield TN20 . . . . .40 A2
  Portslade-by-Sea BN41 . .162 C7
  Rottingdean BN2 . . . . . .165 F1
  Rye TN31 . . . . .93 C5
  Seaford BN25 . . . . .180 E2
West St Leonards
  Cty Prim Sch TN38 . . . .158 FB
West St Leonards Sta
  TN38 . . . . .158 F7
West Street La TN21 . . . .81 F2
West Terr
  Eastbourne BN21 . . . . .184 F2
  Herstmonceux BN27 . . . .93 A5
West Undercliff TN31 . . . .93 A5
West View Hastings TN34 .160 B6
  Hove BN3 . . . . .163 C8
  Lindfield RH16 . . . . .51 B6
  Seaford BN25 . . . . .180 E2
West View Cotts TN34 . . .51 B6
West View Gdns RH19 . . .10 E8
West View Terr BN9 . . . . .168 D2
West Way BN3 . . . . .141 D4
Westaway Dr TN39 . . . . .157 A4
Westbourne Cl BN23 . . . .163 A7
Westbourne Gdns BN3 . .163 A7
Westbourne Gr BN3 . . . .163 A7
Westbourne Pl BN3 . . . . .163 A7
Westbourne St BN3 . . . . .163 A7

Westbourne Villas BN3 . .162 F6
Westbrook
  Forest Row RH18 . . . . .11 E3
  Saltdean BN2 . . . . .177 C6
Westbrook La TN35 . . . . .114 E5
Westbrook Terr TN2 . . . . .8 D1
Westbrook Way BN42 . . .161 F7
Westcliff Mansion BN20 . .188 FB
Westcombe 1 BN1 . . . . .163 E7
Westcourt Dr TN39 . . . . .156 E5
Westdean Ave BN9 . . . . .179 A5
Westdene Cty Prim Sch
  BN1 . . . . .142 C5
Westdene Dr BN1 . . . . . .142 C5
Westdown Ho BN21 . . . .185 A2
Westdown La TN19 . . . . .61 A3
Westdown Rd BN25 . . . .180 D4
Westgate Rd BN22 . . . . .143 E4
Westerham Rd BN23 . . . .174 D1
Westerings The 4 TN21 . .82 A6
Westerleigh Cl TN38 . . . .159 A8
Western Ave BN26 . . . . .173 B7
Western Espl BN3, BN41 . .162 D6
Western Gdns TN6 . . . . . .38 D8
Western Rd Bexhill TN40 .157 C3
  Burgess Hill RH15 . . . . .72 E3
  Crowborough TN6 . . . . .38 C7
  Eastbourne BN22 . . . . .185 B4
  Hailsham BN27 . . . . . . .132 B7
  Haywards Heath RH16 . .50 F4
  Hove BN1, BN3 . . . . . . .163 E5
  Hurstpierpoint BN6 . . . . .97 A7
Western Road
  Cty Prim Sch BN7 . . . . .146 C8
Western St BN1 . . . . .163 D5
Western Terr 21 BN1 . . . .163 E5
Westfield Ave BN2 . . . . . .166 D3
Westfield Ave N BN2 . . . .166 D3
Westfield Ave S BN2 . . . .166 D3
Westfield Cl Brighton BN1 .143 A4
  Eastbourne BN23 . . . . .185 E6
Westfield Cres BN1 . . . . .143 A5
Westfield Cty Prim Sch
  TN35 . . . . .114 E4
Westfield La TN35,TN37 . .136 C8
Westfield Rd BN25 . . . . .180 E4
Westfield Rise BN2 . . . . .166 E3
Westgate St BN7 . . . . . . .123 C1
Westham 18 BN2 . . . . . .164 F5
Westham Cl TN39 . . . . . .156 E3
Westhill Dr BN24 . . . . . .175 F6
Westhill Dr TN15 . . . . . . .72 E3
Westland Ct BN41 . . . . . .162 A7
Westlands Rd RH16 . . . . .51 B5
Westlords BN21 . . . . .184 C8
Westmeston Ave BN2 . . .177 B6
Westminster Cl BN23 . . .185 E6
Westminster Cres TN34 . .137 A4
Westmoreland Ct TN38 . .135 F3
Westmoreland Ct TN22 . .78 C5
Westmorland Cl
  8 Hove BN3 . . . . .184 B7
  Hove BN3 . . . . .163 E7
Westmount Cl BN42 . . . .161 D8
Westpoint BN8 . . . . .76 C7
Westville Rd TN39 . . . . . .157 A4
Westway TN2 . . . . .9 D7
Westway Cl BN41 . . . . . .140 E4
Westway Gdns BN41 . . . .140 E4
Westwood Rd TN4 . . . . . .7 C5
Wharf Rd
  Eastbourne BN21 . . . . .184 F3
  Hove BN3 . . . . .162 D6
Whatlington Rd TN33 . . .112 E7
Whatlington Way TN38 . .135 D2
Wheatfield Ct TN37 . . . . .136 C5
Wheatfield Way BN2 . . . .143 E3
Wheatland Cl BN10 . . . . .167 B2
Wheatsheaf Ct RH15 . . . .72 E5
Wheatsheaf Gdns BN7 . .123 E2
Wheatsheaf La RH17 . . . .50 A6
Wheel Farm Bsns Pk
  TN35 . . . . .114 D4
Wheel La TN35 . . . . .114 D3
Wheeler Ct RH16 . . . . . . .50 F2
Wheeler La TN22 . . . . . . .57 D6
Wheelers Lane Cotts
  TN22 . . . . .57 D5
Wheelwright Cl BN22 . . .173 D4
Wheelwright La RH15 . . .73 D1
Whichelo Pl BN2 . . . . . . .164 C6
Whiffens Cl BN27 . . . . . .132 A6
Whin Croft Pk TN6 . . . . . .37 D8
Whipping Post La BN2 . .165 F1
Whippingham Rd BN2 . .164 C7
Whippingham St BN2 . . .164 C8
Whistler Cl BN1 . . . . .142 F1
Whitbread Cl BN23 . . . . .174 B4
White Bear Pas 3 BN1 . . .8 A2
White Chys TN6 . . . . .26 A1
White Ct BN26 . . . . .170 F2
White Hill BN7 . . . . .123 C1
White Hill Ave TN39 . . . .156 E4
White Hill Cl TN39 . . . . . .156 E4

White House
Cty Prim Sch BN27 . . . . 152 B8
White Lodge Hove BN3 . . . . . 163 C8
Royal Tunbridge Wells TN1 . . . . 8 C4
White Rock TN4, TN37 . . . . 159 E7
White Rock Gdns **7**
TN34 . . . . 159 E7
White Rock
Pleasure Grounds TN34 . .159 E7
White Rock Rd
TN34, TN37 . . . . 159 E7
White St BN2 . . . . 189 C2
White Way Alfriston BN26 . . . .170 F1
Lewes BN7 . . . . 146 B1
White's Cl BN6 . . . . .97 A7
Whitebread La TN31 . . . . .67 E8
Whitecross St BN1 . . . . .189 B3
Whitefield Rd TN4 . . . . .8 A6
Whitefriars Rd TN44 . . . . .160 A5
Whitegate Cl TN4 . . . . .8 A8
Whitegates Cl BN8 . . . . 100 E7
Whitegates La TN5 . . . . .29 D8
Whitegates Pk TN35 . . . . . . 114 D2
Whitehall Par **3** RH19 . . . . . .1 E1
Whitehall Rd BN2 . . . . .164 E5
Whitehawk Cres BN2 . . . . . 164 E5
Whitehawk Cty Inf Sch
BN2 . . . . 164 E6
Whitehawk Cty Jun Sch
BN2 . . . . 164 E6
Whitehawk Hill Rd BN2 . . . .164 D5
Whitehawk Rd
Brighton BN2 . . . . 164 E6
Brighton BN2 . . . . 164 F5
Whitehawk Way BN2 . . . . . . 164 E6
Whitehill CI TN6 . . . . .25 F1
Whitehill Cty Inf Sch TN6 . .26 A1
Whitehill Rd TN6 . . . . .37 F8
Whitehouse Ave TN39 . . . . .157 B7
Whitehouse La TN21 . . . . .81 B4
Whitelot Cl BN42 . . . . .140 E2
Whitelot Way BN42 . . . . .140 E2
Whiterock Rd BN42 . . . . .161 E7
Whitethorn Dr BN1 . . . . .142 B4
Whiteway Cl BN25 . . . . .180 E6
Whiteway La BN2 . . . . .177 A6
Whiteways Cott BN7 . . . . . . 146 D2
Whitfeld La BN8 . . . . 123 C6
Whitley Rd BN22 . . . . .185 B5
Whittingehame Gdns
BN1 .142 F3
Whittington Coll RH19 . . . . . . .1 A4
Whittington's Way TN34 . . .137 B4
Whittle Dr BN23 . . . . .174 A1
Whittlewood Cl TN38 . . . . . .155 C2
Whitworth Rd TN2 . . . . .7 B2
Whybourne Crest TN2 . . . . . . .8 D1
Whydown Hill TN33 . . . . . . .113 C6
Whydown Rd TN39 . . . . .156 B7
Wick Hall BN3 . . . . .163 D6
Wickets The RH15 . . . . .72 F5
Wickham Ave TN39 . . . . .157 B3
Wickham Cl RH16 . . . . .50 E7
Wickham Dr BN6 . . . . .97 C5
Wickham Gdns TN4 . . . . .7 D5
Wickham Hill BN6 . . . . .97 C5
Wickham La BN7, BN8 . . . . . 100 E3
Wickham Rock La TN36 . . . .112 C5
Wickham Way RH16 . . . . .50 E7
Wickhurst Cl BN41 . . . . .140 F2
Wickhurst Rd BN41 . . . . .141 A2
Wickhurst Rise BN41 . . . . . .140 F3
Wicklands Ave BN2 . . . . .177 D5
Widbury TN7 . . . . .2 E4
Widdicombe Way BN2 . . . . .143 E2
Wigmore Cl BN1 . . . . .143 B1
Wigmore La BN3 . . . . .163 C8
Wilbury Ave BN3 . . . . .163 C7
Wilbury Cres BN3 . . . . .163 C7
Wilbury Gdns BN3 . . . . .163 C8
Wilbury Gr BN3 . . . . .163 C8
Wilbury Grange **9** BN3 . . .163 C6
Wilbury Lodge **15** BN3 . . 163 C6
Wilbury Rd BN3 . . . . .163 C8
Wilbury Villas BN3 . . . . .163 C7
Wilby Ave BN42 . . . . .140 E1
Wild Park Cl BN1 . . . . .143 E3
Wild Park Nature Trail
BN2 .143 D3
Wilderness Gdns TN31 . . . . .67 B7
Wilderness La TN22 . . . . .57 C3
Wilderness Pk TN6 . . . . .25 E2
Wilderness Rd BN6 . . . . .97 A6
Wilderness Rise RH19 . . . . . . .2 A6
Wilderness The RH15 . . . . . . .51 B8
Wilderness Wood
(Adventure Pk) TN22 . . . .57 D4
Wilderwick Rd RH19, RH7 . . .2 A5
Wildwood BN23 . . . . .174 C4
Wilfrid Rd BN2 . . . . .165 F8
Wiliamson Cott Homes
BN3 .163 A7
Wilkins Way TN40 . . . . .157 F6
Willard Cl BN27 . . . . .165 F3
Wilkinson Way TN40 . . . . . . .157 F6
Willard Cl BN22 . . . . .185 A6
Willetts Cotts TN3 . . . . .5 C4
Willetts Field BN8 . . . . .127 E8
Willetts La TN3 . . . . .5 C4
William Allen La RH16 . . . . .151 B6
William Parker Sch
(Lower) TN34 . . . . .136 D3
William Parker Sch
(Upper) TN34 . . . . .158 E7
William Rd TN34 . . . . .158 E7
William St Brighton BN2 . . . .189 B2

William St continued
Royal Tunbridge Wells TN4 . . . . 8 A5
Southwick BN41 . . . . 162 B7
William Sutton Ho BN1 . . .189 B2
Williams Ct **7** BN23 . . . . . .174 E1
Williams Rd BN43 . . . . .161 C8
Willicombe Pk TN2 . . . . .8 D4
Willie Cotts BN7 . . . . .123 E1
Willingdon Ave
Bexhill TN39 . . . . .157 A4
St Leonards TN38 . . . . .136 A5
Willingdon Cl
St Leonards TN38 . . . . .136 A5
Willingdon BN20 . . . . .173 B1
Willingdon Ct BN20 . . . . .173 B3
Willingdon Cty Prim Sch
BN20 . . . . .173 B2
Willingdon Dro BN23 . . . . . .174 B2
Willingdon La BN20 . . . . .183 C7
Willingdon Park Dr
BN22 . . . . .173 D2
Willingdon Rd
Brighton BN2 . . . . 143 E1
Eastbourne BN20, BN21 . . . .184 C6
Willingdon Sch BN20 . . . . . .172 F4
Willingdon Trees
Cty Prim Sch BN22 . . . . . .173 D3
Willingdon Way
St Leonards TN38 . . . . .136 A5
Willingdon BN22 . . . . .173 B2
Willingford La TN19 . . . . .61 C2
Willoughby Cres BN22 . . . . .185 C6
Willow Ave BN27 . . . . .129 B1
Willow Bank TN32 . . . . .64 B3
Willow Cl
East Grinstead RH19 . . . . .1 D3
Etchingham TN19 . . . . .63 B8
Heathfield TN21 . . . . .82 B8
Uckfield TN22 . . . . .61 A6
Woodingdean BN2 . . . . .165 E8
Polegate BN26 . . . . 173 A6
Willow Dr Bexhill TN39 . . . . .156 C5
Polegate BN26 . . . . 173 A6
Seaford BN25 . . . . .181 C3
Willow End TN34 . . . . .136 F4
Willow Est The BN9 . . . . .179 E8
Willow Gdns BN6 . . . . .97 A7
Willow Ho BN6 . . . . .97 E5
Willow La TN36 . . . . .118 B6
Willow Mead **8** RH19 . . . .10 F8
Willow Mews TN32 . . . . .64 B3
Willow Pk RH16 . . . . .51 B4
Willow Stream Cl TN35 . . . .115 E3
Willow Tree Rd TN2 . . . . .7 F1
Willow Way BN6 . . . . .97 A8
Willow Wlk
Eastbourne BN22 . . . . .173 D2
Newhaven BN9 . . . . .179 C8
Royal Tunbridge Wells TN2 . . . .8 B8
Willowbed Wlk TN34 . . . . . .136 E5
Willowbrook Way BN6 . . . . . .98 A3
Willowford Cl BN26 . . . . .173 A5
Willowfield Rd BN22 . . . . . . .185 B7
Willowfield Sq TN37 . . . . . . .137 B8
Willowmead TN6 . . . . .37 E8
Willows Rise TN22 . . . . .79 B5
Willows The
Barcombe Cross BN8 . . . . . .101 E5
Brighton BN2 . . . . 189 C5
Burgess Hill RH15 . . . . .73 B5
Hassocks BN6 . . . . .97 E4
St Leonards TN37 . . . . .136 A6
Wilman Rd TN4 . . . . .8 B7
Wilmington Cl
Brighton BN1 . . . . 143 A5
Hassocks BN6 . . . . .97 F4
Wilmington Gdns BN21 . . . .185 A1
Wilmington Par BN21 . . . . . .142 F5
Wilmington Rd
Hastings TN34 . . . . 137 A3
Newhaven BN9 . . . . .179 B6
Seaford BN25 . . . . .180 D4
Wilmington Sq BN21 . . . . . .185 A1
Wilmington St BN2 . . . . .189 C2
Wilmington Way
Brighton BN1 . . . . 143 A5
Haywards Heath RH16 . . . . . .51 A5
Wilmot Ct **6** BN43 . . . . . . .161 C8
Wilmot Rd BN43 . . . . .161 C8
Wilson Ave BN2 . . . . .164 F6
Wilson Gr TN22 . . . . .78 A7
Wilson's Cross BN27 . . . . . . .131 F7
Wilton **1** RH16 . . . . .50 D6
Wilton Rd TN40 . . . . .173 F2
Wilton Ho TN38 . . . . .158 F6
Wilton Rd TN40 . . . . .157 C3
Wiltshire Cl BN23 . . . . .174 E1
Wiltshire Ho **18** BN2 . . . . .189 C2
Wiltshire Way TN4 . . . . .7 C6
Winceby Cl TN39 . . . . .156 C2
Winchcombe Rd BN22 . . . . .185 A4
Winchelsea Cl BN25 . . . . . . .181 C5
Winchelsea La
Cock Marling TN31, TN36 . . .92 C1
Hastings TN35 . . . . 137 E5
Winchelsea Mus TN31 . . . . .137 E4
Winchelsea Rd
Eastbourne BN22 . . . . .185 D6
Guestling Green TN35 . . . . . .137 F7
Hastings TN35 . . . . 137 D4
Rye TN31 . . . . 93 B5
Winchelsea Sta TN36 . . . . . . .92 D1
Winchester Ho BN22 . . . . . .173 E3
Winchester St BN1 . . . . .189 B4
Winchester Way BN22 . . . . .173 C2
Wincombe Rd BN1 . . . . .142 D1
Windermere Cres BN23 . . . .185 C5

Windermere Ct **5** BN2 . . . .164 C6
Windermere Rd RH16 . . . . . . .50 E4
Windgrove Cotts TN33 . . . . .112 C6
Winding Gr TN33 . . . . .112 D6
Winding St **21** TN34 . . . . .160 B4
Windlesham Ave
BN1, BN3 . . . . .163 E6
Windlesham Cl BN41 . . . . . .141 A1
Windlesham Ct **6** BN1 . . .163 E7
Windlesham Gdns
BN1, BN3 . . . . .163 E7
Windlesham Rd BN1 . . . . . . .163 E8
Windlesham Sch BN1 . . . . . .163 E8
Windmill Ave BN6 . . . . .97 F3
Windmill Cl
Eastbourne BN21 . . . . .184 D6
Heathfield TN21 . . . . .82 B8
Hove BN3 . . . . .141 F2
Windmill Ct
Royal Tunbridge Wells TN2 . . . .8 C3
Winchelsea Beach TN36 . . . .118 B6
Windmill Dr Bexhill TN39 . . .157 B6
Wolfe Cl TN6 . . . . .38 A6
Burgess Hill RH15 . . . . .73 A4
Windmill Gn BN42 . . . . .174 C5
Windmill La
Ashurst Wood RH19 . . . . .11 C7
Cousley Wood TN5 . . . . .30 C8
Durgates TN5 . . . . .29 E4
East Grinstead RH19 . . . . .1 D3
Friston BN20 . . . . 183 A1
Windmill Par BN42 . . . . .140 E1
Windmill Pl BN26 . . . . .173 A5
Windmill Rd
Polegate BN26 . . . . 173 A6
Southwick BN42 . . . . .140 E1
St Leonards TN38 . . . . .136 B2
Royal Tunbridge Wells TN2 . . . .8 C3
Windmill Terr **2** BN2 . . . .189 C3
Windmill View BN1 . . . . .143 B7
Windmill Way TN36 . . . . .118 B7
Windmills Cty Jun Sch
BN6 . . . . .98 A3
Windover Cres BN7 . . . . .123 A2
Windover Way BN22 . . . . . . .173 B3
Windsor Cl
Eastbourne BN23 . . . . .174 C3
Haywards Heath RH16 . . . . . .50 E2
Hove BN3 . . . . .142 A3
Seaford BN25 . . . . .180 B6
Windsor Ct Brighton BN1 . . .189 A2
Brighton, Withdean BN1 . . . .142 D4
Crowborough TN6 . . . . .26 A1
8 Eastbourne BN21 . . . . .185 B3
Polegate BN26 . . . . 173 A7
Windsor Lodge **5** BN3 . .163 B6
Windsor Pl
Crowborough TN6 . . . . .38 C8
East Grinstead RH19 . . . . .11 A8
Hastings TN34 . . . . 136 E2
Windsor Rd Bexhill TN39 . . .157 B4
Crowborough TN6 . . . . .38 C8
Hailsham BN27 . . . . .152 B6
St Leonards TN37 . . . . .158 F6
Windsor St BN1 . . . . .189 A2
Windsor Way
Polegate BN26 . . . . 173 A7
Winchelsea Beach TN36 . . . .118 C6
Windward Quay **3** BN23 .185 F8
Wineham Way TN40 . . . . . . .157 F4
Winfield Ave BN1 . . . . .142 F6
Winfield Cl Brighton BN1 . . .142 F6
Portslade-by-Sea BN41 . . . . .141 A3
Wingate Cl TN38 . . . . .136 A1
Wingle Tye Rd RH15 . . . . .96 A8
Winkfield Cl TN38 . . . . .50 D5
Winkhurst Way RH15 . . . . . . .73 D1
Winkney Rd BN22 . . . . .173 F3
Winnals Pk RH16 . . . . .50 D5
Winscote Cl TN6 . . . . .25 D1
Winston BN27 . . . . .152 B7
Winston Cres BN23 . . . . .185 D7
Winston Dr TN39 . . . . .156 F4
Winston Scott Ave TN3 . . . . .6 E4
Winterbourne Cl
Hastings TN34 . . . . 159 D8
Lewes BN7 . . . . .146 A8
Winterbourne Hollow
BN7 .146 B8
Winterbourne La
BN7 .146 A8
Winterbourne Mews
BN7 .146 A8
Winterton Way BN43 . . . . . .161 B6
Winton Ave BN2 . . . . .166 C3
Winton St BN26 . . . . .171 A4
Wisden Ave RH15 . . . . .72 F5
Wiseacre TN31 . . . . .20 A3
Wish Ct BN3 . . . . .162 E8
Wish Hill BN20 . . . . .173 B1
Wish Rd Eastbourne BN21 . .185 A1
Hove BN3 . . . . .162 E6
Wish St TN31 . . . . .93 B5
Wish Tower Mus BN21 . . . . .185 A1
Wish Ward TN31 . . . . .93 B5
Wishing Tree Cl TN38 . . . . . .135 F2
Wishing Tree La TN38 . . . . . .135 F1
Wishing Tree Rd N TN38 . . .136 A4
Wiston Cl **12** BN43 . . . . . .161 C8
Wiston Rd BN2 . . . . .165 E8
Wiston Way BN2 . . . . .164 F7
Witham Ct BN43 . . . . .142 D2
Withdean Ave BN1 . . . . .142 D2
Withdean Court Ave BN1 . . .142 D3
Withdean Cres BN1 . . . . .142 E3
Withdean Ct **7** BN1 . . . . .142 E3
Withdean Hall BN1 . . . . .142 E3

Withdean Rd BN1 . . . . .142 D3
Withdean Rise BN1 . . . . .142 D2
Witherenden Rd TN20 . . . . . .41 A1
Withy Bush RH15 . . . . .72 E5
Wittersham Rd Iden TN31 . . .70 B7
Withyham Ave BN2 . . . . .177 C5
Witham Rd
Bexhill TN39 . . . . .156 C2
Groombridge TN3 . . . . .13 F1
Wittersham Rd Iden TN31 . . .70 B7
Potman's Heath TN17, TN30 . .70 A3
Wittersham Road Sta
TN17 .49 D6
Wivelsfield Cty Prim Sch
RH17 .73 F6
Wivelsfield Rd
Haywards Heath RH16 . . . . . .50 E2
Saltdean BN2 . . . . .166 C3
Wivelsfield Sta RH15 . . . . . . .73 C4
Woburn Cl BN27 . . . . .129 A1
Woburn Pl BN1 . . . . .143 F5
Woburn Way BN22 . . . . .173 D3
Wolseley Rd Brighton BN1 . .143 D6
Portslade-by-Sea BN41 . . . . .162 A8
Royal Tunbridge Wells TN4 . . . .8 B7
Wolstead Lodge **3** RH16 . .50 F3
Wolstonbury Cl BN6 . . . . .97 B4
Wolstonbury Cr RH15 . . . . . . .73 B2
Wolstonbury Rd BN3 . . . . . . .163 E7
Wolstonbury Way RH15 . . . . .73 B2
Wolverstone Dr BN1 . . . . . . .143 C2
Wonders La BN7 . . . . .182 C7
Wood Rd RH16 . . . . .50 F3
Wood St East Grinstead RH19 . .1 D1
Royal Tunbridge Wells TN1 . . . .8 B4
Wood's Pas **4** TN34 . . . . . 160 B4
Woodbourne Ave BN1 . . . . . .143 A4
Woodbrook Rd TN34 . . . . . . .136 F2
Woodbury Ave RH17 . . . . .73 A4
Woodbury Cl
East Grinstead RH19 . . . . .11 B8
Royal Tunbridge Wells TN4 . . . .8 B5
Woodbury Park Gdns TN4 . . .8 B5
Woodbury Park Rd TN4 . . . . .8 B5
Woodcombe TN34 . . . . .136 F4
Woodcote Rd RH18 . . . . .11 F2
Woodcrest Rd RH15 . . . . .72 F1
Woodcroft RH15 . . . . .72 F1
Woodcroft Dr BN21 . . . . .184 C7
Woodcutters RH17 . . . . .51 F3
Woodgate Mdw BN7 . . . . . . .99 E7
Woodgate Rd BN22 . . . . .185 C5
Woodhams Cl TN33 . . . . . . .112 D5
Woodhill Pk TN2 . . . . .7 E6
Woodhouse Cl BN3 . . . . .162 E7
Woodhouse Rd BN3 . . . . . . .162 E7
Woodingdean
Cty Prim Sch BN2 . . . . . . .165 C8
Woodland Ave
Burgess Hill RH15 . . . . .73 C4
Eastbourne BN20 . . . . .173 C1
Hove BN3 . . . . .142 B3
Woodland Cl
Burgess Hill RH15 . . . . .73 C4
Hove BN3 . . . . .142 B4
Woodland Dr BN3 . . . . .142 B3
Woodland Mews TN21 . . . . . .82 B6
Woodland Par BN3 . . . . .142 B3
Woodland Rd TN4 . . . . .8 C7
Woodland Rise TN40 . . . . . . .157 E4
Woodland Vale Rd
TN37, TN38 . . . . 159 C8
Woodland Walks TN33 . . . . .113 B5
Woodland Way
Brighton BN1 . . . . 142 F4
Crowborough TN6 . . . . .37 F8
Crowhurst TN33 . . . . .134 F4
Fairlight Cove TN35 . . . . .138 E4
Woodlands Cl
Hailsham BN27 . . . . .152 C5
Hove BN3 . . . . .142 B4
Woodland Wlk BN2 . . . . .165 D4
Woodlands Hove BN3 . . . . . .142 C2
Romford TN2 . . . . .9 F7
Woodlands Cl
Hailsham BN27 . . . . .152 C2
Heathfield TN21 . . . . .82 B5
Peacehaven BN10 . . . . .167 B1
Uckfield TN22 . . . . .78 D8
Woodlands Rd
East Grinstead RH19 . . . . .2 A4
Haywards Heath RH16 . . . . . .50 F4
Woodlands The
Brighton BN1 . . . . 142 E5
Hastings TN35 . . . . 136 E5
Woodlands Way TN34 . . . . . .136 E6
Woodleigh Rd RH15 . . . . .73 C4
Woodmans Oak TN33 . . . . . . .88 A3
Woodpecker Cres RH15 . . . . .72 D3
Woodpecker Dr BN27 . . . . . .152 A8
Woodpecker Rd BN23 . . . . . .174 B2
Woodpecker Way TN42 . . . . .78 D5
Woodridge Cl RH16 . . . . .51 A3
Woodruff Ave BN3 . . . . .142 C2
Woods Green Cotts TN5 . . . .29 F7
Woods Hill Cl RH19 . . . . .11 D6
Woods Hill La RH19 . . . . .11 D6
Woods Ho BN2 . . . . .163 A8
Woodsgate Ave TN40 . . . . . .157 C6
Woodsgate Pk TN39 . . . . . . .157 B6
Woodsgate Way TN2 . . . . .9 B6
Woodside Crowborough TN6 . .25 E2
Kilndown TN17 . . . . .32 F8
Woodside Ave BN1 . . . . .142 D2

Woodside Cl TN2 . . . .
Woodside Lodge BN1 142
Woodside Rd Pembury TN2 . . . .
Rusthall TN4 . . . .
Woodside Terr BN26 15
Woodside Way BN27 152
Woodslands Cl BN6 9
Woodslands Rd BN6 9
Woodspring Cl TN3 13
Woodstock RH19 . . . .
Woodstock Rd TN39 156
Woodvale Cl TN39 15
Woodville Cl **8** TN39 15
Woodville Rd TN39 15
Woodward Cl BN23 18
Woodwards RH15 7
Woolven Cl RH15 7
Worcester Cr
6 Eastbourne BN23 17
1 Hove BN3 17
Worcester Villas BN3 162
Wordsworth Dr BN23 17
Wordsworth Rise **8** RH19 . . . . .
Wordsworth St BN1 16
Workhouse La TN36 11
Worsham La TN40 15
Worsted La RH19 1
Wray Cl RH19 1
Wren Cl Burgess Hill RH15 . . .72
Heathfield TN21 82
Wren Ct Battle TN33 11
St Leonards TN38 13
Wrentham Ho RH15 . . . .
Wrenn Ave BN42 17
Westwood Cl TN40 15
Westwood Rd TN40 15
Wrotham Cl
Eastbourne BN23 17
Hastings TN34 13
Wrosham Rd BN23 17
Wyatts La RH17 3
Wyberlye Rd RH15 7
Wybourne Rise TN2 1
Wychperry Rd RH16 54
Wychurst Gdns TN40 15
Wyck Ct BN41 16
Wykeham Cl TN34 15
Wykeham Rd TN34 15
Wykeham Terr BN1 18
Wykeham Way RH15 . . . .
Wynberg Cotts TN6 3
Wyndham St BN2 16
Wynnes Mews BN3 16
Wynnstay RH15 7
Wysshe The BN45 11
Wythwood RH16 5

Y

Yardley St BN1 18
Yates Cl TN31 9
Yeomans BN8 12
Yew Ct **11** BN19 . . . .
Yew La RH19 . . . .
Yew Tree Cl
Broyle Side BN8 12
Hastings TN34 13
Heathfield TN21 8
Yew Tree Cotts
Burgess Hill RH15 7
Groombridge TN3 . . . .
Yew Tree Rd TN4 . . . .
Yewtree La TN6 3
Yielding's Cl BN21 18
York Ave
East Grinstead RH19 1
Hove BN3 16
York Bldgs **6** TN34 15
York Ct BN26 15
York Gdns **3** TN34 15
York Gr BN1 18
York Hill BN1 18
York Ho BN41 16
York Pl Brighton BN1, BN2 . . .18
Hove BN3 16
York Rd Bexhill TN40 15
Burgess Hill RH15 7
Eastbourne BN21 18
Hove BN1, BN3 16
Peacehaven BN10 1
Royal Tunbridge Wells TN1 . . . .
St Leonards TN37 13
York Villas BN1 18
Yorkshire Ct BN20 18
Youl Grange BN20 14
Youngsmere Cl BN1 14
Yvonne Robertson Ho
TN40 15

Any feature in this atlas can be given a unique reference to help you find the same feature on other Ordnance Survey maps of the area, or to help someone else locate you if they do not have a Street Atlas.

The grid squares in this atlas match the Ordnance Survey National Grid and are at 500 metre intervals. The small figures at the bottom and sides of every other grid line are the National Grid kilometre values (**00** to **99** km) and are repeated across the country every 100 km (see left).

To give a unique National Grid reference you need to locate where in the country you are. The country is divided into 100 km squares with each square given a unique two-letter reference. Use the administrative map to determine in which 100 km square a particular page of this atlas falls.

The bold letters and numbers between each grid line (**A** to **F**, **1** to **8**) are for use within a specific Street Atlas only, and when used with the page number, are a convenient way of referencing these grid squares.

Example *The railway bridge over DARLEY GREEN RD in grid square B1*

Step 1: Identify the two-letter reference, in this example the page is in **SP**

Step 2: Identify the 1 km square in which the railway bridge falls. Use the figures in the southwest corner of this square: Eastings **17**, Northings **74**. This gives a unique reference: **SP 17 74**, accurate to 1 km.

Step 3: To give a more precise reference accurate to 100 m you need to estimate how many tenths along and how many tenths up this 1 km square the feature is (to help with this the 1 km square is divided into four 500 m squares). This makes the bridge about **8** tenths along and about **1** tenth up from the southwest corner.

This gives a unique reference: **SP 178 741**, accurate to 100 m.

Eastings (read from left to right along the bottom) come before Northings (read from bottom to top). If you have trouble remembering say to yourself "Along the hall, THEN up the stairs"!

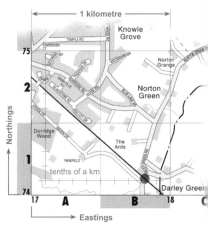

Addresses

Name and Address	Telephone	Page	Grid reference